ISRAEL–PALESTINE ON RECORD

ISRAEL–PALESTINE ON RECORD

HOWARD FRIEL AND RICHARD FALK

VERSO

London • New York

First published by Verso 2007

1 3 5 7 9 10 8 6 4 2

Verso
UK: 6 Meard Street, London W1F 0EG
USA: 180 Varick Street, New York, NY 10014-4606
www.versobooks.com

Verso is the imprint of New Left Books

ISBN-13: 978-1-84467-109-0

British Library Cataloguing in Publication Data
A catalogue record for this book is available from the British Library

Library of Congress Cataloging-in-Publication Data
A catalog record for this book is available from the Library of Congress

Typeset in Bembo by Hewer Text UK Ltd, Edinburgh
Printed and bound in the USA by Quebecor World Fairfield

CONTENTS

INTRODUCTION

Our focus in this book is upon the (mis)representations of the Israel-Palestine conflict in the editorial and news pages of the *New York Times*. We base our conclusions mainly on the findings of an intensive study of the coverage for the period 2000–2006. Although this is a relatively thin slice of time compared to the overall history of the conflict, it is long enough to reveal a pattern that applies to Israel-Palestine relations during the last several decades. The study enables an understanding of the detrimental effects of these (mis)representations on the prospects for peace between these two long-suffering peoples, but more broadly it casts a long, dark shadow across the failure of the *Times* to hold Israel—and as suggested in our earlier volume *The Record of the Paper* (2004), the United States—accountable under international law when it embarks on controversial foreign policy initiatives. And in this instance, even more tellingly, we examine the *Times'* steadfast refusal to consider the relevance of Palestinian rights under international law despite their direct bearing on the merits of the conflict and the contours of a fair and sustainable solution.

This emphasis on Israel-Palestine is due partly to the importance of resolving this conflict and partly to call attention to the insidious partnership between the United States and Israel which has rested in recent years on their joint repudiation of international law constraints on foreign policy, an orientation that is given crucial cover by the *New York Times*. If the *Times* lived up to its responsibilities to be informative and impartial in its treatment of the conflict, it would pay close attention to the connections between foreign policy and international law; its attentiveness would exert a constructive influence on the whole media climate. Despite its august stature, the *Times'* reporting and editorializing on the Israel-Palestine conflict lacks credibility in relation to the professed standards of the newspaper, and yet because of the paper's reputation and authority it exerts an unwarranted influence on public attitudes. In addition, the liberal image of the *Times* gives the American government added room for maneuver when it takes such one-sided positions that correspond with the imbalances of American foreign policy.

Our study of these issues evaluates the coverage accorded the conflict in recent years. It relies primarily on comparisons between the way the *New York Times* reports and editorializes specific issues and incidents, especially those involving violence and civilian casualties, and the treatment of the identical subject matter by respected human rights organizations, including those in Israel. We do not contrast the approach taken by the *Times* with the reporting of Arab media or nongovernmental organizations that might be expected to slant their interpretations to ensure an anti-Israeli interpretation (or at least would be so perceived). Rather, we rely on such widely trusted organizations as Human Rights Watch, Amnesty International, and B'Tselem that are inclined to give Israel the benefit of the doubt and offer criticism of specific situations only when the evidence is over-whelming. In addition, we also rely substantially on the Israeli news media, especially the highly regarded liberal newspaper *Ha'aretz*, which is occasionally referred to as "the *New York Times* of Israel." What is particularly disturbing to us are the major gaps between these reports and the treatment of the same issues provided to the *Times'* readers.

This conclusion is reinforced by another set of comparisons, including a consideration of the irresponsibly vitriolic writings of Alan Dershowitz, which are accorded respectful deference in the *Times* despite their extreme polemical character. We do not discuss the related failure of the *Times* to report upon the strong critiques of Israeli behavior made by such renowned scholars as Edward Said or Noam Chomsky. While Dershowitz's polemics are accorded respect, the far more thoughtful, reliable, and documented writings of Said and Chomsky for the most part are ignored.

As in *The Record of the Paper* our guiding conviction is that international law should be respected by all governments, especially in the area of war and peace. We take this position on the basis of a belief that order sustained by law is more likely to achieve justice than order based on relative power. We also insist that abiding by inter-national law has practical benefits: adherence to international law is the best and most consistent way to promote national interests and uphold national security given contemporary world conditions. If the United States had been law-abiding in its foreign policy, it would have avoided both the Vietnam and the Iraq fiascos. Israel, too, would benefit, including most recently by avoiding the defeat inflicted upon it in the Lebanon War. In this respect, attitudes of governments and their supporters which continue to treat international uses of force as matters merely of national discretion not only violate international law but also overlook recent lessons of history.

This introduction seeks to give background for the more systematic consideration of differing perspectives on the relative responsibility of the parties and their respective claims under international law. It also tries briefly to provide a context for assessing "the blame game" played by governments and the media to explain which side is responsible for the failures of the peace process. Part of our indictment of the *Times'* approach is its failure to give readers a true grasp of these vital matters.

The Israel–Palestine conflict stretches back at least to the establishment of the state of Israel in 1948, and its roots go back much further to the Balfour Declaration of 1917 by which the British Foreign Secretary formally endorsed the Zionist project to establish a Jewish homeland in the territory of Palestine. Palestine was soon to be directly governed by British authority under a special international arrangement, known as the "mandates system" established after World War I. The man-dates system was a hybrid arrangement, a compromise between colonial rule and political independence, and it was relied upon especially to deal with the territories in the Middle East which had previously belonged to the collapsing Ottoman Empire. It is illum-inating to realize that the conflict actually traces back to the late nineteenth century, when the world Zionist movement launched its campaign to encourage Diaspora Jews to settle in Palestine. While we have no interest in adding yet another version of this historical narrative that has been so often set forth from diverse perspectives, it is essential to appreciate the extent to which the respective historical memories of both Israelis and Palestinians help explain why it is almost impossible to find common ground to resolve the main issues in dispute. These contradictory attitudes and historical narratives are dominated by the Holocaust on one side and the 1948 mass dispossession of Palestinians (the *nakba*) on the other. These attitudes and narratives are fixed in the respective political consciousness of the two peoples, so it is crucial to find some neutral criteria to help resolve the major issues in dispute. One of the potential contributions of international law is precisely this ability to supply such neutral criteria; to deprive citizens of the awareness of this possibility is to impoverish our understanding of how to overcome the tragic standoff between these two long-embattled peoples.

The Israel-Palestine conflict has been the most sensitive and, in our view, the most misrepresented foreign policy issue in the United States for some decades. We contend that the unwillingness to view the conflict through the lens of international law has contributed significantly to both an anti-Palestine bias and an inflated sense of Israeli entitlements. This has been reinforced by a distorted public perception of the relative responsibility of the parties under international law for both the sustained violence and the related failures, despite repeated attempts, to find a fair solution to the conflict.

Our attempt in this book is to provide as objectively as possible an appropriate understanding of the main issues, which we believe is most accurately achieved by paying close attention to the assessments made by the world's leading international and Israeli human rights organizations. What is disturbing—and central to our argument—are the discrepancies between such balanced assessments and the biased presentation, featuring a consistent rejection, of the same material by the *New York Times*. These discrepancies concern both the presentation of the factual circumstances of the conflict and the attribution of legal responsibility for various practices. This volume and its predecessor take as their special mission the underscoring of the contention that responsible journalism must devote sustained attention to the relevance of international law in conflicts involving violence and encroachments on fundamental human rights. Beyond the journalistic critique, it is our hope to make clear that respect for international law as a foundation for a resolution of the conflict and an eventual reconciliation of Israelis and Palestinians would greatly benefit *both* peoples, as well as restore some respect for the global leadership role of the United States. The *Times* in our judgment is guilty both of ignoring international law when it conflicts with US foreign policy and of relying upon its authority when it supports official positions adopted in Washington.

More specifically, framing the conflict in relation to international law would emphasize the territorial baselines of 1967, which both sides have formally acknowledged by declaring their acceptance of United Nations Security Council Resolutions 242 and 338. These unanimously backed resolutions call upon Israel to withdraw unconditionally from the Palestinian territory occupied in 1967, giving Israel no legal or moral basis for claiming that it is entitled to keep part of the land or receive something of value from the Palestinians in exchange for its withdrawal. The fact that the Palestinians have authoritatively acknowledged these 1967 boundaries as the foundation for the establishment of two future states living in peace with one another constitutes an enormous and almost totally unappreciated, even unnoticed, historical concession by Palestinian leaders. It means that the Palestinian mainstream is effectively prepared to agree that the Israeli state would occupy 78 percent of the original Palestine, leaving the Palestinians with the remaining 22 percent. The extent of this concession can be grasped by recalling that the earlier American-backed UN partition agreement of 1947, which the Palestinians and their Arab neighbors rejected at the time, gave the Palestinians about 47 percent of the total territory in dispute. Of course, Palestinian extremists do not support such a territorial accommodation, but neither do Israeli extremists agree to renounce their claims to even the residual 22 percent of the Palestinian mandate, and even the Israeli mainstream wants to seize permanent control over part of this Palestinian fragment of the original mandate so as to incorporate the illegal settlements blocs into Israeli territory.

The Palestinians' willingness to start from 1967, rather than 1947 or earlier, gives Israel an excellent opportunity to move forward toward peace and reconciliation, but it is one that Israeli public opinion has never taken properly into account or appreciated. The Israeli position throughout the conflict increasingly has been to encroach on the Palestinian territorial reality, including violating Palestinian private property rights, continuing with its expansive settlement policy, and in recent years constructing a security wall on Palestinian territory. In effect, such Israeli encroachment amounts to a further abridgement of the already severely abridged Palestinian right of self-determination. Defiantly, Israeli leaders insist that such "facts on the ground" represent the necessary and only acceptable starting point for peace negotiations. It is notable that this central feature of the evolution and context of the contending positions is never mentioned in the pages and pages of coverage devoted to the conflict and so-called peace process by the *New York Times*.

Instead, assessments of the reasonableness of the behavior of the two sides habitually start from the de facto realities of Israeli occupation, which is treated as the baseline from which compromises should be made. This leads to the Palestinians being perceived by American public opinion as consistently unreasonable and rejectionist. In effect, Palestinians are criticized for their refusal to accept substantial reductions of their territorial domain (22 percent of historic Palestine) and their unwillingness to lend legitimacy and permanence to the great majority of Israeli settlements unlawfully established on Palestinian territory—as well as in and around Jerusalem, whose metropolitan area has been illegally and massively expanded by annexing surrounding Palestinian land—since 1967 during the prolonged Israeli occupation. The unlawfulness of these settlements in occupied Palestinian territory is established by Article 49, paragraph 6 of the Fourth Geneva Convention of 1949, a position endorsed by the United Nations on a variety of occasions and affirmed by international law experts.

At the same time the *New York Times* lends credibility to the contention that it is the Israelis who are being "generous" in their negotiating position when they agree to withdraw from some of the currently occupied territory, thereby allowing the Palestinians eventually to establish their own state on a portion of that fraction of their residual 22 percent of the original territorial domain covered by the Palestinian mandate. During the Camp David negotiations in July 2000, Israeli Prime Minister Ehud Barak was repeatedly called "courageous" for his reported willingness to agree to Israeli withdrawal from slightly more than 90 percent of the West Bank, while Yasir Arafat was reviled as being disinterested in peace because of his eventual and understandable refusal to accept such an offer. The *Times* never provided the necessary context in relation to the territorial issue that seemed to be at the core of the conflict, and this meant that there was no way for ordinary readers to understand that it was the Palestinians who had been generous by their willingness to base the search for peace on the 1967 borders, thereby implicitly renouncing, in part, their claim to the full implementation of their right of self-determination under international law. It is true that the Palestinians did not help their cause by their own reluctance to emphasize this fundamental concession or by their failure to provide a set of counter-proposals to those put forward first by Barak and then by US President Bill Clinton. It seems likely that Arafat was not eager to advertise Palestinian weakness and that any acknowledgement that

Palestinian leaders were prepared to give up their wider territorial entitlement would have caused an intense Palestinian backlash. Such considerations, however, are no excuse for the failure of the *Times* to look behind the negotiating postures of the parties and examine the undisclosed features of the basic situation.

Analogous (mis)perceptions of the relative merits of Israeli and Palestinian claims have also been encouraged by a similar one-sided coverage of such fundamental issues as the Palestinian right of self-determination, sovereignty over Jerusalem, the treatment of Palestinian refugees claiming a right to return, and the future of Israeli settlements on the West Bank. In each instance, the international law perspective lends credence to Palestinian claims of rights and casts doubts on the legitimacy of Israel's political "needs" in Palestinian territory.

We are certainly not contending that this set of circumstances impeding a balanced understanding of the Israel-Palestine conflict and a fair settlement has been *caused* by the *New York Times*. The US government has consistently used its influence to shape public understanding in this country so as to reinforce positions favored by Israeli leadership, while the pro-Israeli lobby in the United States has been very effective in exerting a variety of pressures supportive of Israeli diplomatic and public relations goals. We do argue, however, that the *New York Times* has contributed significantly to this unfortunate situation by its failure to cover the conflict in an impartial manner. Given the prestige of the newspaper and its reputation for objective journalism, this tilting toward Israel reinforces a set of (mis)perceptions damaging to the Palestinian struggle for self-determination and consistent with Israel's effort to impose a solution that denies fundamental Palestinian rights as embodied in international law.

As with *The Record of the Paper*, our position rests on an insistence that competing claims associated with an international conflict can only be properly resolved by acknowledging the relevance of international law. This does not mean that parties must always defer altogether or agree mechanically to outcomes resulting from relevant rules of international law; some flexibility in the application of international law could result from diplomatic compromises that took into account competing moral and political considerations. What is unacceptable— what the *New York Times* has done—is to ignore the relevance of international law altogether, particularly in view of the extent to which overlooking international law in this case is mainly helpful to Israel's political and territorial claims.

As we seek to demonstrate by this assessment of the *Times'* coverage over the last several years, this neglect of international law reveals a double standard with respect to the prominence given to uses of unlawful force by the two sides, as well as an attempt to resolve the conflict on the basis of negotiations. In a comprehensive assessment of the peace process, Dennis Ross, the chief American negotiator, seemingly shares the approach taken by the *New York Times*. In his book, *The Missing Peace*,[1] instead of illuminating the complicated diplomatic process, Ross mainly wanted to show that he persistently leaned on the Palestinian negotiators to give in on contested issues. He was obviously preoccupied with providing the Israeli negotiators and political leaders with outcomes that would appease Israeli public opinion.

Seeing the peace process through Ross's eyes reveals that the Palestinians, particularly Arafat, were treated as obtuse (or worse), for not accommodating these supposed Israeli needs by subordinating their own goals, however reasonable and legitimate. At the same time, it was taken for granted that Palestinian concerns about security and public expectations were frivolous, if not irrelevant. Again, it might have been expected that the *Times* would balance such governmental one-sidedness by looking at the circumstances and negotiating postures of both sides in a balanced fashion—instead, the *Times'* approach parallels Ross's main argument that it was the fault of the Palestinians that an end to the conflict was not reached at Camp David, and later at Taba, during the closing hours of the Clinton presidency.

Not only does this refusal by the *Times* to consider international law or to evaluate the diplomatic tactics of the two sides seriously bias perceptions of the conflict, but it also refrains from passing judgment on the role of an American foreign policy built around a strange combination of claims: to be both a steadfast ally of Israel and an impartial intermediary between the two parties. Since at least 1967 the United States has approached the conflict almost always on the basis of a strategic commitment to Israel rather than by distinguishing between the respective rights and duties of the parties. Our perspective is rooted in the conviction that the values of a democratic society and of a peaceful and equitable world order depend on a willingness by all political actors, especially those who purport to be world leaders, to shape their foreign policy with a due regard for the restraints of international law.

From this standpoint, the quality of news media coverage is evaluated by the extent to which it takes account of international law. We acknowledge that such a standard of evaluation is not widely shared at this point, but we believe that it is an imperative for a democratic society whose legitimacy depends in the final analysis on adherence to the rule of law. In this spirit, it seems to us that it is reasonable to expect that responsible print media—and especially the *New York Times*, which occupies such an exalted reputation in the public mind—would at least expose its readers to the relevance of international law in the course of addressing controversies associated with international conflicts and foreign policy. The evidence we present establishes overwhelmingly that the *Times* currently refuses even to acknowledge the relevance of international law unless it reinforces the paper's pro-Israeli bias, in which case Palestinian violations of law are given great attention. This selectivity in the treatment of international law establishes the bias of the *Times* beyond any reasonable doubt.

This introductory chapter sets forth in summary form the relevant dimensions of international law. In addition to the more general indictment indicated in the previous paragraph, we criticize the *Times* more specifically for its unwillingness to acknowledge the degree to which the central Palestinian claims in the conflict are solidly supported by international law, as well as the contrary extent to which the Israeli negotiating position or unilateral initiatives depend on ignoring Palestinian rights under international law and validate an existing set of illegal circumstances (especially, occupation and settlements) as the proper foundation for a political compromise. We are also critical of the *Times* for its unbalanced treatment of the ongoing struggle between an occupying power imposing its will for four decades on a hostile and abused civilian population and the resistance mounted by this population.

The *Times* has generally gone along with the Israeli contention that its uses of force are reactive and prompted by legitimate security concerns; the *Times* routinely condemns Palestinian force, even if directed at military targets and personnel, as a species of "terrorism." By criticizing this distinction, we do not intend to whitewash Palestinian violence or altogether dismiss Israeli security concerns, but we are insisting that the behavior of both actors should be appraised equally by reference to the rules of international law, which are quite clear in identifying the respective rights and duties of the parties under conditions of occupation. Central to this appraisal is the underlying unlawfulness of Israel's refusal to withdraw—as agreed by unanimous Security Council decision—and its related ongoing creation of conditions in the West Bank which illegally and intentionally complicate any future compliance with the obligation to withdraw, as well as unacceptably diminish the Palestinian right of self-determination. In this regard, we note, especially, the construction and expansion of settlements which continue up to the present day, as well as the development of an exceedingly expansive network of roads to service these settlements. These actions signal to the Palestinians an Israeli refusal to ever dismantle the large settlement blocs constructed on the Palestinian side of the Green Line, the post-withdrawal boundary.

Our argument proceeds on two levels: it is a critique of the manner in which the Israel-Palestine conflict has been reported by the *Times* over the course of the period 2000–2006, and it presents a template based on respect for international law, which we believe should guide responsible journalism in a democratic society whenever foreign policy or international conflict issues are present. Such an approach could be applied by other news organizations in many national settings, including by the British newspapers the *Independent* and the *Guardian* and the Israeli newspaper *Ha'aretz*—excellent news organizations that we have relied on heavily in this volume. News and commentary in these newspapers would be enhanced even further with a more conscious and consistent integration of international law into their editorial policies. Due, however, to the global projection of American power and influence, and in light of its influential relationship to the Israel-Palestine conflict, we are convinced that highlighting the deficiencies of the way in which the *New York Times* has handled these issues is especially illuminating.

Although the historical background of the conflict shapes attitudes toward the behavior of the two sides and raises at every stage important issues of international law, we will not look back further than 2000 except to the extent necessary to clarify existing claims of rights as of 2006. At the same time, we do recognize that the present dimensions of the conflict and the sources of legal guidance are grounded in pre-2000 expressions of legal assessment. In other words, while ignoring the evolution of the conflict since 1917, the international law criteria pertaining to the rights of the two sides were mainly established in the period after World War II and prior to 1967. The current factual setting continues to be largely a result of the outcome of the Six-Day War in 1967 and subsequent developments associated with the Israeli occupation of the West Bank, Jerusalem, and Gaza. Some Israeli jurists have insisted that these territories are not "occupied territory" as the term is understood in international law because there was not a clear sovereign entitlement, and hence Israel is not subject to international humanitarian law in the course of the occupation. However, this view has not been taken seriously outside of Israel and in fact was unanimously rejected by the International Court of Justice (World Court) in an Advisory Opinion issued in 2004.

At the time of the 1967 war, although Jordan was administering East Jerusalem and the West Bank and Egypt was administering Gaza, neither possessed sovereign authority, which was not clearly transferred after the collapse of the Ottoman Empire. The overwhelming consensus of international legal opinion, however, is that Israel is an occupying power as that term is understood in international law in relation to the lands taken by Israeli military action in 1967.

Our study of the *Times'* coverage shows, first of all, that important facts are inadequately covered and more selectively reported than those presented by several respected human rights organizations. Secondly, we argue that these misleading portrayals of the facts have undermined a balanced understanding of the respective rights of the Israelis and Palestinians under international law and have thus clouded thinking about a fair and reasonable outcome to negotiations. We also present a brief discussion of the fundamental claims relating to the overall dispute from the perspective of international law, which, aside from the period of the Camp David peace talks in summer 2000, are not directly raised by the daily dynamics of occupation and resistance. We then set forth the international law issues that do arise in the daily administration of occupied Palestinian territories. As a preliminary matter, we offer a brief primer below of the main issues involved from the perspective of international law.

Right of Self-Determination. The Palestinian people enjoy a right of self-determination, which has been treated in recent decades as the most fundamental of all legal rights, underpinning specific rights. This right of self-determination was given its most authoritative formulation in common Article I of the leading instruments of human rights opened for ratification in 1966: the International Covenant on

Political and Civil Rights and the International Covenant on Economic, Social and Cultural Rights. The right of self-determination was also unanimously affirmed by the UN General Assembly in Resolution 2625, the very influential Declaration on Principles of International Law Concerning Friendly Relations Among States adopted in 1970. The applicability of the right of self-determination to the Palestinian struggle has been frequently and explicitly affirmed by the General Assembly, usually over the opposition of the United States and Israel, in such resolutions as 2535 (1969); 2649 (1970); and 3236 (1974). It is impossible to evaluate the reasonableness of the responses by the two sides to proposed solutions of the conflict without taking into full account the Palestinian right of self-determination.

Territorial Rights. The original international approach to a territorial division of Palestine was a partition plan agreed upon at the United Nations and endorsed in late 1947 by the General Assembly in Resolution 181(I). This division allocated about 53 percent of the land to Israel, established an international trusteeship for Jerusalem under UN administration, an economic union of the two entities, and free transit between them. This partition plan was immediately rejected by the Palestinians and neighboring Arab governments, leading to the 1948 War, which led to the expulsion by Israel of hundreds of thousands of Palestinians, the destruction of more than 600 Palestinian villages in the area under Israeli control, and the dramatic expansion of Israeli territory. This rejection, although seemingly imprudent in view of later developments, did reflect a rather widely held view at the time that the UN partition plan violated the Palestinian right of self-determination that seemed to create an entitlement to the entire mandate of Palestine. It was the outcome of this war that established the so-called Green Line that became the internationally acknowledged boundary of Israel; the Green Line was subsequently recognized by Palestinian leadership in 1988 as the basis for territorial division needed for a *viable* two-state solution.

To give effect to this vision of peace would require Israel to withdraw completely from the additional Palestinian territory it occupied after 1967. Withdrawal on this basis was prescribed by unanimous Security Council Resolutions 242 (1967) and 338 (1973). Every subsequent negotiation for a settlement of the conflict—until 2000—has demanded an Israeli withdrawal to the Green Line, with minor adjustments, and the establishment of a Palestinian state on the previously occupied land. How the question of the Israeli settlement blocs and security wall will be handled in the future is uncertain: perhaps it will be addressed by negotiations or by way of Israel's effort to dictate a solution on its own. It is our contention that unless the solution approximates what was prescribed in Resolution 242, the result will not be treated as legitimate and will not be accepted by the Palestinians. Nothing less can even approximate at this late stage of the conflict the realization of what remains the most fundamental legal issue at stake, the Palestinian right of self-determination.

Refugees. From the time of the mass and coerced departure of Palestinians from the territory on which the state of Israel was established in 1948, the issue of Palestinian refugees has been a fundamental concern for Palestinians—it is almost regarded as a sacred grievance that cannot be abridged by political forces. The refugee issue has also been a source of intense emotional controversy, as it relates directly to the tension between unconditional Palestinian demands to recover their homes and deep-seated Israeli fears of the demographic impact of returning Palestinians on the identity of the country as a "Jewish state."

In accordance with customary international law, in 1948 the UN General Assembly, in Resolution 194, called upon Israel to arrange for the repatriation of those Palestinians who had fled or been expelled; at the time this appeared to be a diplomatic condition attached to Israel's admission to the United Nations as a member state. This Palestinian right of return has remained an intensely emotional issue for both sides. Almost all Israelis insist that there can be no literal implementation of the Palestinian right of return. Israelis argue instead that a right of return should be confined to a right to return to Palestine. In contrast, the Palestinians insist that Resolution 194 did not so circumscribe their right of return, and international law definitely confirms the Palestinian understanding of the right of return. Palestinians are also angered by Israel's unconditional policy of allowing any person of Jewish identity, wherever in the world they reside and even in the absence of any family or other prior contact with Israel, to settle permanently in Israel whenever they so desire. As a matter of law, it would seem that the Palestinian refugees clearly have the right to settle in Israel and thereby return to their former homes, but it is highly uncertain after such a lapse of time to what extent such a right would be exercised if it were made available to Palestinian refugees. It is also possible that a political solution could be worked out at some point, probably within a comprehensive settlement, by limiting the annual influx of Palestinian refugees to Israel and by compensating Palestinians if they choose to remain outside or return to a Palestinian state. As matters stand, international law supports the Palestinian claimed right of return as expressed by General Assembly Resolution 194.

Security Resolution 242, adopted in 1967, not only called for Israeli withdrawal from occupied Palestinian territory, but also demanded "a just settlement of the refugee problem." By failing to affirm Palestinian rights of return in so many words, this resolution took a step away from the earlier insistence in Resolution 194 upon strict Israeli implementation of international law on the refugee issue. It has been contended that by using this phrasing the UN took note of Israeli concerns and thus indicated a willingness to work out an arrangement that was more flexible than follows from the clear mandate of international law. Whether ordinary Palestinians understood at the time that their rights as refugees were being traded away seems highly unlikely, but the intention within the Security Council seems to have been to give some ground to Israel on refugees but to hold firm on the question of land, and consequently of withdrawal. With the passage of time, this firmness has been badly eroded by Israel's sustained settlements in the West Bank with US support. This pattern of behavior has effectively denied the Palestinians any realistic prospect of realizing their right of self-determination even in its much curtailed form of an entitlement to 22 percent of historic Palestine.

From Israel's perspective at least 80 percent of the settlements—whether their establishment was motivated by religious zeal or to take advantage of subsidized living—are slated for incorporation into Israel if an eventual settlement is negotiated or imposed. The rest of the settlements are regarded as temporary and are still deemed useful to Israel as future bargaining chips, removable by Israel when the price is right.

Jerusalem. Israeli officials declared after the 1967 war that Jerusalem would remain a unified city under Israeli sovereign control. Ehud Barak expressed Israeli intentions to his public just prior to the peace negotiations at Camp David in 2000: Jerusalem was one of four Israeli security "red lines" that could not become the subject of a negotiated compromise; in his words, the city would remain "a united Jerusalem under our sovereignty for eternity, period."[2] In a series of UN resolutions, including 252 (1968), 267 (1969), and 298 (1971), Israel was censured for taking various measures intended "to change the status of the City of Jerusalem including expropriations of land and properties, transfer of populations and legislation aimed at incorporation of the occupied" portion of the city. Resolution 298 called these changes "totally invalid" and incapable of changing "the status" of the city. The future of Jerusalem is also of concern to the Islamic (and Christian) world, as well as to the Palestinians, with strong objections registered to the prospect of Israeli control of access and protection of Muslim sacred sites within the city.

The main elements of conflict between the two peoples, if interpreted in accordance with international law, overwhelmingly support the substantive claims of the Palestinians with respect to a final settlement. This support is also fully consistent with an array of resolutions passed by both the Security Council and the General Assembly. If Israel were to show respect for international law and UN authority, it would withdraw from the territories occupied in 1967, including from its settlements in East Jerusalem, and would dismantle all other settlements, as well as exhibit a willingness to negotiate a just way to resolve the refugee issue and other outstanding questions (such as border security and water rights). These underlying conditions of a reasonable settlement should inform impartial journalistic coverage of the conflict on a daily basis, but especially at those times when moves are made to establish what Security Council Resolution 242 calls "a just and durable peace."

There is a series of separate international law issues that arise from the specific realities of the Israeli occupation, which has now lasted for forty years, itself a biblical interval. The occupation defies the authority of international law and the United Nations, which has repeatedly demanded a timely Israeli withdrawal. In view of the refusal by Israel to withdraw, Palestinian resistance has been mounted, giving rise to a debate about the right and scope of a Palestinian right of resistance.[3] A Palestinian claim to a right of resistance is strengthened by the abusive and unlawful daily character of the occupation, as well as Israel's refusal to apply the 1949 Geneva Conventions and 1977 Geneva Protocols that contain the rules governing a belligerent occupation of this character. Israel is also bound by the basic obligations set forth in these important legal instruments because their rules and standards are part of customary international law—that is, they are obligatory independent of any formal consent to an agreement. This position is made clear in the famous Common Article 3 of the Geneva Conventions.

It is quite remarkable, as we demonstrate in the pages ahead, that the *New York Times* has never even acknowledged these dimensions of the Israel-Palestine conflict. This omission leaves even sophisticated readers with the impression that the Palestinians are the initiators of violence and wrongdoing, and that the Israelis are merely responding to insurgent violence within their own territory. There is some admission in the *Times'* coverage that Israeli violence is, on occasion, excessive or ill considered, but not in a manner that takes note of the highly questionable legality of the occupation itself.

This section, again as a preliminary brief on the issues discussed at length ahead, briefly outlines some Israeli occupation practices that seem clearly to be in violation of international humanitarian law.

Protection of Civilians. It seems correct to conclude that the primary goal of international humanitarian law is to protect civilian life. Article 3 of the Fourth Geneva Convention imposes an unconditional obligation "in all circumstances" to treat civilians "humanely." This general directive is set forth more specifically in relation to military operations in Article 51 of Protocol I,[4] which prohibits uses of force that fail to discriminate effectively between military and civilian targets. Article 51(7) specifically forbids "attacks against the civilian population or civilians by way of reprisals."

Excessive Force. Independent inquiry has consistently found that Israel has used excessive force to punish resistance activities, including responding to stones thrown by children with deadly fire. A basic standard embodied in customary international law is the requirement that force be used in a manner that is *proportional* to the provocation.

Collective Punishment. Article 33 of the Fourth Geneva Convention explicitly forbids "[c]ollective penalties" and punishment "for an offense he or she has not personally committed." Israel has imposed collective punishments in many forms throughout the occupation, with one particularly resented practice being house demolitions that penalize the families of individuals accused of engaging in anti-Israeli violence, whether directed at military or nonmilitary targets. Other frequent collective punishments imposed as reprisals involve onerous curfews that obstruct Palestinian access to food and medicine, as well as disrupt employment relations and impose intense stress. On frequent occasions Palestinian universities and schools, as well as entire refugee camps, have been arbitrarily closed, often for long periods, causing severe hardship. Furthermore, there is abundant evidence that Palestinian civilians are seriously inconvenienced, as well as routinely harassed and humiliated, at the many checkpoints situated throughout the occupied territories which make travel within the West Bank a hazardous and onerous undertaking.

Settlements. Settlements established by the occupying power are viewed by international humanitarian law as illegal encroachments on the rights of an occupied people, interfering with their eventual right of self-determination. Article 49(6) of the Fourth Geneva Convention specifically prohibits an occupying power from establishing settlements composed of its nationals and more generally prohibits population transfers that alter the character of the occupied territory. As of the end of 2006, Israel has established at least 200 settlements, many heavily armed and protected by Israel Defense Forces (IDF) deployments, throughout the West Bank and Jerusalem; these settlements are inhabited by more than 400,000 Israelis. The term "settlement" is misleading; these Israeli communities are really armed enclaves imposed on a hostile and alien population. Because many of the settlements are situated near densely populated Palestinian areas, there are many daily points of friction. Much of the violence that occurs is connected to the provocative presence of these settlements, which generates settler violence, anti-settlement activism, and numerous incidents at IDF checkpoints that are often situated for the security of these communities. From the Palestinian viewpoint, these settlements are illegal encroachments on Palestinian territory; they are also manifestations of Israeli bad faith in relation to an eventual peace based on two coexisting sovereign states.

Water Rights. Israel has for many years been diverting large quantities of water from aquifers under the West Bank for use in Israel and controlling Palestinian access to the water. Water scarcity is a major concern in the region, and it is inconsistent with the legal duties of an occupying power to alter patterns of beneficial use of valuable resources in occupied territory.

Targeted Assassinations. The Fourth Geneva Convention in Articles 64–78 makes detailed provisions for allegations of criminality associated with individuals living in occupied territories. No punishment can be carried out by an occupying power "except after a regular trial" (Article 71). Considerable attention is given in the treaty to limiting the discretion of an occupying power to impose a death sentence at the end of a trial. Despite these restrictions, Israel has with great frequency carried out lethal assaults against individuals suspected of contributing to or encouraging anti-Israeli violence. There is often no way to verify if those targeted are in fact directly linked to terrorist activities. These assaults have resulted in a large number of completely innocent bystanders also being killed, deaths inadequately explained by Israeli authorities as "collateral damage."

Right of Resistance. It is against such a background that Palestinian acts of resistance should be judged. Such judgment would include distinguishing between violence directed against Israeli military forces and targets, as well as armed settlers and settlements, and violence deliberately targeting civilians (as in many instances of suicide bombing). As with Israeli violence against Palestinian civilians, there is no legal defense of Palestinian violence aimed at civilian targets, whether in the occupied territory or in Israel itself.

It is not necessary by way of conclusion to do more than underscore the extent to which the *Times* has left unchallenged the Israel–US insistence on excluding international law from the "peace process" based upon the 1993 Oslo Declaration of Principles,[5] as well as later attempts to negotiate an end to the conflict, including at the Camp David summit in July 2000 and in the 2003 "Roadmap."[6] The effect of not adhering to international law on the most fundamental issues in controversy has been to push the bargaining process toward compromise based on Israeli "facts" in Palestinian territory, most of which exist within various degrees of illegality. Instead of insisting on the implementation of Palestinian rights under international law as the starting point for negotiations, diplomacy effectively has bracketed claims favorable to the Palestinians and thereby required the weaker side to give up both its legal entitlements and its only potential bargaining leverage. Neglecting Palestinian rights—rights of which the Palestinian population is well aware—gives to any proposed solution a quality of illegitimacy. It is clear that the strong in this case are imposing their will on the weaker party, and for this reason a solution reached under such circumstances would be challenged at some future point even if accepted by the Palestinian leaders of the moment. Israelis may receive a temporary respite from the conflict by inducing a weak Palestinian leader to accept a bargain that neither realizes Palestinian rights under international law nor shows how the sacrifice of such rights was reasonably offset by corresponding adjustments. Again, our purpose is not to dwell upon the diplomatic dimensions of the relationship between Israelis and Palestinians, but rather to insist that unless the *Times'* coverage is responsive to these issues, the newspaper cannot convey to its readers the sort of facts and analysis that are necessary for an informed perspective of the conflict.

It is our hope to show that the *Times'* coverage of events bearing on the Israel-Palestine conflict is consistently pro-Israeli in character and that this bias is reinforced by overlooking the international law dimensions of the conflict that tend to favor the Palestinians. The outlook of the United States government and the American people bears directly on whether a fair solution to this long-standing conflict can be achieved in the years ahead. We believe that a fair solution is highly unlikely without a more impartial presentation of the facts from the US news media, and without the realization that it is unreasonable to expect the Palestinians to make peace if their rights under international law are being pushed aside. It is not that the Palestinians hold international law in great esteem or that its strictures are beyond criticism, but at present there is no better way to gauge whether grievances, demands, or one side's "facts" are valid without testing their validity against the rules and standards of international law. As the world has become more globalized, the importance of according attention and respect to international law grows correspondingly. So too grows the obligation of responsible journalism to convey our changing world to its readers with attention to international law— especially with respect to violent conflicts that bring suffering to many people.

Part One

Facts Under Ground

1

The *New York Times* and The Human Rights Organizations

The front page of the *New York Times* for September 29, 2000, featured two photographs: one depicted Palestinians throwing stones in the direction of the second photograph, which showed Ariel Sharon walking in Jerusalem's Old City. There was no accompanying front-page article, but the caption for both photographs read: "The Likud Leader Ariel Sharon visited the sacred site Jews call Temple Mount and Muslims call Haram al Sharif. Palestinians responded violently, and there were injuries."

The front-page photograph and caption were thus the *Times'* first report on what would become the second Palestinian *intifada*.[7] The *Times'* coverage of the Israel-Palestine conflict over the next several years consistently featured a dual focalization: (a) a general editorial emphasis on reporting and condemning Palestinian violence, particularly Palestinian suicide bombings inside Israel, and (b) a disinclination to report or condemn a much higher magnitude of Israeli violence and lawlessness in occupied Palestinian territory. Our analysis of the *Times* is thus focused less on inaccuracies in news coverage and commentary, though a few such inaccuracies can be identified and inevitably occur. Rather, we allege serious shortcomings in the *Times'* coverage of Israel's policies in the occupied territories with respect to important facts and applicable law, especially compared to the substantial reservoir of valuable information generated by the United Nations, the major human rights organizations that monitor Israel's conduct in the West Bank and Gaza Strip, and the British and Israeli press.

While much of what the *New York Times* actually prints about Israel's conduct is technically accurate within the narrow context of a given article or editorial, its coverage is far more insular than one might expect from the most important newspaper in the world's leading democracy. Thus, Ariel Sharon's "visit" to the Temple Mount/Haram al Sharif was a narrowly accurate—he did go there—but misleading characterization of what Sharon did on that day and its implications at the time. And the manifest stone-throwing of the Palestinians was also a fact, though Sharon's massive but unseen and unmentioned security entourage reflected more awareness of the Israeli provocation than what the *Times* front page revealed.[8] Overall, the enduring pattern of the *Times*' maximalist coverage of Palestinian violence and minimalist coverage of Israeli violence obscures the magnitude of Israel's transgressions.

The unevenness of the *Times*' coverage is substantial enough that it veils a major fact about the conflict: Israeli violence against Palestinians far exceeds Palestinian violence against Israelis. This is true even for the period September 2000 to December 2006, which saw a sustained series of Palestinian suicide bombings inside Israel. While the *Times* provided comprehensive and mostly accurate coverage of the vast majority of Palestinian suicide bombings in Israel, as the predominant representation of the conflict these reports, featured as such, were misleading, given that many more Palestinians were killed by Israelis within this period.

The *Times*' coverage is also deficient in situating Israeli violence within the applicable framework of international humanitarian law,[9] including the Fourth Geneva Convention, as established by authoritative human rights organizations—including the International Committee of the Red Cross, Amnesty International, Human Rights Watch, and B'Tselem: The Israeli Information Center for Human Rights in the Occupied Territories. In fact, the *Times* rarely mentions the Fourth Geneva Convention as applied to Israel's occupation of the West Bank and Gaza. Nor does the *Times* seem otherwise aware of, informed by, or concerned with this basic framework of international law that applies to Israel's occupation of the West Bank and Gaza.

As every major human rights organization and numerous UN General Assembly and Security Councils resolutions have established, the Fourth Geneva Convention is the principal instrument of international law that applies to Israel's occupation of the Palestinian territories. In addition to its applicability, the Convention prohibits nearly all of Israel's conduct reported in this book, including Israel's "excessive" use of lethal force, beatings and abuse, house demolitions as collective punishment, administrative detention and torture, as well as Israel's settlements in the West Bank. With respect to the Convention's applicability to Israel's occupation, B'Tselem observes:

The Fourth Geneva Convention deals with the protection of civilians during war or under occupation, and therefore relates to Israel's actions in the Occupied Territories. The Convention prohibits, among other things, violent acts against residents of occupied territory, the taking of prisoners, injury to the civilians' dignity, acts of retaliation against them, collective punishment, and mass or individual deportation. The Convention also protects children by ensuring maintenance of relations between family members who have been separated as a result of war, protects property, provides safeguards for detainees and prisoners, and states many other protections. The Convention also sets due process standards for criminal trials conducted against residents of occupied territory, and prohibits occupying states from settling its citizens in occupied territory.[10]

Thus, we can identify at the outset two major problems with the *New York Times*' coverage of the Israel-Palestine conflict: the *Times*' relative failure to report Israeli violence in the occupied territories, and its consistent refusal to identify Israel's violations of international humanitarian law in the territories.

The claim that more Palestinians than Israelis have been killed and injured is fully documented by the major human rights organizations monitoring the situation. For example, according to B'Tselem, from September 29, 2000, to November 30, 2006, Israeli personnel, primarily security forces, killed 4,032 Palestinians.[11] For the same period, 1,017 Israelis were killed by Palestinians.[12] Included in these statistics are 808 Palestinian children (younger than eighteen years of age) who were killed by Israelis, and 119 Israeli children killed by Palestinians.[13] This means that nearly four times as many Palestinians were killed, including nearly seven times as many Palestinian children. B'Tselem statistics for 1987 to 2000 reflect a similar reality: Israelis killed 1,491 Palestinians, including 304 Palestinian children; Palestinians killed 186 Israelis, including four Israeli children.[14]

In terms of journalistic emphasis, however, the *New York Times* has focused predominantly on the killing of Israelis by Palestinians. For example, from September 29, 2000, to December 31, 2005, the *New York Times* published about fifty front-page articles on Palestinian suicide bombings and other terrorist acts,[15] in addition to twenty-five articles on Palestinian terrorism reported elsewhere in the front section.[16] This reporting accounted for the vast majority of Palestinian suicide bombings and other terrorist acts inside Israel's borders throughout the period, therefore reflecting most killing of Israelis by Palestinians. In contrast, there was much less emphasis in the *Times* on the far more numerous Israeli killings of Palestinians in the occupied territories during the same period.

In addition, the first Palestinian terrorist bombing inside Israel within this period did not occur until November 22, 2000; that is, nearly two months after Israeli security forces had killed 236 Palestinians, including 86 children, and injured more than 9,000 additional Palestinians, according to the Palestinian Red Crescent Society, and as reported in an important report issued by the UN Human Rights Commission.[17] (A Palestinian car bomb in East Jerusalemem killed two Israelis at an outdoor market on November 3, 2000.) Reports by the UN and major human rights organizations of steadily escalating Palestinian casualties in the weeks and months after September 29, 2000, corroborate these figures. The *Times*, consistent with its practice of underemphasizing Israeli violence and Palestinian casualties, only briefly noted or ignored the reports altogether.

On October 7, 2000, one week after the September 29 start of Palestinian demonstrations against the Israeli occupation, the UN Security Council issued a resolution that cited "80 Palestinian deaths and many other casualties" following "the provocation carried out at the Haram al-Sharif in Jerusalem on 28 September 2000" by Sharon. The resolution—the United States under President Bill Clinton abstained from the vote—"condemn[ed] acts of violence, especially the excessive use of force against Palestinians."[18]

The resolution prompted a cluster of related articles in the *Times*, many featuring criticism of the Security Council for censuring Israel.[19] However, the initial article in the series, printed on page 20 of the front section, focused on the draft resolution itself and the situation in the territories that prompted it. The *Times'* William A. Orme Jr. had visited a hospital in East Jerusalem on October 3 and interviewed its director, who noted "the high number of upper body injuries" to Palestinians brought to the hospital. The director of another hospital told Orme of treating "18 Palestinians who were shot in the eye with rubber projectiles," and he said that "most of the damaged eyes were left sightless." Orme noted that between September 29 and October

3, "at least 42 Palestinians have been killed in the clashes, including 13 children." He also reported "for the first time since peace talks led to the creation of the Palestinian Authority six years ago, Israelis have fired on civilians from helicopter gunships used [sic] armor-piercing missiles."[20] Orme's article was an early exception to the pattern of reporting which would emerge.

Subsequent reports by human rights organizations documented a steady increase in Palestinian casualties in the early months of the intifada. On October 19 Amnesty International reported that "since 29 September 2000 more than 100 Palestinians, including 27 children, were killed by the Israeli security forces." Amnesty also reported that "September/October 2000 is not the first time when excessive use of lethal force by the Israeli security forces has claimed Palestinian lives; protesters and bystanders, including many children, died during the 1987–1993 intifada, in September–October 1996, in May 2000, and on many other occasions." Amnesty also noted, referring to the round of killings current at the time:

> [Amnesty International] believes that these practices have continued, among other reasons, because of the lack of any investigation by the Israeli Government into the circumstances surrounding past cases of excessive use of force and the failure to bring the perpetrators to justice and bring about a change of practice in the use of force by the security forces in the wake of such killings in order to meet international human rights standards.[21]

The Times ignored this report except for the following two sentences, which were printed nearly a week after the report was issued in an article under a headline about another matter: "International groups have criticized Israel for too much shooting during riots, and for stepping up its response too quickly from nonlethal riot control techniques to lethal ones. Amnesty International, in a recent report, said Israel was using combat techniques when it should be using policing methods to disperse violent disturbances."[22]

Also in October 2000, Human Rights Watch issued a report that found "a pattern of repeated Israeli use of excessive lethal force during clashes between its security forces and Palestinian demonstrators in situations where demonstrators were unarmed and posed no threat of death or serious injury to the security forces or to others." In cases involving Palestinian gunfire, "use of lethal force by the Israel Defense

Forces (IDF) was indiscriminate and not directed at the source of the threat, in violation of international law enforcement standards." The report continued: "A particularly egregious example of such unlawful fire is the IDF's use of medium-caliber bullets against unarmed demonstrators in the West Bank and Gaza Strip, and in some instances, such as the Netzarim Junction in the Gaza Strip, against medical personnel. These military weapons, which inflict massive trauma when striking flesh, are normally used to penetrate concrete and are not appropriate for crowd control."[23] The *Times* ignored this report by Human Rights Watch.

On November 3, 2000, Physicians for Human Rights (PHR) reported, "Since the renewed crisis in the Middle East erupted in late September, there have been at least 160 deaths and over 5,000 injuries, the vast majority of which have been Palestinian." The physicians "found that the Israel Defense Force has used live ammunition and rubber bullets excessively and inappropriately to control demonstrators," that "fatal gunshot wounds in Gaza reveal that approximately 50% were to the head," and "this high proportion of fatal head wounds suggests that given broad rules of engagement, [Israeli] soldiers are specifically aiming at peoples' heads." The group reported "of the 31 Palestinians killed in Gaza between September 30 and October 24, 38% were under the age of 18." In addition, "of the first 1,134 injuries reported in the combined West Bank and Gaza data, 2% were under the age of 9, 14% were under the age of 15, and 17% were 16 through 18 years of age."[24]

Echoing reports by Amnesty International and Human Rights Watch that Israel had resorted to combat methods to respond to Palestinian demonstrations, PHR analyzed the wounds of hospitalized patients (looking at X-rays, bullets removed after surgery, and post-mortem examinations) and found that Israeli security forces were using M-16s, AK-47s, and Luger handguns against stone-throwing or unarmed Palestinian demonstrators; they also used 50-caliber ammunition rounds fired from guns mounted on helicopters and tanks, in addition to rubber bullets and rubber-coated steel bullets. The physicians reported that "numerous independent eyewitness accounts from PHR interviews and other reliable reports have documented that most of [the Palestinians] who have been shot were not carrying or using firearms." In one instance, "on October 24, PHR physicians witnessed a demonstration on the outskirts of Ramallah where they saw IDF soldiers fire live and rubber ammunition at Palestinian civilians when they could see no evidence of Palestinians using firearms."[25]

In its review of the PHR report, the *Times* summarized a number of the main findings, including, as reported by the *Times*, a "pattern of the Israeli Army's using live bullets to wound and disperse unarmed [Palestinian] rioters," that the army "used live ammunition and rubber bullets excessively and inappropriately" and "appeared to be shooting to inflict harm, rather than solely in self-defense," that "most of the dead in Gaza" are killed "by high-velocity bullets from a M-16, the standard Israeli Army rifle," that "thirty-eight percent of the deaths were of children younger than 18 and 14 percent younger than 15," and that "half the fatal gunshots in the Gaza cases that it studied were to the head."[26] Despite these serious findings, which were consistent with similar findings by Amnesty International and Human Rights Watch, and which by this time reflected a consensus among at least these major human rights organizations that the Israeli government was engaged in a policy of excessive use of lethal force in the Palestinian territories, the *Times'* article on the Physicians for Human Rights report was published on page 8, rather than the front page. More than half the article was devoted to the death of a Palestinian man which PHR had judged was the result of a traffic accident, not wounds inflicted by the Israeli army, as many Palestinians had charged.[27]

On November 29, 2000, the UN High Commissioner on Human Rights, Mary Robinson (who had been president of Ireland from 1990 to 1997), issued an extensive report on the human rights situation in the Palestinian territories. Her report was based on her trip to the region from November 8 to 16, which included visits to Israel, Egypt, Jordan, the Gaza Strip, and the West Bank. After meeting with more than seventy officials, Robinson reported, in understated fashion, "it was explained that the anger and frustration of the present Intifada stemmed from the lack of implementation [by Israel] of the key United Nations Resolutions, especially General Assembly Resolutions 181 (II) and 194 (III) and Security Council resolutions 242 (1967), the continuing [Israeli] encroachment on [Palestinian] land for settlements, and what was perceived as a peace process which had not addressed the Palestinian claims of a State with East Jerusalem as its capital and some recognition of the right of return of refugees." Robinson continued: "An inescapable conclusion is that much of the present situation has to do with the daily reality of life under the occupation, including what Palestinians see as the numerous daily humiliations imposed upon them." Robinson reported that "the most persistent allegation brought to the attention of the High Commissioner was that Israeli security forces have engaged in excessive force, disproportionate to the threat faced by their soldiers." In addition to citing estimates from the Palestinian Red Crescent Society that 236 Palestinians had been killed and 9,353 injured from September 29 to November 23, she also cited figures from the Palestinian Authority's Minister of Health, who estimated that 6,958 Palestinians in the West Bank and Gaza had been injured from September 29 to November 9 and that 40 percent of these injuries were to children. Robinson also reported: "According to Red Cross/Red Crescent [from September 29 to November 20], 86 children had been killed and over 3,000 [children] injured, two to three hundred of whom, it is estimated, will have permanent disabilities."

Robinson also visited al-Shifa Hospital, the largest hospital in the Gaza Strip, and met with forty-five patients, including children. She reported:

> A 15-year-old, now a paraplegic, informed the High Commissioner that he was shot by Israeli soldiers while he was demonstrating and throwing stones in the industrial zone close to the Eretz checkpoint. He had joined other teenagers after school to express his anger following the death of one of his schoolmates the previous day. A 14-year-old wounded in the arm and leg explained that he had gone to throw stones in revenge after a classmate had been shot and blinded in both eyes, and the doctor accompanying the High Commissioner confirmed he had treated the other boy.

She traveled as well to the Rafah Palestinian refugee camp in southern Gaza, where she inspected private houses and apartments "that had been heavily damaged by [Israeli] gunfire and/or rocket attack, particularly at night." She reported:

> The owner of one house in Rafah told the High Commissioner that she had been obliged to leave her house, within a few minutes, when she realized that an Israeli tank had already started to destroy part of the house. A farm owner told the High Commissioner that Israeli soldiers had destroyed his greenhouses and his family residence during the night of 29 October. Water wells have reportedly also been destroyed in actions carried out by settlers or Israeli forces. The High Commis-

sioner saw that a number of fields of fruit-bearing trees, particularly olive trees, had been cleared in the occupied regions. The High Commissioner was told that, in many cases, these orchards and fields represented the entire livelihood of dozens of families.

Robinson reported that "the destruction of family dwellings has left more than a thousand [Palestinian] children without homes, often in situations of food shortage and without access to medical care," and she noted that "many children suffer from psychological and social problems as a direct consequence of the current situation." Robinson wrote: "Children themselves explained to the High Commissioner their fear of leaving their homes or, in some cases, of going back to their homes, and of difficulties sleeping."

The High Commissioner also visited Hebron, a Palestinian city in the West Bank. Hebron's population is approximately 130,000 Muslims and 400 Jewish settlers. In 1997 Hebron was divided into two sections: "H1," with a population of 100,000 Muslims and administered by the Palestinian Authority, and "H2," with a population of 30,000 Muslims in addition to the 400 Jewish settlers, which is administered by the Israeli occupation commander. Even though the Jewish settlements were built and remain in violation of international law and the settlers represent a fraction of Hebron's population, about 20 percent of the entire city—the H2 sector—is under Israel's control to guarantee the security and privileges of the settlements. With respect to Hebron, Robinson wrote:

> Since the first week of October [2000], the IDF has imposed a curfew on 30,000 Palestinians living in the H2 zone, which has had an enormous impact on the enjoyment by Palestinian residents of their basic human rights. As a result of the curfew, thousands of families and their children live under virtual house arrest, confined to their homes for all but a few hours per week. During the hours when the curfew is not imposed the use of motor vehicles by Palestinian residents is forbidden, requiring residents to walk considerable distances to purchase food supplies, as shops in the Hebron H2 zone are also affected by the curfew.
>
> Workers from the Hebron H2 zone have been prevented from reaching their places of work, whether in Israel or in the occupied territories. Restrictions on freedom of movement make it increasingly difficult for the Palestinians in the H2 zone to meet their most basic

needs, such as food supplies and medical care, and Palestinian children cannot attend school. In this regard, the High Commissioner was informed that 32 schools had been closed since the beginning of the events, preventing some 15,000 pupils from exercising their right to education.

The curfew does not apply to the 300 to 400 Israeli settlers living in the H2 zone of the city and the settler school remains open. To ensure the safety of those settlers, the IDF maintains a large presence in that part of Hebron. Three schools and several Palestinian houses in the H2 zone have been taken over by the IDF and turned into military posts.

Robinson met with Hebron's mayor and other officials from the H1 zone, who told her "that since October [2000], 20 Palestinians had been killed in Hebron, of whom 5 were under 18 years of age, and that many houses, stores and facilities had been damaged, without compensation." She also reported that "allegations were made [by these officials] that settlers were involved in violence against and harassment of Palestinian residents, with the tacit consent of the IDF."[28]

On November 28 the *Times* published an article by Barbara Crossette, a veteran UN–based reporter, who briefly summarized Robinson's report, including her recommendation that international monitors be sent to the West Bank and Gaza—a proposal supported by the Palestinian leadership and human rights organizations but rejected by Israel. Crossette wrote: "The Palestinian push to raise demands on Israel seems at times to work at cross-purposes with Secretary General Kofi Annan's efforts to build a balanced role for himself and the organization in the region. He has made great efforts to help end Israel's isolation at the United Nations and to reduce the routine vilification that it receives from a majority of Arab and developing nations." Crossette also wrote: "The call for monitors or further international action in Israel and the occupied territories has been roundly rejected by [Israeli] Prime Minister Ehud Barak's government. Israel views those proposals as ploys by the Palestinians and their international supporters—led in the United Nations by Egypt, Malaysia, and Pakistan—to expand the roles of the United Nations and the European Union in the Mideast and to reduce the importance of American leadership."[29] Thus, the essential import of an authoritative fact-finding mission presenting evidence of considerable Israeli misconduct in the Palestinian territories got lost; instead, it was associated with supposed excessive demands made on Israel (as in the sound proposal to place UN monitors in the territories) and the "routine vilification" of Israel at the UN, which presumably applied to Robinson's report as well.

The reports by the major human rights organizations summarized above document Israel's use of excessive lethal force in the occupied territories beginning September 29 but before November 22—that is, before the first Palestinian bombing (a remote-detonated car bomb) inside Israel since the beginning of the *intifada*. The Palestinian bombing on November 22 killed three people and wounded several others, including a one-year-old girl. Earlier that day, Israeli security forces killed nine Palestinians.[30] Nevertheless, the *Times* quoted without comment Israel's Prime Minister Ehud Barak's assertion that he would "get even" with the Palestinians, despite the fact that Israel had already killed and injured hundreds of Palestinians by that point.[31]

The next Palestinian bombing in Israel, a suicide bombing, did not occur until March 4, 2001. This bombing, and the front-page coverage in the *New York Times*, began the long train of such bombings in Israel, which was generally given front-page coverage in the *Times*. As in the case of the November 22 Palestinian bombing, reports by human rights organizations of extensive Israeli human rights violations in the Palestinian territories preceded the March 4 bombing but were either ignored by the *Times* or mentioned minimally without further interest. In a December 2000 publication, B'Tselem reported that "from 29 September to 2 December 2000, Israeli security forces killed 204 Palestinian civilians and 24 Palestinian security forces, and wounded approximately 10,000 Palestinians." With respect to Israeli casualties, B'Tselem reported that 29 Israelis (civilians and security force personnel) had been killed by Palestinians within the same time period, and 118 Israeli civilians had been injured.[32] This B'Tselem report—in which Israel's most respected human rights organization documented a massively disproportionate scale of Israeli violence in the first two months of the Palestinian *intifada*—was ignored by the *New York Times*.

On March 16, 2001, a UN Human Rights Commission report was issued pursuant to a fact-finding visit from February 10 to 18. This report estimated that 311 Palestinians had been killed and 11,575 Palestinians had been injured since September 29, 2000; it also estimated that 47 Israelis had been killed and 466 injured since September 29. Among the 311 Palestinians killed, the report noted that 84 were Palestinian children, with 5,000 Palestinian children injured. The report also estimated that, among the 47 Israelis killed, one child was killed and 15 had been injured.[33] This UN Human Rights Commission report, once more documenting excessive use of force by Israel in the occupied territories, was again ignored by the *New York Times*.

Thus, prior to March 4, 2001, when the first Palestinian suicide bombing in Israel since September 29 took place, hundreds of Palestinians had already been killed and thousands injured, with little news coverage or critical commentary in the *Times*. In contrast, the Palestinian suicide bombing of March 4, 2001, was reported on the *Times'* front page, including a front-page photograph of grieving Israelis and a photo caption citing Israeli witnesses "scream[ing] for vengeance."[34] Thus began a pattern of coverage in the *New York Times* (in the period September 2000 to December 2006) which highlighted Palestinian violence against Israelis while minimizing much greater Israeli violence against Palestinians.

The pattern of excessive Israeli force receiving only modest coverage in the *Times* continued well beyond March 2001. For example, Amnesty International issued annual reports in 2001–2006, each with a section on Israel and the occupied territories, and each criticizing Israel for its excessive use of lethal force against Palestinians in the West Bank and Gaza. As far as can be determined, the *Times* ignored each of these annual reports on Israel and the Palestinian territories. For example, in its annual report for 2001 (covering events in 2000 and in particular the first few months of the *intifada*) Amnesty International reported that "more than 300 Palestinians were killed by the Israeli security forces; most were unlawfully killed during the new Intifada."[35]

In its annual report for 2002 (covering events in 2001) Amnesty began documenting persistently disproportionate lethal violence against Palestinians, including the rising number of Palestinian children killed, even as the toll among Israelis began to increase due to the onset of the Palestinian bombings inside Israel. With this report Amnesty also began to document other dimensions of Israeli misconduct, in addition to excessive lethal force, which were common throughout the second *intifada*, including beatings and abuse, administrative detention, torture, targeted assassinations, house demolitions, and prolonged closures and curfews:

More than 460 Palestinians were killed during 2001 by the Israeli security forces; most were unlawfully killed. Among the victims were 79 children and 32 individuals targeted for assassination. More than 2,000 Palestinians were arrested for security reasons. There were widespread reports of police brutality. Palestinian detainees frequently reported that they were tortured or ill-treated during interrogation. At the end of the year at least 40 people were under administrative detention. At least 33 [Israeli] conscientious objectors were imprisoned during 2001. Hundreds of Palestinians from the Occupied Territories were tried before military courts in trials whose procedures fell short of international standards. Collective punishments against Palestinians included closures of towns and villages, demolition of more than 350 Palestinian homes and prolonged curfews. Palestinian armed groups killed 187 Israelis, including 154 civilians.[36]

Amnesty's annual report for 2003—covering events in 2002, a year that witnessed extensive Palestinian suicide bombings in Israel—indicated that, even in this context, Israeli security forces killed more than twice as many Palestinians, with both sides brutally killing many children:

At least 1,000 Palestinians were killed by the Israeli army, most of them unlawfully. They included some 150 children and at least 35 individuals killed in targeted assassinations. Palestinian armed groups killed more than 420 Israelis, at least 265 of them civilians and including 47 children, and some 20 foreign nationals, in targeted or indiscriminate attacks. Prolonged closures and curfews were imposed throughout the Occupied Territories and more than 2,000 homes were destroyed. Thousands of Palestinians were arrested. Most were released without charge, but more than 3,000 remained in military jails. More than 1,900 were held in administrative detention without charge or trial, and some 5,000 were charged with security offences, including involvement in attacks against Israelis. More than 3,800 were tried before military courts in trials that did not meet international standards. Ill-treatment of Palestinian detainees was widespread. Israeli soldiers used Palestinians as "human shields" during military operations. Certain abuses committed by the Israeli army constituted war crimes. These included unlawful killings, obstruction of medical assistance and targeting of medical personnel, extensive and wanton destruction of property, torture and cruel and inhuman treatment, unlawful confinement and the use of "human shields". The deliberate targeting of civilians by Palestinian armed groups constituted crimes against humanity.[37]

Amnesty's annual report for 2004, covering events in 2003, continued to document a high level of casualties on both sides, with Palestinians, however, suffering three times the number of people killed:

The Israeli army killed around 600 Palestinians, including more than 100 children. Most were killed unlawfully—in reckless shooting, shelling and bombing in civilian residential areas, in extrajudicial executions and through excessive use of force. Palestinian armed groups killed around 200 Israelis, at least 130 of them civilians and including 21 children, in suicide bombings and other deliberate attacks. Increasing restrictions on the movement of Palestinians imposed by the Israeli army throughout the Occupied Territories caused unprecedented poverty, unemployment and health problems. The Israeli army demolished several hundred Palestinian homes and destroyed large areas of cultivated land and hundreds of commercial and other properties. Israel stepped up the construction of a fence/wall, most of which cut deep into the West Bank. As a result, hundreds of thousands of Palestinians were confined in enclaves and cut off from their land and essential services in nearby towns and villages. Israel's expansion of illegal settlements in the Occupied Territories continued, further depriving Palestinians of natural resources such as land and water. Thousands of Palestinians were detained by the Israeli army. Most were released without charge, hundreds were charged with security offences against Israel and at least 1,500 were held in administrative detention without charge or trial. Trials before military courts did not meet international standards. Allegations of torture and ill-treatment of Palestinian detainees were widespread and Israeli soldiers used Palestinians as "human shields" during military operations. Certain abuses committed by the Israeli army constituted war crimes, including unlawful killings, obstruction of medical assistance and targeting of medical personnel, extensive and wanton destruction of property, torture and the use of "human shields". The deliberate targeting of civilians by Palestinian armed groups constituted crimes against humanity.[38]

In its annual report for 2005 (covering 2004) Amnesty reported that Israeli security forces had killed nearly seven times as many Palestinians in 2004 than the number of Israelis killed by Palestinians that year:

> The Israeli army killed more than 700 Palestinians, including some 150 children. Most were killed unlawfully—in reckless shooting, shelling and air strikes in civilian residential areas; in extrajudicial executions; and as a result of excessive use of force. Palestinian armed groups killed 109 Israelis—67 of them civilians and including eight children—in suicide bombings, shootings and mortar attacks.[39]

According to this report, in 2004 the Israelis killed more Palestinian children (150)—"recklessly" and "unlawfully"—than the total number of Israelis killed (109) by Palestinians. This report also noted that "the Israeli army destroyed several hundred Palestinian homes, large areas of agricultural land, and infrastructure networks," and that "Israel continued to expand illegal settlements and to build a fence/wall through the West Bank, confining Palestinians in isolated enclaves cut off from their land and essential services in nearby towns and villages." The report also noted that "Israeli settlers increased their attacks against Palestinians and their property and against international human rights workers."[40]

Amnesty's annual report for 2006 (covering 2005) reported that this pattern of killing and violence continued, with many more Palestinians than Israelis killed:

> Israel withdrew its settlers and troops from the Gaza Strip and dismantled four small settlements in the northern West Bank. However, it continued to build and expand illegal settlements and related infrastructure, including a 600km fence/wall, on Palestinian land in the occupied West Bank. Military blockades and restrictions imposed by Israel on the movement of Palestinians within the Occupied Territories continued to cause high unemployment and poverty among the Palestinian population. There was much less violence between Israelis and Palestinians, although attacks by both sides continued. Some 190 Palestinians, including around 50 children, were killed by Israeli forces, and 50 Israelis, including six children, were killed by Palestinian armed groups. Israeli forces carried out unlawful attacks and routinely used excessive force against peaceful demonstrators protesting against the destruction of Palestinian agricultural

land and the Israeli army's construction of the fence/wall. Israeli settlers frequently attacked Palestinian farmers, destroying orchards and preventing cultivation of their land. Israeli soldiers and settlers responsible for unlawful killings and other abuses against Palestinians and their property generally had impunity. Thousands of Palestinians were arrested by Israeli forces throughout the Occupied Territories on suspicion of security offences. Israeli conscientious objectors continued to be imprisoned for refusing to serve in the army.[41]

Taken together, Amnesty's annual reports indicate that from September 29, 2000, to December 31, 2005, Israelis killed more than 3,000 Palestinians, while the Palestinians killed more than 900 Israelis. This generally corroborates B'Tselem's statistics, cited above, that from September 29, 2000, to November 30, 2006, Israelis killed 4,032 Palestinians, while Palestinians killed 1,017 Israelis.[42]

While the *New York Times* covered none of Amnesty's annual reports from 2001 to 2006 on Israel and the occupied territories, which documented extensive Israeli violence against Palestinians, it did publish dozens of front-page stories on Palestinian suicide bombings during these years, as well as numerous editorials condemning those bombings. Nor did the *Times* cite or describe, with a few exceptions, dozens of other important reports issued by Amnesty International from September 2000 to December 2005.[43] These reports addressed in detail issues that were summarized in Amnesty's annual reports. These numerous reports were mostly ignored in the news pages of the *New York Times,* nor were there any editorials critical of Israel's policies in the West Bank and Gaza which were guided by or which cited any of Amnesty's reports. Nor did the overall substance and tone of the *Times'* news coverage and editorial-page commentary reflect the massive violations of international humanitarian law by Israel that are documented in these reports.

A notable exception was a brief series of six news articles in the *Times* by Joel Greenberg who, from early September to early November 2002, cited reports that were issued at the time by Amnesty International, Human Rights Watch, and B'Tselem. In the first article of this series Greenberg cited Amnesty International in the context of a decision by Israel's Supreme Court that allowed the IDF to expel the siblings of a Palestinian man accused of planning a suicide bombing. The Court ruled that the forcible expulsion of these individuals from the West Bank to Gaza did not violate international law. However, as Greenberg wrote: "Amnesty International contended that 'unlawful forcible transfer' of Palestinians under Israeli occupation constituted a war crime under the Fourth Geneva Convention and the Rome Statute of the International Court of Justice."[44]

A month later, citing an Amnesty International report, Greenberg wrote:

> Amnesty International released a report today that accused the Israeli Army and Palestinian armed groups of "utter disregard for the lives of children and other civilians" in the last two years of violence.
>
> The report said that 250 Palestinian children and 72 Israeli children had been killed by the end of August and that both Israel and the Palestinians had failed to bring those responsible to justice.[45]

Greenberg referred to the same Amnesty report a few days later:

> The latest violence came as the London-based rights group Amnesty International issued a report this week asserting that both the Israeli Army and Palestinian armed groups were killing children with impunity.
>
> The United Nations Committee on the Rights of the Child called on Israelis and Palestinians today to "refrain from using and/or targeting children in the armed conflict," which it said had been marked by "acts of terror on both sides."
>
> Amnesty International said more than 250 Palestinian children had been killed from the outbreak of the violence in September 2000 to the end of August this year. Seventy-two Israeli children have been killed, 70 percent of them in suicide bombings, it said. About 7,000 Palestinian children and hundreds of Israeli children have been wounded.
>
> The overwhelming majority of Palestinian child victims were killed when "members of the Israeli Defense Forces responded to demonstrations and stone-throwing incidents with excessive and disproportionate use of force, and as a result of the IDF's reckless shooting, shelling and aerial bombardments of residential areas," the report said.
>
> It asserted that most of the children were killed when the lives of soldiers were not at risk.
>
> The report said both the Israeli and Palestinian authorities had

consistently failed to punish those responsible for the killings, contributing to the persistence of such practices.[46]

Two weeks later, citing hospital sources as well as witnesses and
Palestinian authorities, Greenberg wrote:

> Israeli tanks battling Palestinian gunmen fired cannon and machine
> guns into the densely populated Rafah refugee camp in the southern
> Gaza Strip today, killing at least 6 people and wounding 60 others, the
> director of the local hospital said.
>
> The Palestinian leadership, in a statement released in Gaza, called
> the killings a "new massacre" and said that eight people had been
> killed. There were unconfirmed reports that two of the bodies had yet
> to be recovered.
>
> The latest bloodshed came days after the Bush administration
> expressed deep concern over a significant rise in Palestinian civilian
> casualties during Israeli military operations. Last week, 17 Palestinians
> were killed during an Israeli raid on the town of Khan Yunis in the
> Gaza Strip.
>
> After today's shelling, witnesses said, dismembered bodies were
> pulled from the rubble of refugee dwellings and body parts littered the
> alleys. The dead included a 4-year-old girl, a 15-year-old boy, two
> women and two men, said Dr. Ali Musa, the director of Rafah
> Hospital. He said that half of the wounded were seriously hurt.[47]

In the same article, Greenberg cited Amnesty International in addition
to B'Tselem. He wrote:

> Stepped-up Israeli military operations in the Gaza Strip in recent
> weeks, which the army says are meant to pursue militants, have taken a
> mounting toll on civilians. In the West Bank, prolonged curfews on
> Palestinian cities, often enforced with gunfire, have also caused a steady
> stream of civilian casualties.
>
> Human rights groups have accused Israeli forces of reckless shooting
> and shelling in residential areas.
>
> In a report issued this month on the killing of children in the current
> conflict, the London-based human rights group Amnesty International
> accused Israeli forces of reckless shooting and shelling in Palestinian
> residential areas. The Israeli rights group B'Tselem said in a separate
> report on Wednesday that soldiers using gunfire to enforce curfews

had killed 15 Palestinians over the last four months, 12 of them under the age of 16.

However, Prime Minister Ariel Sharon, speaking to reporters at the end of a visit to Washington, saw things differently. The Israeli Army, he told reporters, "has the highest level of morality in the world, and it is making supreme efforts not to harm civilians."[48]

Two weeks later, on November 4, Greenberg cited Amnesty International again. He began the article as follows:

A new report by Amnesty International contends that Israeli forces committed war crimes in Jenin and Nablus this spring during a large-scale offensive in the West Bank, killing Palestinians unlawfully, blocking medical care, using people as human shields and bulldozing houses with residents inside.

The report was formally submitted to Israeli officials today.

"The information in this report suggests that the Israeli Defense Forces committed violations of international law during the course of military operations in Jenin and Nablus, including war crimes, for which they must be held accountable," the new report says in its conclusion.

A report issued by the group in July called attacks by Palestinian militants on Israeli civilians crimes against humanity.

A spokesman for the Israeli Foreign Ministry called the report one-sided, asserting that it "ignores the fact that Israel is in the midst of an armed conflict that was imposed on it."[49]

Greenberg concluded the article as follows:

The 76-page Amnesty International study, which used stronger language than a similar report in July by the United Nations secretary general, focuses on Israeli Army actions between April and June in Nablus and Jenin in the West Bank. It is based on interviews with witnesses, medical crews and aid workers, visits to sites of the fighting, autopsies by a forensic specialist and assessments by a military expert.

The Jenin refugee camp and the old city in Nablus were the scenes of the fiercest fighting and the heaviest losses on both sides during the Israeli offensive, which began at the end of March after a series of suicide bombings and deadly shooting attacks in Israel.

Citing accounts by witnesses and on-site investigations by Amnesty

International delegates, the report describes incidents in which un-armed Palestinian civilians were fatally shot in custody or while in their homes. In one incident on April 6, a man was shot and killed after he was seized with other men in the Jenin refugee camp, the report says. In another incident, the previous day, a woman was killed when soldiers used explosives to blow open the door of her house as she went to open it.

In Nablus, again on April 6, eight members of a single family were killed, including three children, their pregnant mother and an 85-year-old grandfather, when their house was bulldozed.

The report says soldiers used people as human shields, forcing them to walk in front of soldiers and to enter homes and rooms suspected of being booby-trapped or of sheltering gunmen.[50]

Greenberg's writings at the time also included a November 1 article about a report by Human Rights Watch on Palestinian terrorism in Israel. Greenberg began this article as follows:

A report by Human Rights Watch on Palestinian suicide bombings calls the attacks crimes against humanity and criticizes the Palestinian Authority for failing to act effectively to stop them.

The 170-page report, to be issued Friday, says Yasir Arafat and the Palestinian Authority bear a "high degree of responsibility" for the attacks and have "contributed to an atmosphere of impunity" that has allowed the bombings to continue.

But the report said no evidence was found indicating that Mr. Arafat or other senior Palestinian officials were themselves behind the bombings. Prime Minister Ariel Sharon of Israel and other Israeli officials have repeatedly accused Mr. Arafat and the Palestinian Authority of active involvement in the violence, a charge the Palestinians have denied.[51]

In short, Greenberg was reading the reports issued by human rights organizations at the time. And with six stories in two months citing reports from Amnesty International, B'Tselem, and Human Rights Watch, Greenberg was obviously making an effort to incorporate these reports into his coverage of the conflict. Although these organizations also condemned Palestinian crimes (including suicide bombings), their reports focused predominantly on Israel's conduct, given its far broader violations of international humanitarian law in the occupied territories, and Greenberg's reporting reflected that fact.

However, Israel's "war crimes" in the territories, or reports that the IDF shoots Palestinian children with impunity, or that Israel also practices "terrorism" in the course of the conflict are not the customary focus of the *Times'* coverage, and the stories by Greenberg—a native Israeli accustomed perhaps to the much less stifled coverage of the Israel-Palestine conflict in the Israeli press—were out of place with the overall pattern of coverage at the *Times*. The anomalous character of Greenberg's reporting was underscored further when he left the *Times* for the *Chicago Tribune* in November 2002—two weeks after the last of these six reports—with no publicly announced explanation to our knowledge. Greenberg's departure abruptly ended the brief experiment of integrating reports by Amnesty International and other human rights organizations into the *Times'* coverage of the conflict.

It seems reasonable to expect that the leading newspaper in the United States, supposedly the world's leading democracy and defender of human rights, would regularly cover in some detail reports by the most authoritative human rights organizations in the world, especially as they involve concerns over which the US has the most influence—that is, its own policies and those of its key allies. Given that the United States is Israel's chief political, military, and financial supporter, it also seems reasonable that the *Times* would cover such reports, because they regularly charge Israel with committing serious crimes and because the United States is closely associated with Israel's conduct in fact and world opinion.

For example, at the height of Israel's "unlawful" and "excessive" use of force against the Palestinians in the West Bank and Gaza immediately after September 28, 2000, Amnesty International, in a press release issued on October 19, "called on the US government to cease all transfers of attack helicopters to Israel, including the pending sale of Apache helicopters, until Israeli authorities demonstrate that the helicopters will not be used to commit human rights violations in Israel and the Occupied Territories and the areas under the control of the Palestinian Authority." Amnesty reported "that US-supplied helicopters have been used to violate the human rights of Palestinians and Arab Israelis during the recent conflict in the region." William F. Schulz, executive director of Amnesty International USA (AIUSA), stated:

Given the close military relations between the U.S. and Israeli governments and the Israeli use of helicopters provided by the U.S. in recent incidents, AIUSA today urged the U.S. government to use its influence to insist that the Israeli forces abide by international human rights standards on the use of force and firearms.

"The Israeli government has been using U.S.-supplied helicopters to commit human rights violations during its recent round of conflict with the Palestinians, and the U.S. government must accept some responsibility for how such weapons are used," said Schulz. "We urge the U.S. government to suspend all attack helicopter transfers to Israel immediately. We also urge the U.S. to support Amnesty International's call for an impartial international investigation, led by the United Nations, into the serious human rights abuses that have taken place in the region over the last few weeks."[52]

At the time the Federation of American Scientists also reported, with more specificity, the transfer of US weaponry to the government of Israel while it was unlawfully using such weapons against Palestinians: "Since the outbreak of renewed violence [on September 29], the U.S. government has authorized the sale of an additional 52 F-16I fighter jets, 9 AH-64D Apache Longbow attack helicopters, 23 AH-1F attack helicopters, and 59 UH-60L Black Hawk utility helicopters."[53] Consistent with its practice of mostly ignoring violations of international law by the United States and Israel, as well as not reporting important facts that underscore or facilitate such violations, the *New York Times* hardly reported and seldom (if ever) condemned these critical US weapons transfers to Israel.

In short, the *Times'* coverage of the Israel-Palestine conflict is generally at odds with Amnesty International's coverage of the conflict. This represents, in effect, a significant split between the leading liberal news organization in the United States and the world's foremost human rights organization with respect to the human rights dimension of the Israel-Palestine conflict. This is not to say that the *Times* never mentions a human rights organization or report, that it supports every policy of Israel in the West Bank and Gaza, or that the human rights organizations have a crystal ball that provides perfect insight. The fault lines, however, are clear enough. Whereas international humanitarian law is the standard of analysis at Amnesty International and the other rights groups, that standard is of little concern at the *Times*, to the detriment of its news coverage and editorial-page commentary.

It is also worth noting the generally consistent findings, grounded in legitimate sources of law, issued by the major human rights organizations in contrast to the inconsistent counsel from the *Times'* editorial page. For example, the *Times* editorial page supported the US invasion of Iraq throughout fall 2002, withdrew that support a few days before the apparently imminent attack on Iraq in March 2003, supported the invasion again soon after it was initiated, then muddled its support as the quagmire set in.[54] Similarly, the *Times* supported the Israeli invasion of Lebanon in summer 2006, then qualified its support when the invasion led to large-scale civilian casualties and became identified within Israel with political and military ineptitude.[55] Rather than having a history of consistent observance of international law, leading to reliable editorial guidance in response to illegal and imprudent threats of force, the *Times'* editorial page instead has a long-standing habit of supporting such threats—and the unlawful force that follows—in the frenzied early stages of crises and acute conflict. The policy disasters that follow lead to the predictable turnabouts in the *Times'* editorials.

While Israel is entitled to its territorial borders as recognized under international law, it is not entitled to occupy the West Bank and Gaza and thus deny the Palestinians their right to self determination on those territories as recognized under international law. This simple working editorial policy for the *Times'* editorial page would legitimately fix its opposition, in principle, to Israel's illegal occupation of the West Bank (and Gaza), its illegal annexation and extensive illegal settling of East Jerusalem, its illegal settlements in the West Bank, its illegal separation barrier on Palestinian territory, its illegal de facto annexation of territory in the West Bank via the settlements and separation barrier, its illegal shootings, beatings, and abuse of Palestinians, its illegal torture of illegally detained Palestinians, and so on. It is also illegal for Palestinians to bomb or otherwise attack Israeli civilians. With all of this illegality, all covered by international law, lying at the center of the conflict, it's simply not possible for the *New York Times* to ignore international law and still cover the conflict impartially and competently, as it claims to do. This pattern of neglect is consistent with a pro-Israel bias, because international law overwhelmingly supports Palestinian claims on the main issues in dispute between the two sides.

In addition to Amnesty International and B'Tselem, Human Rights Watch (HRW) has reported that Israeli violence greatly exceeded

Palestinian violence from September 29, 2000, onward. Thus, in its section on Israel and the occupied territories in its annual report for 2001, HRW began as follows:

Within three weeks, more than 120 Palestinians were killed and over 4,800 injured in clashes with Israeli security forces that began on September 29 [2000]. Most of the deaths were the result of excessive, and often indiscriminate, use of lethal force by Israel Defense Forces (IDF) soldiers, police, and border police against unarmed civilian demonstrators, including children. The casualties were disproportionately on the Palestinian side, but two Israeli soldiers were beaten to death by a Palestinian mob.[56]

In its annual report for 2002 HRW stated:

Many civilians were among the over seven hundred Palestinians and over two hundred Israelis who, by November 2001, had been killed in the violence that followed the eruption of clashes between Israelis and Palestinians in September 2000. In addition, some 16,000 Palestinians and some 1,700 Israelis were injured in the violence. The conflict was marked by attacks on civilians and civilian objects by both Israeli security forces and Palestinian armed groups. Both Israeli and Palestinian authorities failed to take the necessary steps to stop the security forces under their control from committing abuses, and failed to adequately investigate and punish perpetrators.[57]

Its report for 2003 noted:

The violence that erupted beginning in September 2000 intensified in 2002. Civilians increasingly paid the price for repeated, egregious violations of international humanitarian law by the Israel Defense Forces (IDF) and Palestinian armed groups. At least 1,949 Palestinians and 637 Israelis were killed between September 2000 and late October 2002, the majority civilians, including 292 Palestinian and seventy-nine Israeli children.[58]

HRW's annual report for 2005 noted that "armed attacks and clashes in the course of the year brought casualties since September 2000 to well over three thousand Palestinians and nearly one thousand

Israelis killed, and more than 34,000 Palestinians and six thousand Israelis injured."[59] And HRW's annual report for 2006 reported: "Since the beginning of the current *intifada* in September 2000, Israel has killed nearly three thousand Palestinians in the West Bank and Gaza, including more than six hundred children. During the same period, Palestinian fighters have killed more than nine hundred Israelis inside Israel and in the OPT [occupied Palestinian territory]. Most of those killed on both sides were civilians."[60]

These annual HRW reports—all ignored by the *New York Times*—confirm what Amnesty International and B'Tselem had also reported: Israel has killed and injured many more Palestinians since September 2000 than the number of Israelis killed and injured by Palestinians. The *Times* also ignored dozens of HRW reports and press releases issued since September 2000 on Israeli and Palestinian human rights violations.[61] While HRW was often critical of the conduct of the Palestinians in its reports, it issued more reports that were critical of Israel, due to the larger scale and broader scope of Israel's violations of international humanitarian law.

One striking statistic in the Amnesty International, Human Rights Watch, and B'Tselem reports is the number of Palestinian children killed by Israeli security personnel. According to B'Tselem's statistics, from September 29, 2000, to September 15, 2006, Israeli security forces killed 764 children seventeen years of age and younger.[62] The evidence indicates that most of these children were not only "unlawfully" killed, as these human rights organizations reported, but brutally killed. A Switzerland-based human rights organization, Defence for Children International (DCI), which was established in 1979 during the International Year of the Child and has consultative status with the United Nations Economic and Social Council (UNESCO), the United Nations Children's Fund (UNICEF), and the Council of Europe,[63] has documented the cause of death of many Palestinian children killed by Israeli security forces. On December 31, 2000, DCI issued a report that included "complete information on the Palestinian children killed in the First Quarter of the Intifada (29 September 2000–31 December 2000)." The list of children killed "includes those Palestinians under the age of 18 years who were killed as a direct result of Israeli military and settler presence in the Occupied Palestinian Territories."[64] The DCI chart of Palestinian children killed is reproduced below.

DATE	NAME	AGE	RESIDENCE	CAUSE OF DEATH
30 September	Mohammad Jamal Mohammad Al-Dura	11	Al-Breij/Gaza	Live bullet to multiple places
30 September	Nizar Mohammad Eida	16	Deir Ammar/Ramallah	Live bullet to chest
30 September	Khaled Adli Insooh Al-Bazyan	15	Nablus	Exploding bullet to head
1 October	Samir Sidqi Tabanja	12	Nablus	Live bullet to chest
1 October	Sarah 'Abdel Atheem 'Abdel Haq	18 mos.	Talfit/Nablus	Live bullet to head. *Killed by Israeli Settlers*
1 October	Hussam Bakhit	17	Balatta Refugee Camp/Nablus	Live bullet to head
1 October	Iyad Ahmad Salim Al-Khoshashee	16	Nablus	Live bullet to multiple places. *Iyad's body was found Sunday in the hills surrounding Nablus, but he is believed to have died on Saturday.*
1 October	Sami Fathi Mohammad Al-Taramsi	16	Sheikh Radwan/Gaza	Live bullet to chest
1 October	Mohammad Nabeel Hamed Daoud	14	Al-Bireh/Ramallah	Live bullet to head
2 October	Wa'el Tayseer Mohammad Qatawi	16	Balatta Refugee Camp/Nablus	Live bullet to eye
2 October	Muslih Hussein Ibrahim Jarad	17	Deir Balah/Gaza *Killed in Um Al-Fahim*	Live bullet to chest
2 October	'Aseel Hassan 'Assalih	17	'Arrabeh Al-Batouf/Upper Galilee	Live bullet to neck
3 October	Hussam Ismail Al-Hamshari	16	Tulkarem	Exploding bullet to head
3 October	Ammar Khalil Al-Rafai'i	17	Al-Maghazi/Gaza	Hit by missile in the head
4 October	Mohammad Zayed Yousef Abu 'Assi	13	Bani Sahla/Gaza	Live bullet to chest
6 October	Saleh Issa Yousef Al-Raiyati	17	Rafah/Gaza	Live bullet to head
6 October	Majdi Samir Maslamani	15	Beit Hanina/Jerusalem	Exploding bullet to head
6 October	Mohammad Khaled Tammam	17	Tulkarem	Live bullet to chest
8 October	Yousef Diab Yousef Khalaf	17	Al Breij/Gaza	Died from injuries sustained on 2 October, shrapnel to head.
11 October	Karam Omar Ibrahim Qannan	17	Khan Younis Refugee Camp/Gaza	Rubber coated steel bullet to chest
11 October	Sami Hassan Salim Al-Balduna	17	Tulkarem Refugee Camp	Live bullet to chest
12 October	Sami Fathi Abu Jezr	12	Rafah/Gaza	Died from injuries sustained on 11 October, Live bullet to head
16 October	Mo'ayyad Osaama Al-Jawareesh	14	Aida Refugee Camp/Bethlehem	Rubber coated steel bullet to head
20 October	Mohammad 'Adil Abu Tahoun	15	Tulkarem	Live bullet to multiple places
20 October	Samir Talal 'Oweisi	16	Qalqiliya	Live bullet to chest
20 October	'Alaa Bassam Beni Nimra	16	Salfit	Live bullet to chest
21 October	Omar Ismail Al-Abheisi	15	Deir Balah/Gaza	Exploding bullet to chest
21 October	Majed Ibrahim Hawamda	15	Ramallah	Exploding bullet to head
22 October	Wa'el Mahmoud Mohammad Imad	13	Jabaliya Refugee Camp/Gaza	Live bullet to head
22 October	Salah Al-Din Fawzi Nejmi	16	Al-Maghazi Camp/Gaza	Live bullet to chest
23 October	Ashraf Habayab	15	Askar Refugee Camp/Nablus	Exploding bullet to head. *Died from injuries sustained 16 October.*

24 October	Iyad Osaama Tahir Sha'ath	12	Khan Younis/Gaza	Live bullet to head. *Died from injuries sustained 21 October.*
24 October	Nidal Mohammad Zuhudi Al-Dubeiki	16	Hai Al-Darraj/Gaza	Exploding bullet to abdomen.
26 October	'Alaa Mohammad Mahfouth	14	Arroub Refugee Camp/Hebron	Live bullet to head. *Died from injuries sustained on 6 October.*
27 October	Bashir Salah Musa Shelwit	16	Qalqiliya	Live bullet to chest.
29 October	Husni Ibrahim Najjar	16	Rafah/Gaza Strip	Live bullet to head.
31 October	Shadi Awad Nimir Odeh	17	Hai Zaitun/Gaza Strip	Live bullet to head.
1 November	Ahmad Suleiman Abu Tayeh	17	Shatti Refugee Camp/ Gaza	Live bullets and exploding bullets to multiple places.
1 November	Mohammad Ibrahim Hajaaj	14	Sheja'aya/Gaza	Live bullet to head.
1 November	Ibrahim Riziq Mohammad Omar	14	Shatti Refugee Camp/ Gaza	Live bullet to chest.
2 November	Khaled Mohammad Ahmad Riziq	17	Hizma/Jerusalem	Live bullet to multiple places.
2 November	Yazen Mohammad Issa Al-Khalaiqa	14	Al-Shiyoukh/Hebron *Killed in Bethlehem*	Live bullet to back.
4 November	Rami Ahmad Abdel Fatah	15	Hizma/Jerusalem	Exploding bullet to multiple places.
4 November	Hind Nidal Jameel Abu Quweider	23 days old	Hebron	Tear gas inhalation.
5 November	Maher Mohammad Al-Sa'idi	15	Al-Breij/Gaza	Live bullet to head
6 November	Wajdi Al-Lam Al-Hattab	15	Tulkarem	Exploding bullet to chest
6 November	Mohammad Nawwaf Al-Ta'aban	17	Deir Balah/Gaza	Live bullet to chest
7 November	Ahmad Amin Al-Khufash	6	Marda/Salfit	Run-over by Israeli settler
8 November	Ibrahim Fouad Al-Qassas	15	Khan Younis/Gaza	Live bullet to eye. *Died from injuries sustained on 5 November.*
8 November	Faris Fa'iq Odeh	15	Hai Zaitun/Gaza	Live bullet to head.
8 November	Mohammad Misbah Abu Ghali	16	Khan Younis Refugee Camp/Gaza	Live bullet to chest.
8 November	Ra'ed Abdel Hamid Daoud	14	Heras/Salfit	Exploding bullet to multiple places
9 November	Mahmoud Kamel Khalil Sharab	17	Khan Younis/Gaza	Live bullet to back
10 November	Osaama Mazen Saleem 'Azouqah	14	Jenin	Live bullet to chest
10 November	Osaama Samir Al-Jerjawee	17	Hai Al-Daraj/Gaza	Live bullet to chest
11 November	Musa Ibrahim Al-Dibs	14	Jabalia Camp/Gaza	Live bullet to chest
12 November	Mohammad Nafiz Abu Naji	16	Sheikh Radwan/Gaza	Live bullet to chest
13 November	Yahya Naif Abu Shemaali	17	Khan Younis/Gaza	Live bullet to chest
14 November	Saber Khamis Brash	15	Al 'Amari Camp/ Ramallah	Live bullet to chest
14 November	Mohammad Khatir Al 'Ajli	13	Hai Sheju'a/Gaza	Exploding bullet to head
15 November	Ibrahim Abdel Raouf Jaidi	15	Qalqiliya	Live bullet to chest
15 November	Jadua Munia Mohammad Abu Kupashe	16	Al Samua/Hebron	Live bullets to multiple places.
15 November	Ahmad Samir Basel	17	Tel Al-Howwa/Gaza	Live bullet to chest

15 November	Mohammad Nasser Mohammad Al-Sharafe	17	Nasser/Gaza	Live bullet to head
15 November	Jihad Suheil Abu Shahma	12	Khan Younis/Gaza	Live bullet to head
15 November	Ahmad Said Ahmad Sha'aban	16	Jalama/Jenin	Exploding bullet to abdomen
16 November	Samir Mohammad Hassan Al-Khudour	17	Al-Fawwar Refugee Camp/Hebron	Exploding bullet to chest
17 November	Rami Imad Yassin	17	Zeitun/Gaza	Live bullet to chest
17 November	Mohammad Abdel Jalil Mohammad Abu Rayyan	16	Halhoul/Hebron	Live bullet to head
19 November	Abdel Rahman Ziad Dahshan	14	Sabra/Gaza	Live bullet to chest
20 November	Ibrahim Hassan Ahmad Uthman	17	Tel Al-Sultan/Gaza	Live bullet to chest
21 November	Yasser Taleb Mohammad Tebatitti	16	Tulkarem *Killed while on vacation. Family lives in Saudi Arabia.*	Live bullet to chest
22 November	Ibrahim Hussein Al-Muqannan	14	Khan Younis/Gaza Strip	Live bullet to head. *Died from injuries sustained on 20 November*
23 November	Maram Imad Ahmad Saleh Hassouneh	3	Jalazone Refugee Camp/Ramallah	Tear gas inhalation
24 November	Aysar Mohammad Sadiq Hassis	15	Jenin	Exploding bullet to eye.
24 November	Majdi Ali Abed	15	Sheju'a/Gaza Strip	Live bullet to head. *Died from injuries sustained on 17 November.*
26 November	Ziad Ghaleb Zaid Selmi	17	Habla/Qalqiliya	Live bullets to multiple places.
26 November	Mahdi Qassem Jaber	16	Habla/Qalqiliya	Live bullets to multiple places.
28 November	Karam Fathi Al-Kurd	14	Khan Younis/Gaza Strip	Live bullet to head *Died from injuries sustained on 23 November.*
29 November	Mohammad Abdullah Al-Mashharawi	14	Gaza	Live bullet to head. *Died from injuries sustained on 26 November.*
30 November	Walid Mohammad Ahmad Hamida	17	Teku'a/Bethlehem	Live bullet to chest.
30 November	Shadi Ahmad Hassan Zghoul	16	Hussan/Bethlehem	Run-over by Israeli settler.
1 December	Mohammed Salih Mohammad Al-Arjah	12	Rafah/Gaza Strip	Live bullet to head.
5 December	Ramzi Adil Mohammed Bayatni	15	Abu Qash/Ramallah	Live bullet to eye.
8 December	Mohammad Abdullah Mohammad Yahya	16	Kufr Rai/Jenin	Hit by missile.
8 December	Alaa Abdelatif Mohammad Abu Jaber	17	Al-Maghayeer/Jenin	Hit by missile.
8 December	Ammar Samir Al-Mashni	17	Beit Or Al-Tahta/Ramallah	Live bullet to head
8 December	Mu'ataz Azmi Ismail Talakh	16	Dheishe Refugee Camp/Bethlehem	Live bullet to head
9 December	Salim Mohammad Hamaideh	12	Rafah/Gaza	Live bullet to head
11 December	Ahmad Ali Hassan Qawasmeh	15	Hebron	Live bullet to head
20 December	Hani Yusef Al-Sufi	14	Rafah/Gaza	Shrapnel to head
22 December	Arafat Mohammad Ali Al-Jabarin	17	Sa'ir/Hebron	Live bullet to head
31 December	Mo'ath Ahmad Abu Hedwan	12	Hebron	Shrapnel to head

CLINICALLY DEAD				
The following Palestinian children have been declared clinically dead.				
DATE	NAME	AGE	RESIDENCE	INJURY
30 September	Khaled Hameed	17	Rafah/Gaza	Live bullet to head
30 September	Mohammad Nawaf Abu Owemer	13	Deir Balah/Gaza	Live bullet to head
30 September	Mohammad Sami Al-Hummos	14	Rafah/Gaza	Live bullet to head
5 November	Ghazaleh Joudet Jaradat	14	Sa'ir/Hebron	Rubber coated steel bullet to head
11 November	Hamad Jamal Al-Faraa	13	Khan Younis/Gaza Strip	Live bullet to head

CHILDREN DEATHS AS A RESULT OF THE ISRAELI IMPOSED CLOSURE				
DATE	NAME	AGE	RESIDENCE	CAUSE
13 October	Alaa Osaama Hamdan	10	Assawiya/Nablus	Died from a severe lung infection after Israeli soldiers prohibited her father from passing through a checkpoint to transport her to a hospital.

The causes of death listed in this chart, for child after child—and in other DCI charts issued pursuant to this one[65]—are not consistent with Israeli claims that these deaths are regrettable but accidental. This is nothing less than the state-sanctioned murder of Palestinian children by Israeli security forces, no significant aspect of which is reported or commented upon by the *New York Times*.

In addition, DCI issued a report that listed Palestinian child deaths for a twelve-year period beginning in 1990. In this report, DCI noted: "Over the last ten years Palestinian children have been the continual target of Israeli aggression and violence. From 1990–2001, 492 Palestinian children were killed as a direct result of actions taken by Israeli soldiers, settlers or undercover agents." One of the charts published in this report is reproduced below:

Year	Palestinian Children Killed By Israeli Soldiers, Settlers or Undercover Units	Percentage of Total Palestinian Deaths Represented by Children
1990	45	29.8%
1991	42	40%
1992	35	24.6%
1993	54	29.67%
1994	39	27.08%
1995	10	22.7%
1996	29	40.27%
1997	17	85%
1998	14	51.85%
1999	4	50%
2000	105	35.96%
2001	98	21.26%

With respect to this chart, DCI observed that "a cursory examination of these figures indicates that despite a relative decline in aggregate child deaths from 1997–1999, Israeli forces have consistently targeted Palestinian children since 1990."[66] Despite extensive study of the IDF's shooting of Palestinian children, we found no references to any reports by Defence for Children International in the *New York Times*.

While it may not be practical for the news and editorial pages at the *Times* to cover every report issued by the human rights organizations mentioned in this chapter, there is no apparent justification for ignoring their main findings, including the established fact—supported unanimously by Amnesty International, Human Rights Watch, and B'Tselem—that Israeli violence against Palestinians exceeds even Palestinian violence against Israelis. There is even less justification when the *Times* depicts Palestinian violence—in opposition to what the human rights groups have reported—as the dominant source of violence in the conflict.

2

The British and Israeli Press

In addition to minimizing its coverage of reports from the major human rights organizations, the *Times* also manages to minimize its coverage of day-to-day episodes of Israeli violence against Palestinians. Other respected news organizations, including in the UK and Israel, do a better job of covering these incidents, and their reports help explain how so many Palestinian children are shot by Israeli security forces. For example, in January 2006 the British newspaper the *Guardian* reported that a nine-year-old Palestinian girl "was behaving in a suspicious manner reminiscent of a terrorist," according to the Israeli army, because "she got too close to the border fence" that separates the West Bank from Israel. For this reason, an Israeli soldier "fired several bullets into the child," hitting her in the neck and stomach. The girl's mother told the *Guardian*: "We have no idea why she went there [toward the wall] but she was a child. She was so small. She was nine years old. She didn't wear a *hijab* [a headscarf]. It was clear she was just a young girl. This is hatred."[67]

The Israeli newspaper *Ha'aretz* reported the girl's shooting as follows:

> The IDF said troops spotted a Palestinian carrying a large bag near the border fence. Suspecting that it contained explosives, the troops called on the person to stop and fired warning shots in the air. After the person did not heed the calls and moved closer to the border, the soldiers fired again and shot the person dead, an IDF statement said.[68]

The IDF account, as reported in *Ha'aretz*, is worth examining. Even if a very young girl were carrying a large bag near the border fence, no legally or morally acceptable rules of engagement would permit a resort to lethal force against a child under such circumstances. Furthermore, no explosives were found, and even the IDF reported no such finding. It is also notable that the IDF statement disingenuously referred to a "Palestinian" and a "person" as its terrorism suspect, rather than a small girl.

According to the *Guardian's* account, the girl "was the second child killed by the Israeli army last week." In the earlier incident, Israeli soldiers "shot 13-year-old Munadel Abu Aalia in the back as he walked along a road reserved for Jewish settlers with two friends." The *Guardian* reported that "the [Israeli] army said the boys planned to throw rocks at Israeli cars, which the military defines as terrorism."[69] Apparently the dead boy never got the chance to throw stones—he was shot before any were even thrown.

A few weeks later, in mid-February, *Ha'aretz* reported that IDF soldiers shot dead a mentally handicapped nineteen-year-old Palestinian man who was carrying a toy gun. *Ha'aretz* reported: "This is the latest in a number of incidents of IDF soldiers shooting to death Palestinians carrying toy guns," the bearers of which are usually children. "Three months ago," according to the newspaper, "IDF soldiers shot dead a 12-year-old boy in the Jenin refugee camp who was carrying a toy gun." An IDF soldier "opened fire from inside a jeep and hit Al-Khatib [the young boy] in the head." In addition, in January 2006 IDF soldiers killed another twelve-year-old Palestinian boy in a village east of Jenin. The soldiers "were driving through the village when local youths began congregating and throwing stones at their jeep." The soldiers said the boy "aimed a rifle at them that resembled in design and size an M-16 assault rifle. The soldiers opened fire and killed" the boy.[70] Note that even the IDF rendition of these episodes alleges no actual gunfire from the boys before the Israeli soldiers shot and killed them.

In early March 2006 an "Israel Air Force aircraft" killed two young boys—an eight-year-old and his fifteen-year-old brother—in addition to a 24-year-old man in the Gaza Strip. The three Palestinians were bystanders in a missile attack against a car carrying two suspected Islamic Jihad militants, both of whom also were killed. An aunt of one of the men killed, who also happened to be near the scene of the missile attack, suffered a heart attack and died. Israel routinely assassinates suspected Palestinian militants in this manner, often killing and maiming incidental onlookers, as in this case. This practice of "targeted assassinations" is a clear violation of international humanitarian law and is condemned by every major human rights organization. Expressing no regret for the loss of life, Israeli Prime Minister Ehud Olmert stated with respect to this incident: "The war on terror will be conducted in full strength as it is being conducted in every corner, in every place in the Gaza Strip and everywhere else."[71]

With few or no arrests or serious investigations into the killing of Palestinian children by Israeli security personnel, the Israeli government does very little to punish or prevent such incidents. Thus, predictably, two weeks later, in mid-March 2006, Israeli soldiers shot and killed another small Palestinian child. According to *Ha'aretz*, Israeli border police shot dead a ten-year-old girl while reportedly seeking the arrest of wanted Islamic Jihad militants; Israeli sources told *Ha'aretz* that the girl was inadvertently hit by shots fired at a Palestinian taxi trying to evade an Israeli roadblock. *Ha'aretz* reported: "But Kamal Zaed, the girl's uncle who was driving the car, said three [Israeli] men ran toward the car and before he could turn off the engine they fired on him." The uncle said: "The first bullet hit my niece. She got a bullet in the head from the very beginning." Even assuming that the Israeli description of events was accurate, it alleges no prior Palestinian gunfire. *Ha'aretz* also cited condemnation of the shooting by the British government: "The British Foreign Office condemned Israel over the weekend after Border Policemen operating in the West Bank village of Yamoun on Friday shot a 10-year-old Palestinian girl to death."[72]

Two weeks after this incident, in early April 2006 Israeli soldiers shot and killed another Palestinian child, in this instance a thirteen-year-old boy, and wounded two other children in the Qalandiyah refugee camp north of Jerusalem. According to Palestinian sources cited by *Ha'aretz*, "an IDF Jeep entered Qalandiyah after 5 P.M. Clashes broke out, Palestinians began attacking the jeep with stones and IDF troops responded with gunfire, the Palestinians said." According to Israeli sources cited in the same article, "soldiers opened fire when the children attempted to vandalize the separation fence next to Qalandiyah. The soldiers followed the routine procedure to arresting a suspect. However, after the children fled the scene, the soldiers reportedly opened fire."[73] Thus, by the IDF's own account, IDF soldiers opened fire a second time and killed a thirteen-year-old boy for running away after the IDF had opened fire on the boy the first time. Given these incidents and many others, it appears that Israel's rules of engagement permit Israeli soldiers to shoot and kill Palestinian children who wander toward the separation barrier, vandalize the separation barrier, throw stones, think about throwing stones, ride in taxicabs, or run away from Israeli soldiers.

A week after this thirteen-year-old boy was killed, *Ha'aretz* reported that IDF artillery hit a family home in Beit Lahia, a town in the northern Gaza Strip, killing a twelve-year-old Palestinian girl and injuring her pregnant mother, who was admitted to a hospital "in serious condition." *Ha'aretz* reported "thirteen other members" of the girl's family, "including toddlers, children, and teenagers were injured."[74] With respect to the same incident, the *Jerusalem Post* reported that the girl killed by the IDF was an eight-year-old, and "thirteen others were wounded"—all children—"ranging from one year old to 17."[75] Israel had been shelling Gaza for several days in response to Qassam rocket attacks by Palestinian militants on southern Israel.[76] Investigating this incident, *Ha'aretz* reported that the IDF had reduced the "safety zone" that its artillery shells must maintain around Palestinian communities—the zone had been reduced from 300 meters to 100 meters. The paper noted that because the fragmentation range of such shells is 100 meters, "the decision [to reduce the zone] clearly endangers civilian lives." *Ha'aretz* also reported that, although such shelling had killed seventeen Palestinians in the Gaza Strip from April 7 to 10, "widespread shelling of Gaza would continue," according to the IDF.[77]

On April 11 Amnesty International issued a press release that called upon the Israeli army "to end immediately its air bombardment and shelling of civilian residential areas in the Gaza Strip."[78] On April 16 *Ha'aretz* reported "six human rights organizations appealed [to] the High Court [of Israel] to cancel a regulation which allows Israel Defense Forces artillery to fire shells at targets up to 100 meters away from Palestinian houses."[79] Similarly, on April 16 B'Tselem reported that "three Israeli human rights groups and two Palestinian organizations jointly wrote to the Israeli Minister of Defense and Chief of Staff demanding the cancellation of the decision to reduce the 'safety zone' for artillery fire on the Gaza Strip, due to the danger it poses to the civilian population and its cost in human lives."[80]

On April 18 *Ha'aretz* reported that "an IDF artillery shell killed 16-year-old Palestinian Mahmoud Ovayed and wounded two others in the northern Gaza Strip town of Beit Lahiya." The newspaper said "the youths were standing in an open field in the northern part of Beit Lahiya when they were hit by the shell."[81] On April 30 *Ha'aretz* reported that seven Palestinians "were injured from Israel Defense Forces artillery fire" in an incident the day before. The injured casualties included three children, ages fourteen, five and three.[82]

On May 1 *Ha'aretz* reported that "Israel Defense Forces troops Monday morning killed a Palestinian woman during a raid on a suspected militant hideout in the West Bank city of Tulkarm." IDF soldiers had surrounded a house where a Palestinian was hiding, whereupon "the troops spotted a figure moving inside the house and opened fire," killing Eitef Zalat, a woman in her forties.[83] The *Jerusalem Post* added "her two daughters were also wounded in the incident and were being treated in the hospital."[84] On May 1 *Ha'aretz* reported that "some of the [IDF] bullets penetrated the house, fatally wounding Eitef Zalat." On May 2 *Ha'aretz* reported that several witnesses said Zalat was shot in the head while standing near a window of her home during the incident, which involved an elite IDF unit conducting an arrest raid, and that one of her children was "moderately to seriously injured by the gunfire."[85]

These incidents and other day-to-day atrocities like them are regularly reported by Israeli newspapers. While we do not expect the *Times* to focus its coverage to the same extent, its news reports and editorials nevertheless overall do not reflect the cruel and vicious realities of Israeli violence in the occupied Palestinian territories. In contrast, the three Palestinian suicide bombings that occurred during this period—January to May 2006—were prominently covered in the news and editorial pages of the *Times*.[86]

While persistent readers of the *Times* will find an occasional story about Israeli soldiers killing Palestinian civilians, the *Times* regularly and prominently publishes stories about Palestinians killing Israelis. This pattern of coverage by the *Times*—and the US news media in general—creates an impression that Palestinians are responsible for most of the violence in the Israel-Palestine conflict. This widely held notion benefits Israel in several important ways: it gives it the pretense of a morally superior position in the conflict; it gives it a substantial political advantage in the United States which deflects attention from its illegal occupation of Palestinian territory; and it allows actual and de facto annexations of Palestinian territory to seem almost reasonable.

The manner in which the *Times* manages to obscure Israel's confiscation of Palestinian territory was illustrated in its coverage of Prime Minister Ehud Olmert's "convergence plan," announced in early 2006. A January 25, 2006, news article in the *New York Times* reported, "In his first major policy address since becoming Israel's acting prime minister, Ehud Olmert said that he backed the creation of a Palestinian state, and that Israel would have to relinquish parts of the West Bank to maintain its Jewish majority." In his speech Olmert said: "We support the establishment of a modern, democratic Palestinian state. The existence of two nations, one Jewish and one Palestinian, is the full solution to the national aspirations and problems of each of the peoples." Olmert also stated, as the *Times* reported: "The choice between allowing Jews to live in all parts of the land of Israel [which in the sense intended here includes the West Bank] and living in a state with a Jewish majority mandates giving up parts of the land of Israel. We will not be able to continue ruling over the territories in which the majority of the Palestinian population lives."

Also without clarification, the *Times* reported two weeks later that "Acting Prime Minister Ehud Olmert said on a television interview broadcast on Tuesday that he wanted to set the country's permanent borders, with Israel giving up significant parts of the West Bank but keeping the largest Jewish settlement blocs," identified as "Ma'aleh Adumim, just east of Jerusalem, with about 30,000 residents; Gush Etzion, several miles south of Jerusalem, with more than 20,000 residents; and Ariel, north of Jerusalem, with close to 20,000 residents." The *Times* reported, again without comment, that "Mr. Olmert also said Israel would need to maintain a presence near the West Bank border with Jordan."[87]

Taken together, these two major policy statements by then Acting Prime Minister Olmert indicated with new specificity Israel's intention to annex land on the Palestinian side of the Green Line near Jerusalem, which includes the Israeli settlement blocs mentioned above, in addition to Palestinian land along the Jordan Valley. Left out of these two news reports is the fact that the land claimed by Olmert belongs to the Palestinians under international law. Also omitted, pointedly, are any maps depicting the Olmert "withdrawal" plan, which would demonstrate Israel's plan to illegally annex Palestinian territory.

The *Times*' tacit endorsement of the misleading Israeli "withdrawal" from the West Bank continued in a news article by its veteran Israel-based correspondents, Steven Erlanger and Greg Myre, who wrote about the Israeli Knesset election on March 28: "Israelis voted Tuesday to bring to power a new centrist party, Kadima, which is committed to a further pullout from the occupied West Bank." By voting for Kadima, they wrote, "Israelis turned away from the right." Erlanger and Myre also wrote, again quoting Olmert without comment, that because Israel was "prepared to compromise" by giving up "parts of our beloved land of Israel," referring again to the recognized state of Israel plus all of the West Bank, the Palestinians too should "accept only part of their dream" and thus relinquish those portions of West Bank land staked out by Olmert. Thus, by participating in the strategic deception that Olmert's "withdrawal" from the West Bank constitutes a rejection of the Israeli right wing, and by conveying with no comment Olmert's appeal to the Palestinians to accept "only part of their dream" to retain the West Bank in a peace agreement with Israel, the *Times'* two most experienced reporters on Israel in effect lent support to the plan to annex West Bank territory.[88]

One day after the report by Erlanger and Myre appeared, a *New York Times* editorial on the March 28 Knesset election with the misleading title, "West Bank Withdrawal," observed:

> Israeli voters have endorsed the idea of withdrawing from the West Bank. We're not happy with Mr. Olmert's proposal of a unilateral withdrawal. But at this point, we're heartened by anything that leads to an Israeli withdrawal from land that the Palestinians must control if the area is ever going to evolve into two peaceful, co-existing states.[89]

It is true only in the narrowest sense that by voting for the Kadima and Labor parties many Israeli voters endorsed "withdraw from the West Bank," given that Olmert was planning to withdraw from *some* Palestinian territory. Overall, however, the editorial's characterization of the Olmert plan as a "West Bank withdrawal" is misleading, since the plan's core featured Israel's annexation of West Bank territory.

The *New York Times*, in news articles and an editorial, failed to report the obvious fact that Olmert's "withdrawal" plan featured an Israeli annexation of Palestinian territory. In contrast, the *Ha'aretz* columnist Gideon Levy correctly observed that Olmert's plan is often mistakenly reported by the news media, as we just demonstrated, as a left-of-center policy. Levy wrote:

> While pundits and opinion polls indicate a seeming shift leftward, with a majority for the establishment of a Palestinian state and evacuation of settlements, the real political map has taken a sharp turn to the right.
>
> The three large parties' platforms—Kadima, Labor, and the Likud, seemingly center, left and right—are completely united in their agreement about keeping the large settlements in Israel's hands . . .

Suddenly we have woken to a new consensus. It is not clear how this right-wing consensus was established. Once there was a consensus over Jerusalem—now it has spread to half the West Bank—yet it's called "a move to the left."

Israelis have in fact moved to a position of "give peace no chance"—saying no to a just agreement, no to a Palestinian state. Since when has the size of the settlements determined their moral and legal standing? Whoever votes for one of the large parties must know he is casting his ballot for annexation.[90]

Similarly, also writing in *Ha'aretz,* Israeli journalist Amira Hass described in detail what the *New York Times* chose to briefly mention but not investigate, that is, Israel's de facto annexation of the Jordan Valley in the West Bank:

While the international community busied itself with the disengagement from the Gaza Strip last summer, Israel completed another cut-off process, which went unnoticed: In 2005, Israel completed a process of cutting off the eastern sector of the West Bank, including the Jordan Rift Valley, from the remainder of the West Bank.

Some 2,000 Palestinians, residents of the West Bank, are prohibited from entering the area, which constitutes around one-third of the West Bank, and includes the Jordan Rift, the area of the Dead Sea shoreline and the eastern slopes of the West Bank mountains.

This picture of such a large Palestinian area being absolutely cut off from the rest of the West Bank has emerged from tours and talks *Ha'aretz* has conducted in the area over a period of a number of weeks, from testimonies gathered by the B'Tselem human rights organization and reports from officials from the UN Office for the Coordination of Human Affairs.[91]

In addition to Hass' report, a *Ha'aretz* editorial opposed any such de facto Israeli annexation of the Jordan Valley. As the editorial noted, "in a graduated process determined primarily by security considerations, the Israeli government has, over the last few years, almost totally severed the West Bank from the Jordan Valley, and transformed the Jordan Valley area into a Jewish region." In opposition to this process, the editorial argued "the Jordan Valley settlers are part of an obsolete political worldview that saw obstruction of passage from the east into Israel as an existential security need, and the settlers as those who would defend the border." The editorial concluded: "Between the eastward expansion of Ma'aleh Adumim, the westward expansion of the Jordan Valley communities and the expansion of the settlement blocs toward the Green Line, the Palestinians are left with no territory on which to establish a state."[92]

A similar report on Israel's apparent annexation of the Jordan Valley was published by the British newspaper the *Guardian*:

> Israel has effectively annexed the Jordan Valley—about a third of the occupied West Bank—by barring almost all Palestinians from entering the region, a respected Israeli human rights group said yesterday. The group, B'Tselem, points to a system of permits and checkpoints that has expanded over recent months to keep most Palestinians out of the valley. It says this and other measures that are forcing residents to leave the area appear to be a step towards seizing the land for Israel.[93]

Likewise, a front-page headline in the British newspaper the *Independent* read: "The New Israel: Election Victory Gives Ehud Olmert a Mandate to Implement His Controversial Plan to Redraw Border and Annex Palestinian Territory."[94]

Thus, upon reading the Israeli and British press—but not the *New York Times*—we learn that in the first few months of 2006 Israeli security forces shot, killed, and wounded several Palestinian children with impunity, and that Israel's top political leaders openly announced a detailed plan to annex territory on the Palestinian side of the Green Line. These events somehow transpired without informative coverage in the *Times*' news pages or opposition from the editorial page.

Pursuant perhaps to the absence of opposition to (or even much knowledge of) Olmert's annexation plans in the United States—the only country capable of pressuring Israel to rescind such plans—Israel moved in May 2006 to expand and apparently include additional West Bank territory within Israel's final borders. Consistent with the pattern already established, such plans were reported in the Israeli press but not the *New York Times*, even though in this case the reports preceded by only a few days Olmert's official state visit to the United States. On May 21 *Ha'aretz* reported that "[Israeli] Defense Minister Amir Peretz has approved expansion of four West Bank settlements," and that "most of the settlements involved are located [on the Palestinian side] close to the pre-1967 war Green Line border."

Ha'aretz reported that Israel's military commander in the occupied territories, Major-General Yair Naveh, "signed orders expanding by 60 dunams [15 acres] the jurisdictional area of Givat Ze'ev, a northern suburb of Jerusalem located just inside the West Bank," and "Naveh also signed orders allowing expansion of Oranit, just over the Green Line near Kfar Sava." In addition, Naveh "signed orders allowing expansion of the northern Jordan Rift Valley settlement of Maskiyot, where the government plans to provide homes for settlers evacuated last summer from the Gaza enclave of Shirat Hayam." And "most recently, Naveh signed an order enlarging by 400 dunams [100 acres] the jurisdictional area of Beitar Ilit, a Haredi settlement in the Gush Etzion area."[95]

The *Jerusalem Post* cited this planned expansion of settlements and reported that the Beitar Ilit settlement expansion "would connect it to Israel proper," an indication of permanency for this settlement, and by implication, the others. The *Post* reported that Yariv Oppenheimer, general director of Peace Now, "condemned the expansions, saying they were apparently an attempt to take more Palestinian land ahead of Olmert's plan to lay down final borders by 2008."[96] *Ha'aretz* also cited Oppenheimer as saying, "in the back rooms and far from the public eye, the government of Israel has chosen to expand the settlements"; he also said that the expansions were an attempt "to steal more Palestinian land." The *New York Times* ignored reports of these planned expansions of Israeli settlements and provided its readers with little insight into how subversive the settlements are to prospects for a fair solution to the conflict.

Two days later, on May 23, the *Jerusalem Post* reported "Prime Minister Ehud Olmert's plans for the division of the West Bank involve the dismantling and relocation of [only] 20 to 30 settlements, and not the previously assumed evacuation of the vast majority of the settlements on the far side of the security barrier." Citing statements issued by a spokesman for Olmert, the *Post* reported that the spokesman's "comments suggest the retention of many more [Israeli] settlements [in the West Bank] than previously indicated."[97] This *Post* report and the previous one from *Ha'aretz* clearly signaled that the Olmert government's claims to Palestinian territory were even more expansive than what had been indicated earlier in January and March.

The *Times* ignored these reports as it had ignored earlier ones. The paper continued to report, in two front-page stories on May 24 and May 25, that Olmert's plan was an Israeli "withdrawal" from the West

Bank. Thus, on the front page for May 24 the *Times* reported: "President Bush offered conditional support on Tuesday [May 23] for Israeli ideas for a substantial withdrawal of settlers from the West Bank, but insisted that the new prime minister, Ehud Olmert, first exhaust all possibilities for a negotiated peace." The only reference in this article to Israel's annexation intentions was "what the Palestinians would call an Israeli land grab of occupied territory."[98] The obvious takeaway message here is that Olmert's plan to unilaterally and illegally annex West Bank territory is legitimate, whereas Palestinian opposition is frivolous.

On May 25 the *Times'* front page again referred to the Olmert plan as an Israeli withdrawal from the West Bank:

> The new prime minister of Israel, Ehud Olmert, left Washington for home late Wednesday [May 24] a pretty happy man. He was embraced by President Bush and reassured about Iran, and he received 16 standing ovations from a joint meeting of Congress for a speech that was strong on emotion and rhetorically tough on terrorism.
>
> More important, Mr. Olmert received just enough presidential support for his main initiative—another unilateral pullback of Israeli settlers from a large portion of the West Bank—to satisfy an Israeli public that craves American support and respect.
>
> Mr. Bush hailed Mr. Olmert's "bold ideas" and said they "could be an important step toward the peace we both support."[99]

These reports in the *Times*, which celebrated Olmert's "withdrawal" plan, disregarded Palestinian rights by never mentioning that the West Bank belongs to the Palestinians under numerous UN resolutions and that Israel has no right to any unilateral decisions to take parts of it for itself. The reports also wrote over the coincidental release of Amnesty International's 2006 annual report on May 23, which included this horrifying paragraph in the section on Israel and the occupied territories:

> In November [2005] an Israeli army company commander was acquitted of all charges in relation to the killing of a 13-year-old girl, Iman al-Hams. She had been shot dead by Israeli soldiers in October 2004 in Rafah in the southern Gaza Strip while walking near a fortified Israeli army tower opposite her school. According to an army communication recording of the incident, the commander had stated that

"anything that's mobile, that moves in the zone, even if it's a three-year-old, needs to be killed." Neither the commander nor any other soldier was charged with the girl's murder as the court accepted that the commander had not breached regulations on when to open fire. The court focused on whether he had acted improperly by repeatedly shooting at the child as she lay injured or dead.[100]

While the *Times* took care to note the emotional standing ovations that the US Congress gave to Israeli Prime Minister Ehud Olmert, it didn't bother to mention this passage or the others concerning Israel in Amnesty's report.

The acquittal of the Israeli commander who shot the Palestinian girl is one of the clearest indications, among many, that IDF soldiers shoot Palestinian children with impunity. His acquittal is even more outrageous given the recorded evidence which revealed that Israeli soldiers identified the shooting victim as a young girl and then apparently chased her down before she was shot multiple times by the commander. In November 2004 a report in the *Independent* described the events as recorded by the tape:

> Israeli soldiers continued firing at a Palestinian girl killed in Gaza last month well after she had been identified as a frightened child, a military communications tape has revealed.
>
> The tape is likely to be crucial in the prosecution case against the men's company commander, who faces five charges arising from the killing of Iman al-Hams, 13, in the southern border town of Rafah on 6 October.
>
> It shows that troops firing with light weapons and machine guns on a figure moving in a "no-entry zone" close to an army outpost near the border with Egypt had swiftly discovered that she was a girl.
>
> In the recorded exchanges someone in the operations room asks: "Are we talking about a little girl. She's running defensively eastwards, a girl of about 10. She's behind the embankment, scared to death."

Four minutes after this communication, the Israeli observation post reported, as recorded on the tape, "I think that one of the positions took her out. . . . She's not moving right now." The commander then tells his men, after firing at the girl with an automatic weapon and declaring that he has "confirmed" the killing, that "anyone who's mobile, moving in the zone, even if it's a three-year-old, needs to be killed."

The *Independent's* report continued: "The [Israeli] soldiers said that the commander had fired two shots at the girl from close range as she lay on the ground before withdrawing, turning and 'emptying his magazine' by firing some 10 bullets at her body." The Israeli army stated that the shooting was a mistake and that the girl was carrying a bag "that the soldiers had thought contained explosives" but "was found to contain schoolbooks." Her family, according to the *Independent*, was "at a loss to explain why she had wandered into a dangerous prohibited zone" but said she "was on her way to school at the time."[101]

There were numerous reports of the shooting in the British press,[102] and several references to it in the back pages of the *New York Times*.[103] The coverage of the girl's shooting in the *Times* was less comprehensive than reports in the British newspapers. For example, both the *Independent* and the *Guardian* reproduced detailed portions of the recorded conversations among the Israelis soldiers involved in the incident; the *Times* produced a very small portion: "The Israeli television network Channel Two broadcast a surveillance tape that had recorded the incident. The network said a voice heard saying, 'I carried out verification of the kill,' was that of the captain."[104] Even though the *Times'* Greg Myre had reported that "Palestinian hospital officials in Rafah have said she was hit by 15 to 20 bullets"[105] and that "Palestinian doctors who saw the girl's body said she had been hit by at least 15 bullets,"[106] the *New York Times* editorial page ignored the incident, not even bothering to demand an independent investigation.

The ongoing Israeli killing of Palestinian civilians, including children, and the absence of any legal accountability in Israel for their murders is almost inexplicable in a democracy that supposedly is governed by the rule of law. There is, however, a plausible explanation. The first can be discerned from statements that are made throughout Israeli society indicating a low regard for Palestinian life. For example, the *Independent* reported in June 2006 that "Ehud Olmert, the Israeli Prime Minister, expressed 'deep regret' for army operations that have killed 14 Palestinian civilians in Gaza in just nine days but said the lives of Israeli citizens threatened by Qassam attacks were 'even more important.' "[107] In 2001 the *New York Times* reported that Olmert, who was mayor of Jerusalem at the time, said that so-called "illegal" Arab homes in East Jerusalem were "a cancer and a plague."[108]

In summer 2006, after an Israeli soldier was captured on June 25 in southern Israel across the Gaza border and after two other Israeli soldiers were captured on July 12 in northern Israel by Hezbollah militants, the *Jerusalem Post* published an editorial about these events and Israel's considered options in response:

> Life is about choices. Life in Israel, alas, is all about excruciatingly difficult choices. Terrorism—by design—cruelly creates for its victims any number of no-win situations, precipitating the painful choices that flow from them. Do we bomb an apartment building where a wanted killer is hiding, knowing civilian lives will invariably be lost in the process? Do we react harshly to an incursion of our borders, aware that this reaction will put our forces even further in harm's way? Do we follow our instincts and ignore international pleas to show restraint, straining our already-tenuous relationships with other countries?
>
> Perhaps the most complex dilemma we face is when IDF soldiers are kidnapped and taken to hostile territory, the situation that now confronts us with the abduction, first, of Gilad Shalit [from southern Israel], and now, of Ehud Goldwasser and Eldad Regev [from northern Israel].
>
> Invariably, the abductors seek to trade them for large numbers of Arab terrorists being kept in our jails, creating yet another impossible quandary.[109]

The next sentence appears to establish a sound assumption from which to begin the consideration of such questions: "On the one hand, every life is precious beyond measure, a world unto itself, the highest of values." However, the following sentence demonstrates that the *Post* was speaking only about Israeli lives: "Each of our soldiers is pure gold, worth hundreds, even thousands of the enemy."[110] This statement from the editorial page of a leading Israeli newspaper, published within weeks of the statement from Prime Minister Olmert cited above, appears to reflect a racist view of Palestinians—among these Israelis at least.

In his book *Pity the Nation: The Abduction of Lebanon*, which reports on the conflicts and wars in Lebanon over the past two decades—including the Israeli invasion and occupation of Lebanon and its bombing of Beirut in 1982, which resulted in many thousands of Palestinian and Lebanese casualties—Robert Fisk described a discussion with an Israeli soldier about the magnitude of those casualties:

> "There are terrorists down there and in the camp on the right," the young soldier said, waving his hand in the general direction of west Beirut. He had lived in France for most of his youth, emigrating to

Israel only six years earlier, and he spoke English with a strong French accent. In the autumn, he was due to commence his first term at law college in Jerusalem. But now he was a soldier, he had fought his way up from southern Lebanon through Tyre and evidently knew that not everyone approved of what his army had done in the past ten days. He had seen the ruins of Sidon.

"It was not really beautiful, I guess," he said. "But one has to do one's job."[111]

Fisk wrote: "But did he not think, we asked, that perhaps the destruction and slaughter in Lebanon these past days—almost 10,000 people were now estimated to have been killed—has been somewhat out of proportion to that wrought on northern Israel?" The Israeli soldier responded:

"It is not the difference between one dead and a thousand dead," he said. "It hurts as much. Seeing dead children and women here is not really nice but everyone is involved in this kind of war—the women too—so we can't always punish exactly the right people because otherwise it would cost us a lot of deaths. And for us, I guess—I hope you understand this— the death of one Israeli soldier is more important than the death of even several hundred Palestinians. We don't play football. I mean it's not quantity of deaths—it's what we are trying to do. I hope there is going to be peace in Lebanon and if it costs a lot of lives, well that's it."[112]

Although Fisk was recording the soldier's comments, "the soldier seemed quite unconcerned about the microphone I was holding in front of him." Fisk asked him about the Palestinians:

The Israeli soldier sighed slightly, as if he knew the question had been coming all along. "Listen," he said, "I know you are recording this but I would like to see them all dead. You may send this anywhere you like: I would like to see all the Palestinians dead because they are a sickness everywhere they go."[113]

The soldier's racist statements appear to be supported by Israeli policies and conduct. In an April 2001 report, Israel's Public Committee Against Torture in Israel (PCATI), issued a report on Israel's apparent torture of Israeli and Palestinian Arabs:

The affidavits and the other information collected by the Public Committee Against Torture in Israel reveals that the police, the GSS [Israel's General Security Service] and other authorities grossly violated the basic human rights of persons in their custody after their detention during the events of September–October 2000. In particular, the following rights were infringed: the right not to be subject to discrimination on the grounds of race or nationality; the right not to be subject to torture or to other forms of cruel, inhuman or humiliating punishment; the right to due process of law; and the right of children to special treatment and protection.[114]

PCATI then issued a list of "comments on the violations," the first of which was titled: "The Right Not to Be Subject to Discrimination on the Grounds of Race or Nationality." As the report noted, "we saw fit to mention and illustrate this aspect as the first and foremost of PCATI's findings" since it represents "the broader context" of the discrimination. PCATI then stated:

The roots of the violent and humiliating behavior of security force personnel toward these citizens during the events lie, we believe, in the racist prejudices rife in the Jewish sector in Israel, and in a manifestation of discrimination that reflects nothing less than full-fledged racism.

A racist and hostile attitude toward the Palestinian minority in Israel runs like a thread through all the findings quoted here. It is difficult to imagine the personnel of the police, GSS or other authorities acting with such gross violence, abuse, humiliation and infringement of rights toward Jewish detainees. It is difficult to fully understand such behavior, and it will surely be impossible to end it, without appreciating that, for the police and GSS personnel, the fact that detainees are Arabs or Palestinians (or, to use the euphemism, "security detainees") seems to unleash a response legitimizing the inhuman treatment of these detainees.[115]

PCATI then noted, "To exemplify the gravity of this situation, we shall quote a selection of statements from the affidavits—all repugnant, and some abhorrent—made by police and GSS personnel to [Arab] Israeli citizens while the latter were in their custody." The committee listed the statements as follows:

- "Filthy Arabs."
- "You're lying Arabs . . . we're going to expel you to the Territories and to Jordan."
- "You're a terrorist, a son of a dog, a filthy Arab . . . even dogs hate the Arabs."
- "Start praying, say 'Allah akbar,' because we're going to kill you in ten minutes."
- "Call to your Muhammad to help you, because you're going to die."
- "You should lower your heads every time a Jew passes."
- "Filthy Arabs, terrorists, Arafats, we'll educate you."
- "The shoes of a Jew you threw stones at are worth millions of Arab souls."[116]

There is additional evidence of anti-Arab racism in Israel. In March 2006, in the context of Knesset elections in Israel and referring primarily to Ariel Sharon's "disengagement" from the Gaza Strip, a *Ha'aretz* correspondent wrote the following story in anticipation of a plurality victory by Sharon's Kadima party and his political protégé Ehud Olmert:

"To return territory and kill Arabs" is a favorite expression of the "ranch forum" of Ariel Sharon's advisers. In 2000, when adman-strategist Reuven Adler and company reshaped and polished Sharon's image, a rule was made: The public likes leaders who show diplomatic moderation and military toughness, who return land and kill Arabs. Sharon followed the rule during his five-year reign, and his heir-apparent, Acting Prime Minster Ehud Olmert will do the same.[117]

In addition to the racism evidenced by such statements, Israel is one of the few western democracies that has a reportedly racist political party as a member of its legislative body. The party, Yisrael Beiteinu, was formed in 1999 by Avigdor Lieberman, its chairman. In spring 2006 Yisrael Beiteinu nearly joined Olmert's governing coalition in the Israeli cabinet. In summer 2003 Lieberman reportedly proposed loading Palestinian prisoners onto buses and taking them to a place "whence they will not return," and according to another report, he said that the prisoners should be drowned in the Dead Sea.[118] In 2006 Lieberman's party called for denying Arab and other non-Jewish Israeli citizens the right to live in Israel on grounds of religion and race, as well as proposing the transfer of Arab Israelis to Palestinian territory.[119]

Despite these attitudes, Ehud Olmert, the prime minister-designate, seriously considered including Lieberman and his party in his governing coalition. In April 2006, a month after the Knesset elections, *Ha'aretz* reported that "it appears that the Labor Party, the Pensioners Party, Yisrael Beiteinu, Shas and United Torah Judaism are inching closer to joining the government," and "Olmert wants the right-wing Yisrael Beiteinu Party to join the government."[120] A month later the *Independent* reported that "a right-wing Israeli party leader," identified in the article as Avigdor Lieberman, "yesterday called for the execution of Israeli Arab politicians who had contacts with Hamas or failed to celebrate the state's independence day, overshadowing the swearing-in of the new [Israeli] coalition government"[121] (from which Yisrael Beiteinu and Lieberman were momentarily excluded). By October, Lieberman formally signed a coalition agreement with Olmert, "bringing the far-right Russian immigrant-based party into the government," making him the newly created Minister of Strategic Threats.[122] A week later, Lieberman stated that Israel should operate in Gaza "like Russia operates in Chechnya."[123]

In the context of the imminent Knesset election in March 2006, and in the midst of the Lieberman controversy in Israel, *Ha'aretz* columnist Gideon Levy wrote about Israel's growing tolerance for racist policies and politicians:

> An absolute majority of MKs in the next Knesset do not believe in peace, nor do they even want it—just like their voters—and worse than that, don't regard Palestinians as equal human beings. Racism has never had so many open supporters. It's the hit of this election campaign.
>
> One does not have to be Avigdor Lieberman to be a racist. The "peace" proposed by Ehud Olmert is no less racist. Lieberman wants to distance them [the Palestinians] from our borders. Olmert and his ilk want to distance them from our consciousness. Nobody is speaking about peace with them, nobody really wants it. Only one ambition unites everyone—to get rid of them, one way or another. Transfer or wall, "disengagement" or "convergence"—the point is that they should get out of our sight. The only game in town, the "unilateral arrangement," is not only based exclusively on our "needs" because of a sense of superiority, but also leads to a dangerous pattern that totally ignores the existence of the other nation.[124]

In its coverage of the Israeli election campaign in early 2006, the *New York Times* mentioned Avigdor Lieberman and Yisrael Beiteinu on a few occasions. In a March 8 news article, the *Times'* Steven Erlanger mentioned the party, its founder, and its platform in an inappropriately upbeat and even negligent manner:

> One of the big surprises so far has been the new right-wing party aimed at Russian-speaking voters, Yisrael Beiteinu, or Israel Is Our Home, led by Avigdor Lieberman. A former top aide to Mr. [Benjamin] Netanyahu, he combines a tough line on the Palestinians with a strong focus on social welfare.
>
> Mr. Lieberman, a native of Moldova and an immigrant to Israel in 1978 at age 20, urges a land and population swap, handing Israeli Arabs in large Israeli cities to the Palestinians in return for keeping large Israeli settlements in the West Bank.[125]

Given that Israeli Arabs, who are citizens of Israel, have expressed no desire to relinquish that citizenship, and that the Palestinian Authority has rejected the notion of any such transfer of Israeli Arabs, one might ask Lieberman—and Erlanger, for that matter—how one would go about "handing Israeli Arabs to the Palestinians" without a forcible transfer in violation of international humanitarian law. It is quite stunning that a *Times'* correspondent would appear to find this proposal so agreeable.

Apparently no one at the *Times* was offended—or perhaps they didn't notice—since Erlanger repeated his reference to the "swap" two weeks later. Referring to an Israeli voter, Erlanger reported that he was "torn between Mr. Olmert's Kadima and Avigdor Lieberman's Yisrael Beiteinu, a hawkish Russian-oriented party that wants to swap Arab Israeli towns for West Bank settlements."[126] After mentioning without comment a few days later that Olmert was considering Lieberman as a coalition partner,[127] and that Lieberman might ultimately become a member of Olmert's coalition,[128] the polite references to Lieberman in the *Times* were dropped in a news article on May 5, which reported:

> Avigdor Lieberman, leader of the right-wing Yisrael Beiteinu Party, started a heated argument when he said that Arab members of Parliament who recently met with Hamas should be tried on treason charges, and that he hoped they would be executed.

"The Second World War ended with the Nuremberg trials and the execution of the Nazi leadership," Mr. Lieberman said. "Not only them, but also those who collaborated with them. I hope that will also be the fate of the collaborators in this house."

Several Arab legislators called his remarks racist.[129]

While the *Times'* editorial page at the time apparently found no reason to condemn the proposals by Lieberman to drown Palestinian prisoners in the Dead Sea, transfer Israeli Arabs (presumably forcefully) to the West Bank, or execute Arab members of Israel's Knesset, the Anti-Defamation League (ADL), in contrast, issued a statement condemning Lieberman's call to execute the Knesset members:

> The Anti-Defamation League expresses grave concern over the inciteful statements made by Yisrael Beitenu head MK Avigdor Lieberman. In an address to the Knesset on May 4, Lieberman called for executing Arab legislators who met with Hamas leaders. He said he hoped they would meet the same fate as those who collaborated with the Nazis and who were condemned to death at the Nuremberg trials.
>
> While there is legitimate concern about Israelis meeting with the leadership of the Hamas terrorist organization, this does not justify Lieberman's horrendous and provocative call for their death. Neither is there justification for equating his political foes with the collaborators of the Nazis. Lieberman, in fact, displays an ignorant perversion of history since only Nazis were tried at Nuremberg, not collaborators.
>
> But his dangerously inflammatory language has no place in Israel, particularly as a public leader speaking on the floor of the Knesset. Israeli leaders like Lieberman who are looked upon as role models should refrain from such generalizations and defaming speech.[130]

This statement apparently represented a turnabout at the ADL with respect to Lieberman, given that two weeks earlier the American-Jewish newspaper the *Forward* reported that the ADL's national director, Abraham Foxman, "wouldn't have a problem" with a cabinet post for Lieberman in Olmert's government. The *Forward* reported:

> Foxman said he was unconcerned about the possibility of a Cabinet post for Lieberman: "If they [Olmert's Kadima Party] make the deal [to include Lieberman], we [the ADL] wouldn't have a problem with

it. I find [Lieberman] to be a person one can discuss and debate and argue and disagree [with] and I don't think we have a problem and I don't think the American Jewish community will."[131]

A few months later *Ha'aretz* reported that Effi Eitam, a member of Israel's National Union–National Religious Party, "said that the great majority of Palestinians in the West Bank should be expelled, and that Arabs should be ousted from Israeli politics as a fifth column and 'a league of traitors.' " The *Ha'aretz* report continued:

> It was the first time that Eitam, who heads the Religious Zionism faction within the National Union, has publicly supported deportation of Palestinians, a concept espoused by assassinated National Union founder Rehavam Ze'evi as "transfer."
> "We will have to expel the great majority of the Arabs of Judea and Samaria," Eitam urged, referring to the whole of the West Bank.
> According to Eitam, experience showed that Israel cannot give up the area of the West Bank. "It is impossible with all of these Arabs, and it is impossible to give up the territory. We've already seen what they're doing there."
> Turning to the subject of Israeli Arabs, Eitam said: "We will have to take another decision, and that is to sweep the Israel Arabs from the political system. Here, too, the issues are clear and simple."

While Yossi Beilin, head of the left-wing Meretz party, criticized Eitam's remarks as "incitement to racism," an Arab Knesset member, Mohammed Barakeh, said "the measures proposed by Eitam are already being implemented" and that the Palestinians "are witness to many steps to push them aside and expel them from their homeland."[132]
Beyond Avigdor Lieberman and Effi Eitam, there is additional reported evidence of anti-Arab racism in Israel. In a 2002 report on Israel's settlement policies in the West Bank, B'Tselem observed that "Israel has created in the Occupied Territories a regime of separation based on discrimination, applying two separate systems of law in the same area and basing the rights of individuals on their nationality." The report continued: "This regime is the only one of its kind in the world, and is reminiscent of distasteful regimes from the past, such as the Apartheid regime in South Africa."[133]
The B'Tselem report also cited real-estate marketing campaigns, described in a *Ha'aretz* article, as further evidence of an apartheid-like

policy. The marketing efforts, about which B'Tselem comments below, encouraged Israelis to move to settlement communities in the West Bank for the purpose of assimilating Palestinian territory into the state of Israel:

> This deliberate and systematic process of assimilation obscures a number of fundamental truths about the settlements: the "communities" mentioned in the [Ha'aretz] article are not part of the State of Israel, but are settlements established in the West Bank—an area that has been occupied territory since 1967. The fundamental truth is that the movement of Israeli citizens to houses and apartments offered by the real estate markets in these "communities" constitutes a violation of the Fourth Geneva Convention. The fundamental truth is that the "state-owned" land mentioned in the article was seized from Palestinian residents by illegal and unfair proceedings. The fundamental truth is that the settlements have been a continuing source of violations of the human rights of the Palestinians, among them the right to freedom of movement, property, self-determination, and improvement in their standard of living. The fundamental truth is that the growth of these settlements is fueled not only by neutral forces of supply and demand, but primarily by a sophisticated governmental system designed to encourage Israeli citizens to live in the settlements. In essence, the process of assimilation blurs the fact that the settlement enterprise in the Occupied Territories has created a system of legally sanctioned separation based on discrimination that has, perhaps, no parallel anywhere in the world since the dismantling of the Apartheid regime in South Africa.[134]

In summary, there is substantial evidence of anti-Arab racism in Israel which may explain in part why Israeli security forces kill Palestinians with very few consequences for IDF soldiers, their commanders, or higher-ups in the military and civilian chain of command. While the *Times* appropriately covers controversies involving charges of anti-Jewish racism,[135] there is little or no coverage in the *Times* of anti-Arab racism among Israelis.

Although the *Times* underreports the deaths and injuries of Palestinian Arabs, this is not likely the result of any specific anti-Arab bias, since the *New York Times* underreports non-Arab fatalities as well, including US and British victims of Israeli violence. For example, throughout April 2006 there was no mention in the *Times* of the death of a young

British citizen named Tom Hurndall killed by an Israeli sniper in Gaza while trying to protect Palestinian children who feared the same fate. If the *Times* had reported on Hurndall, they would have reported—as did the British and Israeli press—the findings of a British investigative inquest that he had been murdered by an IDF soldier.

The findings of the inquest jury were announced three years to the month after the 21-year-old Hurndall was shot on April 11, 2003. About a week earlier, on April 5, 2003, Brian Avery, a 24-year-old US citizen from Albuquerque, New Mexico, was shot in the face by Israeli soldiers as he walked out of a house in Jenin in the West Bank. On March 16, less than three weeks before Avery was shot, Rachel Corrie, a 23-year-old US citizen from Olympia, Washington, was run over and crushed to death in Gaza by a US-made bulldozer operated by Israeli soldiers; Corrie had positioned herself between the bulldozer and a Palestinian home that the IDF soldiers were about to raze.

When these incidents are viewed together, the facts are immediately suggestive. Hurndall, Avery, and Corrie at the time were members of the International Solidarity Movement, an unarmed, nonviolent organization that seeks to nonviolently impede IDF operations in the occupied territories, including stopping the shooting of Palestinian civilians and the demolition of Palestinian homes—and within a thirty-day period in early 2003, three of its members were brutally shot or bulldozed by IDF soldiers. None of this apparently intrigued the *Times,* which initiated no investigations and published no editorials about these episodes. While the British government belatedly investigated the incident involving Hurndall, in response to the skillful and determined investigation conducted by Hurndall's parents, neither the Bush White House nor the US Congress ever investigated the cases involving its citizens (Corrie and Avery), despite being urged to do so by the victims' families. And while British news organizations investigated and reported the Hurndall case, the news and editorial pages of the *New York Times,* the leading US news outlet, were nearly silent with respect to the Americans Corrie and Avery. Beyond preliminary accounts[136]— and with the exception of the *Times'* cultural interest in a play based on Corrie's life[137]—the paper seemed eager to forget about the fact that US citizens had been maliciously killed and maimed by Israeli soldiers. In short, as the facts in these cases were slowly outed (as detailed below), and the more insight they provided into the brutal nature of the Israeli occupation, the more conspicuously silent the *Times* became.

★   ★   ★

On April 11, 2006, the *Independent* reported that a British coroner, Dr. Andrew Reid, had called upon British Attorney General Lord Goldsmith "to consider the prosecution of five senior Israeli officers after an inquest jury found that a British student [Hurndall] had been murdered by one of their soldiers." According to the newspaper, Hurndall, a photojournalism student who had traveled to Gaza with other peace activists, "was trying to save children from a volley of bullets when he was hit in the head in April 2003." He died nine months later in a hospital in London at the age of twenty two.[138]

By ignoring the British inquest,[139] the *Times* deprived its readers not only of the inquest jury's verdict, but also of the statement by Tom Hurndall's father who, confronted with Israel's stonewalling, exhaustively investigated the circumstances of his son's death. Upon hearing the inquest jury's verdict, Anthony Hurndall stated: "Our view is this soldier [who shot Tom Hurndall] was doing no more than what was expected of him. It has become very clear to me that shooting civilians was a regular [Israeli] army activity in that area."[140]

Also on April 11, the *Guardian* similarly reported that Lord Goldsmith "was called on to seek war crimes charges against five Israeli officers after an inquest jury found that a soldier under their command intentionally killed a British peace activist in Gaza. Tom Hurndall, 22, died after being shot in broad daylight by an Israeli soldier who later said his commanders had issued orders allowing him to shoot even unarmed civilians." Hurndall was shot, the *Guardian* reported, as he "tried to rescue children who froze in fear after the [Israeli] soldier had opened fire."[141]

On April 9, 2006, just prior to the announcement of the inquest jury's decision in the Hurndall case, the *Observer*, the British Sunday newspaper, published a summary of events involved in the Hurndall shooting, which began as follows:

> Just before midday on 11 April 2003, an Israeli sniper opened fire on three [Palestinian] children as they played in a dusty, makeshift playground in Rafah, deep in the fag end of the Gaza Strip. The youngsters froze. A young English photographer [Hurndall] dashed to the scene, carrying the traumatized body of a small boy to safety. Hurndall returned into the line of fire. As he bent to scoop a small girl away from the fizzing bullets, a bullet thudded into the side of his head.[142]

More than a year earlier, in January 2005, the *Observer* published findings of its own investigation of the Hurndall shooting, an "episode that has strained diplomatic relations between Britain and Israel and raised fresh concerns over Israeli policies towards the Occupied Territories." The *Observer* reported:

> An Observer investigation into the shooting has uncovered allegations of missing evidence, fabricated testimony and a[n] [Israeli] military cover-up. Disquiet is mounting among British government officials whose repeated requests [to Israeli authorities] for evidence that could determine if Hurndall was shot deliberately have been rejected. The missing documents, understood to include an Israeli military police inquiry, could mean a manslaughter charge for the man who shot Hurndall being upgraded to murder.
>
> In addition, the North London coroner, Dr Andrew Reid, whose inquest into Hurndall's death has been adjourned until the trial is over, has said he is "outraged" that an agreement to share vital evidence with Israeli authorities was broken. After passing on his findings, including detailed pathology reports, to Israeli officials, he was told that nothing would be given in return. Similarly, a [British] Metropolitan Police investigation to determine the wider events surrounding Hurndall's death—whether there was systematic shooting at civilians in the Occupied Territories— has been refused permission to extend its inquiries into Israel.[143]

Israel's noncooperation with the British investigation was almost certainly related to the fact, reported by the *Observer*, that "Sergeant Wahid Taysir, the sniper who killed Hurndall, has already said a policy of shooting at unarmed civilians existed at the time."[144]

Prior to the inquest jury's decision in April 2006, the *Times'* scant coverage of the Hurndall shooting three years earlier had simply noted what witnesses to the shooting had reported, in addition to Israeli denials of wrongdoing. In his original statement about the incident, the Israeli soldier who shot Hurndall claimed he had shot at a man in military fatigues who was firing at Israeli soldiers with a pistol. This was untrue, and the Israeli soldier eventually recanted the statement. Another false statement about the shooting, issued by the Israeli government, was printed in the second paragraph of a brief report in the *Times* the day after Hurndall was shot:

> An Israeli sniper shot and critically wounded a British activist today as he tried to protect Palestinian children near a roadblock in the southern Gaza Strip, his organization said, citing witnesses.

The Israeli Army said it was investigating the report. But it said it knew of only one instance in which soldiers shot in that area today, to kill what the army said was an armed Palestinian who had opened fire on an Israeli post.[145]

As in many other news reports the *Times* published about Israeli violence in the territories, the paper was content in this instance to simply pit witnesses who are somehow tainted through their associations—in this case with a peacenik group, the International Solidarity Movement—against the official statements of the Israeli government. Reports such as these, where rote quotes of conflicting accounts (and little else) are printed, are regarded as the gold standard of American journalism—that is, a balanced report. Predictably, the *Times* reports two sides of a story in this fashion from the occupied territories. In this particular case, however, as in many others, a third, fourth, fifth, and sixth side of the story emerged—the private investigation undertaken by Tom Hurndall's parents, the investigations conducted by the British press, the British coroner's inquest with which Israel refused to cooperate, and the inquest jury's decision. The *Times* neglected to report these aspects of the story as they developed. Also, with respect to what should be a general journalistic principle when government personnel resort to a lethal use of force against unarmed civilians, the burden of proof must lie disproportionately with the government to show that the use of force was justified. Thus, the *Times*' decision simply to record a set of conflicting statements in cases such as these, where one side represents the Israeli government in the absence of any additional inquiry or investigation, does nothing to compel accountability.

Furthermore, the evidence indicates that Israeli authorities also issued false statements with respect to the Avery and Corrie incidents and that the *Times* printed these statements as well, without follow-up or investigation, as indicated in the passages below:

[Hurndall] was the second activist from the International Solidarity Movement to be shot in less than a week. Last Saturday night, Brian Avery, 24, of Albuquerque, was shot in the face and seriously wounded when he stepped into the street during an Israeli curfew to investigate gunshots in the West Bank city of Jenin.

Members of the group said an Israeli armored vehicle had opened fire on him. *An Israeli security official said that there were gun battles in the area at the time and that Mr. Avery might have been struck by a Palestinian bullet.*

On March 16, another American member of the group, Rachel Corrie, 23, was crushed to death by an Israeli Army bulldozer as she tried to stop it from demolishing a home in Rafah. Witnesses said Ms. Corrie had been clearly visible, *but the [Israeli] army said its investigation showed that the driver never saw her.*[146] (Italics added)

Evidence and witness accounts reveal that the above statements from Israeli authorities are almost certainly untrue. Nevertheless, they serve an important purpose. For Israel, they momentarily deflect blame and accountability as the news cycle quickly sweeps the story away. For the *Times*, they provide pretexts for balanced and fair coverage. However, with respect to journalistic oversight, the practice of printing such statements as a presumptively sufficient counterweight to eyewitness evidence of state-sanctioned murder is deeply flawed and easily exploited. To be clear, such statements from the Israeli government—if those are the statements issued—need to be published, but they should not be the last word, as they too often are in the *Times*.

Without having to face any obvious burden of accountability, least of all in the US press, such statements from Israel fail to meet even minimal standards of credibility and decency. Thus, a nine-year-old Palestinian girl acted like a terrorist when she wandered toward the separation barrier and so she had to be shot in the neck and stomach by Israeli soldiers. The incident is not investigated and no one is arrested and tried. A thirteen-year-year-old Palestinian boy who apparently thought about throwing stones at Israeli soldiers thus acted like a terrorist and had to be shot in the back by Israeli soldiers. The incident is not investigated and no one is arrested and tried. A Palestinian cab driver allegedly runs an Israeli checkpoint in Palestinian territory and so his young niece in the back seat had to be shot in the head. The incident is not investigated and no one is arrested and tried. Idealistic US and British peace activists are bulldozed or shot by Israeli soldiers, and the best the *New York Times* can do is to pair denials of responsibility with eyewitness accounts. Consistently, the *Times* then lets the story die, echoing the deaths of Israel's victims.

Brian Avery, "an American pro-Palestinian activist," as James Bennett wrote in the *New York Times*,[147] was shot by an Israeli soldier in April

2003. As the two-year anniversary of that event approached, the Israeli newspaper *Ha'aretz* published an investigative report titled "Who Shot Brian Avery?" The *Ha'aretz* report summarized events leading up to the shooting as follows:

> At the end of March [2003], Avery decided to go to Jenin, where he joined a local ambulance team and worked shifts, as necessary. He planned to remain in the territories for about a year, and afterward to return home, tell people what is happening here, and then return here again for a while. On Shabbat, April 5, Avery was staying in a rented apartment in Jenin, which he shared with other ISM [International Solidarity Movement] activists. With him was Jan Tobias Carlson from Sweden, a senior ISM activist.
>
> Jenin had been under curfew since Friday, and Avery did a shift of 17 hours straight in the ambulance. He spent Shabbat sleeping. In the afternoon he awoke and went up to the roof of the building, where he sat with Carlson and two Palestinian friends. At about 6 P.M., the sound of approaching military vehicles was heard, followed a few minutes later by two or three rounds of firing. Avery and Carlson went down into the street.
>
> "We were afraid that there were children in the area, and thought that it would be a good idea to go down and keep them away from there," testified Carlson later. "Brian was wearing a vest with the word 'Doctor' written in phosphorescent colors in English and Hebrew, front and back."
>
> "We made our way cautiously in the direction of the central junction in Jenin," says Avery. "At the time, four of our friends from ISM were approaching from another direction, after we spoke to them over the phone and arranged to meet at the junction in order to find out the reason for the shots. When we arrived at the junction, we saw that a tank and an APC [armored personnel carrier] were approaching us. We stopped, and stood with arms outstretched to show them that we weren't armed. We moved aside in order to allow them to pass, and stood right under a street lamp, which was already lit. When they were 30 meters from us they shot a volley of 15–20 bullets, while they were driving.[148]

The unarmed Avery was shot in the face. "That was one of the severest injuries I have ever seen," Carlson said. Another eyewitness, Lasse Schmidt, told *Ha'aretz* that "the entire left side of Avery's face was only attached at the ear."[149]

The *Ha'aretz* piece, which fairly described the International Solidarity Movement as "a coalition of groups and individuals whose goal is to support Palestinians' nonviolent resistance to the occupation," noted that Israeli Superintendent Shlomo Sagi, identified as "spokesman for the Judea and Samaria [West Bank] district of the Israeli Police," said with regard to the ISM and other such groups that "beyond occasional arrests in demonstrations over the separation fence, we do not encounter problems of violence or illegal weapons on the part of international activists in the territories."[150]

The 4,000-word article in *Ha'aretz* on the Avery shooting was fair and informative, and it treated the case of a US citizen shot by an Israeli soldier with more concern and respect than the leading newspaper in the United States, which covered the Avery incident with a few sentences in the middle of two news articles with headlines about other issues.[151]

Because Israel's forty-year occupation of the West Bank and Gaza Strip violates international law, the Palestinians living in those territories have a right under international law to resist the occupation. If Palestinian terrorism that targets and kills Israeli civilians is not a legally or morally permissible option within the framework of a right of resistance—and we argue that it is not—then other forms of resistance must be legally available. Clearly, at a minimum, nonviolent resistance to the occupation is an acceptable option from a legal and moral standpoint. The so-called pro-Palestinian US and British members of the International Solidarity Movement who were attacked by Israeli soldiers were engaged in nonviolent resistance against numerous operational aspects of Israel's occupation, including the demolition of Palestinian homes as "collective punishment" (one among many Israeli occupation practices that violate international law). Citing the United Nations Relief and Works Agency for Palestinian Refugees (UNRWA), B'Tselem reported in 2005 that from September 2000 to September 2004 Israel destroyed 2,370 Palestinian housing units in the Gaza Strip, leaving approximately 22,800 Palestinians homeless.[152]

With respect to Israel's demolition policy, B'Tselem reported that "since the beginning of the al-Aqsa intifada [September 29, 2000], Israel has employed a policy of house demolition, uprooting of orchards, and destruction of farmland in the Gaza Strip. This policy has been used mostly in areas surrounding [Israel's] settlements [in Gaza], on both sides of the bypass roads [that link the settlements to

Israel and other settlements] along which the settlers drive, and around army posts, mostly along the Egyptian border." The B'Tselem report continued:

> The destruction of many hundreds of acres of agricultural land based on the claim that Palestinians fired from these lands, and the demolition of entire residential neighborhoods on the charge that some of them contained tunnels, constitute excessive injury to the civilian population. This action is illegal. Israel's policy, which is carried out against people whom Israel does not contend were involved in attacks on Israeli civilians or security forces, constitutes collective punishment. Despite these violations of international humanitarian law, Israel refuses to compensate Palestinians whose property was damaged in these actions.[153]

B'Tselem also reported that "the scope of house demolitions and destruction of farmland is especially extensive along the border between Rafah and Egypt,"[154] a strip of land along which Israel at the time had an array of IDF posts. This gives context for the incident in which Rachel Corrie was run over and killed in Rafah on March 16, 2003, by an Israeli bulldozer used for house demolitions and farmland destruction. At the time, Corrie had placed herself between the bulldozer and a Palestinian home that was about to be destroyed.

The initial account of Corrie's death in the *New York Times*, published on March 17, provided a substantial amount of detail. The *Times'* Greg Myre reported that "an Israeli Army bulldozer today crushed to death an American woman who had kneeled in the dirt to prevent the armored vehicle from destroying a Palestinian home in the southern Gaza Strip, witnesses and hospital officials said." Myre added that Corrie "was among eight Americans and Britons who had been acting has [*sic*] 'human shields' to try to stop the almost daily house demolitions by Israeli forces in Rafah, a town on Gaza's border with Egypt." Quoting witnesses from the International Solidarity Movement, Myre wrote "at the time Ms. Corrie was run over, she was in an open area in front of the house." The witnesses reported that "the bulldozer came from some distance away, and 'there was nothing to obscure the driver's view.' "[155] Photographs showing Corrie on the ground immediately after being run over support the statement given to Myre that the bulldozer came from some distance away with nothing to obscure its view.[156] Thus eyewitnesses and photographs taken at the time clearly undermine the statement given by Israeli authorities about the incident, as reported by Myre, that "the driver of the bulldozer had not seen the woman."

Based on Myre's account describing the possibly deliberate killing of a US citizen by Israeli soldiers, the *New York Times* editorial page had sufficient grounds to call for an independent investigation into Corrie's death—but it neglected to do so. Although the Israeli government reportedly conducted an internal investigation of the Corrie incident, no such report was ever publicly issued. On March 16, 2005, the two-year anniversary of the killing of Rachel Corrie, Amnesty International issued a press release that "called on Secretary of State Condoleezza Rice to support an independent investigation of [Corrie's] death." The press release noted that the investigation "conducted by the Israeli Defense Force failed to resolve contradictions between the official IDF position and eyewitness testimonies." Amnesty reported that "while the US government has assisted in the investigations into cases of US citizens killed by Palestinian armed groups, it has failed to do so in Corrie's case, raising the appearance of a double standard."[157] The *Times'* editorial page not only neglected to call for an independent investigation, it published no editorials at all on the killing of a US citizen by a US-made bulldozer operated by the US-supported Israeli military.

When the British documentary filmmaker James Miller was shot on May 3, 2003, within weeks of the Hurndall, Avery, and Corrie episodes, the *Times* covered this incident by printing a seventy-five-word excerpt from Reuters, which included a claim by the Israeli army that Miller was shot accidentally while Israeli troops were returning Palestinian fire. The Reuters dispatch printed in the *Times* included the ritualistic denial of blame by the Israeli government:

> Israeli forces in the southern Gaza Strip shot dead a British television cameraman on Friday, military officials and Palestinian witnesses said.
>
> The cameraman, James Miller, who was in the refugee camp of Rafah making a documentary, died after being evacuated by Israeli forces for treatment.
>
> *The Israeli Army said the troops were not trying to hit Mr. Miller but were returning fire while searching for smuggling tunnels and that Mr. Miller was hit in the exchange.*[158] (Italics added)

For the next three years, this would be the only item in the *Times* about the shooting of Miller, with the last word (above) going to the Israeli army. And, as in the Corrie, Hurndall, and Avery cases, Israel's explanation of the Miller shooting was apparently false, as determined in April 2006 by a second British inquest jury. As a Reuters report not picked up by the *Times* on this occasion stated: "An award-winning British cameraman shot dead in the Gaza Strip by an Israeli soldier was murdered, a London inquest found on Thursday [April 6]. James Miller was shot by a member of the Israel Defense Forces in May 2003 in the Rafah refugee camp while making a documentary about Palestinian children caught up in fighting with Israel." The inquest jury, as Reuters reported, also concluded: "It is a fact that from day one of this inquest, the Israeli authorities have not been forthcoming in the investigation into the circumstances surrounding Miller's death."[159]

The *Times'* first and only report for three years on Miller's shooting (the seventy-five-word Reuters report) also compares badly with other contemporaneous reports of the incident. For example, the International Federation of Journalists (IFJ), which represents more than 500,000 journalists in more than 100 countries, issued a press release on May 3, 2006—the day Miller was shot—that stated:

> Only hours after a new global campaign was launched by media leaders demanding that attempts to kill journalists should be made a war crime, a freelance journalist was shot dead in controversial circumstances by Israeli forces in Palestine.
>
> Award-winning cameraman James Miller was filming the demolition of houses for a documentary in the Gaza town of Rafah, the scene of earlier disturbances, when he was shot in the neck. Israeli army spokesmen said he was shot as troops fired in defence, but other witnesses say Miller and two colleagues were simultaneously filming and waving a white flag as they walked toward the tank.[160]

Unlike the *Times*, the IFJ called for an "independent investigation by respected international authorities" into Miller's shooting. Likewise, the Committee to Protect Journalists (CPJ), in a press release dated May 7, 2003—four days after Miller was shot—stated: "We demand a full and transparent investigation into this shocking incident. . . . We believe that the failure of Israeli authorities to conduct serious investigations and punish those who have harmed journalists in the past has fostered a climate of impunity and recklessness among Israeli troops, making indiscriminate fire acceptable."[161]

Not only did the *Times* not call for an investigation into the Miller shooting, it also did not mention at the time of the shooting, as CPJ did, that another journalist had been killed recently by the Israeli army: "Miller is the second journalist to have been killed in the Occupied Territories during the last two weeks. APTN [Associated Press Television Network] cameraman Nazeh Darwazeh was shot in the head by an Israeli soldier at close range while filming clashes between Palestinian youths and Israeli troops in central Nablus on April 19 [2003]." CPJ noted further that, "since May 2002, four journalists have been killed in the Occupied Territories—all by Israeli gunfire."[162]

On May 3, Reporters Without Borders also "voiced its shock at the death of British freelance cameraman James Miller, killed by Israeli gunfire yesterday evening in Rafah in the Gaza Strip." Calling for an investigation into Miller's shooting, it reported that the Palestinian cameraman Nazeh Darwazeh "was struck in the eye by a shot fired by an Israeli soldier" on April 19 and was killed.[163] In contrast to the press releases of these three organizations, the *Times* news pages were content to briefly note that an Israeli soldier had shot a cameraman named James Miller, and that Israeli authorities said that he was accidentally shot in a crossfire. Just as it had ignored the Hurndall, Avery, and Corrie incidents that preceded Miller's death by a few weeks, the *Times* published no editorial on the Miller shooting.

In a lengthy article that appears to have been written for publication in April 2006 (given its focus on the British inquest jury decision on the Miller shooting), the *Times* published its only analysis of the Miller case on June 24, 2006—more than two months after the jury inquest verdict and more than three years after Miller was shot. *Times* reporter Sarah Lyall began the article as follows:

> Three years ago, in an incident that resonates now with the recent killing of seven members of a Palestinian family on a Gaza beach, a documentary filmmaker was shot to death in Gaza.
>
> Then as now, the victims' families blamed the Israeli military, which denied responsibility. A major difference is that the filmmaker, James Miller, was a British citizen, and after some prodding from his family, his government has taken up his cause.[164]

Lyall then wrote, with respect to the competing contentions between Miller's family and the Israeli government about whether the death was a murder or an accident:

> A resolution of sorts came in April at a coroner's inquest here into the death of Mr. Miller, 34, an experienced filmmaker looking into the effects of violence on children for HBO. The jury's verdict was that he was murdered.
>
> The killer was identified as the commander of an armored personnel carrier in the Israeli Army who had admitted firing his gun that night, but no one in Israel has been charged, and many questions raised in the hours after the shooting have never been resolved.[165]

Though Lyle's report was inexplicably late, it was better late than never, given that British Attorney General Lord Goldsmith at the time was still considering whether to take up the Miller and Hurndall cases with Israeli authorities. As Lyall reported, "Lord Goldsmith said he needed 'to consider myself whether there ought to be prosecutions here [London] in either of these cases.' "[166] Although it had effectively spent three years ignoring the Hurndall and Miller cases, it was not too late for the *Times*' editorial page to recommend criminal prosecutions in London; this perhaps would have introduced the issue of Israel's accountability to at least some law with respect to its conduct in the Palestinian territories. The *Times*' editorial page, however, published no such editorial.

These relatively high-profile incidents involving US and British citizens were not particularly easy to ignore, but by doing so the *Times* helped prevent any political damage to the Israeli occupation, confining its coverage of these cases primarily to initial "balanced" accounts provided by eyewitnesses and Israeli authorities. Thus, by practicing what is unfortunately regarded as the gold standard of American journalism—balanced reporting that is rigidly heedless of the people and world around it—the *Times* characteristically left its readers mostly uninformed about these tragic but instructive episodes of the Israeli occupation.

3

Palestinian Testimonies

While Israel's government officials, lobbyists, and intellectuals have a great deal of access to US government officials and the US news media, Palestinian commentators have much less: this obviously gives Israel a public relations advantage inside the US with respect to its policies in the Palestinian territories. When, for example, Hamas won the Palestinian parliamentary elections in January 2006, and a few months later when Israel invaded the Gaza Strip, few Palestinian commentators had access to the US news media to provide a Palestinian point of view with respect to those events.[167] Likewise, few if any Palestinian spokespersons had access to the American people via the news media in order to respond to Prime Minister Olmert's convergence plan, which featured annexation of Palestinian territory, or to respond to Israel's repeated shelling and missile attacks inside Gaza in June 2006, or to respond to Israel's targeted assassinations of Palestinians. In general, the *New York Times* has expended little effort to present the views of Palestinian commentators to the American public.

This shortfall is especially obvious at the *Times*, where the opinion page features Thomas Friedman, who supports with minor exceptions Israel's policies in the occupied territories, and David Brooks, who supports those policies without exceptions. Brooks replaced William Safire, who, like Friedman and Brooks, was in the habit of ringing "Arik" (Ariel Sharon) and "Bibi" (Benjamin Netanyahu) to chat patronizingly about Israel's political and security situation as they saw it. This is in addition to the editorial page, which, like Friedman, supports Israel's occupation policies with an affectation of insight and fairness.

Despite having no access to the US news media, there is at least one category of Palestinians who can and have spoken authoritatively about Israel's conduct in the West Bank and Gaza Strip. These spokespersons and their testimonies are ignored by the *Times*, even though they are readily available to reporters, editors, and opinion-page writers. B'Tselem, for example, whose highly qualified and respected analysts are themselves mostly ignored, has compiled a substantial archive of testimonies from Palestinians about life under the Israeli occupation, including the Israeli use of firearms, beatings and abuse, demolitions of Palestinian homes, destruction of agricultural land, administrative detention, and torture.

Citing even a small fraction of the B'Tselem-collected testimonies from Palestinians can function as an antidote to the repetitive and recognizable manner in which US news organizations, including the *New York Times*, report the conditions and events testified to by the Palestinians below. Nigel Parry, co-founder of Electronic Intifada (EI),[168] described this phenomenon as follows:

> When I lived in Ramallah between 1994–1998, the era of the so-called peace process, I witnessed perhaps 30 clashes between young Palestinians and Israeli soldiers to very consciously document and photograph what transpired. I was sick to my stomach with reading media reports by foreign correspondents that characterized these events along the lines of:
> *Israeli soldiers and Palestinians clashed today in the outskirts of Ramallah. Two Palestinians were killed and four injured.*
> What was problematic about these reports was the utter lack of contextual information that let you know how a stone-throwing protest routinely ended up with dead Palestinian teenagers and children.[169] (Italics in original)

To provide missing contextual information in the *Times'* coverage of Israel's occupation, we reproduce below testimonies from Palestinians who have personally experienced or witnessed Israel's (a) lethal use of force, (b) beatings and abuse, and (c) home demolitions and destruction of agricultural land. Each of these categories has been identified by B'Tselem as involving serious Israeli violations of international humanitarian law in occupied Palestinian territory, and the testimonies below (and many others) are available on its website as evidence to support those charges. (We made no changes to any minor errors in the English-language translations of the testimonies provided by B'Tselem.)

Use of Lethal Force. From September 29, 2000, to December 31, 2005, B'Tselem published numerous reports[170] and testimonies[171] about Israel's use of lethal force in the occupied territories. A few of the testimonies are reproduced or excerpted below, and some are preceded by explanatory summaries.

1. The Testimony of 'Uthman al-Hajin, 50, August 2002.

I own four dunams (1 acre) in a-Sheikh 'Ajalin Neighbourhood in Gaza. On it, I grow vine grapes, figs and vegetables. I also have there a well of sweet water. My father and step mother used to live on that land together with my brother and his children. A year ago, my father was killed in a car accident and since then, I work there and my children help me. We have a house on that land, and during this summer vacation we lived there and picked the grapes and the figs. The house has two rooms, from stone, covered with a tin roof. It was kind of a vacation for the family since a-Sheikh 'Ajalin area is beautiful and have a view to the Gaza coast.

Before the Oslo agreements, the Netzarim settlement [an Israeli settlement] border was about 1.5 km from my land. After the peace process started, and especially after the break of the current intifada, Israel created a safety zone around the settlement and used the lands of the residents in the area. Today, the border of the safety zone is only 300 meters from my land. Tanks are positioned regularly on a sand hill, named a-Taba, next to the safety zone border.

On July this year, about ten [Israeli] soldiers came down from the hill and went north, in the direction of Shemlech family land, which is adjacent to mine. They came to my land and asked my wife and children if we live there. They answered that we are, and told the soldiers that we are picking grapes and figs and then sell them. The officer told my family that they should not be scared. He demanded that we will not come near a-Taba hill and warned them that if anybody will, he will be shot. My wife told him: "we will not allow anybody go to that place, even not the small children." The officer thanked her and returned with the soldiers to the hill.

On Wednesday evening, August 28, after we finished working, Muhammaed Samir al-Hajin, my 18 years old nephew, came to visit us together with my relative Hasem al-Hajin. At around 21:00, I noticed a tank on a-Taba hill. My sons and the two visitors went to sleep under a fig tree which is about eight meters east to the house. Me, my wife and my small children planned to sleep outside, next to the house, about six meters from the place my older sons slept. I went to change my clothes and got ready to sleep. My wife and the small children slept already and the others were lying awake under the tree.

When I went to sleep, I was surprised to hear three shells shot continuously. The shells fell and exploded where my older sons were lying. When the first shell was shot, I heard my sons yelling. My wife woke up, started to shout, and ran to the boys. On her way, two more shells were dropped next to her. I ran away and hide in the west side of the house. When my wife arrived to the place where my sons were, I heard shootings from machine guns. My wife's screams stopped. The shooting stopped after a few minutes and then I crawled towards my small son, Sa'id, in order to save him. I arrived to the place where he was sleeping before, but I could not find him. I started to call him loudly: "Sa'id, Sa'id, Sa'id." At this moment, the tank started shooting again. I crawled back and hide again in the west side of the house. I was confused and didn't know whether to go and save my sons and risk my life or whether to wait for a miracle. I decided that the best thing to do will be to call my relatives from my mobile phone and tell them to call an ambulance . . .

After a while, an UNRWA ambulance arrived. The staff told us that they have permission to evacuate the wounded. The permission was also for the two other ambulances. The three ambulances drove until we arrived to the place where the incident happened and the paramedics went to treat the wounded. One of the paramedics brought my son Sa'id, who was injured in his right shoulder. When I went to help them, I saw my son Salah lying injured on the ground. His voice was very low and with a lot of pain. I picked him up and brought him to the ambulance. I returned to the place and found my wife lying on her face and blood covered all her body. It looks like she was dead but I wasn't sure since her body was still hot. I tried to pick her up but I couldn't. When I did that, I saw a hole in her left hip. Two neighbors arrived and helped me transfer her to an ambulance.

The medical staff saved the life of two injured people, who at the time I didn't know who they were. Me and one of the paramedics saved my relative, Muhammed Samir al-Hajin. The paramedics brought the other injured and I didn't know what was the condition of all my children.

My son Rafaat, aged 23, arrived to save us. He started looking between the trees for wounded, and then the tank shot a shell at him. He ran to the neighbors' land. The tank shot three flares and Rafaat crawled and ran away.

It took about two hours, or less, until the ambulances received the permission to evacuate the injured. I arrived to the hospitals with the ambulances and stayed there until the next day in the afternoon. My sons Ashraf and Nihad, my wife and Muhammed, my relative, were killed. Five others were injured.[172]

2. The Testimony of 'Aref Daraghmeh, 32, August 2002.

The Apache helicopters cited in the testimony below by 'Aref Daraghmeh were sold to Israel by the United States under the terms of the US Arms Export and Control Act of 1994, which stipulates that US-exported weapons shall be used for "legitimate self-defense."[173] With respect to the export of US weapons to Israel, the Federation of American Scientists (FAS) reported in May 2002 that "since 1950, the United States has provided more than $46 billion in grant military aid to Israel, a sum that outstrips military aid to Egypt, America's next largest beneficiary, by at least $20 billion." FAS reported, "Israel has also received many billions more in grant 'economic' aid, loans for military purchases, and used American armaments."[174] Furthermore, in April 2003 the US Congressional Research Service reported "there were unconfirmed reports in February 2001 that the United States was investigating if Israel misused US military equipment during the 2000–2001 'Intifadah,' specifically by using Apache helicopters to assassinate Palestinians suspected of terrorism."[175] To our knowledge, no such investigation was completed or report publicly issued. In July 2002, one month before the incident described in the Palestinian testimony below, the *New York Times* reported:

> A senior State Department official said today that Israel could face "consequences," including possible sanctions on arms sales, if it improperly used American-made weapons during attacks on Palestinian targets.
>
> Richard A. Boucher, the State Department spokesman, said the United States was closely monitoring Israeli actions to ensure they did not violate the Arms Export Control Act, which requires that military items sold by the United States be used solely for "internal security and legitimate self defense."
>
> "We've made quite clear that we're seriously concerned about some of the Israeli tactics, some of the Israeli actions, including targeted killings and actions like this that endanger civilians," Mr. Boucher told reporters today.[176]

92   ISRAEL–PALESTINE ON RECORD

The *Times* said that Boucher's remarks "were prompted by reports that the Israeli military used an American-made F-16 fighter jet to drop a laser-guided bomb into a densely packed neighborhood in Gaza City on Tuesday, killing a Hamas leader and 14 civilians."[177] To our knowledge, this was the last report in the *Times* that mentioned the US Arms Export Control Act as applied to Israel until August 2006,[178] though Israel did not end its policy of "targeted killings" of Palestinians with US-exported weapons, including Apache helicopters and F-16s. Although US law places restrictions on US-exported weaponry to Israel, much of it paid for by US taxpayers, to our knowledge the *Times* has never published an editorial on this subject.

Testimony of 'Aref Daraghmeh, 32.
On Saturday, 31 August 2002, at around 4:30 P.M., I was standing with some people at the entrance of my house, in the eastern neighborhood of Tubas. I saw two Apache helicopters hovering above the neighborhood. One of the helicopters fired a missile, which landed about fifty meters away from my house. The missile landed on the side of the road, near the house of 48 year-old Nahila Salameh Daraghmeh. She was injured by shrapnel. Her 30 year-old brother, Ibrahim, was also injured. Later, another missile hit the house of my neighbor, Ghaleb Mahmud Daraghmeh. The house was partially damaged and Ghaleb's mother, 52 year-old Tanha Jamil Daraghmeh, was injured by shrapnel and was taken to a hospital.

The helicopter then fired a third missile towards a silver Mitsubishi, which had four people in it. The missile hit the trunk and the car spun around its axis. I saw a man stepping out of the car and running away. The three other passengers remained inside. I saw an arm and an upper part of a skull flying out of the car. The car went up in flames and I could see three bodies burning inside it.

Three minutes later, after the Israeli helicopters left, I went out to the street and began to shout. I saw people lying on the ground. Among them was six-year-old Bahira Burman Daraghmeh. She was dead. I remember seeing Bahira two minutes before the attack in one of the nearby stores, buying supplies for her first day of school. I also saw Bahira's cousin, Osama Ibrahim Daraghmeh. He had been hit by shrapnel. He ran about 25 meters and then fell on the ground and died. I saw Osama's mother running towards Bahira, picking her up and heading towards the a-Shifa clinic, which is about 500 meters away. I went to the clinic and saw her screaming after seeing the body of her son, Osama.

I later found out that the attack was meant to assassinate two people who were wanted by Israel. They were inside the car that was hit. One of them managed to escape. The other one, 28 year-old Rafat 'Akab Daraghmeh, was killed.

The other fatalities are: 17 year-old Yazid 'Abd a-Razek Daraghmeh and 16 year-old Sari Mahmud Subeh. I think they had no connection to the two wanted men. I also found out that Rafat Daraghmeh was an activist in the al-Aqsa Martyrs Brigade in Tubas.

All the wounded were transferred to the government hospital in Jenin by a Red Crescent ambulance. In addition, I saw about ten houses which were heavily damaged. The missiles landed in the center of the eastern neighborhood of Tubas.[179]

This account was supported by the father of Osama Daraghmeh, the boy who was killed by the helicopter:

My son, Osama Daraghmeh, was supposed to start the seventh grade. He was born on October 22, 1989, and killed on the first day of the school year. Five minutes before his death Osama bought himself a pair of black jeans and wanted to know what I thought of them. I told him they were great. He was very happy and asked me for some money to buy supplies his teachers asked him to bring to his first day of school. I told him: "Get some rest, and in the evening, you and I will go and buy all the stuff." But Osama insisted on going to the store next to our house, which is about twenty meters away. I let him go, and I wish I hadn't. He went and never came back.

I heard explosions and saw Israeli helicopters. Everyone was scared and confused, but it didn't cross my mind that Osama was killed in these explosions. It was only half an hour later that I was informed of Osama's death. It was the worst news I had ever gotten in my life. They've killed what was dearest to me. I do not know what life will be like without Osama. Why did they kill my son? What danger did he pose to them? What will the soldier that killed my son tell his children? He'll probably be proud and tell them what heroic deed he had done in Tubas, which killed my son and six-year-old Bahira. Israel should know it is killing innocent children. Bahira, my niece, was also killed when she went to buy supplies for her first day of school.[180]

3. The Testimony of Suleiman Muhammad Salameh al-Akhras, 13, July 2001.

With respect to the testimony below, B'Tselem reported: "On Saturday, 7 July 2001, Khalil al-Mughrabi, 11, was killed in Rafah. Two other children, Ibrahim Abu Susin, 10, and Suleiman Abu Rijal, 12, were wounded." In response to questions from B'Tselem about these incidents, an IDF spokesman said that "dozens of Palestinians rioted near Rafah and endangered soldiers' lives," and that "the soldiers acted with restraint and control and dispersed the rioters by using means for dispersing demonstrations and by live gunfire into an open area distant from the rioters." B'Tselem noted that testimonies from a number of Palestinians "contradicted this version of the events."

In response to additional questions from B'Tselem about whether the Israeli army had conducted any investigation into the killings, the Israeli army responded that it had not initiated an investigation because "there was no suspicion of criminal behavior by the soldiers." Attached to this response, "apparently in error," as B'Tselem reported, was the IDF's preliminary inquiry file about these events. Upon reviewing the IDF inquiry file, which concluded "under the circumstances, we have not found any suspicion of criminal behavior on the part of the IDF soldiers, or that there was just cause to open an investigation," B'Tselem reported that "the documents presented in this report raise grave questions about the manner in which the army investigates itself." B'Tselem concluded that "the army conducted a shallow and superficial inquiry, at all stages of the process, and made no effort to understand what injured the children, to determine who was responsible, and to ensure that such incidents would not recur."[181]

Testimony of Suleiman Muhammad Salameh al-Akhras, 13.

Even before the intifada, I used to play soccer with my friends around Yubneh Refugee Camp, in Rafah, close to the Egyptian border. We used to play there because there aren't any other soccer fields in the city, and because the ground is flat and made of concrete, so it's good for playing.

On Saturday, I was playing there with twenty or thirty other children between the ages of ten and thirteen. They are all friends from the neighborhood and from school. We divided into a few teams of six and played a few games in order to give all the children a chance to play. About fifteen minutes before we finished playing, an Israeli tank drove along the border. It arrived from Salah a-Din gate and drove west toward the Tel Zu'arub post, where there is a very tall military tower that overlooks the whole area. After we finished playing, we sat down to rest. Some of us sat alongside the sand piles that are near the border fence. Others sat on the top [of] the piles. While we were resting, the soldiers in the tower suddenly shot a bullet. We didn't hear it until it entered Khalil Ibrahim Muhammad al-Mughrabi's head. Khalil, who was sitting on top of one of the piles, fell down immediately. His head burst and parts of it flew toward the children who were near him.

Then the soldiers opened intense fire from the tower. This time, the shooting was very loud. It sounded different from the bullet that hit Khalil. When we ran north, toward the houses in the refugee camp, two more of my schoolmates were hit. Ibrahim Abu Susin was hit in the stomach and his intestines came out. Suleiman Abu Rijal was hit in the thigh. A number of civilians rushed to the place immediately and evacuated the deceased in a Mercedes public-transport vehicle. An ambulance, which arrived immediately after, evacuated the two wounded to the hospital.

The terrible sight that I saw in this incident shocked me so much that I couldn't speak for six hours.[182]

This account was supported by another witness, Muhammad Salah Hussein al-Akhras, 14:

On the evening of Saturday, I was playing with about thirty more children at a soccer field near the border, in Yubneh Refugee Camp. The game started after the afternoon prayer, i.e. around 5:00 P.M. After a while, a tank drove along the border. It came from the east and drove west, toward Tel Zu'arub and the military tower there. The tank passed by quietly without shooting at us. After we finished playing, we lay on the ground to rest. Some of us sat on the piles of sand near the border. Around 7:10 P.M., I stood up and told the children to leave the place. I was two meters away from Khalil al-Mughrabi. Then I heard a faint sound and saw Khalil's brain flying out of his head and splattering all over my face and clothes. We started running away from the place. While we were running, intensive fire from the tower began. That gunfire resulted in two more children being hit. One of them was my neighbor, Ibrahim Abu Susin. He was hit in the stomach and his intestines came out. The other, Suleiman Abu Zeidan, was hit in the left thigh. Civilians who were there evacuated the deceased and the wounded to the hospital.[183]

By declining even to investigate this incident beyond a preliminary inquiry, B'Tselem concluded that "the message that the Judge Advocate General's office transmits to soldiers is clear: soldiers who violate the Open-Fire Regulations, even if their breach results in death, will not be investigated and will not be prosecuted. This policy grants prior immunity to security forces and allows them to violate the law. Furthermore, it shows utter disregard for human life."[184]

4. The Testimony of Sharif Muhammad Hamed Redwan, 19, November 2001.

The "Open-Fire Regulations" refer to legally established procedures permitting live ammunition fire by Israeli security personnel. B'Tselem reported that Israel modified its Open-Fire Regulations upon onset of the second *intifada* in fall 2000. Prior to the *intifada*, the regulations permitted security personnel to fire live ammunition only in the context of two narrowly defined circumstances: (a) when human life was in jeopardy, in which case security personnel were permitted to shoot only the assailant, and only when "a real threat of the loss of human life or grave bodily harm" was present, and (b) during the apprehension of a suspect, in which case soldiers were permitted to fire at the legs of a person suspected of committing a dangerous crime, but only as a last resort, and only after giving warning and firing in the air.[185] After the outbreak of the *intifada* the IDF changed the Open-Fire Regulations, and according to B'Teslem, they "artificially expanded the term 'life threatening.' " With respect to this change, B'Tselem argued:

The sweeping change in the definition of the situation ignores the substantial number of actions by security forces such as dispersing demonstrations, making arrests, operating checkpoints, that are ordinary policing actions and were defined as such prior to the current intifada. The change in the Open-Fire Regulations' handling of these acts, which themselves have not changed, are unlawful, and the previous Open-Fire Regulations must continue to apply. Security forces' actions are also subject to the international rules on the use of weapons, which provide that security forces may use lethal force only where there is a real and immediate threat to life. Then, too, force is allowed only when strictly necessary and the use of non-lethal means was unsuccessful in removing the danger.[186]

B'Tselem also reported that "during the current intifada, the IDF changed the Open-Fire Regulations numerous times," and "the IDF has not officially published the Regulations and most of B'Tselem's requests to the IDF Spokesperson to obtain information about the changes were not answered." Citing press reports, B'Tselem also reported:

> [T]he [Israeli] army is acting in accordance with a new compilation of open-fire regulations, which is referred to as Blue Lilac. They were prepared a few months before the intifada broke out. These regulations expand the range of situations in which soldiers may open fire, and give the commanders in the field increased flexibility and discretion. The new regulations allow, *inter alia*, firing at the legs of stone throwers, and sniper fire from ambush. In some areas, the procedures for apprehending suspects is nullified, and soldiers are allowed to fire without warning at Palestinian suspects.[187]

B'Tselem also reported:

> During the first months of the al-Aqsa intifada, Palestinians held hundreds of demonstrations near IDF posts. Demonstrations of this sort eventually became less frequent, but did not stop altogether. During some of these demonstrations, Palestinians threw stones and petrol bombs at soldiers, and on occasion, armed Palestinians from within or outside of the demonstrating crowd fired live ammunition at soldiers. It should be emphasized that, based on the view from B'Tselem's observation posts, Palestinian demonstrators did not open fire in the vast majority of demonstrations.[188]

To support this analysis, B'Tselem included a number of "Sample Cases" in its report to illustrate the manner in which Israel security forces used excessive lethal force against Palestinian demonstrators, including children, when no Israel lives were at risk. The testimony that follows is about the death of a fifteen-year-old boy, Wail 'Ali Redwan, who lived in Khan Yunis, a Palestinian refugee camp in the Gaza Strip.

Testimony of Sharif Muhammad Hamed Redwan, 19.

On Saturday, I went to the funeral of the five children from the al-Astal family. It took place at the cemetery east of the Neve Dekalim settlement. After the funeral ended, I heard gunfire coming from west of the cemetery. My friends Rami Mahmud al-Qara and Muhammad Abu Jam'a and I rushed to see what was happening. When we got there, I saw dozens of people throwing stones at the army post, which was located on the fence of the settlement.

Wail 'Ali Redwan was among the stone throwers. He was standing about one hundred meters from the fence and sixty meters from us. I told Rami and Muhammad that I was going to get Wail. I was afraid he would get killed because he was standing in an area where there was no cover. Suddenly, I heard explosions from pressure grenades. They shook the area. Several soldiers who were outside the army post had thrown the grenades from twenty meters east of where Wail was standing. Alongside the soldiers were two tanks and several jeeps. I also saw two snipers hiding behind concrete blocks that were next to the post. The snipers fired single shots at the stone throwers.

I walked toward Wail. As I did, the soldiers opened heavy fire. I looked in the direction from which the firing was coming and then saw Wail, who was fifty meters west of me, bend over and check his leg (I later learned that he had been hit in the leg by a rubber bullet). Then he raised his head and stood straight up. As he did, a bullet hit him in the head. I think that a sniper hit him. Wail did not have a stone in his hand when he was shot. He had only bent over to check his leg.

Because the gunfire was so intense, we couldn't get to Wail quickly enough to help. We had to crawl along the sand. When we reached him, we picked him up and carried him several hundred meters. On the way, we lost our grip and he fell because we had to bend over as we walked; otherwise, we would have been hit by the bullets. Near the Nimsawi neighborhood, we put Wail into an ambulance. It was around 1:30 P.M.[189]

5. The Testimony of Jihad Ibrahim Mahmud 'Abdallah, 13, November 2001.

The testimony below is about the death of Kipah Khaled 'Abdallah, a thirteen-year-old boy who lived in the Daheishe refugee camp in the West Bank.

Testimony of Jihad Ibrahim Mahmud 'Abdallah, 13.

I live with my father, mother, and four brothers and sisters in the Daheishe refugee camp. My uncle Khaled lives next door. His eldest son, Kipah, was my best friend. He was my age, and the two of us were in the eighth grade at the school for boys in the camp.

On Sunday, at about 10:50 A.M., we walked to school together, as usual. We were in the afternoon session, which began at 11:00. When we reached the schoolyard, we were told that a protest march was being organized for three grades (seventh, eighth, and ninth) against Israel's policy of murdering innocent women and children. The march was scheduled to begin at the square of the Church of the Nativity.

Kipah and I got to the square together with the other students at about 12:10 P.M. We marched to the Red Cross headquarters and then to Rachel's Tomb, where we started throwing stones. After a while, we ran into a big area located behind a pottery shop, where there is a blacksmith's workshop. It was rocky, so it was good cover from the bullets of the Israeli soldiers who were firing at us. They also fired tear gas and rubber bullets. Because there was so much tear gas, we had trouble breathing. It was also hard to see what was happening.

At some point, our friend Adham Abu Salim was hit in the right leg by a rubber bullet. We carried him to the road and put him into a Ford car. Then we went back to the area behind the pottery shop. I was standing about fifteen meters from Kipah, who was next to our friend Rami. About 150 meters away was an Israeli bulldozer. It was coming at us from the direction of Rachel's Tomb. The bulldozer stopped at the gas station, around seventy meters from us. About six soldiers got out of the bulldozer and opened fire at us. One of them aimed his rifle and fired. The bullet hit Kipah in the chest and came out of his back. I saw him fall to the ground.

Rami yelled for us to come over. Several other boys and I went to him, and I saw Kipah lying on the ground drenched in blood. We picked him up and ran to a Red Crescent ambulance that was fifty meters away. The paramedic got out of the ambulance and put Kipah inside. Rami went in the ambulance while the rest of us followed on foot to the hospital in Beit Jala.

Later on, Kipah was taken to al-Moqassed Hospital. He died there. The doctors said that Kipah died from a bullet that entered the left side of his chest and struck his heart.[190]

6. The Testimony of Jamal Bassem 'Ali Shahrur, 48, August 2001.

Israel's security forces also use excessive lethal force at checkpoints in the occupied territories. There are approximately 40 permanent checkpoints staffed by Israeli security personnel which severely restrict the movement of Palestinians in the West Bank. In addition, the Israelis have placed more than 400 physical obstacles—including dirt piles, concrete blocks, iron gates, and trenches—that block other roads in the West Bank and further restrict movement.[191] B'Tselem reports that the physical obstacles divide the West Bank into five separate areas that must be traversed via the staffed checkpoints. The nature of the movement restrictions are described in a B'Tselem report:

> The five areas in the West Bank are the North (Jenin, Nablus, and Tulkarm districts), the Center (Salfit, Qalqiliya, and Ramallah districts, and the Jericho enclave), the South (Bethlehem and Hebron districts), the Jordan Valley and the northern part of the Dead Sea (except for the Jericho enclave), and East Jerusalem.
>
> This [checkpoint] system enables Israel to designate use of some of the roads in the West Bank for the primary or exclusive use of Israelis, mainly settlers living in the West Bank. Israel prohibits Palestinian vehicles even from crossing certain roads, which also restricts access to roads that they are not prohibited from using. As a result, travelers in Palestinian vehicles have to get out, cross the road by foot, and find alternate transportation on the other side.
>
> Prolonged checks and searches carried out by soldiers at the staffed checkpoints and the accompanying degradation and long lines deter Palestinians from using even some roads that are open to them. Consequently, there is light Palestinian travel on some of the main West Bank roads, and these roads are essentially used only by settlers.
>
> Israel's policy greatly affects all areas of life for Palestinians in the West Bank and makes it impossible for them to live a normal life. Simple actions, such as shopping, visiting relatives, and going to classes at the university, have become a complicated, and at times impossible, task. . . .
>
> One of the main purposes of the movement restrictions policy is to protect Israeli settlers. Given that the settlements are illegal, the policy only aggravates the situation: it comprehensively and disproportionately impedes the freedom of movement of an entire population in order to perpetuate the settlement enterprise.[192]

In addition, B'Tselem reported that "even before the al-Aqsa intifada, the checkpoints were a focal point for unjustified shooting by soldiers," and "during the first intifada, B'Tselem documented many cases in which soldiers positioned at checkpoints violated the Open-Fire Regulations and shot Palestinians who posed no threat to life."[193]

The testimony below is about the Israeli shooting at a checkpoint of Majid Amjad Jilad, a young child from Turlkarm in the West Bank.

Testimony of Jamal Bassem 'Ali Shahrur, 48.
I was born in Bal'a, Tulkarm District, and moved to Tulkarm as a child. Most of my relatives still live in Bal'a. My daughter 'Abit, 25, is the mother of Majid, who was injured in the incident. She studies computers at the al-Quds Open University. I am not involved in politics and do not belong to any party. Until the al-Aqsa intifada broke out, I had a magnetic card and a permit to enter Israel. . . .

On Friday, at 4:00 P.M., I drove to Bal'a. In the car with me were my wife, two of my children, and my grandson Majid. It was quiet in Tulkarm, and nothing unusual had taken place in the town that day. After driving for a few minutes along the main road leading from Tulkarm to Nablus, when we were about three kilometers from Tulkarm, I came across a dirt roadblock near the Nur Shams refugee camp. The dirt piles blocked most of the road, leaving a space of only two meters on the shoulder of the road on which cars could cross. There were no soldiers around, so we were able to cross it without any problem.

At 4:15, we reached Bal'a. . . . At 8:15, we got back into the car and started back to Tulkarm. I was driving, my wife was sitting in the seat next to me, and the three children were in the back seat. Majid was standing behind my seat, and when I told him to sit down, he said that he wanted to see the road. We reached the area of the dirt piles near the Nur Shams refugee camp. There is a big bend in the road about thirty meters before the roadblock, so it is impossible to see the roadblock until just before you get to it.

I was going about 70 km/h, and when I got around the bend, I saw an armored vehicle near the roadblock, and five soldiers were standing alongside it on the road. Even though it was getting dark, the soldiers did not set up any lights so they could be seen. When I noticed them, I was around thirty meters away. I slammed on my brakes. The car stopped after about five meters. When it stopped, I heard shots being fired at us. Four bullets hit the left side of the front windshield, and one hit the car's left bumper. One of the bullets grazed my shoulder, hit my grandson's elbow, and pierced his abdomen. At first, I didn't realize that he had been wounded, but then I heard the children crying and my wife screaming. I turned the car around and drove toward 'Anbate. The soldiers did not fire any more and did not chase us. . . .

While I turned around to go to 'Anbate, I saw Majid leaning on the seat, blood flowing from his hand and abdomen. My wife told me that he had been wounded and called out his name. He told her that he had pains in his abdomen. My two sons were crying and screaming all the time, even though they had not been hit. I drove very fast, and we got to the 'Anbate municipal building, where there is a medical clinic. I carried Majid in my arms to the first floor, where the clinic is located. The two medics who were there began to treat him and called the Red Crescent in Tulkarm to get an ambulance. Then they put him into a taxi and took him toward Tulkarm, meeting the ambulance at the dirt roadblock near a–Shams, where the soldiers had fired at my car. I drove in my car to Tulkarm. . . . When I arrived, at 9:00, Majid was already in surgery.

Beatings and Abuse. Although B'Tselem also has issued many reports[194] and testimonies[195] about Israeli beatings and abuse of Palestinians in the occupied territories, the *New York Times* ignores this information as well.

In issuing these documents B'Tselem noted that both Israeli law and international law permit the use of "reasonable force in self-defense and for duty-related purposes," including "dispersing rioters, arresting suspects resisting arrest, and preventing a detainee from fleeing." However, B'Tselem also noted that "the acts described in testimonies given to B'Tselem and to other human rights organizations deviate greatly from what the law allows and constitute flagrant violations of human rights." It also reported that the absence of serious investigations of Israeli beatings and abuse of Palestinians sends a message to Israeli security force personnel that "even if the establishment does not accept acts of violence, it will not take measures against those who commit them." This sends a message "that the lives and dignity of Palestinians are meaningless and that security forces can continue, pursuant to the function they serve, to abuse, humiliate, and beat Palestinians with whom they come into contact."[196]

1. The Testimony of Na'ima Musa 'Ali Abu 'Ayash, 48, February 2001.

I live with my husband and children in al-Hijera. The village is located six kilometers south of Hebron, on the road to Beersheva. Our house is around 200 meters north of the road. We have been living in the house, which is four stories and has a red-tile roof, for three years. Construction of the upper floors is not yet completed. Two check-points face our house—one at the entrance to the al-Fawwar refugee camp and the other at the entrance to Dura. Since the beginning of the events, Palestinian children and the army have continuously clashed on the road near the checkpoints. At night, Palestinians and soldiers exchange fire. My children often go onto our roof to watch the clashes.

On Monday, 19 February 2001, around 3:30 P.M. I went up to the second-floor roof to hang the laundry. When I looked in the direction of the checkpoint at the entrance to al-Fawwar, I saw something unusual happening. On the road, near the checkpoint, there were two or three army jeeps. Someone later told me that a child had thrown an object at the soldiers and it landed on the road. I hung up a few clothes and then heard my eight-year-old son, Wasim, and my five-year-old daughter, Asil, shouting below. When I looked, I saw a jeep park near the house and several soldiers rush through the gate and into the yard.

When I went downstairs, I saw that the soldiers had already entered the house. Three of them held my two adult children, Wisam, 24, and Ahmed, who is 20. I saw the painter Zohir 'Asfur and the son of our neighbor, Muhammad al-Khatib, lying on the floor in the front room. The soldiers aimed their weapons at them and ordered them to keep quiet. I heard a shout from the kitchen. A soldier stood at the entrance. I rushed there and saw my daughter Noha, 16, and my son Mu-hammad, 13, trapped in the kitchen with three soldiers. One of the soldiers beat Muhammad and slammed his head against the refrig-erator. The soldier grabbed the child's hair. Noha tried to protect her brother and get the soldier to stop beating him. Muhammad tried to hide behind her, but another soldier pulled her by the hair and also slammed her head against the refrigerator. He told her a number of times to move back and shut up.

I tried to get into the kitchen to protect my two children. The soldier standing at the entrance put his rifle to my head and told me to shut up. I did not listen and tried to push him away and go into the kitchen. The soldier struck me on the right side of my head with his rifle. For several seconds, I was in a daze, and when I recovered, the soldier pushed me into the room opposite the kitchen. He aimed his rifle at me and threatened to shoot if I moved. My little daughter Asil and my son Wasim ran to me, hugged me, and screamed. I estimate that they beat my son and daughter for about ten minutes. While that was going on, several soldiers completed their inspection of the roof and came back down. . . .

After the soldiers were gone, I felt sharp pains in my head. My son-in-law Ghassan Abu Radwan took me by car to 'Alia Hospital, in Hebron, where for two hours I underwent X-rays and treatment. The doctor told me that my skull was fractured.[197]

2. The Testimony of Isma'il al-'Izza, 21, January 2003.

I live with my family in the al-Fawwar refugee camp, which is about seven kilometers south of Hebron. Our house is about 150 meters from the al-Fawwar junction. There are dirt roadblocks at the entrance to the refugee camp. I have a little snack stand on the road near my house. I sell cola, cigarettes, cookies, and sandwiches. Occasionally, whether during the day or night, Israeli soldiers leave their positions at the junction, and come into the camp. They stand near my snack stand, and prevent passers-by from continuing on their way. They shoot at children who curse them or throw stones.

When the soldiers, usually there's three, stand next to my stand, one of them comes in and demands cola and biscuits for him and his colleagues. He takes the merchandise and leaves without paying. This has happened more than ten times in the past month.

The first time it happened, in the beginning of January, soldiers arrived at the stand at about 6:00 A.M. and took cola and biscuits. I asked them to pay and they refused. So I refused to give it to them. One of the soldiers threatened to send me to jail if I didn't give him what he wanted. I stood by my refusal and he demanded that I go with him. The three soldiers led me to a vineyard, about 300 meters from the stand. They ordered me to stand next to the fence that separates the field from the path. The soldier stood next to the fence behind me and suddenly hit me on the back of the head with the butt of his gun. I fell on the ground and couldn't remember what happened next. Later, the owner of the field, of the Abu Ghalion family, told me that he saw me, lying unconscious on the ground. He said he told my family. My brothers, Hassan, 42, and Khalil, age 38, came to the field immediately. It was 8:00, two hours after I had fainted. They took me to the hospital. When we arrived at the hospital, I woke up, got treated, and returned home. Since that incident, I've been scared to refuse the soldiers' demands, and I let them take whatever they want.[198]

3. The Testimony of Muhammad Shaker Da'ana, 13, January 2003.

I live with my family of 14 in Jabel Johar in area H2 in Hebron. I am the tenth child and I study at al-Mutnabi School, which is in the Wadi a-Nasri, about a kilometer from my home.

On Thursday, 23 January 03, at about 8:00 A.M., I left my home to go to school. On the way, I saw an Israeli army jeep drive down the street at top speed. All of the children that were walking on the street ran away as soon as they saw the jeep. I couldn't run because my knee was hurting. The day before I fell when soldiers were chasing us when we were leaving school, and my knee had been hurting since. The jeep stopped next to me and two soldiers stepped out. One of them asked me where I was going, and I said that I was on my way to school. The soldier said, "To school, son of a bitch," and hit me on the forehead with his gun. I fell on the ground, bleeding from the wound in my forehead. The blood covered my entire face. The two soldiers lifted me up and threw me forcefully back on the ground. I crashed into an electricity pole. I started screaming and crying and the soldiers fired in the air. I was on the ground. One of the soldiers picked me up and demanded I get up and spread my legs. He threatened to shoot me if I leave.

I stayed in one place for a few minutes, with my face covered in blood and my coat and clothes stained. I heard someone calling me, but I couldn't go to them because the soldiers where still in the area. When they left me and went to chase other school kids, I approached the man, Maher al-'Ajalouni, whom I knew. He gave me first aid. He cleaned the blood that covered my face and tried to stop the bleeding. Later, a few men carried me home. My father and brothers were still home. My cousin, Mundhar Da'ana, who's a lawyer, took me to Muhammad 'Ali al-Mukhtaseb Hospital, where I was given medical treatment. The doctors stitched my wound with 11 stitches and told me to return to the hospital in case of dizziness or vomiting. . . .

Since the incident, I haven't gone to school because I have severe pains in the legs and head.[199]

Home Demolitions and Destruction of Agricultural Land.
Israeli violence in the occupied territories goes well beyond shootings and beatings. It also includes the illegal destruction of Palestinian homes and property, including farms and orchards. From
September 29, 2000, to December 31, 2005, B'Tselem issued a
number of reports[200] and testimonies[201] pertaining to Israel's policy
of demolishing Palestinian homes and agricultural land. Although
the *Times*' Israel-based correspondents wrote several valuable articles
within this period about the destruction caused by demolitions,[202]
the *Times*' editorial page published no condemnation of the demolitions policy.

In a forty-page document issued in February 2002, B'Tselem
reported, "Since the beginning of the al-Aqsa intifada [September
29, 2000], Israel has demolished hundreds of houses, uprooted
thousands of trees, and destroyed thousands of acres of land in the
Gaza Strip. In almost all cases of demolition, the houses were occupied
and the residents fled when the bulldozers appeared at their doorsteps.
The IDF implemented this policy primarily in the Gaza Strip, near
Israeli settlements, bypass roads, and army posts."[203] In a fifty-page
document issued in 2004, B'Tselem reported, "During the course of
the al-Aqsa intifada, which began in September 2000, Israel has
implemented a policy of mass demolition of Palestinian houses in
the Occupied Territories. In that period, Israel has destroyed some
4,170 Palestinian homes."[204]

Similarly, in May 2004 Amnesty International issued a forty-page
report on Israel's policy of destroying homes and agricultural land in
the Palestinian territories. The press release to the report stated:

> Israel's unjustified destruction of thousands of Palestinian and Arab
> homes as well as vast areas of agricultural land has reached an
> unprecedented level and must stop immediately, Amnesty Interna-
> tional said today.
>
> Over the last three and a half years [since September 2000], Israeli
> armed forces have demolished more than 3,000 homes, leaving tens of
> thousands of men, women, and children homeless or without a
> livelihood.[205]

The press release also reported: "According to the United Nations,
more than 2,000 homes in Gaza have been destroyed in the last three
years and 10 percent of the agricultural land. In the West Bank, almost

90 percent of Israel's fence/wall is being built on occupied territory and at least 600 [Palestinian] homes have been destroyed." The press release continued:

- In the Occupied Territories, demolitions are often carried out as collective punishment for Palestinian attacks or to facilitate the expansion of illegal Israeli settlements. Both practices contravene international law and some of these acts are war crimes.
- Discriminatory planning and building policies make it practically impossible for Israeli Arabs and Palestinians to obtain building permits.
- In Israel, the demolition of homes for lack of building permits in the Arab sector is a recurrent phenomenon, whereas demolition of homes without building permission in the Jewish sector is almost unheard of.
- Forced evictions and house demolitions are usually carried out without warning with families given little or no time to leave their homes and salvage their possessions.
- Most cases of house demolition and destruction of land are not subject to legal supervision or appeal.

Likewise, in October 2004 Human Rights Watch issued a 120-page report on Israel's demolition of Palestinian homes and destruction of agricultural land. The report began as follows:

Over the past four years, the Israeli military has demolished over 2,500 Palestinian houses in the occupied Gaza Strip. Nearly two-thirds of these homes were in Rafah, a densely populated refugee camp and city at the southern end of the Gaza Strip on the border with Egypt. Sixteen thousand people—more than ten percent of Rafah's population—have lost their homes, most of them refugees, many of whom were dispossessed for a second or third time.

As satellite images in this report show, most of the destruction in Rafah occurred along the Israeli-controlled border between the Gaza Strip and Egypt. During regular nighttime raids and with little or no warning, Israeli forces used armored Caterpillar D9 bulldozers to raze blocks of homes at the edge of the camp, incrementally expanding a "buffer zone" that is currently up to three hundred meters wide. The pattern of destruction strongly suggests that Israeli forces demolished homes wholesale, regardless of whether they posed a specific threat, in violation of international law. In most of the cases Human Rights Watch found the destruction was carried out in the absence of military necessity.[206]

Israel's informal policy of refusing compensation to Palestinians for loss of life and property due to unlawful killings and demolitions became a formal policy in July 2005, when the Israeli Knesset passed the "Intifada Law," which (retroactively to September 2000) denies Palestinians a right to sue the Israeli government for damages to people and property inflicted by Israeli security forces.[207] According to the Israeli newspaper, *Yediot Ahronot*, "left-wing activists and international law experts have criticized the 'Intifada Law,' saying the bill was intended to entrench the occupation without paying for the consequences."[208] According to an article in *Ha'aretz*, the law "prevents Palestinians from filing claims for damages for events that took place in 'conflict zones.' "[209] To our knowledge, the "Intifada Law" has never been mentioned in the *Times*' news coverage of the conflict, and there are no editorials in the *New York Times* that condemn it or mention it.

The *Times* did publish a number of news articles from September 2000 to December 2005 on the Israeli demolitions; a few cited B'Tselem spokespersons who were critical of the demolitions from an international law perspective. For example, in May 2003 the *Times*' Greg Myre noted:

> Israel asserts that even its most widely debated practices to try to stem violence can withstand legal scrutiny—the killings of dozens of Palestinian militants, the detention of suspects without charges and the demolition of family homes that belong to the [Palestinians] accused [by Israel] of carrying out attacks against Israelis. But Palestinians and human rights activists say these actions are legally unacceptable, and often amount to collective punishment of Palestinians.
>
> The American legal system is facing similar questions about the treatment of defendants in terrorism cases, in the wake of the September 11 attacks.
>
> Lior Yavne, a spokesman for the Israeli human rights group B'tselem, said that "inside Israel proper, you have a law-abiding state, a proper liberal democracy."
>
> "But once you cross into the Palestinian territories, the situation changes immediately," he said in reference to the West Bank and Gaza. "Whatever is convenient to do in the occupied territories, Israel does without concern for international legal norms."[210]

There are other brief mentions of "collective punishment" and "international law" in the articles on Israel's demolitions of Palestinian homes,[211] including in the *Times* article that reported Israel's announced end to the policy of demolishing Palestinian homes for alleged military purposes. In February 2005 Greg Myre began that article as follows:

> Israel ordered a halt on Thursday to the policy of demolishing the homes of Palestinian militants, a step welcomed by Palestinian and human rights groups.
>
> The decision by Israel's defense minister, Shaul Mofaz, suspends a practice that Israel has employed on and off for decades despite harsh international criticism of it as collective punishment.[212]

While it is true that Israel's practice of demolishing thousands of Palestinian homes was subjected to "harsh international criticism," such criticism did not appear in any editorials in the *Times* within the period examined in this book.

Despite the enormous scale of the Israeli demolitions, especially in southern Gaza, there were few front-page articles about the demolitions in the *Times*,[213] even when, for example, the Israeli army in May 2004 initiated a two-week demolition siege in Rafah in southern Gaza. On May 17 the *Times* reported, "Despite international criticism, Israeli officials said Sunday that they intended to proceed with a plan to widen an Israeli-patrolled lane along the Gaza Strip's border with Egypt by demolishing as many as hundreds of Palestinian homes." The *Times* reported that this "followed fierce fighting late last week in the area, the Rafah refugee camp, during which Israeli forces destroyed 88 buildings, leaving more than 1,000 people homeless."[214]

On May 18 the *Times* reported that "Israeli armored bulldozers reinforced by helicopter gunships advanced early Tuesday into the Rafah refugee camp in the southern Gaza Strip after Israeli troops sealed the camp off for what the army called a large-scale operation to root out militants and weapons smuggling tunnels." The *Times* also reported that "an Israeli helicopter fired missiles that killed at least 11 Palestinians and wounded 30, The Associated Press reported, while bulldozers began knocking down structures at the camp's margins."[215]

On May 20 the *Times* reported that ten additional Palestinians were killed in the siege:

As a throng of Palestinians marched in protest here, an Israeli tank and helicopter gunship opened fire on Wednesday, leaving several people dead, including children, and dozens wounded, Palestinian witnesses said.

The protesters were marching on neighboring Tel Sultan, a Palestinian housing project on Rafah's outskirts. There, for a second day, thousands of Palestinians were held under an Israeli curfew that was enforced with sniper fire, as troops went house to house in a hunt for what the army called suspected militants.[216]

On May 21 the *Times* reported that seven more Palestinians were killed by Israeli fire and that "thousands of Palestinians remained shut in their homes by an Israeli curfew, and relief aid workers said many were running out of food and water."[217]

None of these important reports, written by *Times*' correspondent James Bennett, were published on the front page, and there was no editorial in the *Times* condemning the Israeli siege and destruction. It is, of course, unimaginable that reports about a Palestinian demolitions and murder rampage in any Israeli city or town—one that destroyed hundreds of Israeli homes and left thousands homeless, with a sniper-enforced state of siege, with Palestinian helicopters and tanks (of which the Palestinians have none) opening fire on Israeli demonstrators, killing and injuring dozens of Israelis, including many children—would not have been on the front page of the *New York Times* for days accompanied by editorials condemning Palestinian terrorism.

If in fact such an event were to occur in Israel, it would indeed merit front-page coverage and outraged editorials—so why did this actual siege and demolition, in addition to numerous other similar Israeli sieges and demolitions, not merit front-page coverage and outraged editorials? The *Times* applies two sets of standards to the Israel-Palestine conflict—one that minimizes coverage and condemnation of Israel's full-spectrum violence in the Palestinian territories, and another that headlines Palestinian suicide bombers.

1. The Testimony of 'Adnan 'Abd al-Qarim Suliman Barhum, June 2001.

On Saturday, at 1:30 A.M., I woke to the sound of tanks and bulldozers. I couldn't tell which direction the sound came from. I heard a loud sound of cannon explosions. I opened the window on the eastern side of the house and saw a large army bulldozer about thirty meters away. The bulldozer demolished an irrigation pool and two water-pump sheds belonging to my cousin 'Atta Barhum and me. At that moment, my brother Suliman came to my house. He had fled from his house. He told me that the tanks had entered the property of our neighbor, which is west of our house. While the shelling continued, I took my disabled mother, who requires a wheelchair, and told my wife and children to get out of the house. They were all frightened and hysterical. Throughout the neighborhood there were screams of little children, and adults asking, "Where is my son? Where is my brother? Did they get out?"

When I left the house, I saw a yellow-green beam of light coming from the army tower at Tel-Zo'arub, around eight hundred meters west, directed at all the houses in the area. I left my mother alone on the main road and went to see where my children, my wife, and other relatives were. When I got close to the house, I saw the beam of light shining each time on a different house, and the bulldozer demolishing the house on which the beam was shining.

The Israeli army did not inform us, either before or during the action, of its intention to demolish our house, so we didn't have time to remove our possessions. It was the same for our neighbors. The army closed off the area from 1:30 A.M. with tanks. There were about five tanks and two bulldozers. At 2:00 A.M., the bulldozers began to demolish the houses. Twenty-four families were there, and they all fled. Some of them stayed close to the concrete fence along the border, and some moved about one hundred meters to the north.

At approximately 5:30 A.M., it ended. The army left the area, and I looked for my wife and children. My sister Hanan told me that my wife, who is pregnant, was on the main road and couldn't stand on her feet out of fear and because of the horrible sight of the demolished houses. . . .

Our house that was destroyed had six rooms, two kitchens and bathrooms. It totaled about three hundred square meters. The army also demolished my irrigation pool, the shed with motors and pumps, and a one-hundred-square-meter sheep pen. The pen had six sheep and one of them was killed during the demolition. The bulldozer also uprooted six olive trees that were forty years old.[218]

2. The Testimony of A'adi Jabber 'Ali 'Abid, 43, October 2001.

I own a garage where we take apart cars for spare parts. . . . I was at the garage yesterday with my two sons and the employees. At about 4:00 P.M., an Israeli tank and a gigantic army bulldozer approached from the north along the fence of the [Israeli] settlement. When they reached the garage, the bulldozer began to remove the cars that were outside the fence and pushed them into the garage area. We fled in the direction of the main road. The soldiers gave us no warning and did not tell us to leave. We were afraid that they would shoot us. After some forty-five minutes, when the bulldozer had already left, I went to the garage and saw that all the cars that were outside had been squashed by the bulldozer and put into a big pile.

That night, I was asleep at home, and at midnight or so, my son 'Ala, 21, woke me up and told me that the bulldozers had returned and were destroying the garage. I was surprised because I thought that they had been satisfied with the damage that they had done in the afternoon. Everybody in the house woke up, and I went outside. The residents of the neighborhood were standing in the side streets watching what was going on. I saw a bulldozer accompanied by a tank. The bulldozer destroyed the garage and squashed the cars. At the same time, another bulldozer with a tank alongside drove along al-Bahar Street, proceeded about seven hundred meters, destroyed part of the road, and dug a deep pit in it.

Then the bulldozer turned around and destroyed a fence marking the land belonging to Khalil al-Astel, which was about 120 meters long. It then uprooted close to forty olive trees and date trees that were on the plot of land. The bulldozer drove westward and uprooted about sixty olive trees that were on three dunams belonging to Hamadeh al-Astel. Then it continued to a three-dunam plot belonging to his brother Yunis al-Astel and uprooted about sixty olive trees. The bulldozer then turned to fields on the southern side of the road and destroyed a three-dunam patch on which he grew vegetables, some thirty olive trees, and about ten fig trees.

When it finished, the bulldozer crossed to the northern side of the road and joined the other bulldozer in destroying the garage and the house situated there. Residents gathered in the side streets, and the soldiers in the tanks began to fire bullets and stun grenades. The soldiers at the observation post on the crane did the same. The bullets struck the western windows and walls of my house. They also hit the window of the house of my neighbor Kamel al-'Udi and destroyed his television. Shards from his window fell and struck his Mercedes, breaking its rear window. When the firing started, all of us fled to a safer location so that the bullets wouldn't hit us.

When the two bulldozers finished demolishing the garage, they proceeded east. One of them destroyed the fence of Nazir Farawneh's house, uprooted olive trees in the yard, and knocked down two rooms with a slate roof. The other bulldozer destroyed Wasim al-Habil's house, which was located around fifty meters east of the garage, and two rooms that nobody lived in.

At 2:00 A.M. or so, the two bulldozers and the two tanks drove north, and two other tanks proceeded south. Many residents and I wanted to go to the scene, but soldiers opened fire from opposite the garage. All of us fled.[219]

3. The Testimony of Saleh Hussein Mustafa al-Babli, 47, January 2002.

My house is in the Rafah refugee camp, one meter from the Egyptian border, and west of the Israeli army post at Salah-a-Din Gate. I live with my family of fourteen.

On Thursday, I was woken at about 2:00 A.M. by the sound of tanks and bulldozers that had come from the direction of the Israeli army post. I got out of bed and saw that my sons had also woken up. The bulldozers were approaching the house and we decided to leave immediately. We woke up the others and got out. We managed to proceed a few meters when three bulldozers reached the house. Immediately, one of them started to demolish the house. I stood in the rain for a few moments, unable to believe that I wouldn't ever see my house again. The children were screaming, and one of them asked me to run away because he was afraid I would get hurt. We fled to the adjacent street. I stood there with my wife, children, grandchildren and others in my family and watched for ten minutes as the bulldozer destroyed our house.

Two bulldozers went to the houses adjacent to ours. The children and women screamed and the bulldozers made a lot of noise. All the camp's residents gathered and tried to help the families. We saw people running from their homes. They were dressed in their sleeping garments and were carrying children. The sight was terrifying. The residents gathered in the adjacent street and remained there for about two hours. About thirty minutes before the Israelis finished the demolition work, the soldiers opened heavy fire at the residents who had gathered in the street, and we had to move to narrow side streets to hide. The streets were full of puddles and it was raining all the time.

Then some armed Palestinians arrived. They tried to force the Israelis away, and gunfire ensued for about half an hour. At about 4:00 A.M., the Israeli troops began to withdraw, and I returned to my house to try to save what I could. When I got there, I saw that my house had been completely demolished.[220]

4. The Testimony of Hussam a-Sa'adi, 39, June 2002.

On Thursday, June 20, 2002, Jenin was under curfew. I was at home with my wife Ahlam, age 33 and our five children, Hadil, age 14, Rabi', age 13, Fares, age 12, Mahmud, age 11, and Asil, age 8. My niece, Mona Ibrahim a-Sa'adi, age 22, was visiting us at the house.

The situation in the area was very tense, as the occupation forces were bombing houses, conducting searches and arresting citizens. Around midnight, we heard the army around our house, in the old city. I prepared the family for any situation that might occur, especially as we heard the army was arresting people. I gathered my wife and children, and we all sat in one of the rooms. We were expecting the soldiers to break into the house. The soldiers broke into the home of Marwan and Sofian a-Sukki, which is adjacent to ours. Our house was quiet. We were expecting the soldiers. We left the house lights on so that the soldiers would understand that there were people in it. Suddenly, I heard one of the neighbors saying out loud: "There are people in this house, and children."

At that moment, there was a loud explosion. Parts of the house came down, including the room we were in. It simply caved in on top of us, and we remained beneath the ruins. I was relatively all right, because I had been standing when the explosion happened, so the only part of my body that was under ruins was the lower part. I was shocked and scared. I began calling out my children's names, as they were all under the ruins.

The first voice I heard was Mahmud's. I removed about ten rocks off him. He was scared. I then rescued Asil, who had been hurt in the head and left thigh. I then removed the rocks that were on my legs and came out of the ruins. I continued to look for the rest of the family, shouting in the hope that someone would come to the house to help me. I then rescued my wife, and she began to help me, despite her condition. Together, we rescued Rabi' and Hadil. Hadil came out and began to cry for help. Within ten minutes, only Fares and my niece remained underneath the ruins. The neighbors hurried over and helped us. We managed to get Mona out. She had been hurt in several parts of her body. When we got Fares out, we noticed that his condition was severe. I collapsed. Some of the neighbors told me that they could still hear him speak.

In the meantime, an ambulance arrived. The crew took Fares and the ambulance headed east. . . . When we arrived at the hospital, we found out that Fares had not arrived yet. He finally arrived, about an hour and a half later. He was dead.[221]

Here is what B'Tselem has to say about Israel's policy of demolitions of Palestinian homes and agricultural land for alleged military purposes:

The destruction of many hundreds of acres of agricultural land based on the claim that Palestinians fired from these lands, and the demolition of entire residential neighborhoods on the charge that some of them contained tunnels, constitute excessive injury to the civilian population. This action is illegal. Israel's policy, which is carried out against people whom Israel does not contend were involved in attacks on Israeli civilians or security forces, constitutes collective punishment. Despite these violations of international humanitarian law, Israel refuses to compensate Palestinians whose property was damaged in these actions.[222]

With respect to demolitions of Palestinian home and agricultural land as punitive measures, B'Tselem notes that "punitive house demolitions flagrantly breach international law, which allows destruction of property only when necessary for a military operation."[223]

Despite enormous and mostly illegal Israeli destruction of Palestinian homes, farms, orchards, and livelihoods from September 29, 2000, to December 31, 2006, the New York Times editorial page issued no condemnation of these actions throughout this period.

4

Detention and Torture

On November 23, 2001, the UN's Committee Against Torture issued a report about torture in Israel. The committee is composed of ten independent experts who meet twice a year to make recommendations to various states that have signed and ratified the 1984 UN Convention Against Torture and Other Cruel, Inhuman or Degrading Treatment or Punishment; the group oversees states' compliance with the convention. Each year the committee issues reports on any number of states: in fall 2001, for example, the committee issued reports on Benin, Indonesia, Ukraine, Zambia, and Israel.[224] Among human rights organizations, a report from the Committee Against Torture is viewed as an authoritative assessment of a state's compliance with the Convention.

The report itself is the product of a dialogue with the state under review. As part of this process, the government of Israel submitted a report to the Committee Against Torture describing its compliance with the Convention. This report noted that "Israel signed the Convention [Against Torture] on 22 October 1986 and deposited its instrument of ratification with the Secretary-General of the United Nations on 3 October 1991." It also noted that "the most significant and important new development since the submission of Israel's second Periodic report to the Committee Against Torture was the decision of Israel's Supreme Court in September 1999 concerning investigation methods by the Israel Security Agency."[225]

This statement referred to an important case, *Public Committee Against Torture in Israel* v. *the State of Israel*, in which Israel's Supreme Court ruled that the use of certain interrogation methods by the Israel Security Agency (ISA) involving "moderate physical pressure" was illegal under Israeli law.[226] Between 1987 and 1999, interrogation methods used against persons suspected of terrorist activity involving "a moderate degree of physical pressure"—widely viewed as a euphemism for torture—were assumed to be acceptable. This approach to interrogations in Israel was mainly the result of a 1987 report by an Israeli government commission on Israel's interrogation methods, a group headed by a former president of Israel's Supreme Court, Moshe Landau. The Landau commission, upon investigating the interrogation methods of Israel's General Security Service (GSS, now the ISA, also referred to as "Shin Bet"), concluded that "the exertion of a moderate degree of physical pressure cannot be avoided" when suspected terrorists are involved.[227] The 1999 decision by Israel's Supreme Court, which rejected the Landau commission's de facto allowances for the use of torture during interrogations, is frequently cited by defenders of Israel's detention and interrogation methods.

This was the interpretation of the decision by Israel's Supreme Court in a front-page article in the *New York Times*, which began as follows:

> In a watershed ruling, the Israeli Supreme Court today unexpectedly outlawed the security service's routine practice of using physically coercive interrogation methods, which critics have long denounced as torture.
>
> The court banned several of the General Security Service's techniques for obtaining information from suspected terrorists. They include violently shaking the suspects' upper torsos, forcing them to crouch like frogs and shackling them in contorted positions with sacks over their heads.
>
> The ruling has no precedent in a country where repeated terrorist attacks have long created a perceived conflict between the security interests of the state and the human rights of suspects. Until this decision, the court has shied away from imposing restrictions on security agencies, effectively condoning their practices.[228]

Since 1999, the Court's decision has been cited by several commentators who defend Israel against charges that it still tortures Palestinian prisoners and detainees. For example, in his 2003 book *The Case for Israel*, Alan Dershowitz wrote:

> Israel is the only country in the world whose judiciary has squarely faced the difficult issue of whether it is ever justified to engage in even a modified form of nonlethal torture—akin to the tactics currently being used by the United States on captured al-Qaeda prisoners—in order to obtain information deemed necessary to

prevent a ticking bomb from killing dozens of civilians. On September 6, 1999, the Israeli Supreme Court decided that not only is torture absolutely prohibited but even the types of physical pressure currently being used by the United States—sleep deprivation, forced uncomfortable positions, loud music, shaking, hoods over the head—are prohibited by Israeli law, even in cases in which the pressure is used not to elicit a confession but rather to elicit information that could prevent an imminent terrorist attack. Prior to this decision, the Israeli security services did sometimes employ physical measures similar to those now being used by U.S. authorities against suspected terrorists.[229]

The report cited above by the UN's Committee Against Torture was issued in November 2001, while *The Case for Israel* was published in fall 2003, so Dershowitz clearly had access to the committee's report prior to the publication of his book. However, he ignored the report's findings, which undermined his assessment that the 1999 decision by Israel's Supreme Court "absolutely prohibited" torture in Israel. For example, the report by the Committee Against Torture stated: "While acknowledging the importance of the September 1999 Supreme Court decision, the Committee regrets certain consequences of it," which were listed as follows:

- The ruling does not contain a definite prohibition of torture.
- The court prohibits the use of sleep deprivation for the purpose of breaking the detainee, but stated that if it was merely incidental to interrogation, it was not unlawful. In practice in cases of prolonged interrogation, it will be impossible to distinguish between the two conditions.
- The court indicated that ISA interrogators who use physical pressure in extreme circumstances (ticking bomb cases) might not be criminally liable as they may be able to rely on the "defence of necessity."[230]

Thus, the Court's decision, according to the UN's Committee Against Torture, did not "absolutely prohibit" torture as Dershowitz claimed. The Committee also did not report any cessation by Israel of torture and other cruel, inhuman, or degrading treatment or punishment with respect to interrogations, or with respect to Israeli activities unrelated to interrogations but still prohibited by the UN Convention

Against Torture. In fact, with respect to ongoing Israeli policy and conduct, the 2001 report listed several concerns, including the following:

- Continuing allegations received concerning the use of interrogation methods by the ISA against Palestinian detainees that were prohibited by the September 1999 ruling of the Supreme Court.
- Allegations of torture and ill-treatment of Palestinian minors, in particular those detained in the Gush Etzion police station.
- While noting a substantial decrease since the examination of [Israel's] previous report [1997] in the number of persons held in administrative detention, the Committee continues to be concerned that administrative detention does not conform with article 16 of the Convention [Against Torture].
- The continued use of incommunicado detention, even in the case of children, is a matter of grave concern to the Committee.
- Despite the numerous allegations of torture and ill-treatment by law enforcement officials received by the Committee, very few prosecutions have been taken against alleged perpetrators.
- Israeli policies on closure which may, in certain instances, amount to cruel, inhuman or degrading treatment or punishment.
- Israeli policies on house demolitions, which may, in certain instances, amount to cruel, inhuman or degrading treatment or punishment.
- The judicial practice of admitting objective evidence derived from an inadmissible confession.
- The Committee is also concerned [about] instances of "extra-judicial killings" drawn to its attention.[231]

The Committee then issued eleven recommendations that, if followed, would bring Israel into compliance with the UN Convention Against Torture. These recommendations included:

- The provisions of the Convention should be incorporated by legislation into the domestic law of Israel, in particular a crime of torture as defined in article 1 of the Convention.[232]
- The practice of administrative detention in the Occupied Territories should be reviewed in order to ensure its conformity with article 16 [of the Convention].[233]

- [Israel] should review its laws and policies so as to ensure that all detainees, without exception, are brought promptly before a judge, and are ensured prompt access to a lawyer.
- [Israel] should ensure that interrogation methods prohibited by the Convention are not utilized by either the police or the ISA in any circumstances.
- In view of the numerous allegations of torture and other ill-treatment by law enforcement personnel, [Israel] should take all necessary effective steps to prevent the crime of torture and other acts of cruel, inhuman or degrading treatment or punishment, and institute effective complaint, investigative and prosecution mechanisms relating thereto.
- All victims of torture and ill-treatment should be granted effective access to appropriate rehabilitation and compensation measures.
- [Israel] should desist from the policies of closure and house demolition where they offend article 16 of the Convention.
- [Israel] should intensify human rights education and training activities, in particular concerning the Convention, for the ISA, the Israel Defense Forces, police and medical doctors.
- Necessity as a possible justification to the crime of torture should be removed from the domestic law.
- [Legislative measures] should be taken to ensure the exclusion of not merely a confession extorted by torture but also any evidence derived from such confession.[234]

Also on November 23, 2001, the same day the Committee Against Torture issued these recommendations with respect to Israel and torture, Amnesty International issued a statement: "We now urge the Israeli authorities to immediately implement all of the recommendations of the Committee [Against Torture]." Amnesty also noted: "While the Committee Against Torture recognized the importance of the September 1999 [Israel] Supreme Court decision which banned a number of interrogation methods, it also regretted that the ruling allowed some of those methods—for instance, sleep deprivation—if they are incidental to the interrogation process, and indicated that interrogators who used physical pressure might use the 'defence of necessity.' "[235]

Thus, neither the UN's Committee Against Torture nor Amnesty International viewed the 1999 decision by Israel's Supreme Court as constituting an absolute ban against torture, and both expressed concerns about the ruling. Furthermore, on November 23, the BBC posted an article about the Committee Against Torture, which began:

> The United Nations Committee Against Torture has warned Israel that it has several concerns about the interrogation methods used by the Israel Security Agency against Palestinian detainees.
>
> In its concluding report on Israel, the Committee also said it was unhappy with reports of torture and ill treatment towards Palestinian minors.
>
> The Committee, which is made up of 10 independent experts, said it was worried about methods allegedly used by the Israel Security Forces, which include sleep deprivation and the use of incommunicado detention for both Palestinian adults and children.
>
> Experts also noted that there had been very few prosecutions against alleged perpetrators of torture and that there were several reported instances of "extra-judicial killings."[236]

The *New York Times* printed a brief news article about the UN's Committee Against Torture and Israel's interrogation methods by a Geneva-based correspondent, Elizabeth Olson:

> Appearing before a United Nations committee, Israel defended itself today against accusations by Amnesty International and other groups that it uses methods amounting to torture during the interrogation of Palestinian detainees.
>
> The London-based Amnesty International, in a written report to the Committee Against Torture, said that it had "strong evidence" that Israeli authorities continued to use methods of dealing with detainees that violated international standards even after the Israeli Supreme Court barred such practices.
>
> Those methods, Amnesty International contends, include painful handcuffing, sleep deprivation and forcing prisoners to sit in painful positions or to squat on their haunches for prolonged periods.
>
> The groups making the accusations say such practices would violate the 1987 Convention Against Torture, which requires the 126 countries that have signed, including Israel, to report periodically on their compliance. The groups say their information comes from investigations that include interviews with former prisoners.[237]

Olson included a statement from Israel's delegate to the Committee, who said that a "careful reading" of the Torture Convention "clearly suggests that pain and suffering, in themselves, do not necessarily constitute torture."[238]

In a follow-up report issued in May 2002—which the *Times* did not mention—Amnesty reported: "Amnesty International is concerned that not only have the Israeli authorities ignored the November recommendations of the Committee Against Torture, but also that in every area of concern outlined by the Committee, the Israeli authorities have continued and intensified implementation of policies which amount to torture or cruel, inhuman or degrading treatment or punishment against Palestinians from the Occupied Territories." In this context, Amnesty reported: "The [Israeli] government has failed to implement any of the Committee's recommendations."[239]

Amnesty noted that it "has consistently condemned the deliberate targeting of Israeli civilians by armed Palestinian groups." However, it also noted the international legal standard with respect to torture, as established in the Convention Against Torture, that "no exceptional circumstances whatever may be invoked as a justification for torture." Amnesty then listed its concerns, summarized below, with respect to Israel and torture since November 2001, when the Committee Against Torture issued its recommendations to Israel:

- **Mass arrests and ill treatment**. Since the end of February [2002] more than 7,000 Palestinians have been detained, many of them arbitrarily. Interviews with released detainees and the affidavits of those still in detention show that arrests and detention were accompanied by a consistent pattern of cruel, inhuman and degrading treatment and sometimes torture.
- **Incommunicado detention**. While most of the 2,500 detainees arrested during mass arrests in February [2002] and March [2002] were released within a week, many of the 5,000 detainees arrested during [Israel's] Operation Defensive Shield were held in prolonged incommunicado detention. A new Military Order issued on 5 April 2002 allows an initial period of 18 days incommunicado detention without access to a military judge, who may then extend the prohibition of access to the outside world.
- **Administrative detention**. The use of administrative detention has greatly increased, from some 30 people in November 2001 to more than 1,000 in May 2002.

- **Torture**. Torture, including beatings and prolonged sitting in contorted and painful positions continues to be reported. The State Attorney has authorized special interrogation methods (amounting to torture) to be used in alleged ticking bomb situations.
- **House demolitions**. Large-scale house demolitions have continued to take place since December 2001. More than 500 Palestinian houses, containing more than 2000 Palestinian homes have been wantonly destroyed without any absolute military necessity.
- **Closures**. Closures by the IDF of villages and towns have continued and become even more damaging for the Palestinian population. They deny the right to freedom of movement and have grave economic and social results as well as life-threatening consequences for those prevented or delayed from receiving medical care or reaching hospital.
- **Curfews**. Prolonged curfews, sometimes lasting for weeks, have also caused suffering to the Palestinian population who have been confined to their houses, denied fresh air and normal life for long periods.
- **Trashing and looting**. Amnesty International has documented consistent trashing of private apartments, offices of non-governmental organizations (NGOs) and Palestinian government departments by the IDF. The failure to address this behaviour, to order that it be stopped and to compensate those who have suffered strongly suggested that it was condoned by the IDF command and the Israeli government. There have been many allegations of looting.
- **Use of human shields**. The use of Palestinians as human shields during IDF operations also constitutes cruel, inhuman or degrading treatment or punishment in breach of the Convention.[240]

Meanwhile, also in May 2002, the Tel Aviv–based Public Committee Against Torture in Israel (PCATI), which was a petitioner in the 1999 Israel Supreme Court case, issued its own assessment of torture in Israel pursuant to the 1999 decision. This assessment was co-sponsored by the Jerusalem-based Palestinian Society for the Protection of Human Rights and the Environment, and the Geneva-based World Organisation Against Torture. The concerns expressed by these three organizations were nearly identical to those stated by Amnesty International in its May 2002 report. The three groups, describing Israel's apparent violations of the Convention Against

Torture as an "extremely grave situation," summarized these concerns as follows:

> On 23 November 2001, the [UN] Committee [Against Torture] published its Conclusion and Recommendations following its consideration of Israel's 3rd periodic report, expressing concern over a wide variety of issues and making extensive recommendations as to how Israel should address those concerns. Not only has Israel blatantly ignored these concerned [sic] and totally failed to address them, Israel has greatly exacerbated its violations of the Convention, both quantitatively and qualitatively.[241]

The three organizations then listed concerns they viewed as Israel's violations of the Convention Against Torture: (a) mass arbitrary arrests, (b) violence and humiliation during arrest and in the detention facilities, (c) incommunicado detention, (d) torture and ill-treatment during interrogation, (e) administrative detentions, (f) using Palestinian detainees as human shields, (g) house demolitions, and (h) closures and curfews. The document noted that Israeli and Palestinian organizations "have raised every single matter" cited above "in petitions before Israel's Supreme Court," noting that "to date, however, the Court has taken no steps whatsoever towards putting an end, or at least a temporary halt, to any of the serious violations described above."[242] The *New York Times*, in addition to ignoring Amnesty's report with similar findings, ignored this report as well.

In a report one year later, in May 2003, PCATI reported that "the bodies that are supposed to keep [Israel's] GSS under scrutiny and ensure that interrogations are conducted lawfully," which it identified as the Israeli Supreme Court, the attorney general, and the state prosecutor's office, "act, instead, as rubberstamps for decisions by the GSS." In this regard, the committee reported:

- The High Court of Justice [Israel's Supreme Court] has not accepted even one of the 124 petitions submitted by the Public Committee Against Torture against prohibiting detainees under interrogation from meeting their attorneys during the present Intifada.
- The State Prosecutor's Office transfers . . . interrogees' complaints to a GSS agent for investigation, and it is little wonder that it has not found in even a single case that GSS agents tortured a Palestinian "unnecessarily."

• The Attorney General grants—wholesale, and with no exception—the "necessity defense" approval for every single case of torture.[243]

PCATI also reported that, as of May 2003, Palestinian detainees continued to be "routinely" tortured:

> The study carried out by the Public Committee Against Torture in Israel demonstrates that GSS agents who interrogate Palestinian detainees torture them, degrade them, and otherwise ill-treat them routinely, in blatant violation of the provisions of international law, mainly in the following manners:
> • Violence: Beating, slapping, kicking, stepping on shackles. Bending the interrogee and placing him in other painful positions. Intentionally tightening the shackles by which he is bound. Violent shaking.
> • Sleep Deprivation.
> • Additional "Interrogation Methods": Prolonged shackling behind the back. Cursing, threats, humiliations. Depriving the detainee of essential needs. Exposure to extreme heat or cold.
> • Secondary Methods. Isolation and secrecy. Imprisonment under inhuman conditions.[244]

The PCATI report then noted:

> As a human rights organization, the Public Committee Against Torture in Israel has condemned, and again condemns, any attack targeting civilians, including the terrorist attacks by Palestinians against Israeli civilians. No behavior of the IDF and the GSS, including torture, justifies terrorist attacks. But Israel must understand that to the same extent, no behavior of Palestinians, including terrorist attacks, justifies torture, ill-treatment or other violations of fundamental human rights.[245]

PCATI then "urge[d] the government of Israel to abandon the short-term and destructive 'prevention by any means' approach, which has not brought about the longed-for security and peace to the citizens of Israel. The time has come to try a different path, the path of respect for human rights in general and the rights of detainees and prisoners in particular."[246] In addition to ignoring the May 2002 report by the Public Committee Against Torture in

Israel, the *New York Times* ignored the group's May 2003 report as well.

Despite the fact that the Public Committee Against Torture in Israel is an authoritative voice on torture in Israel, to our knowledge the group was not mentioned in the *New York Times* from September 2000 to December 2006. By ignoring this important organization, the *Times* extends the catalog of human rights organizations that it slights in its coverage of the Israel-Palestine conflict. This is in addition to ignoring Amnesty International's references in its annual reports to "allegations of torture,"[247] "widespread" allegations of torture,[248] and "numerous" allegations of torture[249] in Israel.

Likewise, the *Times* has ignored allegations of torture committed by Israeli authorities as reported by Human Rights Watch in its annual reports. For example, in its report for 2003 Human Rights Watch stated: "Reports of ill-treatment were widespread, including kicking, beating, squalid conditions, and deprivations of food and drink. On September 4, the Public Committee Against Torture in Israel reported that there appeared to be a 'gradual reversion to the use of torture' despite the September 1999 [Israel] High Court decision outlawing its use."[250] In its report issued in 2002, Human Rights Watch reported: "There were new reports of torture of detainees by Israeli security forces after October 2000. The Public Committee Against Torture in Israel, an Israeli nongovernmental organization, reported that Israeli security forces kicked detainees and beat them with rifle butts and other implements, deprived them of food and drink for long periods, exposed them to extreme heat and cold, and used other methods that Israel's High Court of Justice explicitly prohibited in a 1999 ruling, including sleep deprivation and prolonged shackling in contorted positions."[251]

Shortly after Israeli soldier Gilad Shalit was captured on June 25, 2006, by armed Palestinians who had crossed into southern Israel, the *New York Times* reported that "the groups holding him said that before any information on him would be disclosed, Israel must release all Palestinian women in its jails and all Palestinian prisoners under the age of 18." While inexplicably citing no sources, the *Times* also reported "there are 95 Palestinian women and 313 Palestinians under 18 in Israeli jails, of a prison population of about 9,000 Palestinians."[252] Around the same time, a June 2006 newsletter published by the Tel Aviv–based Women's Organization for Political Prisoners (WOFPP) reported "there are, at present, 125 women political prisoners in the Israeli jails," most of them Palestinian.[253]

The *Times* published a number of news articles and opinion pieces mentioning the Palestinian prisoners.[254] However, none of the reporters or commentators at the *Times* bothered to ask who these women and children prisoners might be, how they ended up as prisoners and detainees of Israel, or in what conditions they might be held.

In a July 2005 report titled "Violence Against Palestinian Women," the World Organisation Against Torture (WOAT) and the Public Committee Against Torture in Israel noted:

> There are 8043 Palestinian detainees and prisoners, including 772 administrative detainees in Israeli detention facilities. The Women's Organization for Political Prisoners (WOFPP) reports that there are currently 115 Palestinian women in prison, 6 in administrative detention, 16 of these women are minors. . . . According to WOFPP, in many of the cells, the windows are covered 24 hours a day and there is no light or fresh air. Holding detainees and prisoners inside Israel is in violation of article 76 of the Fourth Geneva Convention that states, "Protected persons accused of offences shall be detained in the occupied country, and if convicted they shall serve their sentences therein," clearly prohibiting the transfer of Palestinian detainees from the OPT [occupied Palestinian territory] to Israel.
>
> Article 76 of the Fourth Geneva Convention also provides that "women shall be confined in separate quarters and shall be under the direct supervision of women." There is uncontested evidence that women prisoners are not necessarily under the supervision of female guards and, more seriously, that women from the Occupied Territories are held in Israeli detention facilities at Hasharon, Telmond and elsewhere.
>
> Like their male counterparts, Palestinian female detainees and prisoners are often held in appalling, crowded conditions, suffer from severe punitive measures and are harshly treated by prison authorities. In addition, many complain of denial of access to proper medical care and education, denial of regular family visits, humiliation, and poor quality of food.[255]

The WOAT/PCATI report included a number of summaries of testimonies and sworn affidavits from imprisoned Palestinian women, including the one below:

> **Asama'a Muhammad Salman Abu Alhija**, a forty-year-old resident of Jenin, was arrested on 11 February 2003. IDF soldiers came to Mrs. Abu Alhija's home and evacuated the family, including five children aged seventeen, fifteen, fourteen, ten and eight, into the cold night. Then they searched the house. Mrs. Abu Alhija was taken to the Kishon detention center where she was left outside for several hours with her hands and feet tied and her eyes blindfolded before she was transferred to the Neve Tirza prison in Ramle. Mrs. Abu Alhija was sentenced to six months administrative detention. According to Mrs. Abu Alhija, she was arrested without having committed any offense; rather, she was arrested in order to put pressure on her husband who was in the Ber Sheva prison. Mrs. Abu Alhija suffered from a malignant growth in her head and had undergone surgery twice in the Almakassad Hospital in Jerusalem in 1991 and in 1999. As a result of the two operations Mrs. Abu Alhija is without sight in her left eye and is prone to severe headaches. Mrs. Abu Alhija had no contact with her family and did not know how her children were doing. The children were at home without their parents. Mrs. Abu Alhija suffered tremendously from the conditions of her imprisonment, the crowded conditions of the cell, the heat and the inedible food. Mrs. Abu Alhija's administrative detention was extended on 10 August 2003 by four additional months. She has since been released.[256]

As this account indicates and as the report itself notes, "some women have been arrested, threatened and ill-treated in order to put pressure on their husbands or other relatives who may be wanted by Israel or who are under interrogation."[257] As the report also indicates, such women who are arrested but not charged may be detained indefinitely.

Another of the summaries included in the WOAT/PCATI report was about a girl who was sixteen-years-old at the time of her arrest and imprisonment:

> **Ayesha Mohammed Ahmed Awad Abiyat**, was arrested on 30 May 2002 in Bethlehem. She was sixteen years old at the time. In a sworn affidavit collected by PCATI attorney Tahreer Atamaleh on 15

May 2003, Ayesha stated that she was attacked by youths near the Church of the Nativity and, when she removed a knife from her pocket to protect herself, one of the boys brought her to the Israeli soldiers who were stationed nearby. The soldiers put her in a tank for two hours and then brought her to a local police station where she was kept on the floor for three hours without water or the possibility of using the toilet. Ayesha stated that, at the station, she was attacked by soldiers who beat her so severely that she had to be taken to a hospital for treatment. From the hospital she was brought to the Etzion Detention Center where she was interrogated from eleven in the morning until midnight. During this time, her hands and legs were manacled and her eyes were kept covered. She further alleges that despite her pleas, she was not given food or drink and not allowed to use the toilet. She stated that her interrogators yelled at her and slapped her and that finally, around midnight, she confessed due to exhaustion and fear. She was brought later to the Russian Compound Detention Center and kept there for eighteen days. On 18 June 2002 Ayesha was transferred to the Neve Tirza prison. On 20 October 2003, she was convicted of possession of a knife and attempting to stab a soldier and sentenced to six years imprisonment and three years suspended sentence.[258]

In addition to reporting the circumstances under which many Palestinian women are arrested and detained by Israeli security personnel, the report also documented cases of Israeli soldiers unjustifiably shooting and killing Palestinian women, documenting a pattern of criminal conduct by Israeli security personnel toward Palestinian women.

In a section titled "Loss of Life During Military Activity," the WOAT/PCATI report noted that "most Palestinian women who lost their lives during military activity by the Israeli security forces were killed near (and sometimes in) their homes or while going about their daily routine." The report notes that Amnesty International, the Palestinian Center for Human Rights, and the Palestinian Red Crescent Society reported, respectively, that from September 29, 2000, to early to mid-2005, 150, 169, and 184 Palestinian women were killed by Israeli security forces.[259]

With respect to "Female Detainees in Interrogation," the report noted that the Supreme Court's 1999 decision, rather than leading to an actual prohibition against torture by Israeli authorities, "left loopholes that enable the General Security Service to use methods of

torture and ill-treatment that they consider a 'reasonable interrogation' in accordance with the ruling, and allow GSS interrogators to
invoke retroactively the 'necessity defense' in lone cases of 'ticking
bombs.' " The overall problem of torture in Israel "is a total, hermetic,
impenetrable and unconditional protection that envelops the GSS
system of torture," and "the achievements of the HCJ [Israel's
Supreme Court] ruling of 1999, which was to have put an end to
large-scale torture and ill-treatment, limiting it to lone cases of 'ticking
bombs,' have worn thin, among other reasons, as a result of the HCJ's
reluctance to enforce international standards which prohibit torture
and ill-treatment under any circumstances."[260] The *Times* ignored this
report from the World Organisation Against Torture and the Public
Committee Against Torture in Israel.

The *Times* has also ignored the issue of Palestinian children imprisoned and detained by Israeli authorities. In a summary of a July
2001 report titled "Torture of Palestinian Minors in the Gush Etzion
Prison," B'Tselem reported:

> The report contains testimonies of ten boys, aged fourteen to
> seventeen, who were arrested between October 2000 and January
> 2001 on suspicion of throwing stones. In most of the cases, the Police
> arrested them at their homes in the middle of the late night and took
> them to the Police station in Gush Etzion, where Police interrogators
> tortured them until morning. The Police objective was to obtain
> confessions and information about other minors.
>
> These are not isolated cases or uncommon conduct by certain police
> officers, and information received by B'Tselem raises the serious
> likelihood that torture during interrogations at the Gush Etzion Police
> station continues.[261]

The report notes how "Israeli security forces, some of them masked
and some with their faces blackened, arrested [the Palestinian minors]
at their homes late at night. In some of the cases, the security forces
made grave threats and acted violently against the minors detained and
their relatives." The report notes that "the security forces also
destroyed property in their houses" and, "in most of the cases, the
security forces beat the detainees while en route to the police station."
The report also notes that "the testimonies indicate that the Israeli
authorities committed numerous human rights violations during the
detention, interrogation, trial, and imprisonment" of the children.[262]

The masks and blackened faces worn by security officials terrorize children and their family members during the course of the arrests. Some of the Palestinian boys who testified noted the fear caused by masked men entering their homes at night to arrest them; in most cases, they were arrested for throwing stones at well-armed Israeli security officials and their vehicles. Hamzeh Za'ul, fifteen, began his testimony as follows:

> On Saturday, 6 January 2001, around 2:30 A.M., I awoke to the sound of an Israeli soldier who ordered me to get up. I opened my eyes and thought that I was dreaming that a soldier was waking me, but there were in fact five masked soldiers standing over me. Their appearance frightened me a lot. I got dressed and they took me outside. On the main road near our house were Israeli soldiers, six large army jeeps, and a white Toyota Police Intelligence vehicle.[263]

Likewise, Mufid Hamamreh, fifteen, testified:

> At midnight on 9 November 2000, fifteen soldiers entered my house. Some of them had masks on and some had colored lines painted on their faces. They were looking for my brother Hasnin and me. Hasnin, who is twenty years old, was not at home. I was asleep in my room.[264]

In nearly every instance, the Palestinian boys who provided testimony to B'Tselem reported severe beatings, amounting to torture, while in detention. In this regard, Mahmud Hamamreh, sixteen, testified as follows:

> They brought me to the interrogation room and the interrogator told me to admit that I had thrown stones. He left the room, came back a few minutes later, and told me: "You had time to think. Do you confess?" I told him that I had nothing to confess. He called two people and they laid me down on the floor. One stepped on me with great force while the other beat me severely all over my body. They beat me for two hours, during which the interrogation continued. The interrogator held an object and said, "This is the Koran, if you swear on it that you did not throw stones, I'll let you go." He brought the object close to my mouth. From the scent, I knew it was a piece of soap, and I swore on it that I had not thrown stones. The interrogator again told me to confess, and when I refused the second time, he again

called to the other two, and they beat me all over my body with truncheons for about an hour. . . . One of them kicked me in the chest, which hurt a lot. I lay on the floor and began to scream. The interrogator came up to me and asked if I was ready to talk. I told him that I had nothing to say. I was taken to the courtyard. There were some thirty soldiers there. The interrogator told me that if I didn't confess, he would tell the soldiers to break my bones. We went back to the interrogation room. I confessed to throwing stones and signed the confession.[265]

Sultan Mahdi, fifteen, also testified about beatings:

The soldiers took me to a room and sat me down on a chair. One of them took off the handcuffs and tied my hands and feet to the chair's legs. My eyes remained covered. About a half an hour later, they removed the blindfold. I saw five or six people in civilian clothes. They asked me questions about my involvement in clashes with soldiers. They asked if I threw stones at army vehicles on the main road. At first, I denied that I did. But two or three of them started to beat me in the face and head. The interrogation lasted for around five hours. I was very tired from sitting all the time on the chair and from the beatings. At the end, they took me to the bathroom near the interrogation room. One of the interrogators grabbed me by the hair and put my head in the toilet. I was frightened. When they took me back to the interrogation room, I decided to confess. I told them that I threw five stones at a settler's vehicle. They wrote up a detailed testimony and forced me to sign it.[266]

In addition to physical beatings and abuse, the Israeli interrogators, according to B'Tselem, also resorted to "threats, curses, and degradation." Ashraf Za'ul, seventeen, testified about receiving such threats:

They brought me to another room. Inside was an officer who identified himself as "Ayub." He said that he was a merciless person and was prepared to kill me if I didn't tell him the name of the young fellows who threw stones. . . . One fellow opened the door and said in Arabic that Ahmad 'Aref Sabatin had died during interrogation. The officer turned to me and said, "What are we going to do with the body of Ahmad Sabatin, what do you say Ibrahim, what do you think? Do you want to change places with Ahmad? I was blindfolded. The interrogator said that he was going to electrocute me and that I would die like Ahmad. I felt the sensation of two iron wires being stuck on me, but nothing happened.[267]

Mufid Hamamreh, fifteen, described how interrogators beat his brother while also issuing threats:

> I was taken back to the cell and that same day, between four and five o'clock in the afternoon, two soldiers came and took me to the interrogation room. There were three interrogators in the room. My brother Hasnin was also there. He had turned himself in the day after I was arrested. Right in front of me, the three interrogators beat my brother, kicking him in the abdomen and legs. One of them burned my brother with a cigarette and told Hasnin that he would shoot me if he didn't confess to everything. Then they took me back to the cell, so I did not know what happened to my brother.[268]

B'Tselem concluded its report on torture at the Gush Etzion police station (located in the Israeli settlement Gush Etzion in the West Bank): "The testimonies in this report represent a shocking picture of torture and maltreatment of minors by Police interrogators."

In addition to ignoring the 2001 B'Tselem report about Gush Etzion, the *Times* also ignored a series of about two dozen reports issued from September 2001 to February 2006 on Palestinian children in Israeli prisons and detention centers. The series, issued by Defence for Children International (DCI), and titled "Children Behind Bars," details the abuse and torture of Palestinian children by Israeli authorities. In the most recent report available at the time of the June 2006 capture of Gilad Shalit—the February 2006 report—DCI described how, after two "13-year olds were arrested for throwing stones at soldiers guarding workers near the [separation] wall," the Israeli soldiers caught the boys "as they were going home after school; they kicked the boys, blindfolded them, tied their hands and put them into the back of a waiting jeep." The DCI report continued:

> The boys were taken [to] a military camp about a kilometre away—visible from the roof of their school. One of the soldiers brought a dog and threatened to let it off the lead so it would maul the boys, other soldiers passing kicked and hit them. Nemer and Zakariya [the two Palestinian boys] were made to stand in the military camp all afternoon

and evening before being taken to the detention centre in Gush Etzion—an illegal settlement between Bethlehem and Hebron.

The boys spent 16 days in Etzion, squashed into a cell with 17 other Palestinians aged between 13–20. The room was so crowded the boys were forced to sleep on the floor. To make matters worse they were only allowed out of the cell to use the bathroom once a day, and only then for half an hour. The remaining 23 hours and 30 minutes were spent locked in the room.[269]

Most of the DCI reports are highly detailed, including analyses of international law and the sentencing of Palestinian minors,[270] the use of Israeli military courts in sentencing Palestinian children,[271] discrepancies in sentencing,[272] prohibited or curtailed family and lawyer visits to children imprisoned or detained by Israel,[273] and poor medical care of Palestinian children imprisoned or detained by Israel.[274] In July 2004 DCI reported that there are "320 Palestinian children who are currently languishing in Israeli prisons and detention centres."[275] All of these reports, and all such reports issued by Defence for Children International, were ignored by the *New York Times* throughout the period (September 2000 to December 2006) covered in this book.

5

Double Standards

Our criticism of the *New York Times'* coverage of the Israel-Palestine conflict is not directed per se at the fifty front-page articles and the twenty-five front-section articles reporting on Palestinian suicide bombs from September 29, 2000, to December 31, 2005. Any bombing targeting civilians is an unacceptable violation of human rights, and on these grounds a Palestinian suicide bombing in Israel is both a hideous and newsworthy event. Rather, our argument is that the *Times* applies a double standard in its coverage which favors Israel, and the newspaper is therefore disproportionately focused on Palestinian violence. This double standard is obvious, given that Israeli violence is without question of a higher magnitude and scale, is brutally applied across the board in Palestinian society, and is heavily subsidized by the United States, making it also a special journalistic responsibility of the *New York Times* to inform its readers about US-supported Israeli conduct.

The double standard at the *Times* runs throughout its coverage of the Israel-Palestine conflict. The United States Congress "emotionally" reacted to Israel's crimes—Israel's illegal occupation, its illegal annexation of East Jerusalem, the separation barrier on West Bank territory, the illegal settlements in the West Bank, the announced plans to annex the main West Bank settlement blocs, the de facto annexation of the Jordan Valley—in May 2006 with standing ovations for visiting Israeli Prime Minister Ehud Olmert. The event transpired without a critical word from the *Times*—in this sense and many others, Israel's crimes are fine, but Palestinian crimes are abhorrent.

And the double standard is pernicious. Israel invades and bombs Gaza in June 2006 in response to a rare Palestinian incursion into southern Israel, whereby two Israeli soldiers are killed and one, Gilad Shalit, is captured. The subsequent Israeli invasion of Gaza was supported by the *Times'* editorial page.[276] A few days before Shalit was captured, however, *Ha'aretz* had quoted an Israeli Air Force (IAF) commander as saying that Israel "carr[ies] out strikes in the Gaza Strip daily."[277] Would the *Times'* editorial page have supported a Palestinian invasion and bombing of Israel in response to Israel's "daily strikes" in Gaza?

Israel also justified the June 2006 Gaza invasion as necessary to stop the Palestinian firing of the Qassam rockets into southern Israel. A few days earlier, however, Human Rights Watch reported that "the IDF has fired more than 7,700 [155mm] shells at northern Gaza since the Israeli withdrawal [from Gaza] in September 2005."[278] Would the *Times'* editorial page have supported a Palestinian invasion of Israel in response to these far more numerous, accurate, and deadly Israeli shells?

Underscoring this point, on June 23, 2006, after Israeli shelling and Apache-fired missiles in Gaza had killed at least fourteen Palestinian civilians, the *Independent* reported that "almost three times as many Palestinian civilians have been killed in Gaza in the past nine days as Israeli civilians in Sderot [in southern Israel] killed by Qassam rockets in five years."[279] Due to Israel's customary denials of responsibility for killing Palestinians, the *Independent*'s estimate—fourteen Palestinian civilians killed—omitted the eight Palestinians killed by Israel's shells on a beach in Gaza on June 9.[280] In addition, despite the Palestinian casualties (the "failures" referred to below), an Israeli air force general, according to the *Jerusalem Post*, stated that "the IDF planned to continue striking terrorists from the air despite the recent failures, although under more stringent guidelines." The *Jerusalem Post* quoted the general: "This is the only way nowadays to strike terror in Gaza."[281] Would the *Times'* editorial page have supported a Palestinian invasion of Israel in response to Israeli terrorism in Gaza?

The details of the Israeli attacks across the Gazan border are even more deplorable. For example, on June 13, nearly two weeks before the Palestinian raid into southern Israel on June 25 that led to the capture of Gilad Shalit, *Ha'aretz* reported that "nine Palestinians, including two schoolchildren, were killed Tuesday when Israel Air Force aircraft fired two missiles in Gaza City at the vehicle of an Islamic Jihad crew heading to fire rockets at Israel." *Ha'aretz* reported that, in addition to the two children, "among the dead were two members of the same family, a father and son," and "also killed were three medical employees on their way to tend to the wounded from an earlier explosion" from the first Israeli rocket fired.[282] Immediately following this incident, the *Jerusalem Post* cited Israel's Defense

Minister Amir Peretz, who said that "Israel will no longer exhibit restraint toward Palestinian terrorists involved in anti-Israeli operations," no doubt cognizant of the fact that Israel's shelling and missile attacks on Gaza were already far deadlier and destructive than anything initiated by Palestinians at the time.[283]

As Israel continued to operate essentially without restraint, on June 20, five days before the Palestinian raid into southern Israel, *Ha'aretz* reported:

> An Israel Air Force strike targeting a car carrying Palestinian militants in the Gaza Strip on Tuesday evening killed two children and a teen and wounded 14 other people, Palestinian witnesses and medics said.
>
> The two children killed in the air strike were five-year-old boy Mohammed Al-Rouka and his seven-year-old sister Nadia Al-Rouka. The teenager was identified as 16-year-old Bilal Al-Hasa.
>
> Seven of the wounded were children and one of them is in critical condition.[284]

Ha'aretz reported that "the strike took place on a narrow and crowded commercial street in the Sheikh Radwan neighborhood of Gaza City," with an obviously high probability of civilian casualties.[285] The very next day, June 21, four days before the Palestinian raid, the Israeli Air Force killed two Palestinian civilians and injured 14 others—all members of the same family—in a missile strike on a Palestinian home in southern Gaza. *Ha'aretz* reported that "the 37-year-old woman killed in the strike, Fatima El-Barbarwi, was seven months pregnant," and "the other casualty was her brother, a 45-year-old doctor named Zakariya Ahmed residing in Saudi Arabia." *Ha'aretz* reported: "Palestinian witnesses said the apparent target of the IAF strike had been a jeep carrying members of the Popular Resistance Committees but the missile struck the house instead."[286]

These Israeli attacks that killed and injured dozens of Palestinians throughout June 2006 proceeded without comment from the *New York Times*' editorial page. Would the *Times*' editorial page have remained silent in response to repeated Palestinian rocket and missile attacks on Israeli beaches and crowded neighborhoods that killed and seriously injured dozens of Israelis?

Nor did the *Times*' editorial page condemn Israel when it was reported in the British newspaper the *Observer* on June 25 that "Israeli forces had detained two Palestinians, who the [Israeli] army said were

Hamas militants, in the Gaza Strip, in what observers said was the first arrest raid in the territory since Israel pulled out of the area a year ago."[287] The detention of the two Palestinian civilians was reported by the *Ha'aretz* columnist Gideon Levy, who wrote that "the IDF kidnapped two civilians, a doctor and his brother, from their home in Gaza" shortly before Palestinians captured Shalit. Levy—but not the *Times'* editorial page—pointed out the double standard embedded in Israel's response to the two episodes:

> The difference between us and them? We kidnapped civilians and they captured a soldier, we are a state and they are a terror organization. How ridiculously pathetic [IDF General] Amos Gilad sounds when he says that the capture of Shalit was "illegitimate and illegal," unlike when the IDF grabs civilians from their homes. How can a senior official in the defense ministry claim that "the head of the snake" is in Damascus, when the IDF uses the exact same methods?[288]

While the free pass given to Israel by the *Times'* editorial page throughout June 2006 also seems "pathetic," it signaled that the leading liberal news organization in the United States would have no problem with the ongoing Israeli killings of Palestinian civilians, before or after June 25, 2006.

Much of the editorial analysis from *Ha'aretz* in response to Israel's repeated attacks inside Gaza was far more responsible than the silence at the *Times'* editorial page throughout June 2006. For example, in commentary published on June 22, the *Ha'aretz* correspondent Amos Harel wrote:

> The story is beginning to repeat itself, and the frequency is troubling.
> For the third time in nine days, Palestinian civilians last night were killed in air force strikes in Gaza. While Israel is busy conducting an internal debate over its role in the deaths of seven civilians at a beach in Beit Lahia in the northern Gaza Strip, the air force killed two more civilians Wednesday—innocents or "uninvolved" using the Israel Defense Forces' dry terminology. Time and again, the air force is making complex excuses whose ultimate argument is that "We did not see the civilians," and "They came into the scene at the last moment."
> The rise in the number of civilian casualties, which the IDF

attributes to coincidence, probably stems from an increase in the frequency of operations in the Gaza Strip, as well as a relaxation of restrictions on firing in the midst of civilian populations.[289]

Also on June 22, a *Ha'aretz* editorial titled "Don't Shoot, Talk," argued as follows:

A sovereign state cannot accept the firing of rockets into its territory, and it does not matter whether the target is Gilo, Kiryat Shmona or Sderot. The ongoing fire at Sderot and the northern Negev is not related to any territorial claim over Gaza, where Israel has withdrawn to the international border. It is another stage in the Palestinian-Israeli struggle, which sometimes becomes violent as each side looks for the other's weaknesses in order to try to defeat it.

It also does not matter at all which organization is doing the firing. The Palestinian Authority has an elected government, and it is responsible for preventing attacks on Israel originating from its territory. But before deciding to escalate the conflict, before marking more and more individuals for assassination, it is appropriate to try the alternative: speaking instead of shooting. It doesn't matter who is more right; it doesn't matter who started it, with whom one speaks or whether speaking has a strategic purpose. Even if conditions are not yet ripe for negotiations on ending the conflict, there is no logical reason not to conduct meetings at every possible level to discuss renewing normal life, halting exchanges of fire, instituting a cease-fire and learning the lessons of the latest round of violence in the endless conflict, before it deteriorates further.

It is as clear as day that the continued killing of Palestinian civilians, including children, will not bring security to the residents of Israel, either in the short term or in the long term—just as firing Qassams at Israeli civilians, including children, in Sderot will not bring Gaza residents a better future.

The Palestinians have an elected government and an elected chairman, and they must decide on their own who will conduct a dialogue with Israel and what the dialogue will be about. On Israel's part, there is no need to boycott any of those involved in the talks or to set preconditions, since at this stage the talks would not be on resolving the conflict, but on bringing the sides closer together and minimizing the flames threatening to ignite a new war. Any attempt to talk—about a hudna [cease-fire] of several days or many years, about a halt to the boycott of the PA [Palestinian Authority] in exchange for a cease-fire, about a halt to the assassinations in exchange for a halt to the Qassams, or any other temporary compromise, even if it does not involve a vision of the end of days—bears at least the option of pragmatic moderation, and hope (albeit slight) for creeping normalization. Any disappointment over failed talks is less painful than counting the corpses of children.[290]

On June 25 Gideon Levy called for the resignation of Israeli Air Force Commander Eliezer Shkedi "for the serial killing of innocent civilians, including babies, children and a pregnant woman," arguing that "the killing is at least a reason for resignation if not prosecution." Levy continued:

Even someone whose moral profile has been so twisted that he cannot see the killing of children as a reason to resign, then the operational failures of the air force—shooting missiles at a house instead of a car, shooting missiles into a crowded street that someone decided was empty, shooting missiles while the wanted men scatter, and shooting a missile that hits two cars instead of one—should lead to the proper conclusion. Is it even conceivable that the IDF would kill 23 civilians (not including the Ghalia family [on the Gaza beach on June 9]), 15 of them by the air force—including three children and a doctor and his pregnant sister in two days—and things would go on as if nothing happened? Is it possible that this serial failure is an orphan? What message is being sent by this behavior to the pilots of the air force—that it is not so bad that innocents get killed? . . .

Once the IDF adopted the stupid method of shooting missiles into densely populated centers, the writing was on the wall that children would be killed. It's not that they were killed by accident. It was inevitable from the start.[291]

In contrast, the first *Times* editorial on the subject of Israel and Gaza did not appear until June 29, after Shalit had been captured, after American officials had weighed in with their outrage about the Shalit capture—but not the Israeli atrocities that preceded it—and after Israel commenced invading and bombing Gaza in response. By way of explanation with respect to the excerpt from the *Times* editorial below, Hamas had adhered to its unilateral cease-fire—who ever mentioned the sixteen-month Hamas cease-fire?—throughout the

IDF shootings of children in the first half of 2006 described above, throughout the 7,700 shells fired by the IDF into Gaza from December 2005 to June 2006, and throughout the numerous assassinations and assassination attempts of Palestinians with Apache helicopters which killed and injured dozens of Palestinians in the same period. Hamas did not first break its cease-fire until June 10, 2006, one day after Israeli shells killed eight Palestinians on a beach in northern Gaza. The June 25 raid into southern Israel leading to Shalit's capture was the second Hamas response to Israeli provocations.

In this context, the *Times'* June 29 editorial blamed Hamas for Israel's disproportionate and illegal military reprisals in response to the June 25 capture of Gilad Shalit, noted that Israel's kidnapping of Palestinian cabinet members was cause for some Alka-Seltzer, nothing more, and also noted that Hamas' just-issued implicit recognition of the state of Israel in pre-1967 borders was only "ironic" and otherwise not encouraging:

> The Palestinians who futilely threw up sand berms on Gaza's main roads to deflect Israeli troop movements were building their defenses in the wrong direction. The responsibility for this latest escalation rests squarely with Hamas, whose military wing tunneled into Israel on Sunday, killed two Israeli soldiers and kidnapped another. This was a follow-up to a declaration earlier this month by Hamas's political leadership that the group's 16-month intermittent cease-fire would no longer be observed.
>
> Under the circumstances, an Israeli military response was inevitable. It should also be as restrained as possible. Israel does not seem to want to reoccupy Gaza, but its reported arrest of several cabinet ministers in the West Bank is unsettling. Bitterness and distrust on both sides are sure to increase, and the already dim prospects for a return to peace negotiations will diminish even further.
>
> Ironically, Hamas has chosen this bleak moment to finally endorse a document that implicitly recognizes Israel within its pre-1967 borders. In a different context that would represent progress. But in a week in which Hamas's military wing has crossed those very borders, it is hard to draw much encouragement. . . .
>
> If things go on like this, Palestinians can look forward to endless rounds of reckless Hamas provocations and inexorable Israeli responses. That is why things must not be allowed to go on like this. It is not just Israel that needs to be delivering that message to Hamas.[292]

If the situation had been considered impartially, the editorial perhaps would have been very different. The Hamas attack on the Israeli soldiers on June 25 did none of the things that Israel had done throughout the month of June: the Palestinian raid into southern Israel was not an indiscriminate attack, did not kill Israeli civilians, did not target Israeli neighborhoods, did not target Israel's government leaders, did not target Israel's vital infrastructure, did not target Israeli government buildings, and did not threaten a humanitarian disaster— all of which characterized Israel's pre- and post-June 25 conduct, which was supported for the most part by the *Times'* editorial page.

Part Two

Laws of Omission

6

International Law

The published reports from various human rights organizations indicate that Israel is engaged in a brutal military occupation of the Palestinian territories. In its coverage of the Israel-Palestine conflict, the *New York Times* has neglected to expose the scale of the occupation's brutality, also ignoring the Fourth Geneva Convention (1949), which is the principal source of international law that prohibits the Israeli conduct described in Part 1.

Israel's conduct in the occupied territories, however, is merely the tactical manifestation of its long-standing strategic goal of expanding its settlements in the West Bank, including East Jerusalem, and eventually annexing Palestinian territory on which the settlements are located. The Fourth Geneva Convention, which prohibits much of Israel's occupation-related conduct, also prohibits these settlements. Article 49(6) of the Convention succinctly states: "The Occupying Power shall not deport or transfer parts of its own civilian population into the territory it occupies." These nineteen words, which outlaw all of Israel's settlements in the West Bank and Gaza and which easily fit into any newspaper editorial or news article, were not printed or cited in the *New York Times* from September 29, 2000, to December 31, 2006—the broadest period covered by this volume. By ignoring the Fourth Geneva Convention, and thus preempting any assessment of the legality of Israel's major tactical and strategic policies in the Palestinian territories, the *Times* has clearly prejudiced its coverage of the Israel-Palestine conflict to the detriment of Palestinian rights and a comprehensive peace.

Even as it has ignored the Fourth Geneva Convention and other sources of international law in its coverage of the Israel-Palestine conflict, the *Times* consistently has favored news sources, opinion-page commentators, intellectuals, and authors who either conditionally support Israel's occupation policies while mostly ignoring international law (the "Liberal Hawks"), or who unconditionally support the occupation and fiercely criticize international law (the "Hawks").[293] Overall, for example, within this framework, the *New York Times* editorial page and the administration of Bill Clinton would be included among the Liberal Hawks, while the *Wall Street Journal* editorial page and the administration of George W. Bush would be considered Hawks.

Although differences in temperament between the Liberal Hawks and Hawks are worth noting, there is in actuality little substantive difference between the two camps. For example, Dennis Ross, a Liberal Hawk, noted in his memoirs that he prioritized Israel's "needs" over Palestinian rights throughout the July 2000 Camp David summit, thus rejecting Palestinian claims to 100 percent (or net 100 percent) of a fully contiguous West Bank.[294] The editorial pages of the *New York Times* and *Wall Street Journal* and Presidents Bill Clinton and George W. Bush have all criticized Yasir Arafat for failing to "compromise" within this framework. Yet President Clinton's principal negotiators, in addition to the president himself, by all accounts disregarded relevant international law throughout the summit and thus neglected the Palestinian right under international law to all of the West Bank, including sovereignty over East Jerusalem. In their published accounts of the July 2000 summit, neither President Clinton, Secretary of State Madeleine Albright, nor chief negotiator Ross mention the Fourth Geneva Convention. Nor do the memoirs by Clinton, Albright, or Ross mention the numerous UN General Assembly and Security Council resolutions—spanning decades and citing the Fourth Geneva Convention—that have declared Israel's settlements in the West Bank and Gaza null and void under international law. The words "international law" are not listed in the indexes of the Clinton, Albright, or Ross memoirs.[295]

The failure of the Camp David summit of July 2000, in our view, was thus grounded in the absence of a fair consideration of Palestinian rights under international law; these rights include the legitimate claim to the West Bank, including East Jerusalem, which (with the Gaza Strip) constitutes 22 percent of historic Palestine (as defined by the pre–1967 war borders). In contrast, Israel's recognized territorial allotment is 78 percent of historic Palestine. Minor territorial adjustments to meet any negotiated recognition of Israel's "needs" could have been proposed by Clinton and Israeli Prime Minister Ehud Barak, with comparable territorial compensation to the Palestinians. But that is not what happened at Camp David.

The failed 2000 summit terminated the Oslo "peace process" of the 1990s. The Palestinians were left greatly disadvantaged territorially at the end of that process given the massive expansion in the 1990s of illegal Israeli settlers in the West Bank. The failure of Camp David under conditions highly adverse to the Palestinians ultimately led to the second Palestinian *intifada* two months later.

The summit failure also marked the end of the Liberal Hawk era in the United States and Israel and the resurgence of the Hawks, largely due to the elections of George W. Bush as US president in November 2000 and Ariel Sharon as Israel's prime minister in January 2001. The Hawk contingent in the United States—especially the *Wall Street Journal* editorial page and Harvard Law School professor Alan Dershowitz—launched a fierce campaign to further undermine Palestinian rights and international law in the context of Israel's occupation by attacking the United Nations (the *Journal*'s editorial page) and Amnesty International and Human Rights Watch (Dershowitz) for issuing reports that were critical of Israel's conduct in the occupied territories. With no countervailing institutional support for international law—either in the Democratic Party or the American news media—the Hawks engaged in a sustained anti–international law, anti–United Nations, and anti–human rights rampage. Policy-wise this approach led to one disaster after another, including the US invasions of Afghanistan and Iraq, the US-supported escalation of Israeli violence in the occupied Palestinian territories, and the 2006 Israeli bombardment of Lebanon.

With respect to Israel, the reports issued by Amnesty International and Human Rights Watch no longer were greeted with mere silence—instead, supporters of Israel's occupation, including Dershowitz and the Anti-Defamation League (ADL), began denouncing these reports as the product of "bias," "bigotry," and "anti–Semitism." The *New York Times,* which rejects international law by omission rather than loud denunciations, did virtually nothing to defend these important organizations while ignoring or barely mentioning their reports. Our review below of statements issued by Dershowitz and the ADL since the onset of the second Palestinian *intifada* in September 2000 reveal the prolific and vicious character of these statements.[296] They also demonstrate, quite ominously, how easily the rule of law and its most prominent proponents can be slandered in the United States when the major news organizations do nothing in response to demagoguery.

In addition, the government of Israel has responded to critical reports from the human rights organizations not by modifying any implicated illegal conduct or policies, but simply by asserting that the relevant law is not applicable to Israel. Thus, alone among more than 180 "High Contracting Parties" to the Fourth Geneva Convention, Israel asserts that the Convention has no official application to its occupation of the Palestinian territories.[297] By disavowing the Convention, Israel places itself above the law that nearly every other country in the world officially recognizes as being applicable to Israel's conduct in the Palestinian territories it occupies.

The American Jewish Congress (AJC) exhibits an approach to the Fourth Geneva Convention similar to Israel's by arguing in a 2002 press release that the Convention needs to be "updated" in order to "unshackle anti-terrorist forces," primarily Israel and the United States. The press release warned that "a single-minded focus on avoiding civilian casualties tends to focus on those civilians who, whether willingly or not, provide cover for terrorists and other wrongdoers, and not on those civilians who are their victims." It also encouraged the Bush administration to seek "a fundamental reexamination" of the Fourth Geneva Convention, not "cosmetic changes or fine-tuning."[298]

Along these lines the New York–based Jewish daily the *Forward* published an article in August 2006 about Israel and the human rights organizations that began as follows:

> As international human rights organizations decry the high toll of civilian deaths suffered in the Lebanon war, America's main organization of Modern Orthodox rabbis is calling on the Israel military to be less concerned with avoiding civilian casualties on the opposing side when carrying out future operations.

The *Forward* reported that "leaders of the Rabbinical Council of America issued a statement prodding the Israeli military to review its policy of taking pains to spare the lives of innocent civilians, in light of Hezbollah's tactics of hiding its fighters and weaponry among Lebanese civilians." The *Forward* continued:

> Because Hezbollah "puts Israeli men and women at extraordinary risk of life and limb through unconscionably using their own civilians, hospitals, ambulances, mosques . . . as human shields, cannon fodder,

and weapons of asymmetric warfare," the rabbinical council said in a statement, "we believe that Judaism would neither require nor permit a Jewish soldier to sacrifice himself in order to save deliberately endangered enemy civilians."

The *Forward* also reported that the American Jewish Congress "is waging a campaign to amend international law, which it views as out of step with fighting terrorism." It noted that the AJC wrote to a US Senate subcommittee in August 2006 that "international law, as it is currently applied by the United Nations, the Red Cross and unofficial international human rights groups, enhances the military capability of irregular forces at the direct expense of states and thus exacerbates the difficulties of nations engaged in asymmetrical warfare."[299]

For its part, the Bush administration (like every preceding administration) officially recognizes the application of the Fourth Geneva Convention to Israel's occupation. However, it supports Israel's violations of the Convention politically, financially, and militarily. For example, in late September 2006—that is, toward the end of Israel's conduct in the territories beginning September 29, 2000, as described in Part 1—*Ha'aretz* reported that the US Congress "approved an additional $500 million for developing joint defense projects with Israel." The money, as *Ha'aretz* reported, "is not part of the regular [US] military aid to Israel, which currently stands at over $2 billion."[300] Both *Ha'aretz* and the *Jerusalem Post* reported that the additional $500 million allocated by Congress was considerably more than the $270 million of additional support sought by the Bush administration.[301] In contrast, with US support Israel effectively quarantined the Gaza Strip and withheld Palestinian tax revenues, the Bush administration cut off financial aid to the West Bank and Gaza, Arab banks declined to transfer funds to Palestinian authorities under US pressure, and the Europeans, also due to US pressure, withheld economic subsidies. The result is that the people of Gaza "are on the edge of starvation" with "signs of desperation everywhere."[302]

The increase in US military and economic support to Israel is startling since Israel's conduct in the Palestinian territories from September 2000 to September 2006 amounted to "grave breaches" of the Fourth Geneva Convention, including "wilful killing, torture or inhuman treatment . . . wilfully causing great suffering or serious injury to body or health, unlawful deportation or transfer or unlawful confinement of a protected person . . . wilfully depriving a protected person of the rights of fair and regular trial prescribed in the present Convention, taking of hostages and extensive destruction and appropriation of property, not justified by military necessity and carried out unlawfully and wantonly" (Article 147). Furthermore, Israel's self-absolution from the Fourth Geneva Convention in fact violates the Convention, since, according to Article 148, "No High Contracting Party shall be allowed to absolve itself" of "grave breaches" of the Convention. By supporting and subsidizing Israel's violations of the Fourth Geneva Convention, the United States itself has violated Article 1 of the Convention, which obligates "the High Contracting Parties [to] undertake to respect and to ensure respect for the present Convention in all circumstances."

By ignoring the Fourth Geneva Convention, the *New York Times* also has failed, journalistically, "to respect and to ensure respect" for the Convention. As previously discussed, from September 29, 2000, to December 31, 2006, the *Times'* editorial page never mentioned the Convention as applied to the Israel–Palestine conflict. The newspaper never published a front page news article (or any article elsewhere in the paper) that examined Israel's occupation in the context of the Fourth Geneva Convention, and no stories' headlines have referred to the Convention. Aside from a handful of incidental references to the Fourth Geneva Convention during this period, the *Times'* news pages, like the editorial page, made no effort to integrate the Convention into its coverage of the Israel–Palestine conflict.[303]

The historical irony of Israel's violations of the Fourth Geneva Convention, in addition to its self-exemption from the Convention, are inescapable, given the law's background. In 1999 a press release issued by the Anti-Defamation League stated:

> The Fourth Geneva Convention on Rules of War [*sic*] was adopted in 1949 by the international community in response to Nazi atrocities during World War II. The international treaty governs the treatment of civilians during wartime, including hostages, diplomats, spies, bystanders and civilians in territory under military occupation. The convention outlaws torture, collective punishment and the resettlement by an occupying power of its own civilians on territory under its military control.[304]

Though Israel ratified the Convention in 1951, "the official stand of the Government of Israel," as Israeli legal scholar David Kretzmer noted, "is that the [Fourth] Geneva Convention does not apply to the situation on the West Bank and Gaza."[305] As Kretzmer and others have pointed out, however, there is virtually no support for the idea that the Fourth Geneva Convention does not apply to Israel's occupation of the Palestinian territories.[306] For example, the International Committee of the Red Cross (ICRC), in an official review of the applicability of the Fourth Geneva Convention in the occupied Palestinian territories in 1999, "reaffirm[ed] the applicability of the Convention to the Occupied Palestinian Territory."[307] About the relevance of the Convention to Israel's occupation dating back to 1967, the ICRC also stated:

> In accordance with a number of resolutions adopted by the United Nations General Assembly and Security Council and by the International Committee of the Red Cross and Red Crescent, which reflect the view of the international community, the ICRC has always affirmed the *de jure* ["as a matter of law"] applicability of the Fourth Geneva Convention to the territories occupied since 1967 by the State of Israel, including East Jerusalem. This Convention, ratified by Israel in 1951, remains fully applicable and relevant in the current context of violence.

The ICRC then "call[ed] upon the Occupying Power [Israel] to fully and effectively respect the Fourth Geneva Convention in the Occupied Palestinian Territory, including East Jerusalem, and to refrain from perpetrating any violation of the Convention." In addition to "call[ing] upon all parties, directly involved in the conflict or not, to respect and to ensure respect for the Geneva Conventions in all circumstances," the ICRC called upon Israel to end its "grave breaches" of the Convention, as enumerated above.[308]

The UN General Assembly and Security Council have repeatedly stated positions identical to those of the ICRC with respect to the applicability of the Fourth Geneva Convention. In numerous resolutions, the General Assembly voted to:

> *Reaffirm* that the Geneva Convention relative to the Protection of Civilian Persons in Time of War, of 12 August 1949 [Fourth Geneva

Convention], is applicable to the Occupied Palestinian Territory, including East Jerusalem, and other Arab territories occupied by Israel since 1967;

Demand that Israel accept the *de jure* applicability of the Convention in the Occupied Palestinian Territory, including East Jerusalem, and other Arab territories occupied by Israel since 1967, and that it comply scrupulously with the provisions of the Convention.[309]

In a resolution issued on December 20, 2001, the General Assembly "express[ed] its full support"[310] for the ICRC declaration issued on December 5, which reaffirmed that the Convention applies to Israel's occupation.

Over the past decades, the UN Security Council has issued several resolutions stipulating the applicability of the Fourth Geneva Convention to Israel's occupation; these resolutions are especially significant because they can be passed only with a supporting vote or an abstention from the United States. In September 1969 a Security Council resolution "call[ed] upon Israel scrupulously to observe the provisions of the Geneva Conventions and international law governing military occupation."[311] In July 1979 a Security Council resolution condemned Israel's settlements in the Palestinian territories as a violation of the Fourth Geneva Convention:

> *The Security Council* . . .
>
> *Considering* that the policy of Israel in establishing settlements in the occupied Arab territories has no legal validity and constitutes a violation of the Geneva Convention relative to the Protection of Civilian Persons in Time of War of 12 August 1949 [Fourth Geneva Convention],
>
> *Deeply concerned* by the practices of the Israeli authorities in implementing that settlements policy in the occupied Arab territories, including Jerusalem, and its consequences for the local Arab and Palestinian population. . . .
>
> *Calls upon* the Government and people of Israel to cease, on an urgent basis, the establishment, construction and planning of settlements in the Arab territories occupied since 1967, including Jerusalem.[312]

In a March 1980 resolution the Security Council reaffirmed its position that the Fourth Geneva Convention applies to Israel's occupation and that Israel's settlements in the occupied Palestinian territories violated the Convention.[313]

Shortly after the onset of the first Palestinian *intifada* on December 9, 1987, the Security Council issued a resolution condemning Israel's excessive lethal use of force in response to the Palestinian demonstrations as a violation of the Fourth Geneva Convention:

> *The Security Council. . . .*
>
> 1. *Strongly deplores* those policies and practices of Israel, the occupying Power, which violate the human rights of the Palestinian people in the occupied territories, and in particular the opening of fire by the Israeli army, resulting in the killing and wounding of defenceless Palestinian civilians;
>
> 2. *Reaffirms* that the Geneva Convention relative to the Protection of Civilian Persons in Time of War, of 12 August 1949 [Fourth Geneva Convention], is applicable to the Palestinian and other Arab territories occupied by Israel since 1967, including Jerusalem;
>
> 3. *Calls once again upon* Israel, the occupying Power, to abide immediately and scrupulously by the [Fourth] Geneva Convention . . . and to desist forthwith from its policies and practices that are in violation of the provisions of the Convention.[314]

One week after the start of the second Palestinian *intifada* on September 29, 2000, the Security Council issued a resolution that simultaneously reaffirmed Israel's obligations under the Fourth Geneva Convention in the Palestinian territories and deplored Israel's use of excessive lethal force in its response to the Palestinian demonstrations:

> *The Security Council. . . .*
>
> *Deeply concerned* by the tragic events that have taken place since 28 September 2000, that have led to numerous deaths and injuries, mostly among Palestinians. . . .
>
> 1. *Deplores* the provocation carried out at al-Haram Sharif in Jerusalem on 28 September 2000, and the subsequent violence there and at other Holy Places, as well as in other areas throughout the territories occupied by Israel since 1967, resulting in over 80 Palestinian deaths and many casualties;
>
> 2. *Condemns* acts of violence, especially the excessive use of force against Palestinians, resulting in injury and loss of human life;

> 3. *Calls upon* Israel, the occupying Power, to abide scrupulously by
> its legal obligations and its responsibilities under the Geneva Con-
> vention relative to the Protection of Civilian Persons in Time of War
> of 12 August 1949 [Fourth Geneva Convention].[315]

UN Security Council resolutions affirming the applicability of the
Fourth Geneva Convention to Israel's occupation of the Palestinian
territories were passed during the administrations of Presidents Richard Nixon, Jimmy Carter, Ronald Reagan, George H.W. Bush, and
Bill Clinton.[316]

The world's leading human rights organizations—Amnesty International, Human Rights Watch, and B'Tselem—concur with the
International Committee of the Red Cross, the UN General Assembly, and the UN Security Council that the Fourth Geneva Convention applies to Israel's occupation of the Palestinian territories.

In a press release issued on December 4, 2001, just prior to the
ICRC's official statement on December 5, Amnesty International
"welcomed the reaffirmation of the principles of the Fourth Geneva
Convention" applied to the occupied Palestinian territories, and the
organization urged the parties to the Convention to "now agree on
concrete measures to ensure respect for the Convention and prevent
further deterioration of the human rights situation in the Occupied
Territories."[317] In a press release issued after the start of the second
Palestinian *intifada*, Amnesty International "call[ed] on all Palestinian
and Israeli armed groups to respect the fundamental principles contained in the Fourth Geneva Convention."[318] And in a press release
issued before the onset of the second *intifada*, Amnesty stated that
"Israel, as a High Contracting Party, has been violating the Fourth
Geneva Convention for more than 30 years, when it carries out willful
killings extrajudicially, when it tortures or when it indiscriminately
uses force."[319]

Likewise, in a major report on the Israel-Palestine conflict issued in
April 2001, Human Rights Watch stated: "Two legal regimes are
directly relevant to Israel's obligations in the Occupied West Bank and
the Gaza Strip. The first legal regime is that of International Humanitarian Law (particularly the Fourth Geneva Convention), which
applies to situations of belligerent occupation as well as situations
where hostilities rise to the level of international armed conflict." In
the "Recommendations" section of the same report, HRW stated:

"To the Government of Israel: Review all military and policing policies applying to the occupied territories of the West Bank and Gaza, including policies on closures, blockades and curfews, to ensure that they are consistent with international humanitarian law and international human rights standards, including the Fourth Geneva Convention."[320] In a report issued one year later, HRW stated: "The Palestinian civilian inhabitants of the occupied West Bank and Gaza Strip are 'Protected Persons' under the Fourth Geneva Convention. They are entitled to extensive protections under the laws of war." HRW then noted:

> Successive Israeli governments have taken the position that the Fourth Geneva Convention does not apply to the West Bank and Gaza Strip and that Israel is not bound by the Convention, a treaty that it has signed and ratified. Instead, Israel takes the position that it will voluntarily abide by the "humanitarian provisions" of the Fourth Geneva Convention. The Convention's defining principle is the obligation to protect and respect civilians: nothing is more humanitarian.
>
> Israel's interpretation is not supported by the Convention's language, nor is it accepted by the body charged with monitoring adherence to the Geneva Conventions, the International Committee of the Red Cross. The ICRC has consistently affirmed the application of the Fourth Geneva Convention in all its statements dealing with the Occupied Territories since Israel's occupation of the West Bank and Gaza. On December 4, 2001, the Declaration of the Conference of High Contracting Parties to the Fourth Geneva Convention reaffirmed the applicability of the Fourth Geneva Convention to the West Bank, Gaza Strip, and East Jerusalem.[321]

And in a letter to President Bill Clinton in July 1999, Human Rights Watch wrote that "Israel, alone among the High Contracting Parties to the Conventions, disputes the applicability of the Fourth Geneva Convention to the lands it occupied in 1967."[322]

B'Tselem also has affirmed the applicability of the Fourth Geneva Convention to the Israeli occupation. In its background section on "International Humanitarian Law (Laws of War)," B'Tselem states: "The Fourth Geneva Convention deals with the protection of civilians during war or under occupation, and therefore relates to Israel's actions in the Occupied Territories."[323]

In addition to the institutions and organizations cited above, the UN's International Court of Justice (ICJ) also has reaffirmed the applicability of the Fourth Geneva Convention to Israel's occupation. In the ICJ's 2004 advisory opinion, *Legal Consequences of the Construction of a Wall in the Occupied Palestinian Territory*, the Court noted that "Israel, contrary to the great majority of the other participants, disputes the applicability *de jure* of the [Fourth Geneva] Convention to the Occupied Palestinian Territory." In a detailed exposition of the Fourth Geneva Convention and the occupied Palestinian territories, in which it cited the ICRC, the UN General Assembly, and the UN Security Council, in addition to responding in detail to Israel's claims that the Convention is not applicable, the ICJ concluded that the "Convention is applicable in the Palestinian territories."[324]

In a concurring opinion in the case, the ICJ's Vice President, Judge Awn Shawkat Al-Khasawneh, wrote:

> 2. Few propositions in international law can be said to command an almost universal acceptance and to rest on a long, constant and solid *opinio juris* as the proposition that Israel's presence in the Palestinian territory of the West Bank, including East Jerusalem and Gaza, is one of military occupation governed by the applicable international legal régime of military occupation.
>
> 3. In support of this, one may cite the very large number of resolutions adopted by the [UN] Security Council and the General Assembly often unanimously or by overwhelming majorities, including binding decisions of the Council and other resolutions which, while not binding, nevertheless produce legal effects and indicate a constant record of the international community's *opinio juris*. In all of these resolutions the territory in question was unfalteringly characterized as occupied territory. . . .
>
> 4. Similarly the High Contracting Parties to the Fourth Geneva Convention and the International Committee of the Red Cross "have retained their consensus", i.e., the Fourth Geneva Convention of 12 August 1949, "does apply *de jure* to the occupied territories."[325]

There is obviously *no* dissent about the application of the Fourth Geneva Convention to Israel's occupation of the Palestinian territories among the authoritative institutions and organizations that monitor the Convention. Yet the *New York Times* continues to ignore the Fourth Geneva Convention in its coverage of the Israel-Palestine conflict, even in the context of Israel's extensive, and extensively documented, violations. The fact that the *Times* chooses to reject by omission any discussion of the Convention in the context of the Israel–Palestine conflict is nothing less than a rejection by the *Times* of the rule of law as it applies to the Israel–Palestine conflict. At least implicitly, the *Times'* stance also supports Israel's self-serving (and groundless) claim that the Convention does not apply to its occupation of the Palestinian territories—a claim for which there is *no* support under international law, as has been painstakingly demonstrated.

This is hardly a "legalistic" issue: the erasure of the Fourth Geneva Convention by the *Times* favors Israel's territorial privileges over Palestinian rights and helps to sway public opinion and policy debates in the United States. Such privileges are shared by advocates of Israel's occupation policies who, as a matter of necessity in the context of what they support, either ignore or assail international law and its sponsoring organizations. The *New York Times*, as it too often does when it really matters—as in its support of the illegal 2003 US invasion of Iraq, and in the context of the Israel–Palestine conflict—concedes the arena of public debate to the proponents of state power over the rule of law in international affairs.

When the International Committee of the Red Cross issued a statement on July 15, 1999, reaffirming the application of the Fourth Geneva Convention to Israel's occupation, the Anti-Defamation League issued a press release that "expressed dismay at the passage" of the resolution. The ADL's opposition was conveyed by its director, Abraham Foxman:

> The passage of this resolution which applies the Fourth Geneva Convention to the "occupied territories" is disruptive to the Middle East peace process, particularly at this time when serious efforts are underway to reinvigorate the process. Moreover, it gives legitimacy to the Palestinian tactic of using the international community to air grievances regarding the Israeli-Palestinian peace process.[326]

Two years earlier, in November 1997, an ADL press release quoted Foxman using nearly identical language in a letter to Switzerland's Foreign Minister stating the ADL's opposition to a similarly proposed conference on the Fourth Geneva Convention and Israel. The 1997 ADL press release stated:

"Not only would such a conference serve to dangerously politicize the standing Geneva Conventions and their important humanitarian purposes," said Mr. Foxman, "but it is our great concern that it would lend legitimacy to the Palestinian tactic of using the international community as a forum for airing grievances regarding the Israeli-Palestinian peace process."

In the letter to the Swiss Foreign Minister Foxman also wrote: "We assure you that such constructive efforts on this matter by the Swiss Government [which formally calls such ICRC conferences] would be greatly appreciated by the Jewish community at this time."[327]

Similarly, in September 1999, a few days before the annual convening of the UN General Assembly in New York, the ADL issued a press release, again using similar language, in which the group opposed a conference on the Fourth Geneva Convention:

> ADL has vigorously opposed convening the Fourth Geneva Convention in regard to Israeli settlements arguing that it could dangerously politicize the international legitimacy and high standings of the Geneva Conventions. It could open a Pandora's box across the globe haphazardly applying the convention to a plethora of nations. Furthermore, it would give credence to the Palestinian tactic of using the international community to air grievances regarding the Israeli-Palestinian peace process, and thereby threatens the peace process itself.[328]

In addition to the press releases, a 1999 "ADL Factsheet" on the Fourth Geneva Convention reiterated the ADL claim that a meeting of the state parties to the Convention "would give credence to the Palestinian tactic of using the international community to air grievances regarding the Israeli-Palestinian peace process, and thereby threatens the peace process itself." The ADL Factsheet also stipulates an important reason why the organization rejects applying the Convention to Israel's occupation: "Israel rejects the interpretation of the 4th Geneva Convention applying it to Israeli settlements in the West Bank and Gaza Strip, stating that those territories were captured in 1967 as a result of a defensive war against countries which had illegally occupied them since 1948."[329]

This last point identifies a major reason for Israel's opposition to applying the Fourth Geneva Convention to its occupation of the Palestinian territories: the Convention outlaws Israel's settlements in occupied Palestinian territory. Because Israel apparently plans to maintain many of these settlements and ultimately annex the Palestinian territory they occupy, they refuse to officially acknowledge the application of the Convention, thereby avoiding any concessions about the illegality of its settlements. In this light, it is clear that it is Israel that is "politicizing" the Fourth Geneva Convention. Likewise, the unseemly "tactic" being deployed here is the ADL's, which supports Israel's unwarranted rejection of the Convention and characterizes the international effort to apply the Convention to Israel's occupation as a Palestinian tactic. Even if it were a Palestinian initiative, the ADL could not legitimately criticize Palestinian efforts to end Israel's illegal conduct by appealing to international law and international authorities as an alternative to Palestinian terrorism.

The ADL's additional claim—that international efforts to apply and enforce the Convention in the occupied territories would "threaten the peace process itself"—also was disingenuous. Those international efforts were initiated in April 1997 by a UN General Assembly resolution that was issued in response to the provocative announcement by Israeli Prime Minister Benjamin Netanyahu in February 1997 that Israel would build new settlements at what the Israelis call Har Homa in East Jerusalem. Thus, Netanyahu's announcement in early 1997, and not the subsequent efforts to affirm the application of the Fourth Geneva Convention to Israel's occupation, was the provocation designed to undermine the Oslo negotiations. While the ADL criticized the UN's effort to apply the Convention in the occupied territories as a "tactic" for "airing grievances regarding the Israeli-Palestinian peace process," Israeli historian Avi Shlaim had a different interpretation of the "tactics" deployed at the time:

> Netanyahu fired the opening shot in the battle for Jerusalem on 19 February [1997] with a plan for the construction of 6,500 housing units for 30,000 Israelis at Har Homa, in annexed East Jerusalem. "The battle for Jerusalem has begun," he declared in mid-March as Israeli bulldozers went into action to clear the site for a Jewish neighborhood near the Arab village of Sur Bahir. . . . The site was chosen in order to complete the chain of Jewish settlements around Jerusalem and cut off contact between the Arab side of the city and its hinterland in the West Bank. It was a blatant example of the Zionist tactic of creating facts on the ground to preempt negotiations.[330]

In addition, the April 1997 General Assembly resolution not only condemned Israel's Har Homa initiative, it also reiterated its established positions that Israel's annexation of East Jerusalem is "null and void," and that "settlements in all the territories occupied by Israel since 1967 are illegal and an obstacle to peace":

> *The General Assembly. . . .*
> 1. *Condemns* the construction by Israel, the occupying Power, of a new settlement in Jebel Abu Ghneim [Har Homa] to the south of occupied East Jerusalem and all other illegal Israeli actions in all the occupied territories;
> 2. *Reaffirms* that all legislative and administrative measures and actions taken by Israel, the occupying Power, that have altered or purported to alter the character, legal status and demographic composition of Jerusalem are null and void and have no validity whatsoever;
> 3. *Reaffirms also* that Israeli settlements in all the territories occupied by Israel since 1967 are illegal and an obstacle to peace;
> 4. *Demands* immediate and full cessation of the construction in Jebel Abu Ghneim [Har Homa] and of all other Israeli settlement activities, as well as of all illegal measures and actions in Jerusalem;
> 5. *Demands also* that Israel accept the *de jure* applicability of the [Fourth] Geneva Convention.

General Assembly resolutions issued later in 1997 (in July and November) similarly denounced the Har Homa settlement and all other Israeli settlements in the occupied Palestinian territories.[331] The ADL's November 1997 press release cited above apparently was designed as a response to the General Assembly's three resolutions in April, July, and November 1997 that were critical of Israel's Har Homa initiative. Considering these facts, it appears that the ADL press release issued in November 1997, in addition to the ones that followed that rejected the application of the Fourth Geneva Convention, were themselves "tactics" to shield Israel's noncompliance with the Convention—which in 1997 included the Har Homa initiative—and undermine negotiations with the Palestinians.

The ADL's "politicization"—the ADL's word—of the Fourth Geneva Convention goes beyond its press releases. In one of its informational documents titled "Advocating for Israel: An Activist's Guide," the ADL provides readers with "What you need to know to fight for Israel's security" and provides guidance on "How to respond to common misstatements about Israel." It then provides pairs of "Misstatement" and "Response," one of which says:

> **Misstatement**: Settlements are a violation of international law.
> **Response**: Settlements, Jewish communities that were established in the West Bank and Gaza Strip after the territories were gained in the 1967 War, do not violate international law.

To support its guidance, the ADL provides a misleading and muddled analysis of the Fourth Geneva Convention in an attempt to demonstrate that Israel's settlements "do not violate international law":

> Critics of Israel frequently cite Article 49 of the Fourth Geneva Convention, which prohibits the forcible transfer of segments of a population of a state to the territory of another state which it has occupied through the use of armed force, as proof of the illegality of settlements. However, Israel maintains that the Geneva Convention, drafted after World War II, was intended to protect local populations from displacement, such as the forced population transfers experienced before and during the war in Czechoslovakia, Poland and Hungary. The situation in the West Bank and Gaza Strip is clearly different. Israel has not forcibly transferred Israelis to these areas. Rather, Israeli settlers voluntarily reside in areas where Jews have historically dwelled.[332]

While it is the case that Article 49(1) of the Fourth Geneva Convention prohibits "forcible transfers," Article 49(6) prohibits "transfers," including voluntary transfers. To our knowledge, no international law authority has ever identified Article 49(1) as the Convention's provision that is applicable to Israel's settlements. Because the Israeli settlements in the occupied Palestinian territories are voluntary, they are covered by Article 49(6), not Article 49(1), and on this basis, are prohibited under the Convention. The ADL's guide to correct "common misstatements about Israel" not only drew the wrong conclusion, but it also presented a misleading analysis of the Convention's relevance to Israel's settlements.

As the previous examples indicate, ADL press releases often shadow important reports issued by the UN and the human rights organizations that are critical of Israel's conduct in the occupied territories.

Though often confusing and inept (or worse), these ADL statements feature intimidation and invective, including implied or outright accusations of anti-Semitism. For example, when the ICRC conference of state parties to the Fourth Geneva Convention issued its statement on December 5, 2001, reaffirming the application of the Convention to Israel's occupation, the ADL issued a press release, similar to its July 1999 press release, that expressed "outrage" and "shock" about the effort to apply the Convention to Israel's occupation of the West Bank and Gaza. Along these lines, the press release featured the following statement by Foxman:

> The re-convening of the Fourth Geneva Convention to censure Israel is a shocking use of a humanitarian mechanism for one-sided political goals. It is mind-boggling that given all the dire circumstances in the world, these nations met for only the second time in the 50-year history of the Fourth Geneva Convention to single out and delegitimize [*sic*] the State of Israel. Switzerland, which called the meeting, and other participating nations have allowed this humanitarian mechanism to be commandeered as a tool in the Arab League campaign to single out and delegitimize the State of Israel.
>
> The absurdities of holding this meeting and passing this resolution are countless. The discussion was held despite the ongoing Palestinian terrorist campaign, which has resulted in one of the bloodiest periods in Israel's history. These countries point to alleged Israeli violations while ignoring Palestinian violence and terror, and the Palestinian rejection of negotiations with Israel aimed at achieving mutual recognition.
>
> ADL has long been opposed to the politicization of humanitarian mechanisms like the Fourth Geneva Convention. This cynical misuse of the Convention's otherwise important mandate sets a dangerous precedent. Such meetings and resolutions do nothing to promote negotiations and security in the Middle East, but serve only to allow elements hostile to Israel to publicly air their grievances before an international audience.[333]

Foxman noted above that the parties to the Fourth Geneva Convention "met for only the second time in the 50-year history of the Fourth Geneva Convention" and that this reflects a bias against Israel. However, Israel's occupation of the Palestinian territories is the world's longest illegal occupation (forty years); meeting only twice during a forty-year period to affirm the applicability of the rules of the Fourth Geneva Convention to that occupation appears to reflect, if anything, a bias against the rights of Palestinians. It is also unclear how applying the Fourth Geneva Convention to Israel's occupation of the Palestinian territories "delegitimizes" the state of Israel, as Foxman argued. And a closer look at what he terms "absurdities" involved in the effort to apply the Fourth Geneva Convention to Israel's occupation reveals a number of discrepancies in his facts. For example, Foxman criticized the ICRC for holding its conference "despite the ongoing Palestinian terrorist campaign, which has resulted in one of the bloodiest periods in Israel's history." He wrote these words in December 2001. However, in its annual report for 2002, Amnesty International reported that more than 460 Palestinians were killed during 2001, including 79 children, and that Palestinian armed groups had killed 187 Israelis, including 154 civilians. While the number of Israelis killed is clearly deplorable and unacceptable, during the year in which Foxman issued the above complaint Israelis killed many more Palestinians. In addition, Foxman wrote that the ICRC statement was issued "despite . . . the Palestinian rejection of negotiations with Israel aimed at achieving mutual recognition"; in fact, negotiations had already failed under Ehud Barak, who was rejected by Israeli voters in the January 2001 election in favor of Ariel Sharon as a demonstration of Israel's post-Oslo rejection of peace negotiations with the Palestinians.

The common ADL tactic, in evidence here and below, is to attach heavy political baggage to reports issued by respected human rights organizations by harpooning them with inflammatory charges of "bias," "bigotry," and "anti-Semitism" as soon as they are released. Tactically, the merits of these charges are irrelevant; the charges themselves are the operative element and they are regularly issued without evidence of any anti-Semitism at the ICRC, Amnesty International, or at any of the human rights organizations mentioned in this volume. As long as the *New York Times* and other major US news organizations are content to let the ADL have the last word about important issues and organizations that the *Times* should be covering, there is little reason for the ADL to discontinue issuing press releases with bullying and misleading headlines, as follows: "Amnesty International Report Biased and Unfair on Situation in West Bank and Gaza" (September 10, 2003); "Anti-Israel Bias at the U.N." (September 2004); "U.N. Human Rights Council Predictably Blames

Israel While Giving Hamas a Pass" (July 6, 2006); "Human Rights Watch: Irrelevant, Immoral on Mideast Conflict" (Abraham Foxman, *New York Sun*, August 2, 2006); "ADL Says One-Sided Human Rights Watch Report Rushes to Judge Israel" (August 4, 2006); "ADL Labels Kofi Annan's Statements on Israel 'Blatantly One-Sided' " (August 9, 2006); "ADL Denounces UN Human Rights Council Anti-Israel Resolution as False and One-Sided" (August 11, 2006); "ADL Calls Amnesty International Report 'Bigoted, Biased, and Borderline Anti-Semitic" (August 23, 2006); "Mearsheimer and Walt Cross the Line from the Academy to Advocacy, Blaming Israel and Its Supporters on an American Muslim Platform" (August 29, 2006).

These ADL statements are typically heavy with accusations, as indicated by their titles, but disingenuous in substance. The intent, apparently, is to discredit critics of Israel's occupation while bypassing the criticism itself. Interestingly, while Amnesty International is supposedly "biased" and Kofi Annan "blatantly one-sided," the ADL, presumably, is neither biased nor one-sided—yet the ADL seldom criticizes Israel's conduct or policies. In the press releases listed above, there is no criticism of Israel, despite clear evidence of major Israeli atrocities and violations of international humanitarian law documented in the reports it criticizes. Similarly, according to the ADL, while Professors John Mearsheimer and Stephen Walt have crossed the line to "advocacy," the ADL itself publishes "Advocating for Israel: An Activist's Guide." Furthermore, while the ADL wields repeatedly and without hesitation the heavy club of bigotry and anti-Semitism, it ridicules Mearsheimer and Walt for speaking "on an American Muslim platform."

Despite the ADL's double standards, there is a clear alignment between the ADL and the US news media when it comes to ignoring facts about Israel's illegal conduct. In a press release issued on August 29, 2006, the ADL cited its findings of a survey of US newspaper editorials on Israel and the Lebanon war in summer 2006. The ADL reported:

> In an informal survey of editorials on the Israel-Hezbollah conflict appearing in 33 of the nation's largest circulation newspapers at the height of the conflict, the Anti-Defamation League (ADL) found that an overwhelming majority of the papers supported Israel's response to Hezbollah's unprovoked attacks and clearly labeled Hezbollah a terrorist organization.

At the same time, U.S. political cartoonists depicted Hezbollah—and particularly Hezbollah leader Sheikh Hassan Nasrallah—as unrepentant terrorists who bore full responsibility for the destruction of Lebanese cities and bloodshed that came about as a result of Hezbollah's attack and Israel's reprisals.[334]

This press release, which is accurate as it applies to the *New York Times* editorial page, merits a closer look, since the *Times'* editorial page could not have simultaneously supported Israel's conduct in Lebanon in July and August 2006, as it did, and also side with the Human Rights Watch and Amnesty International reports that analyzed that conduct from the perspective of international humanitarian law.

A major report on Israel's war in Lebanon was issued on August 3, 2006, by Human Rights Watch; it was not mentioned by the *New York Times* editorial page. The report—"Fatal Strikes: Israel's Indiscriminate Attacks Against Civilians in Lebanon"—documented "serious violations of international humanitarian law by Israel Defense Forces in Lebanon between July 12 and July 27, 2006, while also including the July 30 attack in Qana [in southern Lebanon]."[335]

In an opinion piece published in the *New York Sun* a day before the official release of the report, Abraham Foxman oddly characterized Human Rights Watch as "immoral or irrelevant" for issuing a report a few days earlier on Israel's bombing of a house in Qana in southern Lebanon, which killed at least 28 Lebanese civilians.[336] Foxman's extensive commentary failed to substantively respond to HRW's charge that the bombing in Qana may have been a war crime. The closest Foxman came to actually addressing the report's substance was the following:

> So yes, Israel is striking very hard at Hezbollah and the [Lebanese] infrastructure that allows it to operate and to receive weapons from Iran and Syria. And yes, there are tragically civilian casualties. Israel must do everything in its power to limit these casualties. But it is Hezbollah that has cynically created a dilemma for Israel by embedding their missiles not only in civilian areas, but literally in civilian households.[337]

Similarly, in an August 3 front-page news article titled "Civilians Lose as Fighters Slip into Fog of War," which featured the August 3 report by Human Rights Watch, the *Times*, like Foxman, presented Israel's atrocities as the tragic but inevitable by-product of Hezbollah using Lebanese civilians as human shields, creating an insoluble "dilemma" for Israel:

> Civilian deaths illustrate the raw dilemma of modern warfare, in which a conventional army fights an elusive militia that loads its rocket launchers in family gardens, orchards and on village streets. In Lebanon, the result has been desperate efforts to flee and military miscalculations in the fog of war.[338]

However, not only did Human Rights Watch report that Hezbollah had no involvement in any of the Israeli attacks on Lebanese civilians documented in the report—they found no evidence of Hezbollah loading rocket launchers in civilian households, family gardens, orchards, and village streets prior to or during any of the reported Israeli attacks—but the nature of the numerous attacks by Israeli war planes and helicopters on Lebanese civilians clearly indicated the absence of any mitigating "fog of war" context in most or all of these attacks. The HRW report was very clear on these counts, beginning with the first page of the executive summary:

> The Israeli government claims that it targets only Hezbollah, and that fighters from the group are using civilians as human shields, thereby placing them at risk. Human Rights Watch found no cases in which Hezbollah deliberately used civilians as shields to protect them from retaliatory IDF attack. Hezbollah occasionally did store weapons in or near civilian homes and fighters placed rocket launchers within populated areas or near U.N. observers, which are serious violations of the laws of war because they violate the duty to take all feasible precautions to avoid civilian casualties. However, those cases do not justify the IDF's extensive use of indiscriminate force which has cost so many civilian lives. In none of the cases of civilian deaths documented in this report is there evidence to suggest that Hezbollah forces or weapons were in or near the area that the IDF targeted during or just prior to the attack.[339]

The claims by Foxman and the *Times* that Hezbollah activity was implicated in Israel's attacks on Lebanese civilians are contradicted further by HRW's more extended findings in its August 3 report:

The report breaks civilian deaths into two categories: attacks on civilian homes and attacks on civilian vehicles. In both categories, victims and witnesses interviewed independently and repeatedly said that neither Hezbollah fighters nor Hezbollah weapons were present in the area during or just before the Israeli attack took place. While some individuals, out of fear or sympathy, may have been unwilling to speak about Hezbollah's military activity, others were quite open about it. In totality, the consistency, detail, and credibility of testimony from a broad array of witnesses who did not speak to each other leave no doubt about the validity of the patterns described in this report. In many cases, witness testimony was corroborated by reports from international journalists and aid workers. During site visits conducted in Qana, Srifa, and Tyre [in southern Lebanon], Human Rights Watch saw no evidence that there had been Hezbollah military activity around the areas targeted by the IDF during or just prior to the attack: no spent ammunition, abandoned weapons or military equipment, trenches, or dead or wounded fighters. Moreover, even if Hezbollah had been in a populated area at the time of an attack, Israel would still be legally obliged to take all feasible precautions to avoid or minimize civilian casualties resulting from its targeting of military objects or personnel.[340]

In a letter to the *New York Sun* in response to Foxman's unsubstantiated attack on the Human Rights Watch report on Qana on July 30, Kenneth Roth, HRW's director, wrote:

A critic's first duty is to get his facts right, but not Abraham Foxman. He, embarrassingly, didn't do his homework before launching his broadside at Human Rights Watch. . . . Mr. Foxman, while offering no evidence, blames the hundreds of civilian casualties in Lebanon on Hezbollah's "embedding their missiles not only in civilian areas, but literally in civilian households." Your editorial [August 8], with no greater attention to fact, suggests the same. Hezbollah does sometimes endanger civilians, and that's clearly wrong. But in some two dozen cases examined by Human Rights Watch accounting for what was then a third of the civilian deaths in Lebanon, Hezbollah was nowhere around at the time of the attack.[341]

Most people who read HRW's reports and Foxman's assessment of the organization as "immoral" for issuing such reports would quickly recognize that Foxman, as Roth indicated, hardly bothered with the facts while condemning the human rights organizations for documenting Israel's illegal bombing of civilians in southern Lebanon.

In his public condemnations of Human Rights Watch, Alan Dershowitz also misrepresented the fifty-page August 3 report. About the report, Dershowitz wrote:

> "Who will guard the guardians?" asked Roman satirist Juvenal. Now we must ask, who is watching Human Rights Watch, one of the world's best-financed and most influential human rights organizations? It turns out that they cook the books about facts, cheat on interviews, and put out pre-determined conclusions that are driven more by their ideology than by evidence.
>
> These are serious accusations, and they are demonstrably true.
>
> Consider the highly publicized "conclusion" reached by Human Rights Watch about the recent war in Lebanon between Hezbollah and Israel. This is their conclusion, allegedly reached after extensive "investigations" on the ground:
>
>> "Human Rights Watch found no cases in which Hezbollah deliberately used civilians as shields to protect them from retaliatory IDF attack."
>
> After investigating a handful of cases, Human Rights Watch found that in "none of the cases of civilian deaths documented in this report [Qana, Srifa, Tyre, and southern Beirut] is there evidence to suggest that Hezbollah forces or weapons were in or near the area that the IDF targeted during or just prior to the attack."
>
> No cases! None! Not one!
>
> Anyone who watched even a smattering of TV during the war saw with their own eyes direct evidence of rockets being launched from civilian areas. But not Human Rights Watch. "Who are you going to believe, me or your lying eyes?" That's not Chico Marx. It's Human Rights Watch. Their lying eyes belonged to the pro-Hezbollah witnesses its investigators chose to interview—and claimed to believe. But their mendacious pens belonged to Kenneth Roth, HRW's Executive Director, and his minions in New York, who know how to be skeptical when it serves their interests not to believe certain witnesses. How could an organization, which claims to be objective, have been so demonstrably wrong about so central a point in so

important a war? Could it have been an honest mistake? I don't think so. Despite its boast that "Human Rights Watch has interviewed victims and witness of attacks in one-on-one settings, conducted on-site inspections . . . and collected information for hospitals, humanitarian groups, and government agencies," it didn't find *one instance* in which Hezbollah failed to segregate its fighters from civilians.

Nor apparently did HRW even ask the Israelis for proof of its claim that Hezbollah rockets were being fired from behind civilians, and that Hezbollah fighters were hiding among civilians. Its investigators interviewed Arab "eye witnesses" and monitored "information from public sources including the Israeli government statements." But it conducted no interviews with Israeli officials or witnesses. It also apparently ignored credible news sources, such as *The New York Times* and *The New Yorker*.[342]

This is what Dershowitz wrote, but like Foxman's writings, it does not accurately reflect what the HRW report actually said. With respect to HRW's "conclusion," quoted by Dershowitz as follows—"Human Rights Watch found no cases in which Hezbollah deliberately used civilians as shields to protect them from retaliatory IDF attack"—the very next sentence in the HRW report, which Dershowitz omitted, read:

> Hezbollah occasionally did store weapons in or near civilian homes and fighters placed rocket launchers within populated areas or near U.N. observers, which are serious violations of the laws of war because they violate the duty to take all feasible precautions to avoid civilian casualties.[343]

Thus, it was not the case that HRW reported *no* instances in which Hezbollah used civilians or civilian objects to store weapons or place rocket launchers; rather, HRW reported that no such instances were implicated in the Israeli attacks on Lebanese civilians that were documented in the August 3 report.

In addition, HRW investigated dozens of cases—not "a handful of cases," as Dershowitz wrote—in which it found no evidence of Hezbollah involvement at the time of or prior to Israeli attacks on the civilian targets. By inaccurately citing only "a handful of cases," Dershowitz conveys a false impression that HRW's investigation was less comprehensive than it actually was. His inaccuracy also reduces the number and scale of Israel's attacks on Lebanese civilians where there was no evidence of Hezbollah involvement.

Dershowitz's reproduction of a brief excerpt of what he described as the report's "conclusion" is also of interest: he omitted the preceding two sentences in the report, which were highly incriminating of Israel's conduct, and which were far more suitable to excerpt as representative of the report's conclusion:

> Since the start of the conflict, Israeli forces have consistently launched artillery and air attacks with limited or dubious military gain but excessive cost. In dozens of attacks, Israeli forces struck an area with no apparent military target. In some cases, the timing and intensity of the attack, the absence of a military target, as well as return strikes on rescuers, suggest that Israeli forces deliberately targeted civilians.[344]

While accusing HRW of disingenuously failing to cite evidence of Hezbollah involvement in Israel's attacks on Lebanese civilians, Dershowitz supplied his own evidence to make a case for their involvement. For example, he wrote that HRW "ignored" a *New York Times* story about Hezbollah using civilian shields in southern Lebanon. Here is how Dershowitz began his excerpt from the *Times* report that he accused HRW of ignoring:

> "Hezbollah came to Ain Ebel to shoot its rockets," said Fayad Hanna Amar, a young Christian man, referring to his village. "They are shooting from between our houses."[345]

Rather than ignore the *Times* report, as Dershowitz charged, Human Rights Watch in fact quoted these same words while citing the same report from the *New York Times*:

> Christian villagers fleeing the village of 'Ain Ebel have also complained about Hezbollah tactics that placed them at risk, telling the *New York Times* that "Hezbollah came to [our village] to shoot its rockets. . . . They are shooting from between our houses."[346]

Dershowitz also cited eight other reports from other news organizations that he claimed demonstrated the use of civilian shields by Hezbollah; he produced these articles and the *New York Times* article mentioned above to demonstrate that Human Rights Watch had "cooked the books" by ignoring them. Here are the titles, sources, and dates of four of the eight reports Dershowitz cited:

- "The Battle for Lebanon," *New Yorker*, August 8, 2006;
- "Diplomacy Under Fire," *MacLeans*, August 7, 2006;
- "Hezbollah's Deadly Hold on Heartland," *National Post*, August 5, 2006;
- "Laying Out the Qana Calculation: Disarming Hezbollah Prevents More Crises," *Chicago Tribune*, August 2, 2006.

The obvious problem with Dershowitz citing these four reports while arguing that HRW deliberately ignored them is that all of them were published either after or simultaneous with the August 3 HRW report. (The August 2 article by the *Chicago Tribune* was published while the August 3 HRW report was almost certainly in press.) Once again, one must ponder the substance and methodology applied by Dershowitz in his attacks on Human Rights Watch—in this case accusing it of neglecting to cite articles in its August 3 report that were published after August 3.

The four remaining reports cited by Dershowitz also provided no evidence that Hezbollah used Lebanese civilians or civilian homes or vehicles as shields prior to or during any of the Israeli attacks on civilians in southern Lebanon documented in the HRW report. Looking at these four reports one report at a time, here is the entire excerpt that Dershowitz uses from one of them:

> Days after fighting broke out between Israel and Hezbollah on July 12, [Samira] Abbas said Hezbollah fighters went door-to-door in Ain Ebel, asking everyone to give up their cell phones. "They were worried about collaborators giving the Israelis information," she said.
>
> While she was there, Abbas said, she heard from relatives that her house in Bint Jbeil had been destroyed. She said Hezbollah fighters had gathered in citrus groves about 500 yards from her home.
>
> Mohamad Bazzi, "Mideast Crisis—Farewell to a Soldier; Reporting From Lebanon; Running Out of Places to Run," *Newsday*, July 28, 2006.[347]

Gathering in a citrus grove 500 yards from a civilian home that had been destroyed by an Israeli airstrike hardly constitutes Hezbollah culpability for the Israeli destruction of the house. Dershowitz provided no additional information or excerpts from this report.[348]

This leaves three reports cited by Dershowitz. One of these reports—"Revealed: How Hezbollah Puts the Innocent at Risk; They Don't Care," *Sunday Mail* (Australia), July 30, 2006—apparently pertained to photographs of an anti-aircraft gun taken in "the east of Beirut."[349] While it may or may not have been the case that Hezbollah used civilians as shields in Beirut, the predominant geographic focus of Israeli attacks on Lebanese civilians in HRW's August 3 report was southern Lebanon, which sustained most of the civilian casualties. Thus, this report had little to no relevance to HRW's August 3 report.

This leaves the final two reports cited by Dershowitz. One of these reports was an ambiguous one-line excerpt in a July 28, 2006, communication from a UN post in Naqoura in southern Lebanon. Here is the entirety of what Dershowitz excerpted from that communication:

> It was also reported that Hezbollah fired from the vicinity of five UN positions at Alma Ash Shab, AtTiri, Bayt Yahoun, Brashit, and Tbinin.—United Nations Interim Force in Lebanon (UNIFIL), Naqoura, July 28, 2006 (Press Release)

Presumably, for Dershowitz this single sentence constitutes evidence that Hezbollah used UN positions at these locations in Lebanon as shields that would justify Israeli attacks on those positions. However, the four immediately preceding sentences in the Naqoura communication, which Dershowitz omitted, read as follows:

> There were two direct impacts on UNIFIL positions from the Israeli side in the past 24 hours. Eight artillery and mortar rounds impacted inside an Indian battalion position in the area of Hula, causing extensive material damage, but no casualties. One artillery round impacted the parameter wall of the UNIFIL headquarters in Naqoura. There were five other incidents of firing close to UN positions from the Israeli side.[350]

Thus, the same press release from which Dershowitz squeezed one sentence to vaguely suggest that Hezbollah positions near various UN posts might be implicated in Israeli attacks on such posts in actuality suggests that Israel had attacked UN posts without any reports of Hezbollah positions.

This leaves only one report left among the eight cited by Dershowitz that were supposed to show that HRW had "cooked the books" in its August 3 report. In this final instance, he cited an article from the CanWest News Service in Canada that featured an interpretation of an email written by Major Paeta Hess-von Kruedener of Canada before he was killed by Israeli shelling at the UN post near Khiam in southern Lebanon. Dershowitz excerpted three paragraphs from the CanWest report which describe the contents of the email, and two additional paragraphs with an interpretation of that email by a retired Canadian general. The email by Hess-von Kruedener was written on July 19. In it he wrote: "What I can tell you is this. We have on a daily basis had numerous occasions where our [UN] position has come under direct or indirect fire from both (Israeli) artillery and aerial bombing." And: "The closest [Israeli] artillery has landed within 2 meters (sic) of our position and the closest 1000 lb aerial bomb has landed 100 meters (sic) from our patrol base."[351] According to Dershowitz, the key evidence of Hezbollah involvement—and thus a justification in his mind for the Israeli attacks on the UN post—is this sentence in Hess-von Kruedener's email: "This has not been deliberate targeting, but has rather been due to tactical necessity."[352] CanWest then consulted Canadian Major-General Lewis MacKenzie, who commented, as Dershowitz noted: "What that means is, in plain English, 'We've got Hezbollah fighters running around in our positions, taking our positions here and then using us for shields and then engaging the (Israeli Defense Forces).' "[353]

While it is possible that General MacKenzie's interpretation is accurate, there is no certainty that it is. One day after this CanWest report was published on July 27, the *Toronto Star* reported that MacKenzie had spoken "to a crowd of 8,000 supporters of Israel at a solidarity rally in Toronto two days ago."[354] In addition, while the email by Hess-von Kruedener was dated July 19, the UN post at Khiam was fatally attacked by Israel on July 25, killing Hess-von Kruedener and three other unarmed UN observers from Austria, Finland, and China; assuming that MacKenzie's interpretation of Hess-von Kruedener's email message was correct with respect to events on July 19 or earlier, they were not necessarily applicable to events on July 25. Furthermore, Dershowitz omitted an important response to Hess-von Kruedener's email that was printed in the last three paragraphs of the article he cited:

A senior UN official, asked about the information contained in Hess-von Kruedener's e-mail concerning Hezbollah presence in the vicinity of the Khiam base, denied the world body had been caught in a contradiction.

"At the time [July 25], there had been no Hezbollah activity reported in the area," he said. "So it was quite clear they [Israelis] were not going after other targets; that, for whatever reason, our position was being fired upon.

"Whether or not they thought they were going after something else, we don't know. The fact was, we told them where we were. They knew where we were. The position was clearly marked, and they pounded the hell out of us."[355]

In its August 3 report, Human Rights Watch also reported that the UN post was attacked by Israel on July 25 with "no Hezbollah presence or firing near the U.N. position during the period of the attack." Finally, Reuters reported on September 29 that "Israel used a precision-guided bomb to launch a direct hit on four U.N. peace-keepers killed in southern Lebanon last July, the United Nations said on Friday of its probe into the incident." According to Reuters, the "U.N.-appointed board of inquiry could not affix blame because Israel did not allow the access to operational or tactical level com-manders involved in the July 25 disaster at Khiam," but the UN did provide a senior official who briefed reporters, saying that the Israeli munitions were "precision-guided and meant to hit the targets they hit, which was the United Nations."[356]

In summary, Dershowitz cited nine news articles as evidence—the only so-called evidence that he produced—that Human Rights Watch had "cooked the books" against Israel in its August 3 report. As it turned out, there was no such evidence in these articles to support his charge. Nevertheless, Dershowitz concluded: "Human Rights Watch no longer deserves the support of real human rights advocates. Nor should its so-called reporting be credited by objective news organizations."[357]

While seeking to further discredit the Human Rights Watch report, Dershowitz appeared to impugn HRW's witnesses, apparently on the grounds of their ethnicity, since most HRW witnesses were Arab Lebanese nationals. This apparently is why Dershowitz placed the words "eye witnesses" in parentheses below:

[HRW's] investigators interviewed Arab "eye witnesses" and monitored "information from public sources including the Israeli government statements." But it conducted no interviews with Israeli officials
or witnesses.[358]

In this passage Dershowitz accused HRW of conducting no interviews with Israeli officials or witnesses, yet, in its August 3 report
HRW stated: "Human Rights Watch also conducted research in
Israel, inspecting the IDF's use of weapons and discussing the conduct
of forces with IDF officials."[359] This is the second instance—in
addition to the *New York Times* article that HRW supposedly did
not cite—where Dershowitz falsely accused HRW of ignoring
sources that were in fact cited in its report.

While continuing to impugn HRW's methodology, Dershowitz
wrote, perhaps mistakenly, the word "for" instead of "from" in a key
sentence pertaining to that methodology. Here is what Dershowitz
reproduced as an excerpt from the HRW report, with his mistake in
italics: "[HRW] collected information *for* hospitals, humanitarian
groups, and government agencies." However, the HRW report in
actuality stated that Human Rights Watch had "collected information
from hospitals, humanitarian groups, and government agencies." Thus,
according to the Dershowitz-generated text, HRW's sources for its
report consisted only of Arab "eye witnesses" (quotation marks added
by Dershowitz). In one way or another, he eliminated the *New York
Times*, Israeli officials, hospitals, humanitarian groups, and government
agencies from the list of sources used and cited by HRW in its report.

Lebanon, 2006

It seems quite incredible that Abraham Foxman and Alan Dershowitz would set out to ruin the credibility of Human Rights Watch in order to shelter Israel from public condemnation for its obvious war crimes in Lebanon in summer 2006. At this point, however, we turn to the August 3 HRW report itself to reveal what it actually said, what neither Foxman nor Dershowitz apparently wanted the American people or the US press to consider without the filter of their inaccurate and misleading statements about Human Rights Watch. The section in the HRW report titled "Attacks on Civilian Homes" began as follows:

> Since July 12, when Hezbollah launched an attack on Israeli positions initially killing three Israeli soldiers and capturing two, Israel and Hezbollah have engaged in intense hostilities. Israel has carried out hundreds of strikes against targets in Lebanon, including extensive attacks against Lebanon's infrastructure, private homes and apartment buildings, as well as vehicles moving on roads. Israeli strikes have been especially heavy in Shi'a-dominated areas of Lebanon, considered to be Hezbollah strongholds, including southern Lebanon, the southern suburbs of Beirut, and the Beqaa Valley.
>
> To date, the chief cause of civilian deaths from the Israeli campaign is targeted strikes on civilian homes in villages of Lebanon's South. There has also been large-scale destruction of civilian apartment buildings in southern Beirut, though most of the residents of those buildings had evacuated prior to the attacks. According to the Lebanese Ministry of Social Affairs, the IDF destroyed or damaged up to 5,000 civilian homes in air strikes during the first two weeks of the war. As demonstrated by the case studies below, Israel has caused large-scale civilian casualties by striking civilian homes, with no apparent military objective either inside the home or in the vicinity. In some cases, warplanes returned to strike again while residents and neighbors had

gathered around the house to remove the dead and assist the wounded.[360]

Some of the cases of Israeli attacks on civilian homes reported by HRW are excerpted below. The accounts begin on July 13, one day after the raid inside northern Israel by Hezbollah:

July 13

- On Thursday, July 13, at about 4:00 a.m., Israeli warplanes struck the home of Shi'a cleric Sheikh 'Adil Mohammed Akash, killing the cleric and eleven members of his family. Sheikh Akash was an Iranian-educated cleric and is believed to have been affiliated with Hezbollah, although there is no indication that he took part in hostilities or had a commanding role, either of which might have made him a legitimate military target. The first missile demolished the two-story home in the village of Dweir, located halfway between Saida and Tyre, while a second missile fired minutes later failed to explode. The sheikh and his family had returned to the home just twenty minutes before the strike, an eyewitness who lived nearby told Human Rights Watch. The strike killed Sheikh 'Adil Mohammed Akash; his wife, Rabab Yasin, 39; and ten of their children: Mohammed Baker Akash, 18; Mohammed Hassan Akash, 7; Fatima Akash, 17; 'Ali Rida Akash, 12; Ghadir Akash, 10; Zeinab Akash, 13; Sara Akash, 5; Batul Akash, 4; Nour el-Huda Akash, 2; and Safa' Akash, 2 months. The family's Sri Lankan maid, whose name is not known, also died. There was no evidence of Hezbollah military activity in or around the home, and the village of Dweir is too far from the Israeli border (about 40 kilometers) to serve as an effective launching site for Hezbollah rockets.
- On Thursday, July 13, at about 4:30 a.m., an Israeli air strike demolished the home of 45-year-old Munir Zein, a farmer who also owned the truck used to collect the garbage of the village of Baflay, located some ten kilometers east of the southern port city of Tyre. Villagers interviewed by Human Rights Watch were adamant that Munir Zein had no connection to Hezbollah and that there was no Hezbollah military activity or presence in the area . . . The Israeli air strike demolished the entire Zein home, killing all nine people inside, including three young children and two Kuwaiti nationals, according to two witnesses interviewed by Human Rights

Watch. Those killed were Munir Zein and his wife Najla Zein, 45; their children Ali, 21; Wala, 18; Hassan, 12; Fatima, 9; and Hussain, 5. Also killed were Abdullah el-Tahi, the husband of one of the Zeins' daughters, Huriya, and his father, Heidar el-Tahi, both Kuwaiti nationals visiting their in-laws at the time of the attack. Huriya was in Beirut at the time of the attack. The bodies of most of her family members were recovered, except for that of Munir Zein, which remains buried under the rubble.

- On the morning of July 13, Israeli warplanes fired twice at the two-story home of Na'im Bazi', the late mayor of the village of Zibqine, located some five kilometers north of the Israel-Lebanon border. According to a respected Lebanese human rights activist who personally knew Na'im Bazi' (who died a few years ago), Bazi' and his family were not affiliated with Hezbollah. Human Rights Watch also found no evidence of Hezbollah activity in the area of the home when the attack took place. Twelve members of the family were reportedly killed in the air strike, including six children.

July 15

- At 9:30 a.m. on Saturday, July 15, an Israeli airplane fired at a three-story civilian home in Bint Jbeil, a large town near Lebanon's border with Israel. The strike collapsed the home, killing 80-year-old Haj Abu Naji Mrouj, and his 40-year-old daughter whose name is unknown to Human Rights Watch, and trapping their bodies under the rubble. . . . While villagers were attempting to dig the bodies out of the rubble, an Israeli warplane fired a second missile at the rubble and the rescuers at around 1:15 p.m., killing two male civilians, including 30-year-old Bilal Hreish, a U.S.-Lebanese dual national.

- On Saturday July 15, at about 9:30 p.m., an Israeli Apache helicopter fired into the home of Ibrahim Suleiman, a wage laborer, in the village of Houla, located on the Israel-Lebanon border 25 kilometers east of Tyre. "Neither he nor his children were involved in Hezbollah, nor was there any [Hezbollah] resistance in the town at the time," said Ibrahim Suleiman's neighbor Ali Rizak. The attack demolished the Suleiman home, killing his daughter, Salman Suleiman, 17, and his daughter-in-law, Zeinab, 20, the mother of a four-year-old baby daughter.

July 16

- Between 6 and 7 p.m. on July 16, an Israeli airplane fired into a civilian home in Aitaroun, located just one kilometer north of the Israel-Lebanon border, killing eleven members of the Al-Akhrass family, including seven Canadian-Lebanese dual nationals who were vacationing in the village when the Israeli offensive began. . . . Human Rights Watch obtained the names of eight of the eleven people killed in the attack: Amira al-Akhrass, 23; her children Saya, 7, Zeinab, 5, Ahmad, 3, and Salam, 1; their aunt, Haniya al-Akhrass, believed to have been in her sixties; and two uncles, Mohammed Mahmood al-Akhrass, aged between 70 and 80, and his younger brother, Hassan Mahmood al-Akhrass, about 70.

July 17

- The night after an air strike that killed eleven members of the Canadian-Lebanese Al-Akhrass family, warplanes again struck a civilian home in Aitaroun. . . . The two-story house that had been hit belonged to Hussain Neif Awada, the 34-year-old owner of a shoe shop. His brother Musa Neif Awada, 47, had brought his family to shelter in the stronger basement of Hussain's house. The air strike killed Hussain Awada; his wife, Jamila; and their children, 'Ali, about 12, Hassan, 11, Mahmood, 7, and two younger daughters whose names were not known to the witnesses. Also killed were Musa Awada and his two-year-old son.

July 19

- Around 3:30 a.m. on July 19, at least three Israeli airplanes struck at least thirteen homes in the "Moscow" neighborhood [in Srifa], firing multiple munitions and collapsing the homes on their basements packed with sheltering civilians. . . . From surviving relatives, Human Rights Watch has been able to obtain the names of sixteen persons believed to have been killed in the attack (but whose bodies are still not recovered). Among them are eight members of a single household: Kamil Diab Jaber, a 53-year-old owner of a construction business and a bakery; Mahmoud Jaber, 33; Ali Kamil Jaber, 30; Ahmed Kamil Jaber, 27; Menehil Najdi, 80; Ali Nazal, 28; Ali Za'rour, 30; and Bilal Hamoudi, 31. Also believed killed were three people in the house next to the Jaber family: Abbas Abbas Dakrub, 21; Abbas Dakrub (cousin of Abbas), 18; and Wasim Ghalib Najdi. At least five civilians are believed to have died in a third home belonging to Mohammed Qasim Najdi: Ahmed Najdi, 35, who had just returned to Lebanon from Russia; Hassan Qoreim, 22; Ali Najdi, 30; Mohammed Ali Najdi, 35; and Ali Hassan Sabra, 17.

- At 7 p.m. on Wednesday, July 19, Israeli munitions destroyed the home of Dawood al-Khaled in Debbine Marja'youn (a neighborhood on the outskirts of the southern town of Marja'youn). Dawood's sister, who lived next door, told Human Rights Watch that the strike came from an Israeli Apache helicopter. At the time of the attack, the house was occupied by Dawood; his wife, Hamida; and their six children: Hoda, 14; Fatima, 12; 'Abla, 10; 'Ali, 3; Huweida, 8; and Ahmad, 1. The strike killed Dawood, his daughter, 'Abla, and his son, Ahmad. Hoda and Huweida were gravely injured. Hamida and the other two children, Fatima and 'Ali, were unharmed.

- In addition to strikes from airplanes, helicopters, and traditional artillery, Israel has used artillery-fired cluster munitions against populated areas, causing civilian casualties. According to eyewitnesses and survivors of the attack interviewed by Human Rights Watch, Israel fired several artillery-based cluster munitions at Blida around 3:00 p.m. on July 19. Three witnesses described how the artillery shells dropped hundreds of cluster submunitions on the village. They described the submunitions as smaller projectiles that emerged from their larger shells. The cluster attack killed sixty-year-old Maryam Ibrahim inside her home. At least two submunitions from the attack entered the basement that the Ali family was using as a shelter, wounding twelve people, including seven children. Ahmed Ali, a 45-year-old taxi driver and head of the family, lost both legs from injuries caused by the cluster submunitions. Five of his children were wounded: Mira, 16; Fatima, 12; 'Ali, 10; Aya, 3; and 'Ola, 1. His wife, Akram Ibrahim, 35, and his mother-in-law, 'Ola Musa, 80, were also wounded. Four relatives, all German-Lebanese dual nationals sheltering with the family, were wounded as well: Mohammed Ibrahim, 45; his wife Fatima, 40; and their children 'Ali, 16, and Rula, 13.

July 30

- Around 1 a.m. on July 30, Israeli warplanes fired missiles at the village of Qana. Among the homes struck was a three-story building in which sixty-three members of two extended families had sought shelter. The home collapsed and killed at least twenty-eight people. Sixteen children are among the dead. Initial reports after the attack put the death toll at fifty-four, which was based on a register of sixty-three persons who had sought shelter in the building that was struck, and the rescue teams' ability to locate only nine survivors. Human Rights Watch learned after a visit to Qana that at least twenty-two people escaped the basement, and twenty-eight are confirmed dead. The fate of the remaining thirteen people who hid in the basement is unknown, and village representatives believe they remain buried in the debris.[361]

In each of these reported incidents and many others in which Israeli warplanes and helicopters fired on civilian homes and killed many Lebanese civilians, HRW found no evidence of Hezbollah fighters in the civilian areas targeted.

Nor did HRW find any evidence of Hezbollah fighters implicated in Israel's numerous aerial attacks on Lebanese civilians fleeing southern Lebanon. In its August 3 report HRW reported that "on a daily basis Israeli warplanes and helicopters struck civilians in cars who were trying to flee [southern Lebanon], many with white flags out the windows, a widely accepted sign of civilian status." HRW also reported that "Israel repeatedly attacked both individual vehicles and entire convoys of civilians who heeded the Israeli warnings to abandon their villages." A Lebanese man described to Human Rights Watch his journey from southern Lebanon to Beirut in the midst of Israeli aerial attacks:

We had two vans for four families, eighteen people in all. The journey was very dangerous, with airplanes constantly in the sky. The main road is cut, so we had to go on little side roads or off the road. It took seven hours to Beirut. Just before we reached Tyre, the planes hit a car in front of us, it was still burning when we got there, a civilian car. We saw a total of thirteen cars along the way that had been bombed, often with civilians in them who had died. We saw the dead women and children, and their clothes and mattresses in the car.[362]

A Lebanese woman reported a similar account to Human Rights Watch:

> Neighbors of mine left with a van and two cars, and I went with them. We first stopped at Bint Jbeil at the hospital because there was a plane in the air. When we started again, the plane came and hit the road in front and behind us, just ten meters away from us, with bombs. But we just kept driving. We were flying white flags. Along the way, we saw the dead still inside the cars. I remember well when we approached Soultaniye, there was a Mercedes 300 overturned with dead people inside, we wanted to stop but the driver said we would be hit. There were men, women and children. I remember seeing two dead children. Along the way, we met an old woman who was crying by the side of the road because no one wanted to take her, so we took her with us. There was lots of destruction, all of the gas stations were bombed and we drove as fast as we could. It only got better when we crossed the Litani River [into central Lebanon].[363]

Instead of blaming the Israeli government for these attacks on Lebanese civilian homes and fleeing civilians, Alan Dershowitz blamed the Lebanese government and the Lebanese civilians themselves. In a commentary dated August 7—that is, four days after the August 3 HRW report was issued—and titled "Lebanon Is Not a Victim," Dershowitz refers to the Lebanese civilians killed by Israel as "civilians," using quotation marks, as he did with Arab "eye witnesses," to discredit in this instance the Lebanese men, women, and children who were bombed and killed by Israel in their homes and in their cars. Dershowitz also referred to Lebanese civilians as "collaborators," apparently because a majority voted for or otherwise supported the Lebanese government current at the time. He then implied that these "collaborators"—presumably a majority of Lebanon's adult population—were Israel's legitimate military targets. According to Dershowitz, the hundreds of Lebanese children who were killed and wounded were victims of their own parents, who, as he argued, used them as human shields in their own bedrooms and kitchens:

> It is virtually impossible to distinguish the Hezbollah dead from the truly civilian dead, just as it is virtually impossible to distinguish the Hezbollah living from the civilian living, especially in the south. The "civilian" death figures reported by Lebanese authorities include large

numbers of Hezbollah fighters, collaborators, facilitators and active supporters. They also include civilians who were warned to leave, but chose to remain, sometimes with their children, to serve as human shields. The deaths of these "civilians" are the responsibility of Hezbollah and the Lebanese government, which has done very little to protect its civilians.

Lebanon has chosen sides—not all Lebanese, but the democratically chosen Lebanese government. When a nation chooses sides in a war, especially when it chooses the side of terrorism, its civilians pay a price for that choice. This has been true of every war.

We must stop viewing Lebanon as a victim and begin to see it as a collaborator with terrorism. . . . People make choices and they bear the consequences of choosing to collaborate with terrorism. Lebanon has chosen the wrong side and its citizens are paying the price.[364]

Dershowitz also wrote:

Lebanon has now declared war on Israel and its citizens are bearing the consequences. Lebanon is no more a victim of Hezbollah than Austria was a victim of Nazism. In fact a higher percentage of Lebanese—more than 80%—say they support Hezbollah. The figures were nearly as high before the recent civilian deaths.

This is considerably higher than the number of Austrians who supported Hitler when the Nazis marched into Austria in 1938. Austria too claimed it was a victim, but no serious person today believes such self-serving historical revisionism. Austria was not "Hitler's first victim." It was Hitler's most sympathetic collaborator.

So too with Lebanon, whose president has praised Hezbollah, whose army is helping Hezbollah, and many of whose "civilians" are collaborating with Hezbollah.[365]

Dershowitz here is arguing something quite new in the 100-year-old body of international humanitarian law: he insinuates that people or populations can be classified as combatants not on the basis of their participation in hostilities, but rather because of how they might have voted, how they might have responded in a public opinion survey, or what they might be thinking during an armed conflict.

When, on August 23, 2006, Amnesty International issued a report that documented Israel's destruction of Lebanon's civilian infrastructure by aerial bombardment, Dershowitz called the report "biased," and wrote that Amnesty International was "in a race to the bottom" with Human Rights Watch to see "which group can demonize Israel with the most absurd legal arguments and most blatant factual misstatements." In a manner similar to his charge that Human Rights Watch had "cooked the books" in its August 3 report on Israel, Dershowitz described Amnesty International as a "once-reputable organization" and asserted that Amnesty was "sacrificing its own credibility" when it "misstates the law and omits relevant facts" in its reports on Israel.[366]

Dershowitz also argued that the Israeli targeting and bombing of Lebanon's civilian infrastructure was justified on military and legal grounds and that Amnesty had applied "its own idiosyncratic interpretation of the already vague word 'disproportionate' " when it assessed Israel's bombing of Lebanese infrastructure as a "war crime" under international humanitarian law. Dershowitz wrote—without citing any law himself—that "Amnesty is wrong about the law" when it accused Israel of war crimes and that "Israel committed no war crimes by attacking parts of the civilian infrastructure in Lebanon." Citing his "collaborators" principle, whereby Lebanon's civilians and infrastructure deserved the death and destruction it got from Israel in summer 2006, he wrote: "Israel was, in a very real sense, at war with Lebanon itself, and not simply with a renegade faction of militants."[367]

Like his attack on the August HRW report, Dershowitz's assault on Amnesty's report was apparently designed to discredit the report so that the press and public would disregard it. In fact, Amnesty's August 23 report, which is excerpted below, corroborated HRW's August 3 report in many key respects:

> During more than four weeks of ground and aerial bombardment of Lebanon by the Israeli armed forces, the country's infrastructure suffered destruction on a catastrophic scale. Israeli forces pounded buildings into the ground, reducing entire neighbourhoods to rubble and turning villages and towns into ghost towns, as their inhabitants fled the bombardments. Main roads, bridges and petrol stations were blown to bits. Entire families were killed in air strikes on their homes or in their vehicles while fleeing the aerial assaults on their villages. Scores lay buried beneath the rubble of their houses for weeks, as the Red Cross and other rescue workers were prevented from accessing

the areas by continuing Israeli strikes. The hundreds of thousands of Lebanese who fled the bombardment now face the danger of un-exploded munitions as they head home.

The Israeli Air Force launched more than 7,000 air attacks on about 7,000 targets in Lebanon between 12 July and 14 August, while the Navy conducted an additional 2,500 bombardments. The attacks, though widespread, particularly concentrated on certain areas. In addition to the human toll—an estimated 1,183 fatalities, about one third of whom have been children, 4,054 people injured and 970,000 Lebanese people displaced—the civilian infrastructure was severely damaged. The Lebanese government estimates that 31 "vital points" (such as airports, ports, water and sewage treatment plants, electrical facilities) have been completely or partially destroyed, as have around 80 bridges and 94 roads. More than 25 fuel stations and around 900 commercial enterprises were hit. The number of residential properties, offices and shops completely destroyed exceeds 30,000. Two government hospitals—in Bint Jbeil and in Meis al-Jebel—were completely destroyed in Israeli attacks and three others were seriously damaged.

One paragraph later, the Amnesty report continued:

Amnesty International delegates in south Lebanon reported that in village after village the pattern was similar: the streets, especially main streets, were scarred with artillery craters along their length. In some cases cluster bomb impacts were identified. Houses were singled out for precision-guided missile attack and were destroyed, totally or partially, as a result. Business premises such as supermarkets or food stores and auto service stations and petrol stations were targeted, often with precision-guided munitions and artillery that started fires and destroyed their contents. With the electricity cut off and food and other supplies not coming into the villages, the destruction of super-markets and petrol stations played a crucial role in forcing local residents to leave. The lack of fuel also stopped residents from getting water, as water pumps require electricity or fuel-fed generators.

Israeli government spokespeople have insisted that they were targeting Hizbullah positions and support facilities, and that damage to civilian infrastructure was incidental or resulted from Hizbullah using the civilian population as a "human shields". However, the pattern and scope of the attacks, as well as the number of civilian casualties and the amount of damage sustained, makes the justification ring hollow. The evidence strongly suggests that the extensive destruction of public works, power systems, civilian homes and industry was deliberate and an integral part of the military strategy, rather than "collateral damage".[368]

These excerpts and the excerpts from HRW's August 3 report do not indicate any "fog of war" confusion or imprecision on the part of Israeli warplanes and helicopters, which was how the *New York Times'* characterized Israel's attacks on Lebanese civilians.[369] The fact that such destruction was "deliberate," as Amnesty concluded, is without question, and Israel's highest political and military leaders at the time essentially confirmed this in their public statements. For example, on July 12, hours after Hezbollah had initiated rocket fire from southern Lebanon into northern Israel and had killed three Israeli soldiers and captured two others, *Ha'aretz* quoted IDF officials who "called for an end to the restraint against Hezbollah and said Lebanon should be made to pay a heavy price."[370] On July 12 *Ha'aretz* also reported that Prime Minister Olmert "held the Lebanese government responsible for the [Hezbollah] attack, vowing that the Israeli response 'will be restrained, but very, very, very painful.' " The same article reported that "senior Israel Defense Forces officers said Wednesday [July 12] that 'if the abducted soldiers are not returned we'll turn Lebanon's clock back 20 years.' "[371] As for those civilians in southern Lebanon who were killed by Israeli bombardment in their homes and while fleeing, Human Rights Watch reported that Haim Ramon, Israel's justice minister, said that Israel had given civilians ample time to leave southern Lebanon and that anyone remaining could be considered a supporter of Hezbollah. "All those now in south Lebanon are terrorists who are related in some ways to Hezbollah," Ramon said.[372] It is clear from these statements and others issued at the time that the intent of Israel's highest political and military leaders was to punish "Lebanon," that is, its people and infrastructure, in response to the Hezbollah raid on July 12.

Israel's use of cluster bombs also clearly demonstrated such intentions. On August 30, 2006, Stephen Goose, an experienced military analyst for Human Rights Watch, reported that "Israel used cluster munitions extensively in south Lebanon, with particularly heavy use in the final days prior to the cease-fire," and that "the density of cluster munition contamination in south Lebanon in the immediate post-conflict period appears to exceed that of Iraq, Afghanistan, or Kosovo at the same stage." Goose reported that "as of 29 August [2006], the U.N. Mine Action Coordination Center in South Lebanon had identified 390 individual cluster munition strike locations," and it appeared "that at a minimum tens of thousands of submunitions were used, and possibly hundreds of thousands."[373]

Goose's estimate was confirmed less than a month later when Reuters reported that "Israel scattered at least 350,000 unexploded cluster bomblets on south Lebanon in its war with Hezbollah, mostly when the conflict was all but over, leaving a deadly legacy for civilians, U.N. officials said on Tuesday." Reuters also reported:

> "The outrageous fact is that nearly all of these [Israeli cluster] munitions were fired in the last three to four days of the war," David Shearer, the United Nations humanitarian coordinator in Lebanon, told a news conference in Beirut. "Outrageous because by that stage the conflict had been largely resolved in the form of (U.N. Security Council) Resolution 1701," he said.
>
> The resolution adopted on August 11 halted 34 days of fighting three days later. A truce has largely held since then. Israel denies using cluster bombs illegally.
>
> Chris Clark, manager of the U.N. Mine Action Coordination Center of South Lebanon, said the cluster bomb threat in the south was "extensive and, in my opinion, unprecedented."
>
> While Israel has provided general information about where it believes unexploded ordnance might be, Clark said tactical maps given to the United Nations by Israeli forces withdrawing from the south were "absolutely useless" in clearance efforts.
>
> Only about 17,000 bomblets have been defused so far and the United Nations says clearance work could take up to 30 months. Shearer said cluster bombs had killed or wounded an average of three people a day since the war ended, with 15 killed, including a child, and 83 wounded, of whom 23 are children.
>
> Clearance efforts have so far focused on villages, schools and playing areas, but will soon shift toward farmland, which provides 70 percent of household incomes in the south [of Lebanon], he said. "The cluster munitions are stopping farmers from getting out to their fields and resuming their farming activities," he said.
>
> Cluster bombs have been found on the ground and hanging on

barbed-wire fences and trees, including in citrus, banana and olive groves, Clark said. They have also turned up in the rubble of destroyed buildings, complicating reconstruction efforts. Shearer said it "defied belief" that so many cluster bombs were fired in the last hours of the war.[374]

Neither Alan Dershowitz nor Abraham Foxman condemned Israel's use of cluster munitions in the waning days of the conflict when the cessation of hostilities was known to be imminent. This apparent indication of their own bias may be compared to yet another charge of bias from Dershowitz directed at the August 23 report by Amnesty International:

> The total number of innocent Muslim civilians killed by Israeli weapons during a month of ferocious defensive warfare was a fraction of the number of innocent Muslims killed by other Muslims during that same period in Iraq, Sudan, Afghanistan, Algeria, and other areas of Muslim-on-Muslim civil strife. Yet the deaths caused by Muslims received a fraction of the attention devoted to alleged Israeli "crimes." This lack of concern for Muslims by other Muslims—and the lack of focus by so-called human rights organizations on these deaths—is bigotry, pure and simple.[375]

The charge here is that Amnesty International and Human Rights Watch are guilty of "bigotry" since, according to Dershowitz, they focus their human rights monitoring disproportionately on Israel as compared to Muslim countries such as Sudan and Algeria. This means, presumably, that Amnesty International and Human Rights Watch publish disproportionately more reports critical of Israel than they do of the Muslim countries he identifies—but this is not the case. For example, with respect to Sudan, from September 29, 2000, to September 30, 2006, Amnesty International issued approximately 320 reports on Sudan, compared to 310 on Israel and its conduct in the Palestinian territories and in the 2006 Lebanon war.[376] These figures for both Sudan and Israel refer to reports that Amnesty International designates as "Urgent Actions," "News," and "Reports." Likewise, in the same period Human Rights Watch issued about 210 reports on Sudan and 180 on Israel.[377] Thus Dershowitz, once again, is simply wrong about his facts. In terms of other Muslim countries covered by Amnesty International and Human Rights

Watch, there is no evidence of Amnesty or HRW favoring these countries. While Amnesty International issued 310 reports on Israel from September 29, 2000, to September 30, 2006, it also issued 120 on Saudi Arabia, 169 on Egypt, 178 on Afghanistan, 199 on Pakistan, 291 on Iraq, and 381 on Iran—all Muslim countries. Likewise, while Human Rights Watch issued 180 reports on Israel within the period, it also issued 57 on Saudi Arabia, 86 on Pakistan, 119 on Iran, 137 on Egypt, 253 on Afghanistan, and 266 on Iraq. This means that for the six-year period, Amnesty International issued more reports on Sudan and Iran than it issued on Israel, and Human Rights Watch issued more reports on Sudan, Afghanistan, and Iraq than it issued on Israel.

There is another way to read these figures in the context of the charge from Dershowitz that Amnesty and HRW favor Muslim countries: For the period September 2000 to September 2006, Amnesty International issued about 1,338 reports—almost all of them highly critical—on the Muslim countries cited above, while issuing 310 on Israel. Likewise, for the same period, Human Rights Watch issued about 918 reports—also highly critical—on the same Muslim countries for the same period, compared to 180 on Israel. In summary, there is no evidence of a pro-Muslim, anti-Israel bias at either of these human rights organizations.

As Dershowitz had hoped when he advised news organizations to ignore the reports by Amnesty International and Human Rights Watch,[378] the *New York Times* editorial page, in its coverage of the Lebanon war from July 12, 2006, to August 31, 2006, never mentioned Human Rights Watch or Amnesty International, despite numerous press releases and reports issued by the two organizations. This is not to say that the *Times'* editorial page ignored these reports because Alan Dershowitz told it to—but it does demonstrate that there is little to separate the Liberal Hawks (the *Times*) from the Hawks (Dershowitz). Whereas Dershowitz berates the human rights organizations (with no factual or legal basis) for their reports critical of Israel, the *Times'* editorial page simply ignored the reports, which helped it (and other newspaper editorial pages which also ignored the reports) to receive a commendation for its coverage from the Anti-Defamation League.[379] However, if the ADL had applied a standard for US newspapers that approximated discernible facts and relevant law, as opposed to whether they supported Israel's military actions or not, the marks would not have been so good for the *Times'* editorial page, beginning with its first editorial on July 13, 2006, the day after Hezbollah's July 12 raid into northern Israel.

By roughly 9 a.m. in Israel on July 12, Hezbollah had killed three Israeli soldiers and captured two in its raid on northern Israel. The Hezbollah raid clearly was a provocative and deplorable incident; however, it was also clearly limited and did not threaten the state of Israel. It did not constitute an "armed attack" under international law and thus did not give Israel any legal justification to respond with a massive bombardment and invasion of Lebanon in "self-defense" without UN Security Council authorization. Nevertheless, later that same day (July 12) Israel retaliated with air strikes throughout Lebanon and a ground incursion into southern Lebanon. This response violated international law on at least four counts: (a) it violated Article 2(4) of the UN Charter—the cardinal rule of international law—which prohibits the threat and use of force by states without Security Council authorization (the only exception being a use of force in "self-defense" in response to an "armed attack," "when the necessity for action" is "instant, overwhelming, and leaving no choice of means, and no moment for delibera- tion),"[380] (b) Israel's military reprisals were illegal, given the broad prohibition of the use of force in international affairs, including as retaliation in response to an armed provocation, (c) the massively disproportionate scale of the Israeli reprisals, relative to the original Hezbollah provocation, violated international humanitarian law ("laws of war"), and (d) Israel's failure to distinguish between civilian and military targets in its air strikes and artillery fire also violated international humanitarian law.

Neither in its first editorial on the Lebanon conflict on July 13, nor in any of its several editorials on the conflict thereafter did the *Times'* editorial page ever mention the UN Charter, the international law prohibition against military reprisals, or international humanitarian law; it simply assumed the legality and legitimacy of the Israeli military reprisals. Nor did the *Times'* editorial page clarify—in an international law context or a simple factual one—that Israel's armed reprisals escalated the conflict well beyond the original Hezbollah raid on July 12.

News outlets throughout the day and into the night on July 12 had reported the following events, all preceding the first Hezbollah firing of rockets into Israel in the early morning hours of July 13:

- The "IDF responded to the [Hezbollah] attacks from Lebanon with heavy artillery and tank fire"; "IDF artillery was pounding the fringes of the [Lebanese] villages of Aita el-Shaab, Ramieh and Yaroun in the hills east of the coastal border port of Naqoura"; "Israeli Air Force jets struck roads, bridges and Hezbollah guerrilla positions in southern Lebanon"; "Two Lebanese civilians were killed and a Lebanese soldier was wounded in the IAF air strike on the coastal Qasmiyeh bridge in the south of [Lebanon]."[381]
- "Israeli warplanes and gunboats struck a Palestinian guerrilla base 10 miles south of Beirut late Wednesday [July 12], Lebanese security officials said, in the closest raid to the Lebanese capital since fighting erupted in southern Lebanon after guerrillas captured two Israeli soldiers"; This attack "comes after Israeli warplanes pounded more than 30 targets in southern Lebanon and Israeli leaders promised Lebanon a painful response for the capture of the soldiers."[382]
- "The Israeli Air Force on Wednesday night [July 12] struck at least 40 targets in different places across Lebanon, including bridges and infrastructures along the Litani and Wazzani rivers."[383]
- Referring to the Israeli bombing of Lebanon on the night of July 12, the Associated Press reported: "[Israeli] Air Force Gen. Amir Eshel said the [bombing] campaign was likely Israel's largest ever in Lebanon 'if you measure it in number of targets hit in one night, the complexity of the strikes.' "[384]

In response to these events Hezbollah fired its first barrage of rockets into Israel in the early morning hours of July 13, according to a *Ha'aretz* report: "The [Hezbollah] rocket fire began in the early morning hours of Thursday [July 13], after Israel Air Force jets struck targets across Lebanon following cross-border attacks by Hezbollah during which eight Israel Defense Forces were killed and two others abducted."[385]

Much of the information pertaining to Israel's illegal military reprisals was available by late afternoon New York time on July 12 and thus was available for the *New York Times* editorial page staff to consider as they planned the piece that was published on July 13. The information that Israel had responded to the Hezbollah raid with artillery and tank fire near Lebanese villages, and that its air force had struck roads and bridges and had killed at least two Lebanese civilians, was posted on the *Ha'aretz* website at 4:28 p.m. Israel time (mid-morning in New

York on July 12). The threats issued by Israeli political and military officials cited above were published on the *Ha'aretz* website at 3:33 p.m. and 4:28 p.m. Israel time on July 12 and thus were also available in New York on the morning of July 12. The Associated Press report cited above, which noted that "Israeli warplanes pounded more than 30 targets in southern Lebanon" in response to the Hezbollah raid, was also published at some point on July 12. Thus, despite information indicating Israel had responded to the Hezbollah raid with military reprisals that in fact were illegal and disproportionate on several counts, the *Times'* editorial page on July 13 condemned only the Hezbollah raid, describing it accurately as "horrible behavior," an "unacceptable provocation," and "aggression," while referring, in contrast, to Israel's reprisals as "justifiable":

> Kidnapping Israeli soldiers to use as bargaining chips for the release of Arab prisoners is horrible behavior for groups that claim international recognition and political legitimacy, as Hamas and Hezbollah do. The same applies to lobbing rockets over Israel's borders in the hope that they might kill unsuspecting civilians. In response to such unacceptable provocations, Israeli forces are now engaged in major military operations in Gaza, to the south, and in Lebanon, to the north.
>
> But even when acting justifiably in the face of aggression, Israel best serves its long-term security interests by acting wisely and proportionately. Its guiding principle must always be to focus military actions as narrowly as possible on those individuals, organizations and governments directly complicit in the attacks, while sparing the civilian populations that surround them.[386]

On the same day that this *Times* editorial was published (July 13), the Associated Press reported that during "two days of Israeli bombings" on July 12 and 13, "Israel has hit hundreds of targets in Lebanon" and "had killed 47 Lebanese and wounded 103."[387] Also on July 13, a press release from Amnesty International condemned the attacks against civilians by both Hezbollah and Israel as "a blatant breach of international humanitarian law and amount to war crimes." The director of Amnesty's Middle East Program stated: "Israel must put an immediate end to attacks against civilian infrastructure in Lebanon, which constitute collective punishment."[388] Thus, even as the *Times'* editorial page supported Israel's illegal military reprisals as "justifiable," including with a friendly admonition about "acting wisely and proportionately," Israel had already been charged by Amnesty International with committing "war crimes" in Lebanon by targeting Lebanese civilians and infrastructure.

In contrast to the *Times*, in its editorial for July 13 titled " 'No' to Lebanon War II," *Ha'aretz* advised Israel of "the need for restraint" and warned that "Israel's tremendous power can easily get totally out of control." While appropriately noting that "we cannot accept the scathing attack on Israeli sovereignty" by Hezbollah, it also reasoned as follows:

> The major blow Israel suffered yesterday, the circumstances of which will certainly demand explanations, is particularly harsh primarily because this did not come as a surprise. Hezbollah leader Hassan Nasrallah warned in April that he planned to get back Samir Kuntar, even by force. Israel has refused to release Kuntar, who murdered the Haran family from Nahariya in 1979, until it receives information about MIA Ron Arad. Freeing Kuntar along with the other Lebanese prisoners and captives may have prevented yesterday's kidnapping. It is also possible that if Israel had agreed to the principle of negotiations with the Hamas government, a deal would have been worked out for [Gilad] Shalit's release and for a cease-fire in the south.

While not justifying the Hezbollah raid, the *Ha'aretz* editorial nevertheless noted that Israel's inflexibility in dealing with Hamas and Hezbollah contributed to how they responded (the June 25 raid in southern Israel by Hamas and the July 12 raid in northern Israel by Hezbollah).

In addition, the *Times*' editorial of July 13, while highly critical of the July 12 Hezbollah raid that neither targeted nor killed Israeli civilians, neglected to mention the Israeli bombing of a house in Gaza on July 12—the very same day as the Hezbollah raid—that killed nine members of a Palestinian family in Gaza, including seven children, and wounded another thirty-seven Palestinians, three critically. While the Hezbollah raid was reported on the front page with a four-column headline, the *Times* reported the story of the massacred Palestinian family as a news item on page 14. In that report, the *Times*' Israel-based correspondent Steven Erlanger explained the Israeli attack on the Palestinian house:

> Israeli intelligence identified the correct target—a three-story concrete house on the northern edge of Gaza City where top Hamas

military men were holding a meeting. They included Muhammad Deif, chief of the military wing, sought by Israel for more than a decade, and Raed Saad, his top aide.

The Israeli Air Force hit the target accurately at 3 a.m., collapsing the back of the house into a concrete sandwich, while the front teetered backward, resting on the rubble behind.

But the top men of Hamas's secretive military wing, the most important of the groups that have held a captured Israeli soldier since June 25, escaped, apparently injured, even after another Israeli missile was fired on a car fleeing the scene.

Instead, the bombing killed 9 members of the Salmiyeh family, a father, mother and 7 of the couple's 10 children, ages 7 to 18, who were on the upper floors of the house.

It was another example of Israeli disregard for Palestinian life, in the views of neighbors and onlookers. From Israel's point of view, the meeting was a perfectly justified target and another example of Hamas's irresponsibility in putting civilian lives at risk.[389]

Thus, a distinguishing feature of the New York Times' coverage of the Israel-Palestine conflict—that the paper disproportionately and more prominently reports Palestinian violence against Israelis—also applied in their first day of coverage of the Lebanon war in summer 2006. Whereas the July 12 Hezbollah raid was reported prominently on the Times' front page, the July 12 Israeli bombing of a Palestinian home which killed nine members of a Palestinian family was reported on the bottom of page 14. Whereas the Times condemned the Hezbollah raid in an editorial published on July 13 and in subsequent editorials, the editorial page ignored the bombing of the Palestinian family on July 13. Whereas the Times' editorial page cited the Hezbollah raid as a justification for an Israeli military reprisal, it obviously did not and would not cite the Israeli bombing of the Palestinian family as a justification for a Palestinian military reprisal. Whereas the Times' news article on the Israeli bombing of the Palestinian home meticulously marched its readers through the details of a quasi-justification for the bombing, the Times' news article on the Hezbollah raid conducted no such march; Erlanger's report also omitted the fact that the Israeli assassination attempt of the Hamas official which also involved bombing a Palestinian family is prohibited as a targeted or extrajudicial assassination by international humanitarian law, including the Fourth Geneva Convention.[390]

★　　★　　★

After it voiced support in its July 13 editorial for the onset of Israel's airstrikes in Lebanon in response to the Hezbollah raid of July 12, the *New York Times* editorial page abstained throughout the thirty-four-day conflict from any criticism of Israel's conduct in Lebanon; this was over the course of more than a dozen editorials from July 13–August 31, 2006. After arguing in the July 13 editorial that Israel's military reprisals were "justifiable," the editorial page posited on July 15 that Israel's massively disproportionate and destructive reprisal airstrikes—referred to euphemistically by the *Times* as a "far-reaching military response"—were "legally and morally justified":

> With the circle of violence in the Middle East expanding alarmingly, it is important to be clear about not only who is responsible for the latest outbreak, but who stands to gain most from its continued escalation.
>
> Both questions have the same answer: Hamas and Hezbollah. And Israel needs to be careful that its far-reaching military responses, however legally and morally justified, do not end up advancing the political agenda that Hamas and Hezbollah hard-liners had in mind when they conceived and executed the kidnappings of Israeli soldiers that detonated the fighting.[391]

From this perspective, then, Hamas and Hezbollah were responsible not only for what they did with respect to their actions on June 25 and July 12, but also for what followed—that is, the unnecessary and illegal Israeli escalation of the conflict, the destruction of much of Lebanon's infrastructure, and the killing or wounding of 5,000 Lebanese, the vast majority civilians.

In its editorial on July 18 the *Times* noted, "International diplomacy finally started to stir yesterday in response to the havoc on both sides of the Israeli-Lebanon border," and the paper called on the United States and France to sponsor a UN Security Council resolution "so that the killing and human suffering can stop as soon as possible."[392] There was no criticism of Israel in the editorial.

The next day, July 19, in an editorial on the Group of Eight summit in St Petersburg, the editorial page commented: "On the Middle East, [the Group of Eight nations] uttered familiar platitudes and displayed familiar differences between Washington and Europe. What should have jolted them out of these familiar patterns was the alarming ability to start international conflicts that radical Islamist groups like Hezbollah and Hamas have now shown."[393] There was no criticism of Israel in this editorial either.

In its first paragraph on July 21, the *Times*' editorial page again called for "the fighting to stop" and for "the international community to step in." In a comment, however, that seemed to support the threats of Israel's leaders that it would punish Lebanon for the Hezbollah incursion on July 12, the *Times* explained that a cease-fire was called for because the goal (among others) of "prov[ing] to the Lebanese people the high cost of sheltering" Hezbollah was not attainable by air power alone:

> Israeli officials, with strong backing from Washington, are saying privately that it could take days or even weeks more of pounding to destroy Hezbollah's huge missile stocks, cut off its supply lines from Syria and Iran, and prove to the Lebanese people the high cost of sheltering the terrorist group. It's doubtful that air power will ever be able to achieve those goals, and Israel should not repeat the mistake of occupying Lebanon.[394]

The next editorial was the first in a series that cautiously counseled Israel to stop bombing Lebanon on the grounds that the bombing was bad—for Israel, not Lebanon. Thus, on July 25 the *Times*' editorial page noted:

> Nearly two weeks into the bloody conflict between Israel and Hezbollah, Secretary of State Condoleezza Rice finally made it to the region. . . . Ms. Rice needs to make it clear to Israel that more civilian deaths in Lebanon won't make Israelis safer.[395]

While still maintaining that Israel's bombing of Lebanon was "justified," the *Times*' editorial page argued that it nevertheless was harmful—to Israel, not Lebanon:

> There is a difference between justified and smart. Israel's airstrikes against Hezbollah targets are legitimate so long as Hezbollah wages war against Israel and operates outside the control of the Lebanese government. But the air campaign is now doing Israel more harm than good.[396]

Likewise, on August 1 the editorial page argued that the "mounting civilian casualty toll," which disfavored Lebanese civilians by a 25 to 1 ratio, had done significant damage—to Israel, not Lebanon:

> The mounting civilian casualty toll that would accompany an Israeli offensive of that length would multiply the huge propaganda gains that Hezbollah, Syria and Iran have already reaped and multiply the damage to Israel and the United States.[397]

In each of these instances, the *Times'* editorial page proffers tactical cautions—not criticisms—of Israel's military conduct, while continuing to maintain that the Israeli bombing campaign was justified.

At this point—by August 1, two days after Israel had bombed the house at Qana in southern Lebanon, killing at least 28 Lebanese civilians, with 13 additional civilians missing and unaccounted for—the *Times* editorial page still had no criticism of Israel's bombing campaign in Lebanon. Even with respect to the Qana incident itself, the editorial page remained many shades removed from outrage; using the words "too bad"—as in, "too bad" it happened—by way of mustering even a hint of disquiet over the incident:

> The 48-hour limited suspension of air raids that Washington pressed Israel into declaring was a modest step in the right direction, even though, as it became clear yesterday, it has far too many exceptions. Too bad that even this partial and temporary restraint came only after dozens of Lebanese civilians, many of them children, were killed by an Israeli air raid on the town of Qana.[398]

Following the formula it applied to the Bush administration's threats and use of force against Iraq in 2002–2003—when it supported an invasion on weapons of mass destruction (WMD) grounds, then opposed it just before the invasion, then supported it just after the invasion, then opposed it again—the *Times* likewise took a number of seemingly self-contradictory editorial positions on the Lebanon conflict in 2006. For example, after supporting at the outset Israel's military reprisals, arguing that they were "legally and morally justified," the *Times* ultimately supported the UN Security Council–sponsored cease-fire in Lebanon a month later, commenting at that point that the whole thing was "unnecessary" all along:

It took unconscionably long—almost a month—for the United Nations Security Council to produce a formula to end the fighting in Lebanon. While the diplomats dithered, hundreds of Lebanese and Israelis died, one-third of Lebanon's population was uprooted, and new layers of anger and fear were sown on both sides of the border. . . . This ugly, unnecessary war had many losers and no real winners.[399]

The stance taken in numerous *New York Times* editorials on the 2006 Lebanon war is a classic case study of how the *Times* positions its editorials on both sides of a controversial issue in order to hedge its bets by avoiding a principled position one way or the other. It is a long-standing editorial-page formula that is "balanced" to excess, as the residue of these editorials demonstrates: If the Lebanon war was "unnecessary," as the *Times'* editorial page says above, could it also have been "legally and morally justified," as the editorial page had claimed earlier? How can a thirty-four-day war be "unnecessary" at the end but not at the beginning? Can it be "legally and morally justified" in the beginning, but not at the end? If a war was unnecessary, was the killing "legally and morally justified"? If the *Times* supported a war in the beginning but opposed it in the end, did the *Times* support or oppose the war? If the *Times* supported the US wars in Vietnam and Iraq in the beginning (which it did), but opposed them in the end (which it did), did the *Times* support or oppose those wars? If the *Times* supported Israel's wars in Lebanon in 1982 and 2006 (which it did), but opposed them in the end (which it did), did the *Times* support or oppose those wars? Are there any principles guiding editorial policy at the *Times* when it comes to the United States and Israel? Even in the context of horrendous atrocities, as described in the two examples below, the robots at the *Times* do not flinch and thus do not deviate from the political positioning that is programmed into its editorials.

On July 17, 2006, six days into the Israeli bombing of Lebanon, Human Rights Watch issued a press release that urged the government of Israel to "provide details about a bombing on Saturday [March 15] that killed 16 people in a convoy of civilians fleeing a Lebanese village [Marwaheen] near Israel's border." The press release stated that "under international humanitarian law, all parties to an armed conflict must take all feasible precautions to protect civilians fleeing areas at risk." The HRW request for more details followed an official Israeli government statement about the incident: "Israel Air Force targeted an area near the city of Tyre, in southern Lebanon, used as launching grounds for missiles fired by Hezbollah terror organization at Israel. The IDF regrets civilian casualties while targeting the missile launching area."[400] In its coverage of the Israeli missile attacks on the residents fleeing the southern Lebanese village of Marwaheen, the *New York Times* apparently accepted the Israeli explanation of the incident and made no inquiries itself into the incident (unlike Human Rights Watch).

The *Times'* failure to investigate Israel's missile attack on the Lebanese civilians fleeing Marwaheen was not due to any lack of access to Israeli authorities. On July 16 the *Times* published a front-page photograph of victims from Marwaheen: the caption read, "At least 16 civilians were killed in what appeared to be an Israeli airstrike on a refugee convoy near a southern Lebanese village yesterday." It reported the incident in an accompanying news article:

> A Lebanese civilian convoy was hit near the coastal town of Tyre after fleeing the border village of Marwaheen, resulting in 16 deaths. The Israeli military said the area was a target because Hezbollah had used it to launch missiles, and regretted any civilian casualties. It was the deadliest single attack in the past four days of fighting.
>
> The villagers left after the Israeli military told them to evacuate over a loudspeaker, Reuters reported.[401]

In this article the *Times* quoted or paraphrased Israeli sources at least eighteen times. The day before, on July 15, in the paper's first mention of the incident, Israeli officials were cited eleven times.[402] In each instance, the *Times* reported the basic fact that a civilian convoy had been attacked by Israeli fire, killing many people, but the overall presentation featured mitigating and exculpatory statements, or statements about other matters, from Israeli officials.

Throughout its coverage of Israel's war in Lebanon, the *Times* disproportionately showed a preference for printing official Israeli statements over other sources. In a front-page article on the August 3 Human Rights Watch report—which focused in part on the July 15 Marwaheen massacre—the *Times* cited an HRW source only once, while citing Israeli sources five times as follows:

- "Israel said it believed the [Marwaheen] convoy was transporting rockets";
- "A spokesman for the Israeli Defense Forces in Jerusalem said that the Israeli military believed the convoy 'was transporting weaponry rockets' ";
- "The Israeli Defense Forces, in responses to questions about the incident submitted on Sunday, said 10 civilians had been killed in the attack [on the Marwaheen civilians]";
- "The Israeli Defense Forces spokesman also said the convoy [of Lebanese civilians] had not coordinated its movement with Israel";
- "Israel vigorously denies [that it targets civilians] and says that it has tried to avoid civilian deaths, but that Hezbollah tactics of working among the population make that hard."[403]

The problem here is that each of these statements, citing sources in the Israeli government, is either factually false or otherwise highly problematic. For example, while Israel claimed that ten civilians were killed in the Marwaheen incident, all other sources—including Human Rights Watch; the United Nations Interim Force in Lebanon (UNIFIL), which retrieved the bodies; a photojournalist who was at the scene in the immediate aftermath of the bombing;[404] and surviving witnesses[405]—reported a much higher number of civilians killed. By August 22 the *Times* reported that "the [Marwaheen] convoy was struck by missiles fired by an Israeli helicopter, killing 23 people, including 17 children."[406] While we do not fault the *Times* on its reports of the number of casualties in this instance, we note that the government of Israel inaccurately counted the number of people killed in the Marwaheen massacre and that the *Times* printed Israel's clearly unrealistic estimate of casualties (even though Israel provided no evidence to offset the higher estimate of casualties from virtually every other source).

Nor was there any basis for Israel's claim that the Marwaheen convoy was transporting "weaponry rockets"—no evidence of any rockets was found at the scene of the attack, nor did Israel ever produce any evidence that such weaponry was being transported by the Lebanese convoy. The "weaponry rockets" statements was apparently a refinement of Israel's earlier official statement about the incident: "Israel Air Force targeted an area near the city of Tyre, in southern Lebanon, used as launching grounds for missiles fired by Hezbollah terror organization at Israel. The IDF regrets civilian casualties while targeting the missile launching area."[407] When Human Rights Watch reported that the witnesses they interviewed "did not see any armed person among the bodies,"[408] the Israeli government apparently modified its explanation by charging that the convoy itself was transporting "weaponry rockets," which excluded any reference to Hezbollah fighters. However, no one at the scene of the massacre of the Marwaheen refugees, including the photojournalist interviewed by Human Rights Watch, UNIFIL personnel, or surviving witnesses, reported any evidence of weaponry transported by the convoy.[409]

Israel's claim that the convoy did not coordinate its movements with Israel, put forward as an additional explanation or justification for attacking the civilian convoy, is also disingenuous. Israel had warned the residents of Marwaheen to leave the village and thus would have expected that residents would be on local roads leaving the village. Furthermore, Israel had an obligation under international humanitarian law, as Human Rights Watch reported, to "take all feasible precautions to protect civilians fleeing areas at risk."[410] Instead, Israel literally blew to bits and incinerated twenty-three Lebanese civilians, including 17 children and several women, on the road from Marwaheen. By soliciting and printing numerous statements by the Israeli government about the incident—none of which were held to any factual or legal standards—the *Times* effectively muddled, if not misrepresented, the basic fact that Israel had massacred nearly two dozen Lebanese civilians from the village of Marwaheen.

By doing so, the *Times* muffled any outrage its readers might have felt in response to a more straightforward account of an Israeli Apache helicopter deliberately firing its missiles into a pickup truck loaded with children and women. It also printed official Israeli denials of wrongdoing without conducting even a preliminary investigation. In contrast, British journalist, Robert Fisk wrote two pieces on the Marwaheen massacre. His first report was published in the *Independent* on July 20.[411] For his second article, published several weeks after the incident, he visited and spoke with surviving witnesses of the attack and reported their accounts of what had happened.

> In her last conversation with her husband, Zahra told Mohamed that the four children were having breakfast in a neighbour's house in Um Mtut. "I told her to stay with these people," Mohamed recalls. "I said that if all the civilians were together, they would be protected. My

brother-in-law, Ali Kemal al-Abdullah, had a small pick-up and they could travel in this." First to leave Marwahin was a car driven by Ahmed Kassem who took his children with him and promised to telephone from Tyre if he reached the city safely. He called a couple of hours later to say the road was OK and that he had reached Tyre. "That's when Ali put his children and my children and his own grandchildren in the pick-up. There were 27 people, almost 20 of them children."

Ali Kemal drove north from Marwahin, away from the Israeli border, then west towards the sea. He must have seen the Israeli warship and the Israeli naval crew certainly saw Ali's pick-up. The Israelis had been firing at all vehicles on the roads of southern Lebanon for three days—they hit dozens of civilian cars as well as ambulances and never once explained their actions except to claim that they were shooting at "terrorists". At a corner of the road, where it descends to the sea, Ali Kemal suddenly realised his vehicle was overheating and he pulled to a halt. This was a dangerous place to break down. For seven minutes, he tried to restart the pick-up.

According to Mohamed's son Wissam, Ali—whose elderly mother Sabaha was sitting beside him in the front—turned to the children with the words: "Get out, all you children get out and the Israelis will realise we are civilians." The first two or three children had managed to climb out the back when the Israeli warship fired a shell that exploded in the cab of the pick-up, killing Ali and Sabaha instantly. "I had almost been able to jump from the vehicle—my mother had told me to jump before the ship hit us," Wissam says. "But the pressure of the explosion blew me out when I had only one leg over the railing and I was wounded. There was blood everywhere."

Within a few seconds, Wissam says, an Israeli Apache helicopter arrived over the vehicle, very low and hovering just above the children. "I saw Myrna still in the pick-up and she was crying and pleading for help. I went to get her and that's when the helicopter hit us. Its missile hit the back of the vehicle where all the children were and I couldn't hear anything because the blast had damaged my ears. Then the helicopter fired a rocket into the car behind the pick-up. But the pilot must have seen what he was doing. He could see we were mostly children. The pick-up didn't have a roof. All the children were crammed in the back and clearly visible."

Wissam talks slowly but without tears as he describes what happened next. "I lost sight of Myrna. I just couldn't see her any more for the dust flying around. Then the helicopter came back and started firing its guns at the children, at any of them who moved. I ran away behind a tel [a small hill] and lay there and pretended to be dead because I knew the pilot would kill me if I moved. Some of the children were in bits."

Wissam is correct about the mutilations. Hadi was burned to death in Zahra's arms. She died clutching his body to her. Two small girls—Fatmi and Zainab Ghanem—were blasted into such small body parts that they were buried together in the same grave after the war was over. Other children lay wounded by the initial shell burst and rocket explosions as the helicopter attacked them again. Only four survived, Wissam and his sister Marwa among them, hearing the sound of bullets as they "played dead" amid the corpses.[412]

The *Times* article on August 3 did not attempt to situate the Marwaheen massacre in the context of other nearly identical massacres of other such civilian convoys reported by Human Rights Watch in its August 3 report; these included an Israeli attack on July 23 on the Srour family which killed two adults and severely burned four children (ages fifteen, thirteen, eight, and eight months old) inside their car.[413] Despite such reports, the *Times* packaged its August 3 report about the Israeli attack on the Marwaheen convoy as the by-product of the "fog of war," as the headline reported, when the evidence in the Human Rights Watch report clearly indicated a more deliberate Israeli policy of targeting Lebanese civilians.

The *Times*' "fog of war" front-page headline was published a few days after Israel's attack on the three-story house in Qana on July 30, which killed at least 28 people. The *Times*' coverage of the Qana bombing consumed most of its front page on July 31, though somehow none of the headlines conveyed what had actually happened: "Israel Suspending Lebanon Air Raids After Dozens Die"; "Halt of 48 Hours"; "Rice Visit Is Cut Short—Casualties Include Many Children"; "From Carnage, A Concession"; "Concerned, U.S. Gains Quick Tactical Change"; "Night of Death and Terror for Lebanese Villagers"; "For the Residents, It Is Again a Day When the Children Died." The only indication in the headlines of what had actually happened was reported in the front-page photo caption: "Rescuers moved bodies out of an apartment building in Qana, Lebanon, that was hit by an Israeli missile yesterday. Dozens of people were killed."

Like the *Times*' article on the Marwaheen massacre, its report on the

Qana massacre reported numerous mitigating circumstances as alleged by Israeli officials. The second sentence of the lead front-page story reported that "the strike collapsed a residential apartment building, crushing Lebanese civilians who were sheltering themselves for the night in the basement," but not before beginning with "Israel said the Qana raid was aimed at Hezbollah fighters firing rockets into Israel from the area." Likewise, the very first sentence of the article reported that "one of its [Israel's] raids on the southern town of Qana left dozens of civilians, many of them children, dead on Sunday [July 30], the bloodiest day of the conflict so far," but not before reporting that "Israel agreed to suspend air attacks in southern Lebanon for 48 hours"[414] (which turned out to be untrue, since Israel did not suspend its air attacks in Lebanon).

A few sentences later, also on the front page, the *Times* reported: "One Israeli military official raised the possibility that the building collapsed hours after the strike and that munitions had been stored in the building." The reference to presumably Hezbollah "munitions in the building" not only functioned here as an alternative explanation for why the building was destroyed, it also served as a potential justification for the Israeli attack on the building. However, no evidence was ever found of any munitions or other weaponry in the building, as Human Rights Watch reported on July 30: "None of the bodies recovered so far have been militants, and rescue workers say they found no weapons in the building that was struck."[415] Furthermore, no subsequent reports have indicated evidence of munitions of any kind in the building.

The *Times'* front-page coverage of July 31 also reported that the Israeli government "said that residents had been warned to leave and should have already been gone."[416] This was reiterated inside the front section, where the *Times* reported:

> In a statement, the Israeli Army said it had warned residents of the region and of Qana "several days in advance" to leave their homes. "The responsibility for any civilian casualties rests with the Hezbollah who have turned the suburbs of Lebanon into a war by firing missiles from within civilian areas," the statement said.[417]

Recall that with respect to the Marwaheen massacre, Israel had faulted the refugees from Marwaheen whom it had killed for departing without communicating with them first. In this case, Israel blamed the residents of a house that it had bombed for remaining. Nor was there evidence of any Hezbollah presence or activity at the house before or during the bombing. In a preliminary investigation of the Qana bombing, Human Rights Watch reported that a resident of Qana and witness to the bombing "vigorously denied that any Hezbollah fighters were present in or around the home when the attack took place." The 61-year-old farmer told Human Rights Watch that "all four roads to Qana village had been cut by Israeli bombs . . . which would have made it difficult, if not impossible, for Hezbollah to move rocket launchers into the village."[418]

The *Times* also reported a statement by an Israeli general, who elaborated on the Israeli government statement that munitions inside the home, rather than any direct attack by an Israeli war plane, caused its destruction:

> The Israeli army said it was puzzled that the strike occurred between midnight and 1 a.m., and hit next to the building, but that the building collapsed around 7 a.m. Brig. Gen. Amir Eshel said it was at least possible that the explosion was caused by munitions stored inside the building.[419]

In its preliminary investigation, however, Human Rights Watch reported a description of the bombing by an eyewitness, Muhammad Mahmud Shalhub, the farmer identified above, who contradicted the Israeli government claim that an Israeli bomb may not have been responsible for destroying the house in question:

> Israeli planes began attacking the area in the early evening of July 29, he said, striking more than 50 times. He explained how, around 1 a.m. on July 30, an Israeli munition hit the ground floor of the home:
>> It felt like someone lifted the house. The ground floor of the house is 2.5 meters high. When the first strike hit, it hit below us and the whole house lifted, the rocket hit under the house. I was sitting by the door—it got very dusty and smoky—and we were all in shock. I was not injured and found myself [thrown] outside. There was a lot of screaming inside. When I tried to go back in, I couldn't see because of the smoke. I started pushing people out, whomever I could find.
>
> Ghazi 'Udaybi, another Qana villager who rushed to the house when it was hit at 1 a.m., gave an account consistent with Shalhub's. He and

others removed a number of people from the building after the first strike, he said, but they could remove no one else after the second strike hit five minutes later.[420]

Toward the end of its August 2 report on the Israeli bombing of the house in Qana, Human Rights Watch reported the following:

> The Israeli government initially claimed that the [Israeli] military targeted the house because Hezbollah fighters had fired rockets from the area. Human Rights Watch researchers who visited Qana on July 31, the day after the attack, did not find any destroyed military equipment in or near the home. Similarly, none of the dozens of international journalists, rescue workers and international observers who visited Qana on July 30 and 31 reported seeing any evidence of Hezbollah military presence in or around the home. Rescue workers recovered no bodies of apparent Hezbollah fighters from inside or near the building.
>
> The IDF subsequently changed its story, with one of Israel's top military correspondents reporting on August 1 that, "It now appears that the military had no information on rockets launched from the site of the building, or the presence of Hezbollah men at the time."[421]

This means that what the Israeli government told the *New York Times* and what the *Times* in turn reported on its front page on July 31—that "Israel said the Qana raid was aimed at Hezbollah fighters firing rockets into Israel from the area"—was false. As we noted earlier, this happens repeatedly in the *Times* with respect to statements from the Israeli government (just as it has happened repeatedly with respect to statements from the Bush administration about events in Iraq and Afghanistan). There is no evidence to date that the *Times* intends to apply any fact-checking standards or issue any corrections to such statements from Israeli officials. And just as the *Times'* editorial page never commented on the July 15 Israeli bombing of the Lebanese civilian convoy from Marwaheen, it also never mentioned the July 30 Israeli bombing of the house in Qana.

There was an additional problem in the *Times'* July 31 coverage of Qana. On the front page *Times* reporter Sabrina Tavernise wrote that the bombing of the home in Qana was "a fresh pain in a wound cut more than 10 years ago, when an Israeli attack here killed more than

100 civilians. Many of them were children, too."[422] In their *Times* report on the Qana bombing the same day, Steven Erlanger and Hassan M. Fattah wrote: "In Lebanon, Qana was already nearly synonymous with the killing of civilians. Ten years ago, in an eerily similar attack, Israel, responding to mortar fire, mistakenly shelled a United Nations post in Qana where refugees were sheltering, killing 100 people and wounding another 100."[423] However, the "eerie" aspect of these episodes lies not with the Israeli "mistakes" in bombing the same town; rather, it lies with the fact that Israel can callously bomb civilians in Qana twice in a ten-year interval without appropriate news coverage or editorial condemnation in the *Times*.

Robert Fisk, "by coincidence," in his words, was an eyewitness to Israel's bombing of the UN post in Qana on April 18, 1996. He was traveling at the time in a UN convoy "as it took rations to UN battalions under bombardment across southern Lebanon," and was "scarcely two miles from Qana" when "the first shells" on the UN post there were fired by Israel.[424] The claim in the *Times* that Israel had "mistakenly" shelled the UN post in Qana in 1996 ignores Fisk's investigative and eyewitness account of events on that day. In *Pity the Nation*, his book on Lebanon, Fisk, an expert on Lebanon and the Israeli invasion and occupation of Lebanon from 1982 to 2000, wrote: "Despite the tens of thousands of words written in newspapers and official reports in the aftermath of the [April 1996] Qana killings, this is the first book to give a full and detailed account of the 17 minutes of blood at Qana; indeed, it is the only account of the massacre from the survivors."[425]

Shortly after the Israeli shelling of the UN post at Qana had stopped, Fisk entered its grounds:

> They were the gates of hell. Blood poured through them, in streams, in torrents. I could smell it. It washed over our shoes and stuck to them like glue, a viscous mass that turned from crimson to brown to black. The tarmac of the UN compound was slippery with blood, with pieces of flesh and entrails. There were legs and arms, babies without heads, old men's heads without bodies, lying in the smouldering wreckage of a canteen. On the top of a burning tree hung two parts of a man's body. They were on fire. In front of me, on the steps of a barracks, a girl sat holding a man with grey hair, her arm round his shoulder, rocking the corpse back and forth in her arms. His eyes were staring at her. She was keening and weeping and crying, over and over, "My father, my father."

What in God's name had the Israelis done? Their shells had physically torn these Lebanese refugees apart, bursting in the air to cause amputation wounds, scything through arms and stomachs and legs. The corpses of Sabra and Chatila had been shot, knifed, eviscerated, disemboweled by Israel's Christian militia allies. But this was a butcher's shop. It was so terrible, so utterly beyond comprehension, that I simply could not believe what my eyes were seeing. And the men who fired these shells were Israeli soldiers.

There were heaps of blood-soaked blankets, many containing body parts; some of the Fijian UN soldiers were walking through this slaughterhouse with black plastic bin-liners, picking up here a finger, there a baby's arm. The blue smoke that cloaked us all smelled of charred meat. I kept thinking of Hieronymous Bosch's triptych of hell. A UN soldier stood amid a sea of bodies and, without saying a word, held aloft a decapitated child. "The Israelis have just told us they'll stop shelling the area," another Fijian soldier said. "Are we supposed to thank them?" Behind him, in the wreckage of the UN's battalion's conference room, a pile of corpses was burning. The roof had crashed in flames onto their bodies, cremating them before my eyes. When I walked towards them, I slipped on a human hand.[426]

The UN post in Qana had 600 refugees within its compound on April 18, 1996. More than 100 Lebanese civilians were killed in the Israeli shelling on that day; more than half of those killed were children. According to Fisk's account, Fijian soldiers assigned to the UN post had spotted "three bearded Hezbollah men firing mortars from the old cemetery 350 meters from the UN base" prior to the shelling of the post and "four more Hezbollah men" firing mortars "perhaps 600 meters from the UN compound." Yet, a short time afterward, for nearly twenty minutes Israel's shells were fired directly and continuously into the UN post.

Based on a UN film showing an Israeli surveillance drone flying over the UN camp during the bombardment, Fisk ultimately concluded that the Israeli shelling of the UN post at Qana was not a mistake. At the time the Israelis repeatedly denied to a UN investigator, Dutch Major-General Franklin van Kappen, that a drone was near the UN post. In his report van Kappen wrote: "In response to repeated questions, the Israeli interlocutors stated that there had been no Israeli aircraft, helicopters, or remotely piloted vehicles in the air over Qana before, during, or after the shelling."[427]

The admission or confirmed presence of the surveillance drone above the UN compound would appear to indicate that the Israelis had targeted the post, but the video of the drone was not released by the UN, reportedly due to US pressure to suppress it.[428] Instead, as Fisk wrote: "The Israelis blamed the Hezbollah for the slaughter, claimed that their artillery had fired into the [UN] camp owing to technical malfunctions while shooting at the source of the [Hezbollah] mortars."[429] However, a UN official eventually handed a copy of the film to Fisk, as he relates:

> At the mass funeral of the massacre victims at Qana, I stood on the roof of the shell-smashed base to watch the burials. Many of the young Fijian soldiers around me were weeping. Yes, one of them told me suddenly, he had seen the film. But he couldn't remember if it showed the "drone." In any event, he said, all the soldiers had been forbidden from talking about it. I was deeply depressed. Surely it must be possible to see this film. Surely someone must remember what was on it. Then two days later, I was sitting at home in Beirut when my mobile phone rang. A voice gave me a map reference and added: "1300 hours." I ran to the front room where I kept my files on southern Lebanon, tearing open the large-scale map of the region. The reference was to a crossroads near Qana. I have never driven so fast to southern Lebanon. And at 1300 hours, I saw in the rear-view mirror a UN jeep, pulling up behind me.
>
> A soldier in battledress and blue beret walked up to me, shook hands and said: "I copied the tape before the UN took it. The plane is there. I have made a personal decision. I have two young children, the same age as the ones I carried dead in my arms at Qana. This is for them." And from his battledress blouse he pulled a video-cassette and threw it on the passenger seat of my car. It was, I think in retrospect, the most dramatic individual personal act I have ever seen a soldier take.[430]

Fisk then reported what happened after that:

> I drove at speed back to Beirut and slammed the cassette into my recorder. Zooming into the smoke over Qana, the amateur camera-man caught the explosion of shells above the camp. From the distance the film was taken, it was still possible to make out the individual shellbursts. Norwegian troops can be seen close to the camera. Then

one of them looks into the sky and the camera pans up. There is a buzzing sound and into focus comes the "drone," trailing smoke from its engines, flying low over the [UN] base. As it moves, the sound of explosions can still be heard and a UN radio in the background can be heard. On it, [UN] Commander [Eamon] Smyth is passing on the message that "Fijibatt headquarters is under fire." The camera zooms again and there is the conference room, burning like a torch. So it was all true.

I made stills of the crucial pictures. The UN had no idea I had the film. Nor had the Israelis. But if *The Independent* printed all the details—with photos from the tape—then the UN would be forced to publish its report. There could be no denying these images. My paper did not hesitate. They splashed the story over three pages, leading the paper with the headline "Massacre film puts Israel in dock." I thanked whatever saints protect journalists that I had editors brave enough to publish this. At the same time, and at no profit, we arranged to distribute copies of the tape to every television station which requested it—British, American, French, Arab, and Israeli, all of whom showed the sequence of the "drone" over Qana during the shelling. The UN, mainly on the basis of the film—of which they had, of course, all along had a copy—concluded that the slaughter was unlikely to have been caused by an error, a gentle way of saying it was deliberate. The Israelis, confronted with the film by van Kappen, then changed their story. "In their eagerness to cooperate with the United Nations," they said, they had given wrong information to the major-general. There was indeed a "drone" over Qana, they said, but it was not photographing the camp. It was on "another mission." The Israelis did not say what this "other mission" was. They also said that the pilotless aircraft with its live-time television cameras only arrived after the shelling had ended—a claim the videotape clearly shows to be untrue.[431]

This account thus indicates that despite Fisk's book, the *Independent's* report on the 1996 Qana massacre, numerous other news reports at the time based on the UN film, and the UN's conclusion that the shelling of Qana was unlikely to have been caused by a technical error, in 2006 the *New York Times* nevertheless reported that Israel had "mistakenly" bombed the UN post in Qana in 1996.[432] Furthermore, just as the *Times*' editorial page did not condemn the Israeli bombing of the house in Qana in July 2006, it had no condemnation or comment at all in April 1996 about the Israeli shelling of the UN post in Qana.

On August 1, in the wake of Israel's bombing of the house in Qana, the *New York Times* published arguably the single most important fact in its coverage of the 2006 Lebanon conflict. In the last paragraphs of a front-page story about the Israeli airstrikes of the previous day, *Times* correspondents Craig S. Smith and Steven Erlanger, citing a July 31 column in the Israeli newspaper *Yediot Ahronot*, reported that Israeli Defense Minister Amir Peretz had "relieved the [Israeli] army of restrictions on harming civilian population [*sic*] that lives alongside Hezbollah operatives."[433] To our knowledge, this was the first and last word on the matter in the *Times*.

Indeed, on July 16 IsraelNN.com reported that "Defense Minister Amir Peretz said Sunday [July 16] that IDF troops have been given the go-ahead to set aside routine regulations not to harm civilians, according to Army Radio. Peretz said that civilians in south Lebanon who assist Hizbullah terrorists may also be targeted."[434] The day after Israel's July 30 attack on the house in Qana, as Smith and Erlanger noted in their report, the prominent Israeli columnist Nahum Barnea wrote the following in *Yediot Ahronot*:

> The most pressing question I have is: Did the government, the army, the political echelon and the media not take to blind cheerleading, a move that served only the enemy? The question came up when I heard Defense Minister Amir Peretz explain proudly that he had removed limits on the IDF regulating warfare in areas where civlians live alongside Hizbullah soldiers. I can understand accidentally hurting civilians while fighting a war. But explicit instructions about the civilian population in south Lebanon and the Shiite neighborhoods in Beirut is a rash, fool-hardy action that invited disaster.
>
> We saw the results of that policy yesterday, in the bodies of women and children being carried out of the rubble in Kana. We warned them ahead of time, says the IDF. We dropped leaflets telling them to leave. According to international law we covered ourselves. The generals may consider themselves "covered," either by their understanding of international law or the instructions they received from Defense Minister Peretz. But I, for one, am covered in shame. Anyone who has visited the north in the last couple of weeks can tell you what it's like for civilians during wartime. Those who can leave, do.

Those left behind are the weaker elements of society: the poor, the sick, the elderly, the children, the handicapped. No leaflet is going to make those who have nowhere to go leave their homes.[435]

A few days later, the *Forward* published an article about the instructions that Defense Minister Peretz had issued:

> As Jerusalem defends itself against worldwide condemnation over a deadly air strike that killed dozens of Lebanese children, current and former Israeli officials acknowledge that the Israeli military has loosened the restriction on targeting militants in populated areas.
>
> After an Israeli air force raid Sunday on the Lebanese village of Qana left dozens of civilians dead, many of them children, human rights groups accused Israel of committing a "war crime." Many critics— including Israeli ones—are questioning the military's policy of bombing in densely populated Lebanese areas. As of earlier this week, more than 550 civilians had been killed in Lebanon during the current conflict, with Lebanese officials claiming that the civilian death toll has exceeded 750.
>
> Following the Qana deaths, Israeli authors and intellectuals signed a petition calling for an immediate cease-fire and protesting the killing of civilians. The Association for Civil Rights in Israel called for an official commission of inquiry to investigate the military's bombing policies in Lebanon.[436]

These instructions by Israel's defense minister to disregard rules of international humanitarian law that protect civilians in armed conflict, in addition to the documentation of Israeli war crimes in Lebanon as reported by Human Rights Watch and Amnesty International, are clear indications that Israel in fact rejected and ignored such rules in its campaign in Lebanon. These facts are consistent with statements from Israel's highest political and military leaders that it would punish "Lebanon" for the Hezbollah raid on July 12. Such actions with respect to Lebanon are also consistent with Israel's long-standing rejection of international law as it applies to its own policies and conduct. Israel's disregard of international law is easy to point out:

- It has ignored numerous UN Security Council and General Assembly resolutions to end its occupation in the West Bank and Gaza.

- It has ignored numerous UN resolutions to the effect that its 1967 annexation of East Jerusalem is "null and void."
- It has also ignored numerous UN resolutions condemning its settlements in the West Bank and that urge Israel to withdraw the settlements.
- Israel ignores the prohibition against such settlements in the Fourth Geneva Convention.
- It rejects even the applicability of the Fourth Geneva Convention to its occupation of the Palestinian territories.
- Israel has engaged in "grave breaches" of the Fourth Geneva Convention in the occupied Palestinian territories, which include its excessive use of lethal force, including against hundreds of children.
- Israel's security forces, according to B'Tselem, follow no discernible rules of engagement with respect to their conduct in the West Bank and Gaza.
- Israel ignored the international law prohibition against military reprisals in summer 2006 with respect to both Gaza and Lebanon.
- It violated the UN Charter's prohibition against the use and threat of force without UN Security Council authorization, except in response to an "armed attack," when it threatened Lebanon with massive punishment and then invaded and bombed the country in summer 2006 in response to the Hezbollah raid on July 12.
- Israel not only made little effort in numerous instances to distinguish between combatants and civilians in Lebanon in summer 2006, it also bombed fleeing civilians and reportedly bombed 5,000 civilian homes, killed over 1,000 Lebanese civilians, and wounded many hundreds more, consistent with instructions from its defense minister to disregard legal restrictions on targeting militants and killing civilians.

Israel's total rejection of international law, as it applies to its own conduct, is clear. This basic fact is ignored by the *New York Times* in its coverage of the conflict.

8

Chomsky and Dershowitz

In November 2003, Ethan Bronner, at the time the assistant editorial-page editor of the *New York Times*, reviewed for the *Times* a newly published book by Alan Dershowitz titled *The Case for Israel*.[437] Bronner, the *Boston Globe's* Jerusalem-based correspondent throughout most of the 1990s (and currently the deputy foreign editor of the *Times*), is an expert on the Israel–Palestine conflict.

Given his professional immersion in the issue throughout the past fifteen years and the fact that he is apparently well read on the subject,[438] Bronner no doubt was up to speed on the conflict and related issues in late 2003 when he reviewed the book by Dershowitz. Despite these qualifications, he bypassed errors that were endemic throughout the book, while describing it as "an intelligent polemic" and writing that "Dershowitz is especially effective at pointing to the hypocrisy of many of Israel's critics." Continuing his praise for *The Case for Israel*, Bronner wrote:

> Dershowitz, one of the nation's most accomplished litigators and the author of numerous books on both law and the Jews, knows how to construct an argument. He helps himself here by choosing accusers and accusations that are extreme—Noam Chomsky, who claims that the United States and Israel are the prime sources of evil in today's world, is a favorite.

Bronner also advised "those seeking to rebut the most scurrilous charges against Israel" to read the book.[439]

Bronner's review of *The Case for Israel* is of note not only because his praise for the book does not hold up under scrutiny, but also because it functions as a case study of how the *Times* identifies experts (Dershowitz) and extremists (Chomsky) on the Israel–Palestine conflict. From the perspective of the *Times*' editorial policy, which rejects international law by omission as it applies to the United States and

Israel, it makes sense that Bronner would identify Dershowitz (who assails international humanitarian law and the human rights organizations who monitor compliance with it) as an expert and identify Chomsky (who has argued for decades that all states, including the United States and Israel, should abide by international law) as an extremist. From the perspective of the UN resolutions on the conflict, the applicable sources of international law, and numerous reports from the major human rights organizations, Chomsky's work on the Israel-Palestine conflict is within the mainstream of responsible and authoritative international opinion, and Dershowitz, the Felix Frankfurter Professor of Law at Harvard Law School, lies far outside that consensus.

While applying international law to the Israel-Palestine conflict marks even the most prominent commentators as "extremists" in the *New York Times*, so does an absence of "objectivity" in one's analysis of the conflict. In Bronner's review of *The Great War for Civilisation* (2005), Robert Fisk's splendid book on his career as a journalist covering the Middle East for *The Times* of London and the *Independent*, Bronner criticizes Fisk for supposedly writing without objectivity: "Mr. Fisk has become something of a caricature of himself, railing against Israel and the United States, dismissing the work of his colleagues as cowering and dishonest, and seeking to expose the West's self-satisfied hypocrisy nearly to the exclusion of the pursuit of straight journalism." Bronner also wrote:

> But Mr. Fisk seems to have decided that even striving for objectivity is silly. He approvingly quotes the left-wing Israeli journalist Amira Hass as saying that it is a misconception to imagine journalists can be objective. Journalism's job, she says, is "to monitor power and the centers of power."[440]

With respect to objectivity—a notion that is difficult to pin down in theory or identify in practice at the *Times*—the newspaper has issued no published text about editorial policy and "objectivity" which would permit an evaluation of its theory and practice. Thus we don't actually know to what Bronner refers when he argues that Fisk is not objective. It is evident, on the other hand, that "objectivity" is the Great Wall of China of the *New York Times*, which exists in part to mask the *Times'* institutional biases favoring US power and its sphere of influence (which includes Israel), and as a perch to take shots at those who don't practice the "straight" *Timesian* "objectivity," as in Bronner's criticism of Fisk.

Inadvertently showcasing his own bias, it is noteworthy that Bronner goes after Fisk for factual errors, but he does not do the same regarding Dershowitz.[441] In one pedantic rebuke of Fisk, Bronner wrote: "Mr. Fisk is most passionate and least informed about Israel. He calls Yisrael Harel—a founder of the Jewish settler movement who writes an opinion column—a journalist, as if his views were mainstream."[442] Harel was a co-founder in the early 1970s of Gush Emunim, an ultranationalist settler movement, and he is long-time chair of the Yesha Council, a governing body of the settler movement that succeeded Gush Emunim. He was also editor of *Nekuda*, a right-wing monthly journal of the Yesha Council, and is currently a columnist for *Ha'aretz*. Given Harel's background, is it too far off the mark, or even inaccurate (or relevant) whether Fisk identified Harel as a "journalist" or not? And why would Fisk's only reference to Yisrael Harel in a one-thousand-page book merit any mention in Bronner's review? In addition, the main idea attributed to Harel in Fisk's book—that "two nations cannot live on the small piece of land to the west of the Jordan"—seems to us a fairly mainstream view in Israel.

Continuing his criticism of Fisk, Bronner writes that "his many legitimate points are sometimes warped by his perspective." Bronner continues:

> A good example is a story Mr. Fisk tells of covering the United States invasion of Afghanistan. He was on the border, in Pakistan, when his car broke down and he was set upon by a group of Afghans, who struck his face repeatedly with large stones. Rescued at the last minute, Mr. Fisk says he asked: "Why record my few minutes of terror and self-disgust near the Afghan border, bleeding and crying like an animal, when thousands of innocent civilians were dying under American air strikes in Afghanistan, when the War for Civilisation was burning and maiming the people of Kandahar and other cities because 'good' must triumph over 'evil'?" And so he wrote of his attack in his newspaper: "If I was an Afghan refugee in Kila Abdulla, I would have done just what they did. I would have attacked Robert Fisk. Or any other Westerner I could find."[443]

Perhaps it is only a coincidence that Bronner extracted this specific passage from Fisk's book after it had been published in the *Independent* in December 2001[444] and shortly thereafter pilloried in the *Wall Street Journal* opinion page[445] and by the right-wing commentator Andrew Sullivan.[446] On his web site Sullivan wrote:

[Fisk's] account of his ordeal at the hands of an Afghan mob—a mob that apparently cried "Infidel!" as they attacked and tried to rob him— is a classic piece of leftist pathology. You have to read it to believe it. Even when people are trying to murder Fisk, he adamantly refuses to see them as morally culpable or even responsible. I've heard of self-hatred but this is ridiculous: "They started by shaking hands. We said, 'Salaam aleikum'—peace be upon you—then the first pebbles flew past my face." That sentence alone deserves to go down as one of the defining quotes of the idiotic left. If it weren't so tragic, it would be downright hilarious. Who needs Evelyn Waugh when you have this?[447]

Writing for the *Wall Street Journal,* Mark Steyn, a right-wing columnist for the *Daily Telegraph* (UK) wrote:

[Fisk's] car broke down just a stone's throw (as it turned out) from the Pakistani border and a crowd gathered. To the evident surprise of the man known to his readers as "the champion of the oppressed," the oppressed decided to take on the champ. They lunged for his wallet and began lobbing rocks. Yet even as the rubble bounced off his skull, Mr. Fisk was shrewd enough to look for the "root causes":

"Young men broke my glasses, began smashing stones into my face and head. I couldn't see for the blood pouring down my forehead and swamping my eyes. And even then, I understood. I couldn't blame them for what they were doing. In fact, if I were the Afghan refugees of Kila Abdullah, close to the Afghan-Pakistan border, I would have done just the same to Robert Fisk. Or any other Westerner I could find."

It's not their fault, he insisted, their "brutality is entirely the product of others"—i.e., George Bush, Tony Blair, Donald Rumsfeld, you. And in a flash, the gloom of recent weeks lifted and Mr. Fisk turned in the heady, exhilarating columnar equivalent of a Sally Field acceptance speech: you hate me, you really hate me![448]

Steyn satirizes the "root causes" of the attack on Fisk, but neglects to mention what they might have been. Omitted by Steyn, here is what Fisk actually wrote in the *Independent* about why the Afghans at the refugee camp might not have appreciated his appearance:

> Some of the Afghans in the little village had been there for years, others had arrived—desperate and angry and mourning their slaughtered loved ones—over the past two weeks. It was a bad place for a car to break down. A bad time, just before the Iftar, the end of the daily fast of Ramadan. But what happened to us was symbolic of the hatred and fury and hypocrisy of this filthy war, a growing band of destitute Afghan men, young and old, who saw foreigners—enemies—in their midst and tried to destroy at least one of them.
>
> Many of these Afghans, so we were to learn, were outraged by what they had seen on television of the Mazar-i-Sharif massacre, of the prisoners killed with their hands tied behind their backs. A villager later told one of our drivers that they had seen the videotape of CIA officers "Mike" and "Dave" threatening death to a kneeling prisoner at Mazar. They were uneducated—I doubt if many could read—but you don't have to have a schooling to respond to the death of loved ones under a B-52's bombs.[449]

In the course of their criticism, Steyn, Sullivan, and Bronner all omitted the fact that a US–UK massacre of Afghan prisoners had occurred in the area prior to Fisk's unscripted confrontation with his Afghan attackers. Fisk's report was published in the *Independent* on December 10, 2001. Earlier, the *New York Times* reported that "surrendered Taliban troops staged a revolt today at a prison where hundreds of them were being held under the control of the Northern Alliance, and American warplanes bombed the prison to help quell the uprising. . . . A United States Special Forces soldier at the scene told the BBC that hundreds of prisoners had died in the revolt."[450] On December 1, Agence France Presse (AFP) reported that the US and British governments had turned away demands by Amnesty International and the UN's High Commissioner for Human Rights for an investigation.[451] The *Guardian* also published a lengthy article on December 1 on what it described as a "massacre" at Mazar-i-Sharif.[452] These reports—as well as the statement by Fisk that many of the Afghans had seen reports of the Mazar-i-Sharif massacre on television prior to this confrontation—were ignored by Sullivan, Steyn, and Bronner.[453]

For the record, and in response to Sullivan's characterization of Fisk as a leftist punching bag, Fisk also described in the *Independent* how he punched some Afghans back in response to being attacked:

> I guess at this point I should thank Lebanon. For 25 years, I have covered Lebanon's wars and the Lebanese used to teach me, over and over again, how to stay alive; take a decision—any decision—but don't do nothing.
>
> So I wrenched the bag back from the hands of the young man who was holding it. He stepped back. Then I turned on the man on my right, the one holding the bloody stone in his hand [with which he had hit Fisk] and I bashed my fist into his mouth. I couldn't see very much—my eyes were not only short-sighted without my glasses but were misting over with a red haze—but I saw the man sort of cough and a tooth fall from his lip and then he fell back on the road. For a second the crowd stopped. Then I went for the other man, clutching my bag under my arm and banging my fist into his nose. He roared in anger and it suddenly turned all red. I missed another man with a punch, hit one more in the face, and ran.[454]

Sullivan and Steyn ignored these passages as well, as did Bronner, who signaled with this review that he sought affiliation with the right-wing pundits who had seized upon these same remarks a few years earlier. Bronner then closed his review of Fisk's book with this sentence:

> After reading that [that is, Fisk's encounter with the Afghans described above] and his description of Palestinian suicide bombings as inevitable, you are not surprised to learn that Osama bin Laden urged Americans last year to listen to his interviews with Mr. Fisk because, the mass-murdering founder of Al Qaeda noted, Mr. Fisk was "neutral."[455]

Whatever Bronner intended with these remarks, we did not recall reading, nor could we find, Fisk's use of the word "inevitable" as it applied to his view of Palestinian suicide bombing. We did find Fisk's other references to Palestinian terrorism, and there is nothing to indicate support or tolerance for it, if that is what Bronner intended to imply. After witnessing a Palestinian suicide bombing in West Jerusalem in August 2001 and its resulting human carnage and casualties (which he described in gruesome detail), Fisk wrote: "Many of the corpses are very small. More than half the dead are Israeli children. 'Unforgivable' is the word that comes to mind."[456] Thus, Bronner could have written that Fisk described Palestinian suicide bombings as "unforgivable," a word that Fisk actually used. A page later Fisk wrote about the same incident:

> By now, the Palestinian Authority reacts and its inevitably incompetent—and incomprehensible—spokesmen are trying to remind the world of Palestine's casualties, of a "warmongerer" [*sic*] called Sharon "who wanted only war, not peace." They are saying this at the wrong time, in the wrong place.[457]

Thus, Bronner could have written that Fisk described Palestinian justifications for its terrorism as "incomprehensible," even when at least some Palestinians attempted to justify the bombing as a response to Israeli violence.

The fact is that the British reporter Fisk and the Israeli reporter Hass do attempt to "monitor centers of power," which obviously offended Bronner's journalistic sensibilities. With respect to Hass, here is what Bronner apparently was offended by in Fisk's book:

> Whenever Amira Hass tries to explain her vocation as an Israeli journalist—as a journalist of any nationality—she recalls a seminal moment in her mother's life. Hannah Hass was being marched from a cattle train to the concentration camp of Bergen-Belsen on a summer's day in 1944. "She and the other women had been ten days in the train from Yugoslavia. They were sick and some were dying by the road. Then my mother saw these German women looking at the prisoners, just 'looking from the side.' It's as if I were there myself." Amira Hass stares at me through wire-framed glasses as she speaks, to see if I have understood the Jewish Holocaust in her life.[458]

This explains her "dread of being a bystander,"[459] as Hass wrote, with respect to the manner in which she writes for *Ha'aretz* from the Palestinian territories. Bronner, who works for a major US newspaper that has "looked from the side" as a "bystander" at the initiation of every illegal US foreign-policy disaster since at least Vietnam, is critical of Hass and Fisk for rejecting the "bystander" model of reporting and for writing critically about the brutality of the Israeli occupation.

★   ★   ★

It is also a constructive exercise, with respect to Bronner's objectivity, to compare his thumbs-down review of *The Great War for Civilisation* by Robert Fisk with his favorable review of another book, *The Missing Peace,* by Dennis Ross. In his lengthy telling of the final-status negotiations in mid- to late-2000, Ross described how the initial Israeli offer to the Palestinians at the July Camp David summit included a map of the West Bank that depicted brown areas for Palestinian sovereignty, orange areas for territory to be annexed to Israel, and red for "transitional areas." Ross wrote that by Day 5 of the summit the orange area on the Israeli map "amounted to close to 14 percent of the total of the West Bank outside of Jerusalem."[460]

By Day 6, Ross reported, Israel "had made big moves—on territory, the Israelis would seek 10.5 percent [annexation] of the [West Bank] territory for the [Israeli settlement] blocs," and, "on the eastern border, the Palestinians would have most of the border with Jordan; Israel would retain only a small segment."[461] By Day 7, the Israelis had withdrawn that offer, as Ross wrote: "Now, instead of 10.5 percent, the territory to be annexed was 11.3 percent."[462] By Day 8 Israeli Prime Minister Barak "had presented his bottom lines" and said "he would go to 9 percent annexation in the West Bank with a 1 percent swap opposite Gaza; the Palestinians would get 85 percent of the border with Jordan."[463]

With this information in mind, we can evaluate how the Palestinians responded to the US-backed Israeli approach to the negotiations at Camp David in July 2000, and how Clinton and Ross responded to the Palestinian response. Along these lines, here is how Ross described the scene on Day 5, pursuant to Israel's opening position in which they proposed an annexation of 13 to 14 percent of the West Bank:

> In response to an Israeli map that showed three different colors— brown for the Palestinian state, orange for the areas the Israelis would annex, and red for transitional areas—Abu Ala [chief Palestinian negotiator] was not prepared to discuss Israeli needs unless the Israelis first accepted the principle of the territorial swap and reduced the areas they sought to annex.
>
> The President at first tried to reason with Abu Ala, explaining that he could see "why this map is not acceptable to you. But you cannot say to them, not good enough, give me something more acceptable; that's not a negotiation. Why not say the orange area is too big, let's

talk about your needs and see how we can reduce the orange area and turn it into brown. If we focus on the security aspect and look at the Jordan Valley, we might discuss the security issues and see if we can reduce the orange area." Shlomo [Ben-Ami, Israel's foreign minister and top negotiator] agreed with that approach—thereby signaling that he was open to reducing the orange area, which amounted to close to 14 percent of the total of the West Bank outside of Jerusalem.

Abu Ala continued to resist. As he did, and as he repeated old arguments about the settlements being illegal and the Palestinians needing the 1967 lines, the President's face began to turn red.[464]

Ross failed to note, here and elsewhere in his book, that all of the territory mentioned in the passages above—brown, orange, and red—is Palestinian territory under UN resolutions (22 percent of historic Palestine, compared to Israel's settled claim to 78 percent), and that Israel was claiming an additional 13 to 14 percent of the Palestinian 22 percent, with no legal basis for doing so. Both Clinton and Ross, here and throughout, described the Palestinian territorial claims under the UN resolutions as unreasonable and demonstrating a lack of good faith on the Palestinian side. This was illustrated a few paragraphs later:

> Abu Ala said they did not want to present a map where they gave up their territory; if Israel wanted to justify modifications in the border, it needed to do so with a more reasonable map. I [Ross] could see now that the President was livid. So I stood up and suggested we take a break.
>
> But it was too late. The President had had enough, and he let it rip. He said this was an outrageous approach. He had risked a great deal in having this summit. He had been advised not to take this risk. He disregarded this advice because he felt it necessary to do all he could to reach an agreement. But this was an outrageous waste of his time and everyone else's time. He had offered a reasonable approach that did not compromise Palestinian interests. They lost nothing by trying it, and Abu Ala was simply not willing to negotiate. No one could accept what he was asking for. He would not be part of something not serious, and this wasn't serious, it was a mockery. Arafat had given his agreement to what the President was asking for and now he comes to the meeting and finds an outrageous approach—and he repeated, shouting now, "an outrageous approach."[465]

Then, as Ross reported, "the President stood up and stalked out." A week later President Clinton presented his final ideas to the Palestinians, reducing the orange areas on the Israeli map from 14 percent to 9 percent (with only a 1 percent reciprocal Israeli swap of territory), with little to no Palestinian sovereignty in East Jerusalem, as well as unspecified Israeli "control" of 15 percent of the West Bank's eastern border along the Jordan River. Arafat did in fact reject these parameters at Camp David in July 2000 as the basis of a comprehensive peace agreement with Israel, but he also continued to negotiate with the Israelis and Clinton.

Arafat was nearly uniformly criticized in the United States, including in the *New York Times* editorial page, for rejecting the US parameters that offered the Palestinians 91 percent of the West Bank, an unspecified 1 percent exchange of Israeli land near Gaza, very limited to no sovereignty in East Jerusalem, and Israeli control of the southern part of its eastern border with Jordan. For example, two days after the Camp David summit ended with no agreement, the *Times'* editorial page blamed Arafat for the failure:

> At Camp David, Israel was prepared to consider an American compromise plan that would have given Mr. Arafat a presidential office in the Old City of Jerusalem. It would also have joined some Arab areas of East Jerusalem to Arab suburbs now outside the city to form, in effect, a new, Palestinian-ruled city of Arab Jerusalem. A bridge would have linked these Palestinian-ruled areas to Muslim holy sites in the Old City, guaranteeing unimpeded access to these shrines.
>
> Mr. Arafat, regrettably, showed no interest in this proposal, holding out for full control of all areas of the city formerly under Jordanian rule. Talks on Jerusalem cannot usefully resume until Mr. Arafat shows a greater willingness to compromise.[466]

As it did throughout the Oslo process, the *Times'* editorial page neglected to mention that all of the West Bank belongs to the Palestinians under numerous UN resolutions, that the Israeli settlements are illegal under the Fourth Geneva Convention, and that the US-Israeli parameters in July 2000 did not reflect these stipulated Palestinian rights to territory that the US and Israel were proposing for annexation. Furthermore, the idea that the Palestinian leadership would agree to the terms described in the *Times'* editorial—a ratification of Israel's illegal annexation of East Jerusalem (except for an office for Arafat in the Old City) and a link from one or two autonomous Arab neighborhoods in East Jerusalem to a "new city of Jerusalem" (Abu Dis) that actually lies outside of Jerusalem—is ludicrous. It is also noteworthy that the *Times'* editorial page referred to East Jerusalem as "the city formerly under Jordanian rule," thus in effect dispossessing the Palestinians of their right under international law to self-determination in the illegally annexed city. Given the US emphasis on Israel's "needs" at Camp David over Palestinian rights and the US hostility to even a mention of Palestinian rights under international law, it is clear that Clinton and Ross did not engage the Israelis and Palestinians in an even-handed manner at Camp David. This was a point that the *Times'* editorial page obviously did not make.

Thomas Friedman, the expert on the Israel-Palestine conflict among the *Times'* regular opinion-page columnists, also criticized Arafat. Just as Dennis Ross referred to the "old arguments about the settlements being illegal,"[467] Friedman similarly referred to "repeated Palestinian mantras" with respect to Israel's illegal annexation of East Jerusalem and the legitimate Palestinian claim to the city:

> The reason the Americans were frustrated with Mr. Arafat was that he played rope-a-dope. He came with no compromise ideas of his own on Jerusalem. He simply absorbed Mr. Barak's proposals and repeated Palestinian mantras about recovering all of East Jerusalem.[468]

Friedman, however, conceded the inadequacy of Clinton's proposals to the Palestinians, arguing that "they didn't go far enough." With respect to East Jerusalem, Friedman wrote, "The Palestinians needed three things: First they must have not simply an administrative presence but a sovereign presence in East Jerusalem, over which they have full control and can fly their flag—even if it is just one square block."[469] With that, Friedman and the editorial-page writers demonstrated the range of views published on the *Times'* opinion page. Whereas the editorial page criticized Arafat for not compromising on an offer that provided no sovereignty in East Jerusalem, Friedman advocated a compromise that would give the Palestinians a square block of sovereignty.

Without informative references to the UN resolutions or the Fourth Geneva Convention in the *New York Times'* coverage of the Camp David summit, the paper's readers would have no way of knowing that the Israelis had no legal entitlement to East Jerusalem, to the West Bank, or to its settlements in the West Bank, nor would they have any reason to conclude that the summit failed due to the nonrecognition on the part of the Americans and the Israelis of Palestinian rights with respect to those issues.

Finally, even the final offer at Camp David from President Clinton to the Palestinians of 91 percent of the West Bank with a 1 percent swap represented an unfair offer to the Palestinians. And there is little evidence, beyond Ross's account,[470] that Israeli Prime Minister Ehud Barak ever significantly modified his original position at Camp David of an Israeli annexation of 13 to 14 percent of the West Bank.[471] Citing a Hebrew-language 2004 analysis of the Camp David summit written by Ron Pundak (director of the Peres Peace Center in Tel Aviv) and Shaul Arieli (a retired IDF officer), Noam Chomsky wrote: "In the most careful analysis by Israeli scholars, Ron Pundak and Shaul Arieli conclude that Barak's opening offer [at Camp David in July 2000] left Israel in control of 13 percent of the West Bank, and that a day before the end of the summit the Israeli side still held that position, though Barak's final offer reduced it to 12 percent."[472] In addition, Ross refers repeatedly to "Clinton's parameters" (not Barak's) while describing the final offer to the Palestinians at Camp David. About the map that Ross produced in the front of his book, which depicts a 9 percent Israeli annexation of the West Bank, he wrote, "This map illustrates the parameters of what President Clinton proposed and Arafat rejected."[473]

The evidence indicates further that while Barak showed no flexibility about recognizing a Palestinian right to 22 percent of historic Palestine (which includes 100 percent of the West Bank), Arafat recognized the reality of Israel's settled claim to 78 percent, which was a major Palestinian concession that went unappreciated by Clinton, Ross, and Barak—and the *New York Times*. This concession was noted in 2001, one year after the Camp David summit, by Abu Ala (Ahmed Qurei), the chief Palestinian negotiator at Camp David:

> We have agreed to settle for the borders of 1967. To us this means that we get to keep only 22% of the historic land of Palestine and you get to hold on to all the rest. We have recognized Israel and agreed to its demands for secure borders, security arrangements and cooperation and coordination in security matters. You did not consider this to be a concession on our part. You pocketed this incredible historical con-

cession and made more demands. You wanted massive settlement blocs that would have turned us into a state of cantons, with no access anywhere. This is a situation in which no one would agree to live. We agreed to border adjustments, subject to land swaps. You did not make any concessions, while we accepted border adjustments on both sides, subject to land swaps.[474]

Upon making this concession, the Palestinians, politically, had no others to make, except for minor border modifications to account for some of Israel's "needs" within the framework of an equitable one-to-one territorial swap, which the Palestinians proposed at Camp David, but which, again, Clinton, Ross, and Barak rejected.

Barak apparently revealed almost no willingness to compromise. Instead, as Pundak reports, upon presenting the Palestinians with a map "on the eve of the [Camp David] summit," which depicted a 13 percent annexation of the West Bank, the Israelis told the Palestinians: "This is the map you can get; you will be getting no other map, and the borders of 1967 are not an option."[475] There was in fact no other map forthcoming from the Israelis, a development that left no paper trail of what the Israelis had actually proposed at Camp David, and there is little evidence that Ehud Barak significantly modified this original proposal. Even if he did—and either generated or supported the final proposal at Camp David that Israel would annex 9 percent of the Palestinian West Bank while also offering Arafat no Palestinian sovereignty in East Jerusalem—there was obviously little likelihood that any responsible Palestinian leader could have accepted such an offer.

In *The Case for Israel*, Alan Dershowitz, like the *Times*, perpetuated the claim that Arafat and the Palestinians were responsible for the Camp David failure. With respect to the summit failure, Dershowitz wrote that "Israel has offered the Palestinians every reasonable opportunity to make peace, but the Palestinians have rejected every such offer, most recently at Camp David and Taba in 2000–2001."[476] To support this claim with respect to the 2000 negotiations, he wrote that "the dovish Israeli newspaper *Ha'aretz* editorialized the following after Barak made this offer."[477] Dershowitz then reproduced the excerpt from *Ha'aretz*:

The Palestinians could not ask for a better time to get the best possible peace treaty than right now. But they want more. . . . More than anything else, they want the right of return to be recognized and fulfilled. The Palestinian refugee problem was not caused by Israel; it was caused by Arab states, which have tried, time and again, to use brute force to wipe us off the map.[478] (Ellipses in original)

Dershowitz's footnote to this passage referred to *The Israel-Arab Reader*, edited by Walter Laqueur and Barry Rubin.[479] He identified the origins of this passage as a *Ha'aretz* editorial, but the passage in fact came from an opinion piece by the right-of-center Israeli commentator Yoel Marcus which was published in *Ha'aretz*. Another inaccuracy in this passage is Dershowitz's use of a four-dot ellipsis, which, according to standard usage, indicates that the deleted words span several sentences. In this case, however, the deleted portion amounted to only three words: "They want sovereignty." Because three words is not a lot of words, one can assume that Dershowitz must have deleted them because he did not want his readers to read them. Here is how the passage would have read without deletions (the Dershowitz-deleted words are in added italics):

> The Palestinians could not ask for a better time to get the best possible peace treaty than right now. But they want more. *They want sovereignty.* More than anything else, they want the right of return to be recognized and fulfilled.[480]

With the missing three words included, this passage seems to indicate that the Palestinians were not offered sovereignty in East Jerusalem, which is where the issue is most contentious. Dershowitz apparently did not want this information included in his argument that "Israel has offered the Palestinians every reasonable opportunity to make peace," which is presented elsewhere in *The Case for Israel*:

> I decided to write this book after closely following the Camp David–Taba peace negotiations of 2000–2001, then watching as so many people throughout the world turned viciously against Israel when the negotiations failed and the Palestinians turned once again to terrorism.[481]

> Virtually everyone who played any role in the Camp David–Taba peace process now places the entire blame for its failure on Arafat's decision to turn down Barak's offer. . . . He [Arafat] simply rejected it and ordered preparation for renewed terrorism.[482]

While repeatedly treating the final-status negotiations in 2000 as an undifferentiated process—referring only to "the Camp David–Taba" negotiations in his book—Dershowitz broadly claims that Arafat simply rejected the process and turned instead to terrorism. In his *Times* review of *The Case for Israel*, Ethan Bronner adopted the same position as Dershowitz, beginning with this passage:

> Fifteen years ago, the Israeli scholar Benny Morris coined the term "new historians" to describe a handful of young Israeli writers who were recasting the standard Zionist narrative. Rather than a David-and-Goliath tale of outnumbered idealists miraculously outlasting invading hordes, they said, the story of Israel's triumph was both more explicable and less heroic. Morris and his colleagues shifted the focus of historical inquiry away from the wonder of Jewish national rebirth to military and diplomatic maneuverings on the one hand and Palestinian suffering on the other. . . . They [the new historians] were adjusting their collective narrative to make room for coexistence with onetime enemies. This was a salutary process but it went unreciprocated.

Bronner then took up Dershowitz's analysis directly:

> Israel's new historians were viewed by Arab intellectuals not as an invitation to self-examination but as further evidence that Zionism was a crime. Worst of all, in 2000, when Israel offered Yasir Arafat more than 90 percent of the occupied West Bank and Gaza Strip for a Palestinian state, his rejection was accompanied by a terrorist war that shows no signs of stopping.[483]

Thus, rather than write that Dershowitz "is most passionate and least informed about Israel," as he did about Fisk, Bronner instead concurs with Dershowitz that Arafat initiated a new round of terrorism after Camp David. However, as previously noted, the first terrorist bombing inside Israel after September 29, 2000, did not occur until November 22, 2000; by November 2000, as numerous human rights organizations have shown, Israeli security personnel had killed more than 230 Palestinians, including 80 Palestinian children, and had injured more than 9,000 Palestinians. It is simply not factually accurate, as Dershowitz and Bronner claim, that the Palestinians initiated terrorist violence in the wake of the Camp David failure.

In fact, like the *Times*, Dershowitz barely mentions the human-rights organizations critical of Israel, including Amnesty International, Human Rights Watch, and B'Tselem. One exception was an Amnesty International press release issued in 2002, from which Dershowitz reproduced an excerpt to support his claim that there is no moral equivalence "between those [Palestinians] who deliberately target innocent children, women, and other civilians and those [Israelis] who inadvertently kill civilians in the process of trying to prevent further terrorist acts."[484] The full excerpt of the Amnesty press release is presented below, prefaced by a Dershowitz-paraphrased "accusation" of Israel and then followed by his response:

The Accusation.
There is a moral equivalence between those who *deliberately* target innocent children, women, the elderly, and other civilians and those who *inadvertently* kill civilians in the process of trying to prevent further terrorist attacks.

The Accusers
[Amnesty International]: "*Killing the Future: Children in the Line of Fire*, a new report issued today by Amnesty International, details the way in which Palestinian and Israeli children have been targeted in an unprecedented manner since the beginning of the current *intifada*.

" 'Children are increasingly bearing the brunt of this conflict. Both the Israeli Defense Force (IDF) and Palestinian armed groups show an utter disregard for the lives of children and other civilians,' Amnesty International said today.

'Respect for human life must be restored. Only a new mindset among Israelis and Palestinians can prevent the killing of more children.'

"The impunity enjoyed by members of the IDF and of Palestinian groups responsible for killing children has no doubt helped create a situation where the right to life of children and civilians on the other side has little or no value.

" 'Enough of unacceptable reasons and excuses. Both the Israeli government and the Palestinian Authority must act swiftly and firmly to investigate the killing of each and every child and ensure that all those responsible for such crimes are brought to justice,' the organization stated." (Amnesty International Press Release)

. . . .

The Reality.

[Dershowitz]: Every reasonable school of philosophy, theology, jurisprudence, and common sense distinguishes between deliberately targeting civilians and inadvertently killing civilians while targeting terrorists who hide among them.[485]

In Dershowitz's footnote, he cites the Amnesty International press release with a URL of the Australian branch of Amnesty International, where the release cannot be found; he also inaccurately dates it to 2003—it was issued in 2002. Upon locating the press release, it becomes apparent that Dershowitz omitted its first paragraph, which immediately preceded the portion excerpted in his book. The first paragraph of the Amnesty International press release reads as follows:

> More than 250 Palestinian and 72 Israeli children have been killed in Israel and the Occupied Territories in the past 23 months. When the UN Committee on the Rights of the Child meets to consider Israel's periodic report on Wednesday October 2, Amnesty International calls for a new mindset among the Israelis and Palestinians to prevent the killing of more children.[486]

Thus, Dershowitz omitted the fact, reported in the Amnesty press release, that Israel had killed more than 250 Palestinian children in twenty-three months, even as he argued that Israeli violence was unjustifiably being equated, on moral terms, to Palestinian violence.

Furthermore, while Dershowitz argued that Israeli security personnel "inadvertently" kill Palestinian civilians, the same Amnesty press release stated:

> The majority of Palestinian children have been killed in the Occupied Territories when members of the IDF responded to demonstrations and stone throwing incidents with unlawful and excessive use of lethal force. Eighty Palestinian children were killed by the IDF in the first three months of the *intifada* alone.

The Amnesty press release continued:

> Sami Fathi Abu Jazzar died on the eve of his 12th birthday after being shot in the head by a live bullet fired by Israeli soldiers into a crowd of mostly primary school children. The shooting took place in

the aftermath of a stone throwing demonstration. Six other children were injured by live fire in the same incident. Amnesty International delegates were present in the crowd at the time and concluded that the lives of the soldiers were not in danger.

In the past year Palestinian children have been killed when the IDF randomly opened fire, shelled or bombarded residential neighbourhoods at times when there was no exchange of fire and in circumstances in which the lives of the IDF soldiers were not at risk. Others were killed during Israeli state assassinations, when the IDF destroyed Palestinian houses without warning, and by flechette shells and booby traps used by the IDF in densely populated areas.

The large numbers of children killed and injured and the circumstances in which they were killed indicates that little or no care was taken by the IDF to avoid causing harm to children.

Dina Matar, two months old, and Ayman Matar, 18 months old, were among nine children killed on 22 July 2002 when the IDF dropped a one-ton bomb from an F-16 fighter jet on a densely populated area of Gaza City. The bomb killed 17 people. The aim of the attack was to assassinate a leading *Hamas* activist, who was among those killed. The following day Israel's Prime Minister Ariel Sharon called the attack "one of the most successful operations."

A number of Palestinian children have also died after being held up at IDF checkpoints, and delayed or even prevented from passing through to reach hospital. At least three children have been killed by Israeli settlers. In most cases the IDF does not intervene to protect Palestinians from Israeli settlers, who literally get away with murder.[487]

These passages can be read not only in the context of the claim by Dershowitz that Israeli soldiers "inadvertently" kill Palestinian civilians, but they should also be considered in the context of the claim by Ethan Bronner that Dershowitz "knows how to construct an argument" and that "Dershowitz is especially effective at pointing to the hypocrisy of many of Israel's critics."[488]

In his 2005 book *The Case for Peace*, Dershowitz noted that Norman Finkelstein, a Dershowitz critic,[489] had accused him (Dershowitz) of neglecting to mention human rights organizations in *The Case for Israel,* even as Dershowitz extolled Israel's human rights record throughout that book. He wrote:

Finkelstein claims that in *The Case for Israel* I "never once—I mean literally, not once—mention[ed] any mainstream human rights organization. Never a mention of Amnesty's findings, never a mention of Human Rights Watch's findings, never a mention of B'Tselem's findings . . . none." But a simple check of the index reveals that I repeatedly discuss—and criticize—the findings of these very organizations.[490]

Contrary to his claim, the index to *The Case for Israel* does not list Human Rights Watch. The index does list Amnesty International— once for the press release just discussed, a second time for a one-sentence reference, reproduced in its entirety as follows: "Amnesty International has declared such [Palestinian] terrorist acts to be 'crimes against humanity.' "[491] And the index lists Amnesty a third time for another one-sentence reference, reproduced as follows: "Even Amnesty International—an otherwise wonderful organization, which I support—has contributed to the false comparisons between Israel and outlaw nations that do not respect the rule of law."[492]

The index also lists B'Tselem twice. The first reference is to a B'Tselem report on Israel's targeted assassinations of suspected Palestinian terrorists, which Dershowitz excerpted as follows:

Assassinations have been part of Israel's security policy for many years. Israel is the only democratic country which regards such measures as a legitimate course of action. This policy is patently illegal, according to both Israeli and international law, a policy whose implementation involves a high risk of hurting bystanders and from which there is no turning back even if errors are uncovered after the fact. Israel must cease assassinating Palestinians immediately. (Yael Stein of the Israeli human rights organization B'Tselem)[493]

As Dershowitz indicated in his reply to Finkelstein, he reproduced passages such as this in order to disagree with them as follows: "Targeting the military leaders of an enemy during hostilities is perfectly proper under the laws of war, which is what Israel—as well as the United States and other democracies—has done."[494] Dershowitz cited no legal source to support his contention that the targeted assassinations of suspected Palestinian terrorists "is perfectly proper under the laws of war." In fact, there are only two footnotes for the entire chapter, titled "Is Targeted Assassination of Terrorist Leaders Unlawful?," in which these remarks appear. One footnote cites the B'Tselem report and the excerpt above; the other refers to an Associated Press report by Ibrahim Barzak dated May 31, 2003.[495] This reference included no title for the AP report, and we could not find it.

Dershowitz provides no actual legal argument to refute the contention by Yael Stein, a respected B'Tselem analyst, that Israel's targeted assassinations of suspected Palestinian terrorists violate Israeli law and international law; he also didn't use portions of the B'Tselem report that would have undermined his argument. For example, Stein enumerated several legal concerns—none of which were directly addressed by Dershowitz—including the fact that targeted assassinations violate Israel's Basic Law. Stein also argued that targeted assassinations violate the Universal Declaration of Human Rights and the International Covenant on Civil and Political Rights (which Dershowitz also did not mention). Regarding targeted assassinations and international law, Stein wrote:

In the case of Israel's assassination policy, the State [of Israel] deprives a human being of his or her life without legal sanction, the [Israeli] legal opinion that allegedly permits such a policy is not made public, the decision to take such action is made in the back rooms of the security services and the assassination is carried out with no judicial process. Such a policy constitutes an arbitrary violation of the right to life and a severe violation of international law.[496]

Stein then wrote: "The method Israel uses to carry out the assassination raises a few concerns which, in addition to the legal prohibition, are in themselves sufficient to render the policy illegal." He continued:

The application of the assassination policy carries with it a great risk of injuring persons other than the target. Errors may occur both when selecting the target and while carrying out the assassination.

The decision to assassinate a person is made in back rooms with no judicial process to examine the intelligence information on which it is based. The target of the assassination is not given a chance to present evidence in his defense or to refute the allegations against him. In such circumstances, there is a genuine danger that the information underlying the decision is unreliable or mistaken, with regard to the position held by the person and his actions, and regarding the danger posed. . . .

In addition, errors can occur in the course of carrying out the assassination. First, there is a great risk of harming bystanders. This risk is not hypothetical. Since November 9, 2000 [to January 2001, the date of the B'Tselem report], Israel has killed 15 people while carrying out assassinations, six of whom were not targets. . . . Second, those who carry out the assassination may err in the identification of the victim. Undercover units have killed the wrong person more than once.[497]

Dershowitz cited this B'Tselem report purportedly to specifically refute it, but in a chapter supposedly devoted to the legal status of targeted assassinations, he did not respond to Stein's detailed legal analysis in any substantive manner.

The second and final reference to B'Tselem in *The Case for Israel* is to a single mention of the organization, along with Peace Now, Amos Oz, and Yossi Beilin, "who tend to be quite critical of current Israeli policies" and "are misused outside of Israel by those who would delegitimize and destroy the Jewish state."[498] That is the extent of Dershowitz's references to B'Tselem.

Having reviewed the entirety of Dershowitz's use of the three major human rights organizations as listed in the index to *The Case for Israel*, we can now evaluate his claim that "a simple check of the index [of *The Case for Israel*] reveals that I [Dershowitz] repeatedly discuss— and criticize—the findings of these very organizations." In reality, the index barely mentions them, and much of his analysis about what the organizations report is misleading.

Upon further examination of Ethan Bronner's favorable review in the *Times* of *The Case for Israel*, and his comments that Dershowitz "knows how to construct an argument" and "helps himself by choosing accusers and accusations that are extreme" (Noam Chomsky, in this instance), we must also consider what appears to mark Chomsky as an extremist in Bronner's eyes and in the context of the *New York Times*' coverage of the Israel-Palestine conflict. In this case, it appears to be Chomsky's historically persistent focus on UN resolutions, the Fourth Geneva Convention, international law, and Palestinian rights—not to the exclusion of Israel's rights, but to the inclusion of Palestinian rights.

In Chomsky's most extensive treatment of the conflict, *The Fateful Triangle: The United States, Israel, and the Palestinians* (first published in

1983), he stipulated at the outset a set of "principles" that guided his analysis.

> The first of these is the principle that Israeli Jews and Palestinian Arabs are human beings with human rights, equal rights; more specifically, they have essentially equal rights within the territory of the former Palestine. Each group has a valid right to national self-determination in this territory. Furthermore, I will assume that the State of Israel within its pre-1967 borders had, and retains, whatever one regards as the valid rights of any state within the existing international system.[499]

Given its recognition of Palestinian rights, this is, in fact, an "extreme" statement in the United States. Chomsky's analysis of the conflict in numerous books and other publications is grounded in international law; for the most part, Dershowitz ignores international law, except to denigrate its constraints on Israel's excessive use of force in the occupied territories, its resort to force in the region (most recently in Lebanon in summer 2006) and to discredit the world's most important human rights organizations with false charges. Chomsky recognizes Israel's pre-1967 borders, which are settled borders under numerous UN resolutions and provide Israel with 78 percent of mandatory Palestine and the Palestinians with just 22 percent—this is apparently an "extreme" position, given the fact that neither Dershowitz, the ADL, the United States nor the *New York Times* recognize the Palestinians' 22 percent. Chomsky rejects the legality and legitimacy of Israel's settlements in occupied Palestinian territory in recognition of the Fourth Geneva Convention's prohibition of such settlements and their condemnation in numerous UN resolutions. Dershowitz, the ADL, and the *Times'* editorial page support Israel's settlements in principle, implicitly or explicitly rejecting the applicability of the Fourth Geneva Convention to the Israeli occupation of Palestinian territories. Chomsky does not recognize Israel's annexation of East Jerusalem, which has been declared "null and void" by UN resolutions; Dershowitz, the ADL, and the *Times'* editorial page support, in principle, the annexation of East Jerusalem. Chomsky's analysis of the conflict is informed by the consensus rules and principles as established under UN resolutions and numerous sources of international law; Dershowitz recognizes no such rules and principles as they apply to Israel, and much of his analytical energy is focused on tearing them down. One can thus understand why, for Bronner, Chomsky is the "extremist," rather than Dershowitz.

Bronner's claim that Dershowitz "is especially effective at pointing to the hypocrisy of many of Israel's critics" is also a problem. Dershowitz noted, for example, that it is "misleading" to argue that more Palestinians have been killed than Israelis in the conflict, because "Palestinians count the suicide bombers themselves as victims and ignore the large number of foiled and prevented terrorist attacks against Israelis."[500] However, commentators who assert that more Palestinians have been killed do not cite "Palestinians" as their source; rather, they typically cite the major human rights organizations, including Amnesty International, Human Rights Watch, and B'Tselem. In his chapter, "Why Have More Palestinians Than Israelis Been Killed?," Dershowitz argues that "the Palestinians have willfully tried to kill many more Israelis than they have succeeded in doing, whereas the deaths attributable to Israel have mostly been caused accidentally in a legitimate effort to try to stop terrorism."[501] While no human rights organization has calculated "attempted killings," it is almost certainly the case that the Palestinians have tried to kill more Israelis than they have succeeded in doing. However, the same must also be true on the Israeli side. In his recent book on Dershowitz, Norman Finkelstein, in response to this point, wrote:

> The 3:1 ratio of Palestinians to Israelis killed during the second intifada "[i]gnored," according to Dershowitz, that "Palestinian terrorists had *attempted* to kill thousands more" in attacks thwarted by Israeli authorities. Yet "in the first few days of the intifada," the Israeli newspaper *Maariv* reported, citing Israeli intelligence, "the IDF fired about 700,000 bullets and other projectiles in Judea and Samaria [the West Bank] and about 300,000 in Gaza. All told, about a million bullets and other projectiles were used"—or as one Israeli officer quipped, "a bullet for every child." Should these spent shells also be tabulated as the Israeli army's attempts to kill one million Palestinian children in the first days of the intifada?[502]

Furthermore, Dershowitz incorrectly argued that Arafat ended the promising January 2001 Taba negotiations, which built on President Clinton's "final ideas" presented at the White House in December 2000. Dershowitz argued this point as follows: "Virtually everyone who played any role in the Camp David–Taba peace process now places the entire blame for its failure on Arafat's decision to turn down Barak's offer."[503] As previously noted, this statement is virtually meaningless because it neither identifies a given point in the process nor mentions a specific Israeli offer. Dershowitz continued:

> In a remarkable series of interviews conducted by Elsa Walsh for *The New Yorker*, Prince Bandar of Saudi Arabia has publicly disclosed his behind-the-scenes role in the peace process and what he told Arafat. Bandar's disclosures go well beyond anything previously revealed by an inside source to the negotiations and provide the best available evidence of how Arafat plays the terrorism card to shift public opinion not only in the Arab and Muslim worlds but in the world at large.[504]

Dershowitz then wrote:

> Bandar, who has been a Saudi diplomat in Washington for twenty years and is a high-ranking member of the [Saudi] royal family, served as a crucial intermediary between Arafat and the Clinton administration. He, like nearly everyone else, was surprised at Barak's "remarkable" offer that gave the Palestinian state "about 97% of the occupied territories," the Old City of Jerusalem other than the Jewish and Armenian Quarters, and $30 billion in compensation for the refugees. . . .
> On January 2, 2001—just weeks before the end of Clinton's term—Bandar picked Arafat up at Andrews Air Force Base, went over the Barak proposal, and asked Arafat whether he could ever get "a better deal. . . ."
> Despite Arafat's promises that he would take the deal if Saudi Arabia and Egypt gave him cover, and despite Egyptian and Saudi assurances and Bandar's threats, Arafat rejected the deal and flew home without offering any counterproposals or amendments. As the negotiations faltered, Arafat ordered his terrorist leaders to ratchet up the violence.[505]

Let us examine these passages one deception at a time: Bandar, described by Dershowitz as "an inside source to the negotiations," was not present at any of the final-status negotiations, including those pending at Taba. Thus, the claim by Dershowitz that Bandar enjoyed "insider" status with respect to negotiations is overblown. The insider account that most commentators and scholars cite is not Bandar's in the *New Yorker*, but rather that of Miguel Moratinos, the European Union Special Representative to the Middle East; Moratinos was at the Taba negotiations and wrote an authoritative summary of the negotiations shortly afterward. Dershowitz does not mention Moratinos in *The Case for Israel*, nor does he acknowledge Moratinos's document, first published by Israeli journalist Akiva Eldar in *Ha'aretz* in February 2002.[506] In contrast to Dershowitz's claim that Arafat "rejected the deal" at Taba, Eldar wrote that Yossi Beilin, a leading Israeli political figure who was at Taba, "stressed that the Taba talks were not halted because they hit a crisis, but rather because of the Israeli election" and that "the two sides were discussing arranging a Barak–Arafat meeting in an effort to close the gaps."[507] But that meeting never happened, as Beilin noted:

> The talks at Taba were stopped on Saturday night, January 27 [2001], because Shlomo Ben-Ami and Abu Ala agreed that it would be difficult to reach further breakthroughs at that juncture. It was resolved that the talks would continue in a more limited framework over the next two days, ahead of a possible summit meeting between Barak and Arafat in Sweden on the thirtieth. . . . But a series of events prevented the summit.[508]

With respect to those events, Beilin wrote: "And then on Sunday [January 28], Shimon Peres and Yasser Arafat appeared before a large audience at Davos [Switzerland], and after Peres's speech, Arafat issued a poisonous attack on the Israeli government. He accused Israel of using non-conventional weapons and deliberate economic suffocation, in language reminiscent of the pre-Oslo Arafat."[509] According to Beilin, due to Arafat's speech "the irreversible impression had been created that Arafat was not prepared for a reconciliatory summit meeting." Beilin wrote that "Barak was stunned by [Arafat's] speech and the tone with which it was presented" and that "Arafat attempted to correct himself, and expressed his desire to reach an agreement, but this could not soften the harsh impression he had made." Barak "said that he would not meet with Arafat in light of the Davos speech, but later decided not to close the door on the summit." After no summit invitation had been issued by the Swedish government, and after three Israeli settlers were killed in the West Bank by Palestinians around that time, "Barak announced that there would be no summit meeting with

Arafat."[510] Thus, Barak—not Arafat—cancelled the summit and terminated the peace negotiations.

A major argument in *The Case for Israel*—which Bronner apparently viewed as less problematic than Robert Fisk identifying Yisrael Harel as a journalist—is Dershowitz's claim that Israel occupies a supralegal and supramoral status relative to the Palestinians. In this context, Dershowitz argues that the two sides in the conflict should not be dealt with in an evenhanded way.

> If even-handedness is ever to be achieved within the entire interna-
> tional community, it will only happen if the United States does not
> seek to emulate European conceptions of even-handedness. If the
> United States were ever to become as even-handed as the international
> community has been, it would surely encourage continuing aggression
> against the Jewish state. It would also be morally wrong. Even-
> handedness toward those whose actions are not morally equivalent
> is an immoral and dangerous form of artificial symmetry.[511]

Consistent with his notion that "evenhandedness" in the Israel-Palestine conflict should be abandoned as a matter of principle, in his writings Dershowitz apparently follows his own advice. While the *New York Times* would never be as unambiguous about its own biases as Dershowitz is, it clearly incorporates a rejection of "evenhanded-ness" in its coverage of the conflict. We have already argued this case by noting that the *Times* mostly ignores the major incriminating facts against Israel as reported by the human rights organizations, and it also ignores the UN resolutions and key sources of international law that apply to the conflict. Keep in mind that Dershowitz's rejection of an evenhanded approach to the conflict clashes with Chomsky's "first" principles "that Israeli Jews and Palestinian Arabs are human beings with human rights, equal rights, more specifically, they have essen-tially equal rights within the territory of the former Palestine," and that "each group has a valid right to national self-determination in this territory."[512] This marks Chomsky's "extremism," as Bronner ident-ified it, while sympathetically reviewing a book by Dershowitz that openly rejected an evenhanded approach in Israel's favor.

It also marks, so to speak, two roads in a wood: Chomsky or Dershowitz. International humanitarian law or war crimes? UN resolutions or the illegal annexation of East Jerusalem? The Fourth

Geneva Convention or the illegal settlements? Equal rights or uneven rights? Two states with UN–recognized borders or endless conflict and killing? Bronner's choice is clear: Chomsky is the extremist for supporting international law and an evenhanded application of relevant laws and rights to mediating the conflict, while Dershowitz rejects evenhandedness and constructs "good arguments" on behalf of Israel's illegal policies and conduct. The *Times* itself, like Dershowitz, has rejected an evenhanded and impartial approach to the conflict, including as exemplified by its editorials on Israel's military campaign in Gaza in 2006.

9

Gaza, 2006

As pointed out earlier, the Palestinian raid into Israel on June 25, 2006, which involved Hamas militants, was conducted after numerous atrocities were committed by Israel in Gaza leading up to that point. Few if any of those Israeli attacks, until June 2006, prompted a military response by Hamas, which had been adhering to a cease-fire for sixteen months. Thus, after the Palestinian raid, the *Times'* editorial page would have had far more justification to headline an editorial "Israel Provokes a Fight" than it did for its actual headline, "Hamas Provokes a Fight,"[513] written on June 29 after the Israelis responded to the June 25 raid with a major assault on Gaza. That assault included the Israeli bombing of power plants in Gaza, destruction of bridges,[514] bomb and missile attacks on towns and villages,[515] in addition to the kidnapping of numerous cabinet officials and Hamas members of the Palestinian parliament.[516]

As Israel escalated its response, sustaining its siege and brutal shelling and bombing of Gaza for the next several months, the *Times'* editorial page, in an extraordinary series of un-evenhanded editorials, simply blamed the Palestinians. Like its refusal to criticize the Israeli bombing of Lebanon in summer 2006, the *Times* editorial page also refused to criticize Israel's military campaign in Gaza. Reviewed below are each of the *Times'* editorials on Israel's conduct in Gaza published from the time of the capture of soldier Gilad Shalit (June 25, 2006) up to mid-November 2006, as well as events reported in the intervals between editorials that permit informed evaluation.

Pursuant to the *Times'* June 29 editorial, "Hamas Provokes a Fight," B'Tselem reported on July 3 the following activity of the Israeli Air Force:

> During its operation in the Gaza Strip following the abduction of Cpl. Gilad Shalit, Israeli air force jets have carried out low-altitude sorties over the Gaza Strip in which they intentionally cause powerful

sonic booms. The air force has used sonic booms a number of times since the completion of the Gaza disengagement plan. In the present operation, the air force has caused three or four sonic-boom sorties a night.

The sole purpose of these sorties is to prevent the residents from sleeping and to create an ongoing sense of fear and anxiety. Regarding the sonic booms, Prime Minister Ehud Olmert said that "thousands of residents in southern Israel live in fear and discomfort, so I gave instructions that nobody will sleep at night in the meantime in Gaza." The clear intention of the practice is to pressure the Palestinian Authority and the armed Palestinian organizations by harming the entire civilian population.

Children, in particular, suffer from the sonic booms. In the past, the Gaza Community Mental Health Center reported that the supersonic sorties caused fear among many children, which led to a loss of concentration, loss of appetite, bedwetting, and other disorders. The Center also reported that sonic booms caused headaches, stomach aches, shortness of breath, and other physical effects that appeared among both children and adults. Sonic booms also cause property damage, primarily shattered windows.

The use of sonic booms flagrantly breaches a number of provisions of international humanitarian law. The most significant provision is the prohibition on collective punishment. Article 33 of the Fourth Geneva Convention, which is intended to protect civilians in time of war, categorically states that "Collective penalties and likewise all measures of intimidation or of terrorism are prohibited." The article also states that, "Reprisals against protected persons and their property are prohibited." Air force supersonic sorties also breach the principle of distinction, a central pillar of humanitarian law, which forbids the warring sides to direct their attacks against civilians.[517]

On July 11 B'Tselem reported that six human rights groups in Israel—the Association for Civil Rights in Israel, Physicians for Human Rights–Israel, Hamoked: Center for Defense of the Individual, the Public Committee Against Torture in Israel, Gisha: Center for the Legal Protection of Freedom of Movement, and B'Tselem—demanded that "the [border] crossings in Gaza be opened to allow for the steady and regular supply of fuel, food, medicine, and equipment, including spare parts to operate generators." B'Tselem reported:

During the current military operation in the Gaza Strip the Israeli military has interrupted the supply of fuel to Gaza and kept Gaza's crossings mostly closed to supply of food and other humanitarian goods. The uninterrupted supply of fuel and equipment is necessary for the functioning of Gaza's health and sanitation systems, and Gaza requires a steady supply of food and medicine.

Since Gaza's power station was destroyed on June 28, there is an increased need for fuel to power the generators in Gaza and for spare parts to keep the generators running at such a high capacity. The closure of Karni Crossing has led to shortages in food at a time when, given the difficulty of obtaining electricity to prepare and refrigerate foodstuffs, Gaza requires increased shipments of dairy products, meat, flour, and other goods.

Without a steady supply of fuel and parts, hospitals cannot perform life-saving surgery and treatment plants cannot pump and treat sewage in Gaza. Gaza hospitals have reduced their activities to life-saving procedures. Since the bombing of the power plant, Gaza's water utility has been dumping 60,000 cubic meters of raw sewage into the sea each day, for lack of power and equipment to run the treatment plants, and there is concern that untreated sewage will pollute the aquifer or spill into the streets.

Because of the electricity shortages, stores in Gaza have stopped selling meat and dairy products. Trucks laden with food and medicine have been stuck at Karni Crossing, which has been closed since July 6, including 230 containers from international aid organizations.

Withholding fuel, food, and equipment from Gaza residents constitutes collective punishment, in violation of international law.[518]

On July 8 *Ha'aretz* reported that "A six-year-old Palestinian girl, her elder brother and her mother were killed Saturday evening during an Israeli Air Force strike on a house east of Gaza City, medical sources said."[519]

On July 9 *Ha'aretz* columnist Gideon Levy wrote:

"We left Gaza and they are firing Qassams"—there is no more precise a formulation of the prevailing view about the current round of the conflict. "They started," will be the routine response to anyone who tries to argue, for example, that a few hours before the first Qassam fell on the school in Ashkelon, causing no damage, Israel sowed destruction at the Islamic University in Gaza.

Israel is causing electricity blackouts, laying sieges, bombing and shelling, assassinating and imprisoning, killing and wounding civilians, including children and babies, in horrifying numbers, but "they started."

They are also "breaking the rules" laid down by Israel: We are allowed to bomb anything we want and they are not allowed to launch Qassams. When they fire a Qassam at Ashkelon, that's an "escalation of the conflict," and when we bomb a university and a school, it's perfectly alright. Why? Because they started. That's why the majority thinks that all the justice is on our side. Like in a schoolyard fight, the argument about who started is Israel's winning moral argument to justify every injustice.

So, who really did start? And have we "left Gaza?"

Israel left Gaza only partially, and in a distorted manner. The disengagement plan, which was labeled with fancy titles like "partition" and "an end to the occupation," did result in the dismantling of settlements and the Israel Defense Forces' departure from Gaza, but it did almost nothing to change the living conditions for the residents of the Strip. Gaza is still a prison and its inhabitants are still doomed to live in poverty and oppression. Israel closes them off from the sea, the air and land, except for a limited safety valve at the Rafah crossing. They cannot visit their relatives in the West Bank or look for work in Israel, upon which the Gazan economy has been dependent for some 40 years. Sometimes goods can be transported, sometimes not. Gaza has no chance of escaping its poverty under these conditions. Nobody will invest in it, nobody can develop it, nobody can feel free in it. Israel left the cage, threw away the keys and left the residents to their bitter fate. Now, less than a year after the disengagement, it is going back, with violence and force.[520]

On July 10 *Ha'aretz* reported that "[a]n Israeli Air Force strike on the northern Gaza town of Beit Hanun Monday killed three Palestinian civilians and seriously wounded another." According to Palestinian security sources, "the IAF fired missiles on the teenagers as they were playing soccer in the field outside of the agricultural college in Beit Hanun, near some Qassam launchers that had been set up in the yard."[521]

On July 11 *Ha'aretz* reported that "[a]n 11-year-old Palestinian boy seriously wounded in an Israel Defense Forces strike last week near his home in the northern Gaza Strip died on Tuesday of his wounds."

The same article also reported that "Khaled Wahabeh, an 18-month-old baby who was wounded in the IDF's bombing of Khan Yunis last month, died at a Gaza hospital Monday."[522]

Also on July 11, the *Jerusalem Post* reported that "relief organizations in the Gaza Strip warned of an impending humanitarian crisis Tuesday, with basic supplies dwindling as a result of border closures and military operations. Closed road links and damage to the infrastructure have led to major shortages of basic supplies such as food, water and medicine, United Nations and other nongovernmental organizations said."[523] *Ha'aretz* reported the same day that "[f]our Palestinians have died in recent days awaiting entry into the Gaza Strip on the Egyptian side of the Rafah border crossing, which has been closed for nearly two weeks since the kidnapping of Israel Defense Forces soldier Gilad Shalit." The dead Palestinians were described as a nineteen-year-old woman who was returning from an operation in a Cairo hospital who "died as a result of a severe deterioration in her medical condition as she waited at Rafah," a one-year-old infant who "died of heat stroke," a seventy-year-old man who "suffered a heart attack after waiting nine days to return to Gaza after receiving medical treatment in Egypt," and a fifteen-year-old boy who "died at the crossing after undergoing heart surgery in Cairo."[524]

On July 12 the *Independent* reported that "Israel dropped a quarter-ton bomb on a Gaza home today in an attempt to assassinate top Hamas fugitives, killing nine civilians as Islamic militant leaders got away." The newspaper reported that "the nine dead were all members of the same family, including the parents and seven of their children" and that "rescue workers pulled from the rubble the mangled body of a child, clad in a red T-shirt, whose head was blown open by the blast and whose lower body was torn off."[525] The *Guardian* reported about the bombing that "Israel killed nine members of a family, including two children, during an overnight bomb strike on a house in the Gaza Strip" and that "the two storey house was reduced to rubble and rescue teams frantically searched through the wreckage for survivors while a neighbouring house was close to collapse."[526] In its back-pages report on the bombing, *Times* correspondent Steven Erlanger, while noting that Palestinian witnesses deplored the "Israeli disregard for Palestinian life," then wrote: "From Israel's point of view, the meeting was a perfectly justified target and another example of Hamas's irresponsibility in putting civilian lives at risk."[527] The *Times*' editorial page essentially agreed with that assessment: in its first editorial since June 29

("Hamas Provokes a Fight") on the Israeli military campaign in Gaza, a *Times* editorial for July 13 argued that Israel was "acting justifiably" in both Gaza and Lebanon "in the face of aggression." Upon counseling Israel "to focus military actions as narrowly as possible" to "spar[e] the civilian populations," the editorial commented:

> That is, of course, far easier said than done. Military actions in inhabited areas cannot be fine-tuned. Yet surely the repeated lesson of recent history is that inflicting pain and humiliation on Arab civilians does not make them angry at the terrorists who provoked the violence. It makes them angrier at Israel.[528]

One day later, on July 14, Amnesty International offered a different perspective in a press release on Israel's military campaign in Gaza:

> Amnesty International today urged the Israeli government to immediately cease attacks against Palestinian civilians and civilian property and infrastructure, and to take action to address the growing humanitarian crisis in the Gaza Strip.
>
> The organization condemned attacks such as those carried out by Israeli forces on the night of 11–12 July 2006, when an entire family—Nabil and Salwa Abu Salmiya and their seven children aged between seven and 17—were killed when the Israeli Air Force targeted their home in a densely populated residential district in Jabaliya, north of Gaza City. More than 30 other residents were injured in the attack.
>
> Israeli officials stated that the air strike had targeted Muhammad Deif, a leader of Hamas's armed wing, who was reported to have been in the building at the time and to have been injured in the attack. However, the Israeli government and military officials who ordered and carried out the air attack on the house at about 02:30 am must have known that Nabil Abu Salmiya, a university lecturer and a Hamas member, and his wife and children, would be present at their home and that they and residents of neighbouring houses would be killed and injured.
>
> Such attacks against civilians are prohibited by international law and Amnesty International called for them to cease immediately.[529]

Following their customary and long-standing pattern the *Times* neither mentioned the Amnesty International press release nor noted the international law implications of bombing a home in occupied Palestinian territory with a family in it in the middle of the night.

On July 15, one day after Amnesty International issued its press release, the *Times* editorial page ran its third editorial on the situation in Gaza. In its July 14 press release Amnesty had reported: "In recent weeks dozens of Palestinian women, children and other bystanders have been killed and hundreds have been injured by Israeli air strikes and artillery shelling—including in their homes."[530] In its editorial a day later titled "Playing Hamas's Game," the *Times* commented:

> With the circle of violence in the Middle East expanding alarmingly, it is important to be clear about not only who is responsible for the latest outbreak, but who stands to gain most from its continued escalation.
>
> Both questions have the same answer: Hamas and Hezbollah. And Israel needs to be careful that its far-reaching military responses, however legally and morally justified, do not end up advancing the political agenda that Hamas and Hezbollah hard-liners had in mind when they conceived and executed the kidnappings of Israeli soldiers that detonated the fighting.[531]

The *Times*' editorial page then cautioned Israel "to minimize the damage to civilian bystanders," with the next sentence offering some advice why:

> Here's why: The military chieftains of Hamas and Hezbollah fully understand that their primitively armed guerrillas and limited-range unguided missiles are no match for Israel's world-class military forces. When they engage in provocative operations, like the recent kidnapping of Israeli soldiers and shelling of Israeli towns, they do not expect to win any kind of traditional military victory.
>
> What they more realistically hope for is that the inevitably fierce and devastating Israeli military response will hand them an opportunity to radicalize Arab politics and thereby pressure moderate Arab leaders to distance themselves from Israel and embrace the guerrilla cause.[532]

Not only does this analysis relieve Israel of the responsibility for bombing and killing an entire family in Gaza on July 11—which is what the editorial is responding to indirectly—as well as for the widespread mayhem and destruction throughout the Gaza Strip in response to the capture of Gilad Shalit, but it also mischaracterizes the reported facts with respect to which parties sought to end the hostilities soon after they began. Less than two weeks after Israel initiated its illegal military reprisals in Gaza, *Ha'aretz* reported that "Palestinian Prime Minster Ismail Haniyeh on Saturday called for Palestinian militants and Israel to halt military operations in Gaza after 11 days of fierce fighting left nearly 40 Palestinian militants dead."[533] The *New York Times* also reported that Hamas had sought a cease-fire.[534] *Ha'aretz* reported a day after these reports that senior Hamas members said that "Hamas in its entirety now supports a *hudna*, a long-term cease-fire, and feels that there is a good opportunity for a collective deal between Israel and the Palestinians,"[535] but the Associated Press reported that "Israel rejected the [cease-fire] offer because it did not call for releasing a soldier [Shalit] held by Hamas militants."[536] The *Jerusalem Post* reported that Israeli Prime Minister Ehud Olmert had rejected the cease-fire offer, saying, "This is a war, and it can't be assigned a timetable." Olmert "reiterated that Israel would not negotiate with Hamas, stressing that negotiating with the kidnappers of IDF Cpl. Gilad Shalit would encourage future kidnappings."[537] In contrast, Noam Shalit, the father of the captured Israeli soldier, offered this most discerning statement in *Ha'aretz*: "I know releasing prisoners was on the agenda before the incident [his son's capture], as a kind of gesture, so there is no reason for it not to be on the agenda also after the incident, for the good of releasing a soldier who was sent by the state to the front lines."[538] Furthermore, although Israel kidnapped several cabinet officals and Hamas legislators after the Palestinians captured Shalit, Hamas did not precondition its cease-fire proposals upon the immediate return of its officials. Despite all of these reports about the situation, the *Times*' editorial on July 15 accused Hamas of playing "the provocateurs' game" and of willfully engineering and welcoming— and bearing the responsibility for—Israel's military campaign in Gaza. The editorial noted: "Most Arabs are not blaming Hamas and Hezbollah for provoking these Israeli raids. They are blaming Israel for carrying them out. This is not fair."[539]

Though this editorial may have pleased those (like Dershowitz) who would never criticize Israel's actions, it is hardly world-class commentary, especially compared to a number of Israeli and British commentators who were engaged in analyzing events. For example, the *Ha'aretz* editorial page supported an Egyptian-backed cease-fire proposal, arguing that "diplomacy is the only way out."[540] The *Times*' editorial page mentioned neither the Hamas- nor Egypt-backed ceasefire proposals, nor did it support a UN cease-fire plan at the Security Council, or criticize the US veto of the UN cease-fire resolution.[541]

With the US favoring a continuation of the Israeli military offensive, and with the *Times* in tow, the death and destruction in Gaza continued, as the *Ha'aretz* editorial noted, "with no clear purpose."[542] On July 15 Reuters reported that "Israeli aircraft attacked the Palestinian Economy Ministry and a house in Gaza on Saturday, part of an offensive to free a captured soldier and destroy the institutions of the Hamas-led government. Doctors said one person was killed in the attack on the house and several were wounded. It was not immediately clear who was being targeted."[543]

Also on July 15, Agence France Presse reported that "the Non-Aligned Movement," a 116-nation group, "has condemned as 'disproportionate' Israel's military offensive in Gaza and called for the revival of the stalled Middle East roadmap peace plan."[544] Two days later, AFP reported that Israeli Prime Minister Olmert "vowed to fight the Palestinians until terrorism stops," although the same article reported that the Israeli military campaign "has left at least 87 Palestinians and one Israeli soldier dead since July 5."[545] And the one Israeli soldier killed, as *Ha'aretz* reported, "was accidentally shot by soldiers from his own regiment";[546] thus, there was hardly any Palestinian "terrorism" to stop, as Olmert claimed, since the only side doing the killing was Israel.

On July 20 *Ha'aretz* reported that "Israel Defense Forces soldiers operating in the Mughazi refugee camp on Thursday shot and killed a 13-year-old boy, according to Palestinian sources." "IDF troops killed nine Palestinians," the report continued, "among them five civilians, in its offensive on the camp on Wednesday." The same *Ha'aretz* article also reported:

> The IDF dropped leaflets on towns and villages in the Gaza Strip on Thursday, warning residents that anyone with an arsenal of weapons in their homes would be attacked.
>
> After dropping the leaflets, military officials told the Associated Press that the army was adopting a "new policy" of attacking homes in civilian areas where weapons such as homemade rockets are secretly stored.[547]

On July 21 Agence France Presse reported:

> Four Palestinians were killed as the death toll from Israel's Gaza offensive shot to over 100 and UN Secretary General Kofi Annan renewed calls for an end to "disproportionate" violence.

At least 106 Palestinians and one Israeli soldier have now been killed in the impoverished territory since Israel on July 5 stepped up its operation with the aim of retrieving a missing soldier and stopping militant rocket fire.

The Jewish state has ignored repeated international calls for restraint, and the latest Palestinians to die—a militant from the armed wing of the governing Hamas, and his family—were killed when tank fire hit their home.[548]

On July 26 the Sweden-based Defence for Children International reported that thirty-one Gazan children had been killed in the thirty-one-day Israeli offensive. All of the children save one (a seventeen-year-old) were sixteen years old or younger.[549] This report provoked no editorial in the *Times* condemning Israel's killing of Palestinian children. It is difficult to imagine the *New York Times* editorial page ignoring a report that thirty-one Israeli children had been killed over the course of one month during an illegal Palestinian siege of Israel.

On July 29 the *Los Angeles Times* reported that a three-day Israeli military incursion into Gaza City killed thirty Palestinians and wounded at least seventy-five, leaving "a trail of damaged homes, crushed cars, and uprooted trees."[550] By late July the *New York Times* editorial page had published only three editorials on the situation in Gaza—each criticizing Hamas, none criticizing Israel. The fourth editorial on Israel's military campaign in Gaza would not come for another month and a half in the future.

On July 30 Gideon Levy, one of a handful of excellent Israeli commentators for *Ha'aretz*, wrote:

> In war as in war: Israel is sinking into a strident, nationalistic atmosphere and darkness is beginning to cover everything. The brakes we still had are eroding, the insensitivity and blindness that character- ized Israeli society in recent years is intensifying. The home front is cut in half: the north suffers and the center is serene. But both have been taken over by tones of jingoism, ruthlessness and vengeance, and the voices of extremism that previously characterized the camp's margins are now expressing its heart. The left has once again lost its way, wrapped in silence or "admitting mistakes." Israel is exposing a unified, nationalistic face. . . .
>
> The death we are sowing at the same time [in Lebanon], right now in Gaza, with close to 120 dead since the kidnapping of Gilad Shalit, 27

last Wednesday alone, touches us even less. The hospitals in Gaza are full of burned children, but who cares?[551]

On August 1 the Israeli newspaper *Yediot Ahronot* reported that "a 14-year-old Palestinian teenager and a 24-year-old woman were killed Monday after an IDF shell aimed at a group of gunmen missed its target and struck passersby, according to Palestinian sources." The newspaper reported that the boy took "a direct hit" by the shell, and that the woman, a bystander, "was seriously injured and later died of her injuries." Local residents reported "there were no gunmen or rocket fire at Israeli targets in the area of the incident."[552]

On August 3 the *Jerusalem Post* reported that "IDF troops raided southern Gaza early Thursday, killing at least seven armed operatives and an 8-year-old boy in the latest stage of their month-long offensive, Palestinian officials said."[553]

On August 7 the *Independent* reported that "Israel has arrested a senior Hamas leader at his home in Ramallah"; he was identified as Abdel Aziz Dweik, the speaker of the Palestinian parliament. The newspaper reported that "in addition to regular deadly raids on Gaza, where 1.4 million Palestinians are trapped by an economic blockade, the Israelis have arrested a third of the Hamas government and 36 members of the Palestinian parliament since 26 June."[554]

On August 8 B'Tselem issued a press release: "In July, the Israeli military killed 163 Palestinians in the Gaza Strip, 78 of whom (48 percent) were not taking part in the hostilities when they were killed," and that "the number of Palestinian fatalities in July [2006] was the highest in any month since April 2002." B'Tselem also identified "four cases in which Israel may have committed grave breaches of the laws of war," described as follows:

- **Air Force missile hits group of youths, killing six.**
  On 12 July 2006, a group of youths sought shelter from IDF bombing. Ten of the youths went and hid in a big pit. A missile fired from by [*sic*] an Air Force plane hit the pit, killing six of the youths, five of them minors: Mahmmuad al-'Asar, Ibrahim a-Nabahin and Ibrahim Qatush, age 15, Ahmad Abu Hajaj, age 16, Salah Abu Maktomah, age 17 and Hassan 'Abeid, age 18.
- **IDF fires two shells at residence and kills four members of the family.**
  On 21 July 2006, a few members of the Hararah family went onto

the roof of their house in the a-Sheja'iyeh neighborhood in Gaza City to watch tanks advancing toward the neighborhood. One of the tanks fired a shell at the house. It hit the staircase and killed Muhammad Hararah, 45, the brother of the owner of the house. Almost immediately afterwards, another shell was fired at the same spot, killing the mother of the family, Sabah, 45, and two of her sons, Muamen, 16, and 'Amer, 23.

- **Air Force missile hits horse-drawn cart killing a woman and her grandchild.**
  On 24 July 2006, two youngsters left their family's farm in the Beit Lahiya area after shells had fallen on the farm's land. They went by horse-drawn wagon and on the way picked up two of their family. A missile, fired by an Air Force plane, made a direct hit on the wagon, killing Khairieh al-'Attar, 58 and her grandchild Nadi al-'Attar, 11. Another member of the family, Shadi, 14, was injured.
- **IDF tank shell lands next to housing project, killing three civilians.**
  On 24 July 2006, an IDF fired shell fell next to the a-Nada Towers, a housing project located in the northern Gaza Strip. The shelling killed three civilians, one of them a minor: Saleh Naser, 14, Sadeq Naser, 33, and S'adi Na'im, 29.[555]

On August 25 Reuters reported that "Israeli aircraft bombed the home of a Palestinian militant and what the army said was a weapons depot in the Gaza Strip on Friday, wounding eight people, hospital officials said. A first strike destroyed the home of a local commander from the Al Aqsa Martyrs Brigade in the Jabalya refugee camp. Five civilians near the home at the time of attack where [sic] hurt."[556]

On August 26 the Associated Press reported that "Israeli aircraft fired two missiles early Sunday at an armored car belonging to the Reuters news agency, wounding five people, including two cameramen, Palestinian witnesses and hospital officials said. The Israeli army said it did not realize the car's passengers were journalists and only attacked because the vehicle was driving in a suspicious manner near the Israeli troops in the middle of a combat zone."[557] On August 27 Reuters reported that "the Foreign Press Association described the attack as 'outrageous targeting' of the [Reuters] vehicle and rejected the army's 'excuses,' " and "demanded a full and transparent investigation."[558]

On August 27 Agence France Presse reported that "a [Palestinian] fisherman was seriously wounded late Saturday by fire from an Israeli gunboat, a security source said." AFP reported that "Gaza fishermen have been forbidden from taking to the sea because of fears they could be involved in arms trafficking."[559] AFP also reported that "the Israeli army had seized a Hamas Palestinian lawmaker at his West Bank home, witnesses said, the latest in a string of officials from the ruling Islamist movement to be detained by the Jewish state." AFP reported that "some 20 army jeeps surrounded Mahmud Mesleh's house in the village of Bireh near the city of Ramallah and took him away."[560]

Also on August 27 the Associated Press reported that "a 20-year-old Palestinian man was shot in the head by a sniper in the Shajaiyeh neighborhood of Gaza City, hospital officials said. The army said the man approached troops while he was carrying an anti-tank missile." The AP also reported "a 6-year-old boy was shot in the chest and critically wounded in the same area later Sunday outside his home."[561]

On August 28 the Associated Press reported that "[f]our Palestinian militants were killed early Monday in an Israeli airstrike on central Gaza, Palestinian doctors said. The four men were standing on a street in the Shajaiyeh neighborhood of Gaza City when a missile hit them."[562] Also on August 28 Agence France Presse reported that "Sabet Edwan, 22, was killed by Israeli tank fire near the southern city of Rafah," and "medics discovered the body of another Palestinian, Fathi Abu al-Qumbarz, 50, at his home in Shejaya," who "had been wounded by automatic gunfire while inside his home during Israeli operations in the area." AFP reported that "at least 193 Palestinians and one Israeli soldier have been killed in the Gaza Strip since June 28, when Israel launched a massive offensive to stop rocket attacks and recover a soldier captured by Palestinian militants in a cross-border raid that left two other troops dead." The AFP article also reported that "the latest deaths brought to 5,355 the number of people killed since the start of the Palestinian uprising in September 2000, most of them Palestinians, according to an AFP count."[563]

On August 28 AFP also reported that "six Israeli rights groups on Monday petitioned the country's supreme court to demand the government allow regular food and other essential shipments into the Gaza Strip, with the main export-import terminal closed since August 15. Living conditions for the 1.4 million people in the territory have deteriorated sharply since Israel bombed its only power station on June 28 and after the West ended direct aid when the Islamist-Hamas movement took office."[564]

On August 29 AFP reported that "nine Palestinians were wounded in an Israeli air strike targeting a group of gunmen in an eastern district of Gaza City," and "among the wounded were militants and a 10-year-old child in serious condition."[565]

On August 30 AFP reported that "at least 204 Palestinians and one Israeli soldier have been killed in Gaza since June 28, when Israel launched its offensive to stop rocket attacks and recover the missing [Israeli soldier Gilad] Shalit." AFP also reported that "five Israelis have died as a result of homemade rockets fired from Gaza since the start of the second Palestinian uprising in September 2000, with most of the missiles causing property damage or landing in open spaces."[566]

Throughout the entire month of August (as well as the entire second half of July), the *New York Times* editorial page remained silent with respect to the events documented above, and many others. In contrast, newspaper commentary in Israel, at least in some quarters, was outspoken in opposing Israel's military campaign in Gaza. On August 31, for example, Amira Hass wrote in *Ha'aretz*:

> Let us leave aside those Israelis whose ideology supports the dispossession of the Palestinian people because "God chose us." Leave aside the judges who whitewash every military policy of killing and destruction. Leave aside the military commanders who knowingly jail an entire nation in pens surrounded by walls, fortified observation towers, machine guns, barbed wire and blinding projectors. Leave aside the ministers. All of these are not counted among the collaborators. These are the architects, the planners, the designers, the executioners.
>
> But there are others. Historians and mathematicians, senior editors, media stars, psychologists and family doctors, lawyers who do not support Gush Emunim and Kadima, teachers and educators, lovers of hiking trails and sing-alongs, high-tech wizards. Where are you? And what about you, researchers of Nazism, the Holocaust and Soviet gulags? Could you all be in favor of systematic discriminating laws? Laws stating that the Arabs of the Galilee will not even be compensated for the damages of the [Lebanon] war by the same sums their Jewish neighbors are entitled to.
>
> Could it be that you are all in favor of a racist Citizenship Law that forbids an Israeli Arab from living with his family in his own home? That you side with further expropriation of lands and the demolishing of additional orchards, for another settler neighborhood and another

exclusively Jewish road? That you all back the shelling and missile fire killing the old and the young in the Gaza Strip?

Could it be that you all agree that a third of the West Bank (the Jordan Valley) should be off limits to Palestinians? That you all side with an Israeli policy that prevents tens of thousands of Palestinians who have obtained foreign citizenship from returning to their families in the occupied territories?

Could your mind really be so washed with the security excuse, used to forbid Gaza students from studying occupational therapy at Bethlehem and medicine at Abu Dis, and preventing sick people from Rafah from receiving medical treatment in Ramallah?[567]

On September 2 *Ha'aretz* reported that "IDF troops backed by helicopters entered the northern Gaza town of Beit Hanun and engaged in heavy clashes with Palestinian gunmen. Militants often fire homemade rockets into Israel from the town." The paper also reported that "a resident, Yunis Abu Odah, told local media that bullets fired during the gunfight came through his house and killed his 55-year-old father and 23-year-old brother, while also wounding two of his sisters." *Ha'aretz* reported "it was unclear whether the bullets were fired by IDF troops or Palestinian militants." It also reported, "at the same time, Israel Air Force strikes in a nearby part of Beit Hanun wounded three Palestinians, two of them children, with shrapnel, medics said."[568]

On September 4 the *Independent* reported that "doctors in Gaza are reporting what they say are unexplained injuries among the dead and wounded in operations by the Israeli military."[569] A month later, on October 11, *Ha'aretz* reported: "An investigative report to be aired on Italian television Wednesday raises the possibility that Israel has used an experimental weapon in the Gaza Strip in recent months, causing especially serious physical injuries, such as amputated limbs and severe burns. The weapon is similar to one developed by the US military, known as DIME, which causes a powerful and lethal blast, but only within a relatively small radius." *Ha'aretz* reported that "according to those who testified" to the Italian inquiry, "the wounded were hit by munitions launched from drones." It quoted the head of the emergency room at a hospital in Gaza, who reported that "the legs of the injured were sliced from their bodies 'as if a saw was used to cut through the bone.' "[570] One week later the *Guardian* reported that "doctors in Gaza have reported previously unseen injuries from Israeli weapons that cause severe burning and leave deep internal wounds, often resulting in amputation or death." The *Guardian* also quoted a Gaza doctor from the Al–Shifa hospital who reported "bodies arrived severely fragmented, melted and disfigured" with "internal burning of organs." The *Guardian* reported that "photographs of some of the dead from Shifa hospital showed bodies that had been melted and blackened beyond recognition."[571]

On September 5 B'Tselem reported that "in August 2006, Israeli security forces killed 76 Palestinians, 19 of them minors, in the West Bank and Gaza Strip, 40 of whom (53 percent) did not take part in the hostilities when killed. During the same period, Palestinians killed one member of the Israeli security forces in the West Bank." B'Tselem also reported, "Since the abduction of Cpl. Gilad Shalit, in late June, until the end of August, Israeli security forces killed 226 Palestinians, 54 of them minors, in the Gaza Strip, 114 of whom (among them 46 minors), did not take part in the hostilities when killed."[572]

On September 6 *Ha'aretz* reported that "Israel Defense Forces troops on Wednesday shot and killed a 16–year–old Palestinian boy in the southern Gaza Strip, Palestinian medical officials said." *Ha'aretz* reported "witnesses said he was a civilian, but the IDF denied that, saying soldiers operating in the area had shot a Palestinian who was trying to plant a bomb."[573]

On September 8 Patrick Cockburn wrote in the *Independent*:

Gaza is dying. The Israeli siege of the Palestinian enclave is so tight that its people are on the edge of starvation. Here on the shores of the Mediterranean a great tragedy is taking place that is being ignored because the world's attention has been diverted by wars in Lebanon and Iraq.

A whole society is being destroyed. There are 1.5 million Palestinians imprisoned in the most heavily populated area in the world. Israel has stopped all trade. It has even forbidden fishermen to go far from the shore so they wade into the surf to try vainly to catch fish with hand-thrown nets.

Many people are being killed by Israeli incursions that occur every day by land and air. A total of 262 people have been killed and 1,200 wounded, of whom 60 had arms or legs amputated, since 25 June, says Dr Juma al-Saqa, the director of the al-Shifa Hospital in Gaza City which is fast running out of medicine. Of these, 64 were children and

26 women. This bloody conflict in Gaza has so far received only a fraction of the attention given by the international media to the war in Lebanon.[574]

On September 9 Gideon Levy wrote in *Ha'aretz*:

Abdullah a-Zakh identified his son's body by the belt. The shoes and socks also looked familiar, irrefutable proof that he had lost his son. In the morgue of Shifa Hospital, after hours of searching, he found the bottom part of the boy's body. The next day, when Operation "Gan Na'ul"—"Locked Kindergarten"—ended and the Israel Defense Forces exited the Saja'iya neighborhood of Gaza, leaving behind 22 dead and large-scale destruction, the other body parts were found.

Mohammed was buried twice. He was 14 years old at the time of his death. He was killed last week, three days before the start of the new school year, so he never got to enter ninth grade. Did the planners of the operation give thought to the children who would be killed before giving it the satanic name "Locked Kindergarten"? Did the IDF computer that comes up with the names know that there would be five children and adolescents among the dead? Did they think about the popular song that the operation's name evokes? It was unpleasant, very unpleasant (in the words of the song) this week to see the results of Locked Kindergarten in the Saja'iya neighborhood in the eastern section of Gaza City.

This sprawling, overcrowded residential neighborhood was occupied for almost a week by the IDF. The army wreaked destruction in it. A monstrous bulldozer maliciously potholed a few roads, scarring the asphalt with gaping wounds, for no apparent reason. Houses were hit, street tiling was uprooted, electricity poles were cut down, cars were crushed, dozens of trees were destroyed and 22 residents were killed. For almost a week the tens of thousands of residents lived in terror, some of them unable to leave their homes.[575]

On September 11 *Ha'aretz* reported that "an Israeli Defense Forces tank shell landed near a group of Palestinians in the southern town of Rafah on Sunday, killing a 14-year-old boy and seriously wounding his 19-year-old brother, Palestinian witnesses and medics said." *Ha'aretz* reported that the IDF said the Palestinians were "suspected of planting explosives" and the IDF "fired a tank shell at them."[576]

On September 18, more than two months since its last editorial on Gaza on July 15, the *Times* published an editorial titled "A Real Test for the Palestinians," in which they urged Hamas—not Israel—to "renounce violence" and halt its "rocket and terrorist attacks against Israel":

> After six months of crippling sanctions, Hamas's leaders are trying to figure out the very minimum they need to say—and the even less they plan to do—to end their isolation and salvage their government. Skepticism is more than warranted. But Hamas's admission of weakness could provide at least a chance to quell the violence and resuscitate peace talks. The Bush administration should not squander the opportunity.
>
> The radical Islamist Hamas—which came to power after last January's legislative elections—has been negotiating to form a national unity government with the Palestinian president, Mahmoud Abbas, a moderate, and his Fatah Party. Hamas still refuses to say the words necessary to unlock international aid: that it will renounce violence and recognize Israel's right to exist. Aides to Mr. Abbas warned yesterday that Hamas will have to make some rhetorical concessions—no matter how grudging—before a unity government can hope to win international acceptance.
>
> Words are important. But worrying about who said what should not divert attention from what should be the real test of any Palestinian government: whether it will commit to a genuine cease-fire and use its security forces to halt, rather than abet, rocket and terrorist attacks against Israel.[577]

Perhaps the editorial writers at the *Times* forgot that Hamas had maintained a sixteen-month cease-fire prior to June 25 and that its leaders had proposed a cease-fire in early July to preempt the siege and rampage in Gaza. Nor did the *Times* demand that Israel halt its "rocket and terrorist attacks" in Palestinian territory. The *Times* did not demand supporting a cutoff of all financial assistance to Israel or insist that Israel recognize the right of Palestinian self-determination in Gaza and the West Bank. Nor did the editorial page—in this editorial or any others—demand that Israel end its military campaign in Gaza; it did not question its legality or even its purpose.

With support from the United States and the US news media, including the *New York Times*, there was virtually nothing to stop the

Israeli military campaign in Gaza, which continued with Israeli security forces killing and wounding Palestinians on a daily basis. On October 13 *Ha'aretz* reported that a Palestinian woman was killed, "shot by an Israeli sniper while she was standing outside her home in southern Gaza."[578] On the same day *Ha'aretz* reported that the IDF "targeted the house of a Hamas commander," killing the man's brother and a two-year-old girl.[579] On October 13 the IDF also killed five members of a single family, including a 13-year-old boy, his father, and "three armed Hamas militants," all brothers.[580]

On October 14 Gideon Levy wrote again in *Ha'aretz*:

Let the chips fall where they may, the saying goes, but this time the chip was a terrifying concrete beam that was sent flying into the air hundreds of meters from a house the IDF bombed in the middle of the night. It landed in the bedroom of a 14-year-old girl, Dahm al-Az Hamad. Sometimes children are killed, but this time the girl was her parents' only child. Her mother is paralyzed. Sometimes tragedies happen, but the tragedy of the Hamad family is almost too much to describe.

As Dahm al-Az lay in her mother's embrace, the beam smashed into her frail body and tore it to pieces. Now this long-impoverished and newly bereaved family sits dumbstruck in its tin house in the Brazil refugee camp, at the edge of Rafah. The tin ceiling of the bedroom is still in tatters, the remains of the beam still lie on the floor, while sitting in the plastic chair in the shabby living room, Basama the mother sits and weeps silently. Her wheelchair was also destroyed in the bombing. There is no longer anyone to nurse her, no longer an iota of hope in the home that was suddenly rendered childless. The pilot pressed a button and two powerful bombs, amazingly smart and precise, landed one after the other, sending the beam flying into the air and inflicting a horrific tragedy on the Hamad family, which was already a victim of fate. Regards to the pilot.[581]

On October 18 Reuters reported that "around 250 Palestinians, about half of them civilians, have been killed in Israel's operations in Gaza since June."[582]

In early November the Israelis began a one-week siege of Beit Hanun, a town in northern Gaza from which Qassam rockets were fired on southern Israel. On November 3 *Ha'aretz* reported that IDF soldiers "opened fire on a group of women" who were walking toward a mosque to serve as human shields for Palestinian gunmen who were "holed up there." A forty-year-old woman was killed and several other women were wounded. *Ha'aretz* reported that "a four-year-old boy had died of wounds sustained Thursday by IDF shelling during the [Beit Hanun] operation."[583]

On November 5 *Ha'aretz* reported that "a 12-year-old girl was killed Saturday by Israel Defense Forces sniper fire in the northern Gaza Strip town of Beit Hanun." The newspaper also reported that "large military bulldozers began demolishing homes near a mosque that was the scene of a standoff on Friday," and that "residents of the homes received no warning ahead of time and were seen running for safety."[584]

On November 6 *Ha'aretz* reported that "the International Red Cross on Sunday deplored the killing by the Israel Defense Forces of two 'clearly marked' ambulance workers removing a Palestinian body from an earlier Israeli attack in the Gaza Strip. The paramedics of the Palestinian Red Crescent Society were wearing clearly marked fluorescent jackets and the flashing lights of their ambulance were visible from a great distance when they were hit by Israeli fire after dark on Friday evening, said the International Committee of the Red Cross." In its statement, the ICRC stated that it "is appalled by this failure to protect personnel engaged in emergency medical duties."[585]

Also on November 6 *Ha'aretz* reported: "An Israeli aircraft fired a missile into a town in the northern Gaza Strip on Monday, striking a group of youths on their way to school, killing a 16-year-old." Witnesses and hospital officials "said the missile landed near a school bus in Beit Lahiya." Among the wounded "was a teacher, who was in critical condition" and "as many as seven other civilians, six of them children."[586]

On November 8 *Ha'aretz* reported that "an IDF tank shell killed three people when it hit the Jabalya home of Jamila Shanti, the Hamas legislator who organized a women's protest that allowed militants to escape from a northern Gaza mosque under Israeli siege. Shanti's sister-in-law, who was in the house at the time and unarmed, was killed."[587]

On November 8–9, several news organizations reported the Israeli shelling of a residential area in Beit Hanun. *Ha'aretz* reported, "Israel Defense Forces artillery shells struck a residential area in the northern Gaza town of Beit Hanun early Wednesday, killing at least 19

Palestinians and wounding dozens of others." Witnesses said that "at least seven houses in Beit Hanun were hit."[588] A *Ha'aretz* report later in the day said that "eight children and seven women were among the dead," and that "at least 40 people were wounded."[589] On November 9 the *New York Times* reported that "Israeli artillery shells killed 18 Palestinians, including 8 children and 6 women, at a cluster of houses [in Beit Hanun] on Wednesday, one of the largest single losses of life in Gaza in years." The *Times* reported: " 'Nothing happened,' mumbled Isra Athamnah, 5 years old, who was pocked with shrapnel and in shock. The news her widowed mother, Sanaa, 35, was dead and that she was now an orphan did not sink in." The *Times* also reported the shrieks of a rescue worker: " 'Children! Women! Parents!' said Abu Ahman, 42, a rescue worker who lives on the street and arrived right after the rockets hit. 'I can't find the words that describe this action—legs of children, head of a small girl.' "[590]

In response to this incident, B'Tselem, Amnesty International, and Human Rights Watch all issued statements. B'Tselem commented:

> Even according to the [Israeli] military, the shelling [of Beit Hanun] was not defensive; it was not aimed at Palestinian fire or Qassam rocket-fire that was in progress. The artillery was aimed at what the IDF refers to as a "launching space," i.e., an area from which the army believes that Qassams had previously been fired. . . .
>
> The circumstances involved in the killing of the Palestinians in Beit Hanun, including the fact that the attack was not a defensive action, raise a grave concern that the shelling constitutes a war crime. The Israeli military's contention that they did not mean to harm civilians is meaningless, and cannot justify an action that amounts to a war crime. An investigation conducted by [Israeli] military officials subject to the same chain of command responsible for the action cannot serve as a substitute for a criminal investigation.[591]

In a press release on the Israeli shelling of Beit Hanun, Amnesty International stated:

> The killing this morning of 18 civilians in the Palestinian town of Beit Hanoun, victims of Israeli shelling, was an appalling act, Amnesty International said today. The organization called for an immediate, independent investigation and for those responsible to be held accountable. It said previous Israeli investigations, such as that carried out

into the killings of a Palestinian family on a beach in the Gaza Strip last June, had been seriously inadequate and failed to meet international standards for such investigations, which must be independent, impartial and thorough.[592]

Human Rights Watch also called for an independent investigation, and stated:

[T]he investigation should examine the policy that has led Israel to fire some 15,000 artillery shells into Gaza since September 2005, killing 49 Palestinian civilians and seriously injuring dozens more. A comprehensive investigation should identify issues of individual and command responsibility, including criminal responsibility, for any violation of international humanitarian law committed in the conduct of these artillery operations in northern Gaza.[593]

Human Rights Watch also reported that "since September 2005 alone, Palestinian armed groups have fired around 1,700 homemade rockets into Israel, injuring 36 Israeli civilians." Thus, since the Israeli disengagement from Gaza in September 2005 (up to mid-November 2006), Israel had fired 15,000 artillery shells (155 mm high-explosive projectiles), killing 49 Palestinians and seriously injuring dozens more, while Palestinians had fired 1,700 homemade Qassam rockets, killing no Israelis at the time of this report and wounding 36.[594]

Asked to respond to the shelling of Beit Hanun, which killed at least eighteen people and wounded eighty,[595] Tzipi Livni, Israel's foreign minister, said: "Israel is faced with constant attack by the Palestinian terror organizations, in the form of relentless firing of Qassam rockets at Israeli population centers. Israel has no desire to harm innocent people, but only to defend its citizens. Unfortunately, in the course of battle, regrettable incidents such as that which occurred this morning do happen."[596] As in many other such cases, the Israeli killing of Palestinians did not take place "in the course of battle"—in this case, Palestinians, mostly children and women, were killed in their sleep in their homes. Furthermore, if Israel claims a right to attack Gaza in response to Qassam rocket fire, wouldn't Palestinians, responding to eight times as many rockets that are far more deadly, also have a right to attack Israel? The fact is that neither side has any such right to attack the other in this fashion under the circumstances, but in the *Times*

editorials only one side is condemned and is called upon to stop firing
its rockets.

Ha'aretz published a good deal of excellent commentary following the
Israeli shelling of the Palestinian houses in Beit Hanun. We reproduce
some of that commentary below, in part to compare it with what the
Times' editorial page generated about events in Gaza. The first of the
Ha'aretz commentaries worth noting was an editorial published on
November 9:

> Yesterday, we wrote here that "Israel should declare a complete cease-
> fire in the Gaza Strip for a predetermined period, during which it will
> not engage in any violent actions, neither assassinations nor incursions.
> Simultaneously, it should call on the Palestinians to hold their fire as
> well."
>
> What we feared has come to pass—and for the Palestinians, even
> worse: At least 19 Palestinians were killed yesterday during a sustained
> Israel Defense Forces artillery attack on the town of Beit Hanun. Of
> these, 11 were members of a single family, including women and
> children.
>
> No excuse can justify this atrocity. When artillery batteries aim their
> shells near a residential neighborhood, such a disaster is inevitable, even
> if it is unintentional.
>
> Anyone who fired shells in the direction of civilian houses knows
> very well that he is liable to kill indiscriminately with them.
>
> None of Israel's responses to this catastrophe—expressions of regret
> by the prime minister and defense minister, offers of humanitarian
> assistance to the wounded, the establishment of an inquiry committee
> headed by Major General Meir Kalifi, cessation of the shelling and the
> opening of the Rafah border crossing for a day—can paper over Israel's
> sole responsibility for this fearsome and senseless killing.[597]

Ha'aretz's veteran correspondents, Amos Harel and Avi Issacharoff,
commented on November 10 on the shelling of Beit Hanun:

> Foreign visitors to the Gaza Strip are well acquainted with the band of
> taxi drivers who work at the entrance to the Palestinian side of the Erez
> crossing point. This is a permanent group, a kind of closed guild,
> which is entitled to work there because of the fact that the Shin Bet
> security services do not suspect its members of terrorist activity. Most

of them speak Hebrew, because in the past they worked in Israel or thanks to their close work with Israeli journalists. A few of them know how to recite Jewish prayers by heart. Most of them are inhabitants of the northern Gaza Strip, and this week the long arm of the Israel Defense Forces reached into their homes as well.

It started with A., the regular driver for the Haaretz team, who lives in Beit Hanun. . . . On the fifth day of the operation, A. was arrested, not because he had been involved in terror attacks or the firing of Qassam rockets, but because he is an adult male. The Israel Defense Forces arrested for questioning all of the town's adult males. A. was relatively lucky; he was released in less than 24 hours.

Raad al-Atamna, one of his cabbie colleagues, had a far worse week. Raad lived with his wife and children in the home of his extended family in the Hamad neighborhood, which is on the western edge of Beit Hanun. Early on Wednesday morning he set out for work. A few minutes later, when he was at the entrance to Gaza, his mobile phone rang. His brother Wael informed him that the family home had been bombarded and there were many people injured there; he asked him to call for first aid.

Raad drove back to the house in a frenzy. "You don't understand. It's impossible to forget this sight," he says. "Children without hands, without feet, flung in every corner, tremendous destruction. Our whole family lives there. The stairwell was completely destroyed and in every corner there was someone who was wounded or killed. Blood was everywhere and amputated limbs. Even our neighbors, who came to help, were wounded by the last shells."[598]

Also on November 12, Gideon Levy wrote:

Nineteen inhabitants of Beit Hanun were killed with malice aforethought. There is no other way of describing the circumstances of their killing. Someone who throws burning matches into a forest can't claim he didn't mean to set it on fire, and anyone who bombards residential neighborhoods with artillery can't claim he didn't mean to kill innocent inhabitants.

Therefore it takes considerable gall and cynicism to dare to claim that the Israel Defense Forces did not intend to kill inhabitants of Beit Hanun. Even if there was a glitch in the balancing of the aiming mechanism or in a component of the radar, a mistake in the input of the data or a human error, the overwhelming, crucial, shocking fact is

that the IDF bombards helpless civilians. Even shells that are supposedly aimed 200 meters from houses, into "open areas," are intended to
kill, and they do kill. In this respect, nothing new happened on
Wednesday morning in Gaza: The IDF has been behaving like this for
months now.

But this isn't just a matter of "the IDF," "the government" or
"Israel" bearing the responsibility. It must be said explicitly: The blame
rests directly on people who hold official positions, flesh-and-blood
human beings, and they must pay the price of their criminal responsibility for needless killing. Attorney Avigdor Klagsbald caused the
death of a woman and her child without anyone imagining that he
intended to hit them, but nevertheless he is sitting in prison. And what
about the killers of women and children in Beit Hanun? Will they all
be absolved? Will no one be tried? Will no one even be reprimanded
and shunned?

GOC Southern Command Yoav Galant will say with exasperating
coolness that apparently there was "a problem with the battery's
targeting apparatus," without moving a facial muscle, and will that
be enough? Deputy Defense Minister Ephraim Sneh will say, "The
IDF is militarily responsible, but not morally responsible," and will he
thus exculpate himself?

And who will bear the responsibility for the renewal of the terror
attacks? Only Hamas? Who will be accused of the tumble in Israel's
status and its depiction as a violent, leper state, and who will be judged
for the danger that hovers over world Jewry in the wake of the IDF's
acts? The electronic component that went on the blink in the radar?[599]

And on November 13, Amira Hass wrote:

"It was as if the shells had eyes: Wherever we ran, they followed us,"
said Tahani, Zahar's sister-in-law, whose 12-year-old son Mahmoud
was killed by the second shell. "The first shell woke us. I gathered the
children. The son whose hand I was holding, Mahmoud, is the one I
lost. We didn't know where to go. We ran downstairs, we were
barefoot. My daughter said her feet were burning from the heat of the
explosion. The second shell fell when we were already downstairs. I
went and turned over the children's bodies, to see who was who, until
I found Mahmoud.

"Not even one day had passed since we buried my brother Mazen.
The [Israeli] army detained him and thousands of other men. They

took them for a short interrogation and then released them. He and our cousin were arrested together and freed together. They told them at the detention point in Erez that they could go home. They went home, but there was a curfew. So other soldiers shot him because they violated the curfew. My cousin is in the hospital, seriously wounded. And Mazen, the uncle of my son Mahmoud, is dead.

"Less than one day after we buried his uncle, Mahmoud was lying on the floor among the dead. I tried to wake him, but he did not respond. Then the third shell hit. I fled into the house. The daughter of my brother-in-law also fled, but the shell followed her. My 14-year-old nephew fled and the shell followed him. It exploded, and he saw his hand fall to the floor. Now he is hospitalized in Egypt. Only people without a conscience could do that."

Hayat Athamneh, 55, Tahani and Zahar's mother-in-law, lost three children and two grandchildren in the shelling. "When the shells had enough of us, they went to the house of our relatives, but, thank God, they had fled. When the shells had enough of our relatives, they went to our neighbors. My children also fled, but the shells found them. And my ears started to go deaf from the noise. I could not hear a thing. I could only see. Black smoke, a lot of black smoke."

"And then I saw my son Mahdi, lying here in the west part of the house, near the garden." Athamneh bent down, picked up a blood-stained stone and kissed it. "It is my son Mahdi's blood," she said. "I saw him lying here, his brains on one side and his head on the other."[600]

The response by the *New York Times* editorial page to the Israeli shelling of houses in Beit Hanun on November 8 was quite different from what these commentators in Israel had to say. Like the right-wing factions in Israel who blamed Hamas for the Beit Hanun shelling, the *Times'* editorial blamed Hamas for the Israeli shelling of sleeping Palestinian women and children, with a barely discernible hint of criticism of Israel. Every paragraph in the editorial was problematic, including the gratuitous invocation of "a new wave of terrorist attacks against Americans"—as if a speechwriter for the Bush administration had written the editorial—without specifying where the terrorist "waves" would come from, what the previous "waves" were, and why this was mentioned in the context of an Israeli massacre in Gaza:

There have never been easy answers for how to broker peace between Israel and the Palestinians. But the horrifying price of ignoring the problem was made again this week when errant Israeli tank shells crashed into a Gaza neighborhood, killing 18 people, including seven children, as they slept.

There is more than enough blame to go around. Militants in Gaza constantly lob crude rockets across the border. The Hamas movement—voted into power last winter—is refusing to even implicitly recognize Israel, although doing so would mean resumption of international aid and lessening the desperation of its own people. Hamas's military wing has called for attacks on American targets in retaliation for the Gaza deaths.

And even as he expressed distress for the deaths in Gaza—and called for an immediate meeting with Mahmoud Abbas, the moderate Palestinian president—Prime Minster Ehud Olmert said Israel would continue striking militants, and could not promise that mistakes "may not happen."

Yesterday, analysts were trying to figure out which was the most immediate danger: a new wave of terrorist attacks against Americans, the start of a full-scale Israeli-Palestinian war, or a civil war between Hamas and its rival Fatah if talks on forming a unity government fail.[601]

Unlike the human rights organizations and the Israeli commentators, the *New York Times* did not condemn the Israeli shelling of the houses in Beit Hanun, did not call for an independent investigation, and did not urge the Bush administration to support a UN Security Council resolution condemning the attack. Instead, it condemned Palestinian rockets—nor were the Israeli shells simply "errant," as the *Times'* editorial page claimed, and it was not the first time that such "errant" Israeli shells had killed an entire Palestinian family. None of the regular columnists on the *Times'* opinion page had anything to say about the Israeli shelling of the houses and sleeping people in Beit Hanun, and the news and editorial pages never cited the statements from human rights organizations about the incident. Without any domestic pressure to do otherwise, the Bush administration again vetoed a Security Council resolution calling for a UN–supervised cease-fire and an independent investigation into the Israeli shelling of Beit Hanun.[602]

10

The Road Not Taken

Upon considering *The Record of the Paper*, our first volume on the *Times'* coverage of US foreign policy in the context of international law[603] and this one on Israel's policies in a similar context, we cite the commentary of Yossi Sarid, a columnist for *Ha'aretz*. Sarid, writing soon after the November 2006 elections in the United States, commented: "This Tuesday was a doubly good day: The Democrats won and the Republicans lost." In this piece, he described how he nearly became a US citizen when his parents considered emigrating from Poland to the United States; instead, they chose to settle in Israel. Citing his status as an almost US citizen, Sarid reflected on Bush administration policies—including wiretapping, ignoring the rights of detainees, torture, and the 2003 invasion of Iraq—and he observed that US "moral deterrence has vanished" and that "any war criminal can scrub and launder his misdeeds with US soap."[604]

This comment identified merely one facet of an important point: Given the US disdain for international law, there is little to deter others from disregarding it as well. Why should Israel practice restraint in Lebanon and Gaza when the US demonstrated no such restraint in Iraq? Likewise, why should the Palestinians stop their suicide bombings when Israel shoots and bombs Palestinian women and children? When the US and Israel so thoroughly violate international law, why should Iran be restrained when it threatens—in violation of the cardinal rule of international law, the prohibition against the threat and use of force—the destruction of Israel? When Israel fires artillery shells into Gaza, why shouldn't Palestinians fire Qassams into Israel? When Israel engages in targeted assassinations in Gaza, what keeps Syria from assassinating officials in Lebanon? When Israel has a secret nuclear weapons program, why shouldn't Iran have one? Looking at the situation objectively, the notion that the US and Israel conduct themselves in the world any better than Iran, Syria, or the Palestinians is not supported by the evidence. Yet, as Yossi Sarid sarcastically pointed out, "Washington's ridiculous policy, which it dictates to Israel, too," is that it "doesn't talk to scumbags."[605]

Without the prospect of talks for a final-status agreement on the Israel-Palestine conflict—which hopefully this time around would recognize the legitimate rights of both parties—the alternative is the inevitable next war against Hamas, Hezbollah, Syria, or Iran. A final-status agreement on the conflict might not only prevent major regional war, but it could also clear the way to further steps, including the settlement of territorial claims with Syria and Lebanon, and the outstanding issues in Iran and Iraq could then be addressed in a much different political context than that which exists today. The US and Israeli soap that Iran uses to wash its threats would have mostly melted away.

Similarly, when the *New York Times* ignores international law, other major news organizations, using the *New York Times'* soap, can easily ignore it as well. When a prominent Harvard law professor unfairly attacks the human rights organizations that monitor international humanitarian law, it becomes easier for other commentators to do it too. When President Clinton ignores the applicable UN resolutions and the Fourth Geneva Convention during final-status negotiations, it becomes more difficult for a succeeding president to apply those criteria to peace in the Middle East. The tragic irony, in our view, is that applying international law to each of these areas would have improved Israel's national security, the lives of Palestinians, the *Times'* journalism, academic analysis of the conflict, and prospects for a permanent peace agreement respecting the legitimate rights of all parties involved.

The leadership roles that the United States and the *New York Times* could have taken were roles that they refused—and as a result, the prestige and influence of both have waned. What could have been a world organized around the UN Charter now looks like the US-backed carnage in Lebanon and Gaza and the US masterpiece in Iraq. What could have been a country genuinely organized around the US Constitution now functions as if Vice President Dick Cheney were a founding constitutional author. People ask, "How did things ever get this bad?" Back when it mattered, when a civilized world could have been charted, two roads diverged in a wood, and the US could not travel both. It took the one most traveled by, to its own great harm, and the world's.

Notes

1. Dennis Ross, *The Missing Peace: The Inside Story of the Fight for Middle East Peace* (New York: Farrar, Straus and Giroux, 2004).
2. Clayton Swisher, *The Truth About Camp David: The Untold Story about the Collapse of the Middle East Peace Process* (New York: Nation Books, 2004), p. 15.
3. Richard A. Falk and Burns H. Weston, "The Relevance of International Law to Palestinian Rights in the West Bank and Gaza: In Legal Defense of the Intifada," *Harvard Journal of International Law* 32:129-157 (1991).
4. Protocol Additional to the Geneva Conventions of 12 August 1949, and relating to the Protection of Victims of International Armed Conflicts (Protocol I), 8 June 1977, www.icrc.org.
5. "The Oslo Declaration of Principles," September 13, 1993, the text of which can be found at www.mideastweb.org/meoslodop.
6. "A Performance-Based Roadmap to a Permanent Two-State Solution to the Israeli-Palestinian Conflict," April 30, 2003, the text of which can be found at www.state.gov/r/pa/prs/2003/20062.
7. "*Intifada*" is an Arabic word for "uprising." The purpose of this uprising was to demonstrate against Israel's long-standing occupation of the Palestinian territories. The first *intifada* took place from December 9, 1987, to September 13, 1993.
8. See also "Sharon Touches a Nerve, And Jerusalem Explodes," *New York Times*, September 29, 2000. The article, printed on page 11, reported: "Mr. Sharon entered as a police helicopter clattered overhead and a thousand armed policemen were positioned in and around the Temple Mount, including antiterror squads and ranks of riot officers carrying clubs, helmets and plastic shields. Throughout the tour, Mr. Sharon was ringed by agents of the Shin Bet security service."
9. The International Committee of the Red Cross defines "international humanitarian law" as "compris[ing] the rules which, in times of armed conflict, seek to protect people who are not or are no longer taking part in the hostilities, and to restrict the methods and means of warfare employed." The Geneva Conventions of 1949 and their Additional Protocols of 1977 are the main instruments of international humanitarian law. See "International Humanitarian Law: Answers to Your Questions," ICRC, October 2002, pp. 4, 11, www.icrc.org.
10. B'Tselem, "International Law: International Humanitarian Law (Laws of War)," 2006, www.btselem.org/English.
11. B'Tselem, "Statistics: Fatalities," as of December 18, 2006, www.btselem.org/English. This figure includes 3,930 Palestinians killed by Israeli security forces in the occupied territories, 61 Palestinians killed by Israeli security forces in Israel, and 41 Palestinians killed by Israeli civilians in the occupied territories.
12. Ibid. This figure includes 466 Israeli civilians killed by Palestinians in Israel, 235 Israeli civilians killed by Palestinians in the occupied territories, 87 Israeli security

force personnel killed by Palestinians in Israel, and 229 Israeli security force personnel killed by Palestinians in the occupied territories.

13. Ibid. A "child" is defined by the 1989 UN Convention on the Rights of the Child [Article 1], as any person younger than eighteen years of age.

14. Ibid.

15. "Suicide Bomber Kills 3 Israelis After Deaths of 6 Palestinians," *New York Times*, March 5, 2001, p. A1; "Sharon Orders His First Raid After Bombing," *New York Times*, March 29, 2001, p. A1; "Suicide Bomber Kills 5; Israel Retaliates in Jet Strikes," *New York Times*, May 19, 2001, p. A1; "16 Killed by Suicide Bomber Outside Tel Aviv Nightclub," *New York Times*, June 2, 2001, p. A1; "At Least 14 Dead As Suicide Bomber Strikes Jerusalem," *New York Times*, August 10, 2001, p. A1; "Israelis Grieve, and Strike Back," *New York Times*, August 11, 2001, p. A1; "2 Suicide Bombers Strike Jerusalem, Killing at Least 10," *New York Times*, December 2, 2001, p. A1; "Crackdown Pledge: Arafat Faces Pivotal Test," *New York Times*, December 3, 2001, p.A1; "Israel Breaks with Arafat After Palestinian Assault on Bus in West Bank Kills 10," *New York Times*, December 13, 2001, p. A1; "Latest Attacks Stun Israelis and Dampen Hopes for Peace," *New York Times*, March 4, 2002, p. A1; "Jerusalem Bomber Kills 3 and Shakes U.S. Peace Effort," *New York Times*, March 22, 2002, p. A1; "Up Close, Too Close, to a Suicide Bombing," *New York Times*, March 22, 2002, p. A1; "A Secret Iran-Arafat Connection Is Seen Fueling the Mideast Fire," *New York Times*, March 24, 2002, p. A1; "Bomb Kills at Least 19 in Israel as Arabs Meet Over Peace Plan," *New York Times*, March 28, 2002, p. A1; "U.S. Puts Onus on Palestinians To Stop Terror," *New York Times*, March 30, 2002, p. A1; "Again in Israel, Sabbath Closes in Terror Attack," *New York Times*, March 31, 2002, p. A1; "Sharon Says Israel Is in a War After Suicide Bombing Kills 14; More Tanks Move in West Bank," *New York Times*, April 1, 2002, p. A1; "Bomber Strikes Jews and Arabs at Rare Refuge," *New York Times*, April 1, 2002, p. A1; "2 Girls, Divided by War, Joined in Carnage," *New York Times*, April 5, 2002, p. A1; "At Least 8 Killed in Suicide Bombing on a Bus in Israel," *New York Times*, April 10, 2002, p. A1; "15 Killed by Suicide Bomber; Sharon Cuts Short U.S. Visit After Meeting with Bush," *New York Times*, May 8, 2002, p. A1; "Bomber Disguised as Israeli Soldier Kills 3 in Market," *New York Times*, May 20, 2002, p. A1; "New Arab Bombing in Israel Deepens a Sense of Dismay," *New York Times*, May 28, 2002, p. A1; "At Least 12 Die as Car Bomber Hits Israeli Bus," *New York Times*, June 5, 2002, p. A1; "Israel Attacks Arafat Compound in Swift Response After Palestinian Suicide Bombing Kills 17 in Bus," *New York Times*, June 6, 2002, p. A1; "Israel Acts to Seize Arab Land After Blast; Bush Delays Talk," *New York Times*, June 19, 2002, p. A1; "Jerusalem Blast Kills Six Israelis; Army Raids Start," *New York Times*, June 20, 2002, p. A1; "Palestinians Kill 5 Israeli Settlers in Raid on a Home," *New York Times*, June 21, 2002, p. A1; "Aides to Bush Say Arafat Financed a Terrorist Group," *New York Times*, June 26, 2002, p. A1; "Pair of Bombers Strike in Tel Aviv, Killing 3 in Street," *New York Times*, July 18, 2002, p. A1; "At Least 17 Killed as Militants Bomb Jerusalem Campus," *New York Times*, August 1, 2002, p. A1; "Burst of Attacks from Palestinians Causes 14 Deaths," *New York Times*, August 5, 2002, p. A1; "Suicide Bomber Kills 5 on a Bus in Tel Aviv," *New York Times*, September 20, 2002, p. A1; "Bus Driver's Frantic Struggle Averts Bloodbath in Tel Aviv," *New York Times*, October 11, 2002, p. A1; "14 Die as Bomb-Filled S.U.V. Rams Israeli Bus," *New York Times*, October 22, 2002, P. A1; "12 Israelis Killed in Hebron Ambush Near Prayer Site," *New York Times*, November 16, 2002, p. A1; "At Least 10 Killed in Suicide Bombing of Jerusalem Bus," *New York Times*, November 21, 2002, p. A1; "Pair of Bombers Kill 23 in Israel; Reprisals Begin," *New York Times*, January 6, 2003, p. A1; "Nine Palestinians

and Two Israelis Die in Day of Fury," *New York Times*, January 13, 2003, p. A1; "Suicide Bombing on Bus in Israel Leaves 15 Dead," *New York Times*, March 6, 2003, p. A1; "3 Israelis Killed and 50 Wounded in Blast at Mall," *New York Times*, May 20, 2003, p. A1; "Suicide Blast Kills 16 in Jerusalem; Israel Strikes Gaza," *New York Times*, June 12, 2003, p. A1; "2 Israelis Killed in Suicide Attacks by Arab Bombers," *New York Times*, August 13, 2003, p. A1; "Bombing Kills 18 and Hurts Scores on Jerusalem Bus," *New York Times*, August 20, 2003, p. A1; "In 2 Bombings, Arab Attackers Kill 13 in Israel," *New York Times*, September 10, 2003, p. A1; "Suicide Attacker Kills at Least 19 in North of Israel," *New York Times*, October 5, 2003, p. A1; "Bush Tells Israel It Has the Right to Defend Itself," *New York Times*, October 7, 2003, p. A1; "Suicide Attacker Kills 4 in Israel," *New York Times*, December 26, 2003, p. A1; "Israeli Pathologist Faces Grisly Task after the Bombings," *New York Times*, February 24, 2004, p. A1; "Suicide Bombers Kill 10 in Israel, and Derail Prime Ministers' Talks," *New York Times*, March 15, 2004, p. A1; "Israelis Trudge Home, in Shock After Bombing," *New York Times*, October 9, 2004, p. A1; "Suicide Bombing Kills at Least 4 at Tel Aviv Club," *New York Times*, February 26, 2005, p. A1.

16. "Troops Kill 4 in Gaza; 2 Die in Car Bombing in Israel," *New York Times*, November 23, 2000; "Suicide Bomber Attacks Israeli Bus, Killing a Doctor," *New York Times*, April 23, 2001; "Suicide Bomber Kills 2 Israeli Soldiers; 3rd Is Badly Wounded," *New York Times*, July 17, 2001; "Bush Asks Arafat to Condemn Bombing in Jerusalem," *New York Times*, August 10, 2001; "Militants Vow More Bombing to Avenge Deaths in Gaza," *New York Times*, August 21, 2001; "Man in Orthodox Jew's Garb Sets Off Blast in Jerusalem," *New York Times*, September 5, 2001; "Another Arab Bombing Kills 3 Israelis," *New York Times*, November 30, 2001; "Toxic Traces after Bombing Add to Jitters of Israelis," *New York Times*, December 12, 2001; "Suicide Bomb Wounds 2 Dozen in Tel Aviv Outdoor Mall," *New York Times*, January 26, 2002; "West Bank Suicide Bombing Kills 2 Israelis and Hurts 30," *New York Times*, February 17, 2002; "In Jerusalem, Suicide Bomber Kills at Least 9," *New York Times*, March 3, 2002; "Palestinian Group Says It Will Increase Bombings," *New York Times*, March 23, 2002; "Suicide Bomber, 18, Kills 2 Israelis and Herself," *New York Times*, March 30, 2002; "In Interview, Arafat's Wife Praises Suicide Bombings," *New York Times*, April 15, 2002; "Arab Rakes Israeli Yeshiva with Gunfire; 3 Students Die," *New York Times*, May 29, 2002; "A Morning Commute by Bus Is Transformed into a Shattering Blood Bath," *New York Times*, June 19, 2002; "Suicide Bomber Kills Israeli Soldier, Ending 6 Weeks of Quiet," *New York Times*, September 19, 2002; "Palestinian Subdued and Shot, Yet His Bomb Kills 3," *New York Times*, October 28, 2002; "Bomber Kills 2 and Hurts 30 in Israeli Mall," *New York Times*, November 5, 2002; "A Palestinian Attack Kills 5 on Northern Kibbutz," *New York Times*, November 11, 2002; "In Bus Attack, a Jerusalem Suicide Bomber Kills 6 and Wounds More than 20," *New York Times*, May 18, 2003; "Arafat Calls on Palestinian Militants to Halt Attacks on Israelis," *New York Times*, August 28, 2003; "Gaza Mother, 22, Kills Four Israelis in Suicide Bombing," *New York Times*, January 15, 2004; "Palestinian Bomber Kills 8 and Wounds 50 in Jerusalem," *New York Times*, February 23, 2004; "Twin Blasts Kill 16 in Israel; Hamas Claims Responsibility," *New York Times*, September 1, 2004; "Islamic Jihad Says It Was Behind Bombing in Tel Aviv," *New York Times*, February 27; "Suicide Bomber and 2 Women Die in Attack at Mall in Israeli Town," *New York Times*, July 13, 2005; "Palestinian Suicide Bomber Kills 5 in Israeli Town," *New York Times*, October 27, 2005; "Palestinian Bomber Kills Himself and 5 Others Near Israel Mall," *New York Times*, December 6, 2005; "3 Killed by Suicide Bomber at Checkpoint in the West Bank," *New York Times*, December 30, 2005.

17. "Report of the United Nations High Commissioner for Human Rights and Follow-Up to the World Conference on Human Rights: Question of the Violation of Human Rights in the Occupied Arab Territories, Including Palestine: Report of the High Commissioner on Her Visit to the Occupied Palestinian Territories, Israel, Egypt and Jordan (8–16 November 2000)," United Nations Commission on Human Rights, E/CN.4/2001/114, November 29, 2000, www.ohchr.org.
18. United Nations Security Resolution 1322, October 7, 2000, www.un.org/Docs/sc/unsc_resolutions.
19. "Israelis Criticized for Using Deadly Force Too Readily," *New York Times*, October 4, 2000; "U.S. Abstains in Resolution Condemning Use of Force," *New York Times*, October 8, 2000; "Arab–Israeli Conflict Spreads to Border with Lebanon," *New York Times*, October 8, 2000; "Politely, Lazio and Mrs. Clinton Debate UN and Supreme Court," *New York Times*, October 9, 2000; "Lazio Runs National Ad Campaign to Raise Money for His Senate Race," *New York Times*, October 11, 2000; "Israel Needs an Ally," *New York Times*, October 12, 2000; "Midtown Throng Gathers, Rallying Support for Israel," *New York Times*, October 13, 2000; "Palestinians May Seek General Assembly Vote to Condemn Israel," *New York Times*, October 14, 2000.
20. "Israelis Criticized for Using Deadly Force Too Readily."
21. Amnesty International, "Israel and the Occupied Territories: Excessive Use of Lethal Force," October 19, 2000, www.amnesty.org.
22. "Gun Lessons Are Suddenly All the Rage in Israel," *New York Times*, October 25, 2000.
23. Human Rights Watch, "Israel, the Occupied West Bank and Gaza Strip, and the Palestinian Authority Territories: Investigation into Unlawful Use of Force in the West Bank, Gaza Strip, and Northern Israel: October 4 through October 11," October 2000, www.hrw.org.
24. Physicians for Human Rights, "Evaluation of the Use of Force in Israel, Gaza, and the West Bank: Medical and Forensic Investigation," November 3, 2000, www.physiciansforhumanrights.org.
25. Ibid.
26. "Doctors Back Many Palestinian Accusations, but Not All," *New York Times*, November 4, 2000.
27. Ibid.
28. "Report of the United Nations High Commissioner for Human Rights and Follow-Up to the World Conference on Human Rights; Question of the Violation of Human Rights in the Occupied Arab Territories, Including Palestine: Report of the High Commissioner on Her Visit to the Occupied Palestinian Territories, Israel, Egypt and Jordan (8–16 November 2000)," United Nations Commission on Human Rights, E/CN.4/2001/114, November 29, 2000, www.ohchr.org.
29. "U.N. Rights Chief Proposes West Bank and Gaza Monitors," *New York Times*, November 28, 2000.
30. "Troops Kill 4 in Gaza; 2 Die in Car Bombing in Israel," *New York Times*, November 23, 2000.
31. Ibid.
32. B'Tselem, "Illusions of Restraint: Human Rights Violations During the Events in the Occupied Territories, 29 September–2 December 2000," December 2000, www.btselem,.org.
33. "Question of the Violation of Human Rights in the Occupied Arab Territories, Including Palestine: Report of the Human Rights Inquiry Commission Established Pursuant to Commission Resolutions S-5/1 of 19 October 2000," United Nations Economic and Social Council, Commission on Human Rights, E/CN.4/2001/121, March 16, 2001, http://unispal.un.org/unispal.nsf.

34. "Suicide Bomber Kills 3 Israelis After Deaths of 6 Palestinians," *New York Times*, March 5, 2001.

35. Amnesty International, *Amnesty International Report 2001*, www.amnesty.org.

36. Amnesty International, *Amnesty International Report 2002*, www.amnesty.org.

37. Amnesty International, *Amnesty International Report 2003*, www.amnesty.org.

38. Amnesty International, *Amnesty International Report 2004*, www.amnesty.org.

39. Amnesty International, *Amnesty International Report 2005*, www.amnesty.org.

40. Ibid.

41. Amnesty International, *Amnesty International Report 2006*, www.amnesty.org.

42. B'Tselem, "Statistics: Fatalities," December 2006, www.btselem.org.

43. Amnesty International, "Israel and the Occupied Territories: Excessive Use of Lethal Force," October 19, 2000; Amnesty International, "Israel and the Occupied Territories: Mass Arrests and Police Brutality," November 10, 2000; Amnesty International, "Israel and the Occupied Territories: Imported Arms Used in Israel and the Occupied Territories with Excessive Force Resulting in Unlawful Killings and Unwarranted Injuries," November 17, 2000; Amnesty International, "Israel and the Occupied Territories/Palestinian Authority: Killings and Disrupted Health Care in the Context of the Palestinian Uprising—Medical Letter Writing Action," November 20, 2000; Amnesty International, "Israel and the Occupied Territories: State Assassinations and Other Unlawful Killings," February 21, 2001; Amnesty International, "Israel and the Occupied Territories/Palestinian Authority: The Right to Return: The Case of the Palestinians," March 30, 2001; Amnesty International, "Israel and the Occupied Territories: Broken Lives—A Year of Intifada," November 13, 2001; Amnesty International, "Israel/Occupied Territories: Medical Letter Writing Action: Attacks on Health and Disrupted Health Care," March 14, 2002; Amnesty International, "Israel/Occupied Territories: Update on Attacks on Health Personnel and Disrupted Health Care," April 5, 2002; Amnesty International, "Israel and the Occupied Territories: The Heavy Price of Israeli Incursions," April 12, 2002; Amnesty International, "Amnesty International Statement on the Protection of Human Rights and Humanitarian Law in Israel and the Occupied Territories," April 19, 2002; Amnesty International, "Amnesty International Statement to the United Nations About the Fact-Finding Team Inquiry into the Events in Jenin," April 22, 2002; Amnesty International, "Israel and the Occupied Territories: Statement by Amnesty International," April 26, 2002; Amnesty International, "Universal Jurisdiction: Belgian Court Has Jurisdiction in Sharon Case to Investigate 1982 Sabra and Chatila Killings," May 1, 2002; Amnesty International, "Israel/Occupied Territories: Declaration of Detainees' Rights," May 1, 2002; Amnesty International, "Israel and Occupied Territories: Briefing for the Committee Against Torture," May 14, 2002; Amnesty International, "Israel and the Occupied Territories: Mass Detention in Cruel, Inhuman and Degrading Conditions," May 23, 2002; Amnesty International, "Middle East: Israel and the Occupied Territories and the Palestinian Authority: Without Distinction—Attacks on Civilians by Palestinian Armed Groups," July 7, 2002; Amnesty International, "Middle East: Israel and the Occupied Territories and the Palestinian Authority: Killing the Future: Children in the Line of Fire," September 30, 2002; Amnesty International, "Israel and the Occupied Territories: Shielded From Scrutiny: IDF Violations in Jenin and Nablus," November 4, 2002; Amnesty International, "Israel and the Occupied Territories and the Palestinian Authority: Killing the Future: Children in the Line of Fire—Appeals Cases," November 20, 2002; Amnesty International, "Universal Jurisdiction: Belgian Prosecutors Can Investigate Crimes Under International Law Committed Abroad," February 1, 2003; Amnesty International, "Israel and the Occupied Territories:

Asma Muhammad Suleiman Saba'neh: Letter Writing Action," February 26, 2003; Amnesty International, "Israel and the Occupied Territories: Further Information on Asma Muhammad Suleiman Saba'neh: Medical Letter Writing Action," May 16, 2003; Amnesty International, "Israel and the Occupied Territories: Israel Must Put an Immediate End to the Policy and Practice of Assassinations," July 7, 2003; Amnesty International, "Israel and the Occupied Territories: The Issue of Settlements Must Be Addressed According to International Law," September 8, 2003; Amnesty International, "Israel and the Occupied Territories: Surviving Under Siege: The Impact of Restrictions on the Right to Work," September 8, 2003; Amnesty International, "Israel and the Occupied Territories: The Place of the Fence/Wall in International Law," February 19, 2004; Amnesty International, "Israel and the Occupied Territories: Under the Rubble: House Demolitions and Destruction of Land and Property," May 18, 2004; Amnesty International, "Israel and the Occupied Territories: Torn Apart: Families Split by Discriminatory Policies," July 13, 2004; Amnesty International, "Israel/Occupied Territories: Israeli Settlers Wage Campaign of Intimidation on Palestinians and Internationals Alike," October 25, 2004; Amnesty International, "Israel and the Occupied Territories and the Palestinian Authority: Act Now To Stop the Killing of Children!," November 20, 2004; Amnesty International, "Israel: Conflict, Occupation and Patriarchy: Women Carry the Burden," March 31, 2005; Amnesty International, "Israel/Occupied Territories: Israel—Briefing to the Committee on the Elimination of Discrimination Against Women," June 30, 2005. This list of reports does not include press releases issued by Amnesty International during this period.

44. "Court Says Israel Can Expel 2 of Militants' Kin to Gaza," *New York Times*, September 4, 2002.

45. "With Arafat Siege Lifted, Sharon Faces a New Storm," *New York Times*, October 1, 2002.

46. "More Young Victims Falling on Front Lines in the Mideast," *New York Times*, October 5, 2002.

47. "Palestinians and Israelis Clash in Gaza; At Least 6 Die," *New York Times*, October 18, 2002.

48. Ibid.

49. "Amnesty Accuses Israeli Forces of War Crimes," *New York Times*, November 4, 2002.

50. Ibid.

51. "Rights Group Blames Arafat for Not Halting Suicide Attacks," *New York Times*, November 1, 2002.

52. Amnesty International USA, "Calls for Cessation of All Attack Helicopter Transfers to Israel," October 19, 2000, www.amnestyusa.org.

53. Federation of American Scientists, "Troublesome Transfers in the Works," www.fas.org/asmp/profiles/IsraelTroublesome.html.

54. See Friel and Falk, *The Record of the Paper*, pp. 15–45.

55. See chapter 7 in this volume.

56. Human Rights Watch, *Human Rights Watch World Report 2001*, www.hrw.org.

57. Human Rights Watch, *Human Rights Watch World Report 2002*, www.hrw.org.

58. Human Rights Watch, *Human Rights Watch World Report 2003*, www.hrw.org.

59. Human Rights Watch, *Human Rights Watch World Report 2005*, www.hrw.org. HRW's annual report published in 2004 deviated from the usual format and did not include country reports, so there was no country report on Israel and the occupied territories.

60. Human Rights Watch, *Human Rights Watch World Report 2006*, www.hrw.org.

61. Human Rights Watch, "Investigation Into Unlawful Use of Force in the West Bank, Gaza Strip, and Northern Israel, October 4 Through October 11," October 1, 2000; Human Rights Watch, "Israel/Palestinian Authority: Restraint Urged: Police and Troops Must Protect Civilian Lives," October 4, 2000; Human Rights Watch, "Independent Inquiry Needed in Israeli-Palestinian Bloodshed," October 7, 2000; Human rights Watch, "Research Shows Israeli Pattern of Excessive Force: Palestinian Authority Also Fails in Duty to Protect Civilians," October 17, 2000; Human Rights Watch, "Israel, Palestinian Leaders Should Guarantee Right of Return as Part of Comprehensive Refugee Solution," December 22, 2000; Human Rights Watch, "Israel: End 'Liquidations' of Palestinian Suspects," January 29, 2001; Human Rights Watch, "Palestinian Authority: Halt Executions," January 31, 2001; Human Rights Watch, "Palestinian Authority: Commute Death Sentence," February 12, 2001; Human Rights Watch, "Israel Must Investigate Minibus Killing," February 14, 2001; Human Rights Watch, "Israel: Palestinian Drivers Routinely Abused," February 27, 2001; Human Rights Watch, "Palestinian Authority: Death in Suspicious Circumstances," March 2, 2001; Human Rights Watch, "Israel/Palestinian Authority: International Monitoring Presence Needed," March 28, 2001; Human Rights Watch, "Item 8—Question of the Violation of Human Rights in the Occupied Arab Territories, Including Palestine," March 28, 2001; Human Rights Watch, "Center of the Storm: A Case Study of Human Rights Abuses in Hebron District," April 1, 2001; Human Rights Watch, "Mounting Human Rights Crisis in Hebron: Study Finds Unlawful Killings, Collective Punishment, Failure to Protect Civilians," April 11, 2001; Human Rights Watch, "Israel/Palestinian Authority: Discotheque Bombing Condemned," June 4, 2001; Human Rights Watch, "Israel: Dart Shells Pose Civilian Threat," June 16, 2001; Human Rights Watch, "Israel: Sharon Investigation Urged," June 23, 2001; Human Rights Watch, "Israel/Palestinian Authority: International Monitors a Must: Amnesty International and Human Rights Watch Joint Statement," July 6, 2001; Human Rights Watch, "Israel: Palestinian Academic Rights Violated," July 14, 2001; Human Rights Watch, "Letter to Palestinian Authority President Yasser Arafat: Regarding the Death Penalty for Accused Collaborators," August 2, 2001; Human Rights Watch, "Palestinian Suicide Attack Condemned," August 9, 2001; Human Rights Watch, "PA: Arafat Urged to Commute Death Sentences," August 9, 2001; Human Rights Watch, "Palestinian Authority: Inquiry into Student Deaths Essential," October 11, 2001; Human Rights Watch, "Israel/ Palestinian Authority: Call on Islamic Jihad to Stop Civilian Killings," November 8, 2001; Human Rights Watch, "U.S.: Rights Not 'Optional' in Israel/Palestinian Peace Process," November 16, 2001; Human Rights Watch, "Justice Undermined: Balancing Security and Human Rights in the Palestinian Justice System," November 30, 2001; Human Rights Watch, "Palestinian Authority: End Torture and Unfair Trials," November 30, 2001; Human Rights Watch, "Israel/PA: Bus Attack Condemned," December 14, 2001; Human Rights Watch, "Israel: Opportunistic Law Condemned," March 7, 2002; Human Rights Watch, "Israel: Cease Attacking Medical Personnel," March 9, 2002; Human Rights Watch, "Israel/Palestinian Authority: Protect Civilians, Allow Independent Reporting," May 2, 2002; Human Rights Watch, "Joint Statement Given in Jerusalem: Human Rights Watch, Amnesty International and the International Commission of Jurists," April 7, 2002; Human Rights Watch, "Israel: Allow Access to Jenin Camp," April 15, 2002; Human Rights Watch, "In a Dark Hour: The Use of Civilians During IDF Arrest Operations," April 18, 2002; Human Rights Watch, "Israel: Decision to Block U.N. Inquiry Condemned," April 24, 2002; Human Rights Watch, "Violence in Israel, the Occupied West Bank and Gaza Strip, and the Palestinian

Authority Territories," May 1, 2002; Human Rights Watch, "Jenin: IDF Military Operations," May 2, 2002; Human Rights Watch, "Israel/Occupied Territories: Jenin War Crimes Investigation Needed," May 3, 2002; Human Rights Watch, "Israel/PA: Armed Groups Should Halt Attacks on Civilians," May 9, 2002; Human Rights Watch, "Israel: Decision to Stop Use of 'Human Shields' Welcomed," May 10, 2002; Human Rights Watch, "Jerusalem Bus Atrocity Attacked," June 18, 2002; Human Rights Watch, "Israeli Airstrike on Crowded Civilian Area Condemned," July 23, 2002; Human Rights Watch, "U.N. Jenin Report," August 2, 2002; Human Rights Watch, "Israel/PA: Hamas Must End Civilian Attacks," August 7, 2002; Human Rights Watch, "Erased in a Moment: Suicide Bombing Attacks Against Israeli Civilians," November 1, 2002; Human Rights Watch, "Briefing to the 59th Session of the UN Commission on Human Rights on Israel/Occupied Territories," February 14, 2003; Human Rights Watch, "Israel: Stop Using Flechettes in Gaza," April 29, 2003; Human Rights Watch, "The 'Roadmap': Repeating Oslo's Human Rights Mistakes," May 8, 2003; Human Rights Watch, "International Rights Groups Decry Increased Harassment of Monitors," May 27, 2003; Human Rights Watch, "Israel/PA: Roadmap Needs Rights Component," June 3, 2003; Human Rights Watch, "Israel: Don't Outlaw Family Life," July 28, 2003; Human Rights Watch, "Israel: West Bank Barrier Endangers Basic Rights," October 1, 2003; Human Rights Watch, "Egypt/Israel: Attacks on Civilians Are Unjustifiable Crimes," January 13, 2004; Human Rights Watch, "Israel/Occupied Territories: Briefing to the 60th Session of the UN Commission on Human Rights," January 29, 2004; Human Rights Watch, "Human Rights and Counter-Terrorism: Briefing to the 60th Session of the UN Commission on Human Rights," January 29, 2004; Human Rights Watch, "Israel's Separation Barrier in the Occupied West Bank: Human Rights and International Humanitarian Law Consequences," February 20, 2004; Human Rights Watch, "Israel: West Bank Barrier Violates Human Rights: International Court of Justice Opens Hearings on Barrier Case," February 23, 2004; Human Rights Watch, "Israel: Bush Should Press Sharon on Rights Violations," April 13, 2004; Human Rights Watch, "Israel: End Unlawful Use of Force Against Civilians in Gaza: Israeli Government Should Repudiate Plans for Mass House Demolition," May 19, 2004; Human Rights Watch, "Israel: Strikes to Silence Palestinian Media," July 2, 2004; Human Rights Watch, "Gaza: Killings in Hospital Violate Laws of War," August 3, 2004; Human Rights Watch, "Israel: Release Rights Activist Immediately," August 6, 2004; Human Rights Watch, "Razing Rafah: Mass Home Demolitions in the Gaza Strip," October 18, 2004; Human Rights Watch, "Israel: Despite Gaza Pullout Plan, Home Demolitions Expand: Israeli Forces Destroy Homes to Clear Palestinians From Border," October 18, 2004; Human Rights Watch, "Israel: 'Disengagement' Will Not End Gaza Occupation: Israeli Government Still Holds Responsibility for Welfare of Civilians," October 29, 2004; Human Rights Watch, "Occupied Territories: Stop Use of Children in Suicide Bombings," November 2, 2004; Human Rights Watch, "Israel: Caterpillar Should Suspend Bulldozer Sales: Weaponized Bulldozers Used to Destroy Civilian Property and Infrastructure," November 22, 2004; Human Rights Watch, "Israel: Reject Plan to Demolish Gaza Homes," January 23, 2005; Human Rights Watch, "Israel/Occupied Territories: Human Rights Concerns for the 61st Session of the U.N. Commission on Human Rights," March 10, 2005; Human Rights Watch, "Palestinian Authority: Death Penalty Should Be Abolished," March 31, 2005; Human Rights Watch, "Israel: Bush Should Lay Down the Law on Settlements: Sharon Must Be Told That U.S. Cannot Support Violations of International Humanitarian Law," April 11, 2005; Human Rights Watch, "Israel: Reject Law

Separating Spouses: Discriminatory Law Tears Apart Thousands of Families," May 23, 2005; Human Rights Watch, "U.S.: Bush Should Urge Abbas to Respect Rights," May 26, 2005; Human Rights Watch, "Hamas Must End Attacks Against Civilians: Cease Use of Qassam Rockets," June 9, 2005; Human Rights Watch, "Promoting Impunity: The Israeli Military's Failure to Investigate Wrongdoing," June 22, 2005; Human Rights Watch, "Israel: Bill Would Deny Compensation for Rights Abuses: Palestinians Would Be Excluded from Seeking Remedies in Israel Courts," June 26, 2005; Human Rights Watch, "Knesset Should Reject Amendment to the Civil Wrongs Law," July 27, 2005; Human Rights Watch, "Letter to Senator Clinton on Comments about the Construction of the Wall," November 23, 2005; Human Rights Watch, "Israel: Gaza Power Cut Would Violate Laws of War: Militant Attacks Cannot Justify Unlawful Collective Punishment," December 27, 2005.

62. B'Tselem, "Statistics," September 2006, www.btselem.org.

63. See Defence for Children International home page at http://www.child-abuse.com/childhouse/childrens_rights/dci_what.html.

64. Defence for Children International, "Breakdown of Palestinian Child Deaths (29 September 2000–31 December 2000)," December 31, 2000, www.dci-pal.org. We reproduced the chart as issued, and made no changes for punctuation or style.

65. See www.dci-pal.org/english for other such reports issued by DCI. These reports include the following: "Status of Palestinian Children's Rights," September 28, 2004; "Violations of Palestinian Children's Rights Stemming from the Israeli Occupation," September 24, 2004; "Breakdown of Palestinian Child Deaths (January 2004–April 2004), June 2, 2004; "Breakdown of Palestinian Child Deaths (September 2003– October 2003)," November 19, 2003; "Palestinian Children in the Judicial System, June 2003," July 14, 2003; "Breakdown of Palestinian Child Deaths (1 January–15 June 2003)," July 9, 2003; "Legal Review of Palestinian Child Prisoners for the UN Special Rapporteur, June 2003," June 30, 2003; "Breakdown of Palestinian Child Injuries (1 January–April 2003)," May 10, 2003; "Palestinian Children in the Judicial System, 2002," March 3, 2003; "Breakdown of Palestinian Child Injuries, 2002," February 14, 2003; "Breakdown of Palestinian Child Deaths, 2002," February 12, 2003; "Breakdown of Palestinian Child Deaths (1 January 2002–15 August 2002)," August 20, 2002; "Breakdown of Palestinian Child Deaths During the Intifada (29 September 2000–31 July 2002)," August 17, 2002; "Israeli Practice Towards Palestinian Children, In Violation of UN Convention on Torture and Other Cruel, Inhuman, or Degrading Treatment or Punishment (1984)," May 8, 2002; "Hundreds of Palestinian Children Arrested in the Last Twelve Days, Widespread Reports of Torture," April 9, 2002; "Key Facts: Violations of Palestinian Children's Rights Stemming From the Israeli Occupation," March 23, 2002; "Breakdown of Palestinian Child Deaths Annually (1990–2001)," March 15, 2002; "Violations of Palestinian Children's Rights Stemming from the Israeli Occupation, Report Submitted to Mr. John Dugard, Special Rapporteur of the UN Commission on Human Rights," February 13, 2002; "Breakdown of Palestinian Child Deaths During the Intifada (September 2000–September 2001)," October 14, 2001; "Summary of Attacks on Palestinian Child Political Prisoners by Israeli Prison Guards, Army and Riot Police, September 2001," September 30, 2001; "Breakdown of Palestinian Child Deaths and Injuries in 2001," August 30, 2001; "Violation of Palestinian Children's Rights, Submitted to the UN High Commissioner for Human Rights," November 13, 2000; "An Environment of Terror for Palestinian Children," November 2, 2000.

66. Defence for Children International, "Breakdown of Palestinian Child Deaths Annually (1990–2001)," March 15, 2002, www.dci-pal.org.

67. "Israel's Shooting of Young Girl Highlights International Hypocrisy, Say Palestinians," *Guardian*, January 30, 2006.
68. "Palestinian Medics: IDF Troops Kill Girl Near Gaza Strip Border Fence," *Ha'aretz*, January 26, 2006.
69. "Israel's Shooting of Young Girl Highlights International Hypocrisy, Say Palestinians."
70. "IDF Troops Kill Palestinian Wielding Toy Rifle Near Jenin," *Ha'aretz*, February 15, 2006.
71. "Five Killed in IAF Strike in Gaza, Including 8-Year-Old Boy," *Ha'aretz*, March 6, 2006.
72. "U.K. Condemns Israel for Killing of 10-Year-Old Palestinian Girl," *Ha'aretz*, March 19, 2006.
73. "IDF Kills Palestinian Boy in Clashes North of Jerusalem," *Ha'aretz*, April 3, 2006.
74. "IDF Shelling Kills 12-Year-Old Girl in Her Northern Gaza Home," *Ha'aretz*, April 11, 2006.
75. "Palestinians Turn to UNSC Against IDF Strikes in Gaza," *Jerusalem Post*, April 10, 2006.
76. "Hamas Said Set to Curb Kassams, but Fire Goes On," *Ha'aretz*, April 11, 2006.
77. "IDF to Continue Shelling Despite Civilian Deaths," *Ha'aretz*, April 11, 2006.
78. Amnesty International, "Israel/Occupied Territories: Israel Must Halt Attacks on Gaza Residential Areas—Children Killed," April 11, 2006, www.amnesty.org.
79. "IDF Accused of Knowingly Risking Palestinian Lives," *Ha'aretz*, April 16, 2006.
80. B'Tselem, "Israeli and Palestinian Human Rights Organizations Petition the High Court: Reducing 'Safety Zone' in Shelling of Gaza Strip Is Manifestly Illegal Order," April 16, 2006, www.btselem.org.
81. "IAF Aircraft Fires Missile at Metal Workshop in Gaza Strip," *Ha'aretz*, April 18, 2006.
82. "Seven Palestinians Hurt in IDF Shelling of Gaza Strip," *Ha'aretz*, April 30, 2006.
83. "IDF Troops Kill Palestinian Woman in West Bank Operation," *Ha'aretz*, May 1, 2006.
84. "IDF Confirms Civilian Woman's Death," *Jerusalem Post*, May 1, 2006.
85. "Palestinian Mom Killed, Daughter Hurt in IDF Arrest Raid," *Ha'aretz*, May 2, 2006.
86. "Palestinian Suicide Bomber Wounds 20 in Tel Aviv," *New York Times*, January 20, 2006; "Into the West Bank Abyss: From Student to Suicide Bomber," *New York Times*, January 20, 2006; "Bomber Kills 3 Israelis as Hamas Takes Power," *New York Times*, March 31, 2006; "Suicide Bombing in Israel Kills 9; Hamas Approves," *New York Times*, April 18, 2006; "Israel Plans Response to Tel Aviv Bombing," *New York Times*, April 19, 2006; "The Face of Hamas," *New York Times*, April 19, 2006.
87. "Olmert Says Israel Will Keep 3 Large West Bank Settlement Blocs," *New York Times*, February 8, 2006.
88. "Israeli Voters, by Thin Margin, Support Parties Vowing Pullout," *New York Times*, March 29, 2006.
89. "West Bank Withdrawal," *New York Times*, March 30, 2006.
90. "A New Consensus," *Ha'aretz*, March 19, 2006.
91. "Israel Cuts Jordan Rift from Rest of West Bank," *Ha'aretz*, February 13, 2006.
92. "Obsolete Security Asset," *Ha'aretz*, February 14, 2006.
93. "Israel Excludes Palestinians from Fertile Valley," *Guardian*, February 14, 2006.
94. "The New Israel: Election Victory Gives Ehud Olmert a Mandate to Implement His Controversial Plan to Redraw Border and Annex Palestinian Territory," *Independent*, March 30, 2006.
95. "Peretz Approves Expansion of Four West Bank Settlements," *Ha'aretz*, May 21, 2006.

96. "Israel to Expand W. Bank Settlements," *Jerusalem Post*, May 21, 2006.

97. "Only '20-30 Settlements' to Be Removed," *Jerusalem Post*, May 23, 2006.

98. "West Bank Pullout Gets a Nod From Bush," *New York Times*, May 24, 2006.

99. "2 Cheers for Olmert in Washington," *New York Times*, May 25, 2006.

100. Amnesty International, *Report 2006: The State of the World's Human Rights*, www.amnesty.org.

101. "Israelis Fired on Girl 'Having Identified Her as a 10-Year-Old,' Military Tape Shows," *Independent*, November 24, 2004.

102. "Israeli Army Chief 'Emptied His Magazine' at Girl in Gaza," *Independent*, October 12, 2004; "Gaza Girl Death Officer Cleared," BBC, October 15, 2004; "Israeli Officer: I Was Right to Shoot 13-Year-Old Child," *Guardian*, November 24, 2004; "Not Guilty. The Israeli Captain Who Emptied His Rifle into a Palestinian Schoolgirl," *Guardian*, November 16, 2005.

103. "Israeli Parliament Votes Its Symbolic Displeasure with Sharon's Plan for a Gaza Pullout," *New York Times*, October 12, 2004; "Israeli Military Kills 4 Palestinian Militants in Gaza Operation," *New York Times*, October 14, 2004; "Redeploying in Gaza Strip, Israel Finishes Its Pullback," *New York Times*, October 17, 2004; "Israel Charges Captain in Killing," *New York Times*, November 23, 2004; "Palestinian Girl, 8, Is Killed by Israeli Fire, Father Says," *New York Times*, December 11, 2004; "Israeli Cleared in Death of Arab Girl," *New York Times*, November 16, 2005.

104. "Israel Charges Captain in Killing."

105. "Israeli Parliament Votes its Symbolic Displeasure with Sharon's Plan for a Gaza Pullout."

106. "Israeli Military Kills 4 Palestinian Militants in Gaza Operation."

107. "Olmert: Israeli Lives Worth More Than Palestinian Ones," *Independent*, June 23, 2006.

108. "Israelis Destroy 14 Homes of Palestinian Refugees," *New York Times*, July 10, 2001.

109. "Too High a Price," *Jerusalem Post*, July 13, 2006.

110. Ibid.

111. Robert Fisk, *Pity the Nation: The Abduction of Lebanon,* 4th ed. (New York: Thunder's Mouth Press/Nation Books, 2002), pp. 239–40.

112. Ibid., p. 240.

113. Ibid., pp. 240–41.

114. Public Committee Against Torture in Israel, "Racism, Violence and Humiliation: Findings, Conclusions and Recommendations of the Public Committee Against Torture in Israel Concerning the Behavior of the Security Forces toward Persons Detained during the Events of September–October 2000," April 2001, www.stop-torture.org.

115. Ibid.

116. Ibid.

117. "Analysis: 'Give Back Territory and Kill Arabs,' " *Ha'aretz*, March 15, 2006.

118. "Lieberman Blasted for Suggesting Drowning Palestinian Prisoners," *Ha'aretz*, July 8, 2003.

119. "Lieberman—Nyet, Nyet, Nyet," *Ha'aretz*, March 14, 2006.

120. "Ehud Olmert: Kadima Will Keep Interior Ministry Portfolio," *Ha'aretz*, April 11, 2006.

121. "Israeli Demands Execution of Pro-Hamas MPs," *Independent*, May 5, 2006.

122. "Kadima, Yisrael Beiteinu Formally Sign Coalition Deal," *Ha'aretz*, October 23, 2006.

123. "Lieberman: Treat Gaza Like Chechnya," *Yediot Ahronot*, November 1, 2006.

124. "One Racist Nation," *Ha'aretz*, March 27, 2006.

125. "Israeli Election Campaign Starts in Earnest," *New York Times*, March 8, 2006.

126. "Sharon's Spirit, and Absence, Pervade Election," *New York Times*, March 25, 2006.

127. "Israeli Voters, by Thin Margin, Support Parties Vowing Pullout," *New York Times*, March 29, 2006.

128. "Not with a Bang but a Pop," *New York Times*, March 30, 2006.

129. "His Coalition in Place, Olmert Turns to Setting Israeli Borders," *New York Times*, May 5, 2006.

130. Anti-Defamation League, "ADL Disturbed by MK Avigdor Lieberman's Call to Execute Arab MKs," May 8, 2006, www.adl.org.

131. "Jewish Groups Join in Bid to Aid Arabs, but Spar over Olmert Tie to Rightist," *Forward*, April 28, 2006.

132. "Leftist MKs Blast Eitam's Statements on Arabs, Urge AG to Investigate," *Ha'aretz*, September 11, 2006.

133. B'Tselem, "Land Grab: Israel's Settlement Policy in the West Bank" (summary), May 2002.

134. Ibid.

135. For example: "French Jews Tell of a New and Threatening Wave of Anti-Semitism," *New York Times*, March 22, 2003; "Harvard President Sees Rise in Anti-Semitism on Campus," *New York Times*, September 21, 2002; "The Return of an Ancient Hatred," *New York Times*, April 20, 2002; "The Uncomfortable Question of Anti-Semitism," *New York Times*, November 4, 2001; "Israeli Outrage at Arafat's Speech Makes Talks With Him Even Less Likely," *New York Times*, September 4, 2001; "Palestinians Give U.N. Racism Talks a Mixed Message," *New York Times*, September 1, 2001; "Powell Will Not Attend Racism Conference in South Africa," *New York Times*, August 28, 2001; "U.N. Racism Panel Is Deadlocked on Israel," *New York Times*, August 9, 2001; "Arab League Belligerence," *New York Times*, March 30, 2001.

136. "Israeli Army Bulldozer Kills American Protesting in Gaza," *New York Times*, March 17, 2003; "An Israeli Raid Yields Dead Militant and Innocent Victim," *New York Times*, March 19, 2003; "Israel to Leave Peace Talks Unless Plan Is Amended," *New York Times*, April 6, 2003; "Israeli Trial of a Leading Palestinian Opens with Defiance," *New York Times*, April 7, 2003.

137. See "Play About Demonstrator's Death Is Delayed," *New York Times*, February 28, 2006; "Too Hot To Handle, Too Hot Not To Handle," *New York Times*, March 6, 2006; "Tensions Increase Over Delay of a Play," *New York Times*, March 7, 2006; "Theater Addresses Tension over Play," *New York Times*, March 16, 2006; "Requiem for an Idealist (and a Cause Célèbre)," *New York Times*, March 31, 2006; "Play About Gaza Death to Reach New York," *New York Times*, June 22, 2006.

138. "Activist Was Unlawfully Killed in Israel, Says Inquest Jury," *Independent*, April 11, 2006.

139. According to *Black's Law Dictionary*, an "inquest" is: "1. An inquiry by a coroner or medical examiner, sometimes with the aid of a jury, into the manner of death of a person who has died under suspicious circumstances, or who has died in prison"; and "2. An inquiry into a certain matter by a jury empaneled for that purpose." *Black's Law Dictionary*, 7th ed., s.v. "inquest."

140. Ibid.

141. "Calls for UK to Act Over Britons Shot Dead in Gaza," *Guardian*, April 11, 2006.

142. "Mother's Plea for Justice for Her Slaughtered Son," *Observer*, April 9, 2006.

143. "Parents Fight to Learn Why Israeli Sniper Shot Their Son," *Observer*, January 30, 2005.

144. Ibid.

145. "British Activist Is Reported Wounded by Israeli Sniper in Gaza," *New York Times*, April 12, 2003.
146. Ibid.
147. "Israeli Trial of a Leading Palestinian Opens with Defiance."
148. "Who Shot Brian Avery?" *Ha'aretz*, March 18, 2005.
149. Ibid.
150. Ibid.
151. "Israel to Leave Peace Talks Unless Plan Is Amended," *New York Times*, April 6, 2003; "Israeli Trial of a Leading Palestinian Opens with Defiance."
152. B'Tselem, "Demolition for Alleged Military Purposes: Statistics on Houses Demolished for Alleged Military Purposes," 2005, www.btselem.org.
153. Ibid.
154. B'Tselem, "Demolition for Alleged Military Purposes: Destruction of Houses and Property on the Rafah-Egyptian Border," 2005, www.btselem.org.
155. "Israeli Army Bulldozer Kills American Protesting in Gaza," *New York Times*, March 17, 2003.
156. See http://electronicintifada.net/cgi-bin/artman/exec/view.cgi/7/1248.
157. Amnesty International, "The Killing of Rachel Corrie; Amnesty International Urges Rice to Support Independent Investigation" (press release), March 16, 2005.
158. "Troops Kill British Cameraman," *New York Times* via Reuters, May 3, 2003.
159. "UK Man Shot by Israeli Soldier Was Murdered: Inquest," Reuters, April 6, 2006.
160. International Federation of Journalists, "IFJ Demands End to Military 'Whitewash' After Top Journalist Is Shot Dead in Palestine" (press release), May 3, 2003, www.ifj.org.
161. Committee to Protect Journalists, "CPJ Calls For Full and Transparent Investigation into British Journalist's Death" (press release), May 7, 2003, www.cpj.org.
162. Ibid.
163. Reporters Without Borders, "Israel Army Kills Second Journalist in Two Weeks," May 3, 2003, www.rsf.org.
164. "British Filmmaker's Death in Gaza Continues to Resound," *New York Times*, June 24, 2006.
165. Ibid.
166. Ibid.
167. The *Washington Post*, a notable exception, published the following articles: Mousa Abu Marzook, "What Hamas Is Seeking," *Washington Post*, January 31, 2006 (Marzook is deputy political bureau chief of the Islamic resistance Movement [Hamas]); " 'We Do No Wish to Throw Them Into The Sea,' Interview with Ismail Haniyeh, Palestinian Prime Minister," *Washington Post*, February 26, 2006; Ismail Haniyeh, "Aggression Under False Pretenses," *Washington Post*, July 11, 2006.
168. According to its web site, at www.electronicintifada.net, Electronic Intifada "publishes news, commentary, analysis, and reference materials about the Israeli-Palestinian conflict from a Palestinian perspective."
169. "Does Israel Have a Policy of Killing Palestinian Civilians," *Electronic Intifada*, June 13, 2006, www.electronicintifada.net.
170. B'Tselem, "Events on the Temple Mount—September 29, 2000," December 2000; B'Tselem, "Illusions of Restraint: Human Rights Violations During the Events in the Occupied Territories, September 29–December 2, 2000," December 2000; B'Tselem, "Israel's Assassination Policy: Extra-Judicial Executions," January 2001; B'Tselem, "On Human Rights in the Occupied Territories," June 2001; B'Tselem, "Whitewash: Office of the Military Advocate General's Investigation into the Death of Khalil al-Mughrabi, Age 11, on July 7, 2001," November 2001; B'Tselem, "Excessive Force: Human Rights Violations During IDF Actions in Area

A," December 2001; B'Tselem, "Wounded in the Field: Impeding Medical Treatment and Firing at Ambulances by IDF Soldiers in the Occupied Territories," March 2002; B'Tselem, "Trigger Happy: Unjustified Gunfire and the IDF's Open-Fire Regulations During the al-Aqsa Intifada," March 2002; B'Tselem, "Death in Custody: The Killing of Murad 'Awaisa, 17, in Ramallah, 31 March 2002," May 2002; B'Tselem, "Operation Defensive Shield: Soldiers' Testimonies, Palestinian Testimonies," September 2002; B'Tselem, "Lethal Curfew: The Use of Live Ammunition to Enforce Curfew," October 2002; B'Tselem, "Human Shield: Use of Palestinian Civilians as Human Shields in Violation of the High Court of Justice Order," November 2002; B'Tselem, "Take No Prisoners: The Fatal Shooting of Palestinians by Israeli Security Forces During 'Arrest Operations,' " May 2005.

171. B'Tselem, "Mahmud Ahmad Is Shot by the IDF and Denied Medical Treatment," October 2001; B'Tselem, "IDF Shoots Palestinian Woman in Labor While on Her Way to Hospital," February 2002; B'Tselem, "Border Police Injure Zaher Frihat and His Two Children," June 2002; B'Tselem, "IDF Rubber Bullet Causes Head Injury to Seven-Month Pregnant Woman," July 2002; B'Tselem, "Hebron: IDF Tear Gas Grenade Wounds a 12-Year-Old in the Face," July 2002; B'Tselem, "IDF Gunshot to the Head Kills Ahmad al-Qureni, Nablus," August 2002; B'Tselem, "IDF Use Samir Abu 'Amra and Ahmad Abu 'Amra as Human Shields," August 2002; B'Tselem, "Jabalya: IDF Tank Kills Four Members of a Palestinian Family," August 2002; B'Tselem, "Tubas, Jenin District: IDF Helicopter Missile-Fire Kills Four Palestinian Civilians and Wounds Dozens," August 2002; B'Tselem, "Nazlat a-Sheikh, Jenin District: IDF Gunfire Kills Muhammad Ali Zeid, Age 16," October 2002; B'Tselem, "Nablus: IDF Tank Shell Fire Kills Samar Shar'ab," November 2002; B'Tselem, "Al-Burej Refugee Camp: IDF House Bombing Kills Nuha al-Maqadmeh," March 2003; B'Tselem, "Surda Checkpoint, Ramallah District: IDF Soldiers Damage Khaled al-Bazar's Cart," August 2003; B'Tselem, "Sarra Checkpoint, Nablus District: IDF Soldiers Beat Palestinian and Fire Next to His Head," December 2003; B'Tselem, "IDF Soldiers Shoot and Kill Muhammad Abu Rajab After He Opens the Door for Them," March 2004; B'Tselem, "Deir Qaddis, Ramallah District: IDF Soldiers Fire at Peaceful Demonstrators, Wounding Some," March 2004; B'Tselem, "IDF Soldiers Kill Muhammad Diriyah, Father of Six, When He Opens the Door to House for Them," April 2004; B'Tselem, "IDF Soldiers Shoot and Kill Husni Daraghmeh After He Followed Their Orders and Raised His Hands in the Air," April 2004; B'Tselem, "IDF Soldiers Kill Eleven-Year-Old Palestinian Girl in Nablus," September 2004; B'Tselem, "IDF Soldier Shoot[s] Ibreez al-Minawi, in Nablus," September 2004; B'Tselem, "Suspected Execution of Mahmud Kmel and Use of Palestinians as Human Shields by IDF Soldiers in Raba, Jenin District," December 2004; B'Tselem, "IDF Soldier Shoots and Kills a 14-Year-Old Boy Playing with His Friends in Tubas, North of Nablus," January 2005; B'Tselem, "Security Forces Shoot Twelve-Year-Old Child with Live Ammunition, Beit Liqiya," April 2005; B'Tselem, "IDF Soldier Fires Live Ammunition at Stone-Throwing Youths in Beit Liqiya, Killing Two of Them," May 2005; B'Tselem, "Soldiers Shell House with Residents Still Inside, Setting It on Fire," October 2005; B'Tselem, "IDF Soldiers Shoot and Kill Bilal a-Sha'er, 17, When He Tried to Sneak into Israel to Work, Khan Yunis," November 2005; B'Tselem, "IDF Soldiers Shoot and Kill Sayyed Abu Libdah, 16, When in His Family's Orchard, 600 Meters From the Gaza Perimeter Fence," December 2005.

172. B'Tselem, "Testimonies: Jabalya: IDF Tank Fire Kills Four Members of a Palestinian Family, August 2002," August 2002, www.btselem.org.

173. See Arms Export Control Act, US Department of State, Directorate of Defense Trade Controls, http://www.pmdtc.org/aeca.htm.

174. Federation of American Scientists, "Country Profile: Israel," May 2002, www.fas.org.

175. Congressional Research Service, "Issue Brief for Congress: Israeli–United States Relations," April 4, 2003, http://fpc.state.gov/c4564.htm.

176. "State Dept. Raises Concerns About Israel's Use of U.S.-Made Arms," *New York Times*, July 25, 2002.

177. Ibid.

178. "Inquiry Opened into Israeli Use of U.S. Bombs," *New York Times*, August 25, 2006.

179. "Tubas, Jenin District: IDF Helicopter Missile-Fire Kills Four Palestinian Civilians and Wounds Dozens."

180. Ibid.

181. B'Tselem, "Case Study 13: Whitewash: The Office of the Judge Advocate General's Examination of the Death of Khalil al-Mughrabi, 11, on 7 July 2001," 2001, www.btselem.org.

182. Ibid.

183. Ibid.

184. Ibid.

185. B'Tselem, "Trigger Happy: Unjustified Shooting and Violation of the Open-Fire Regulations During the al-Aqsa Intifada," March 2002, www.btselem.org.

186. Ibid.

187. Ibid.

188. Ibid.

189. Ibid.

190. Ibid.

191. B'Tselem, "Restrictions on Movement: Forbidden Checkpoints and Roads," 2006, www.btselem.org.

192. Ibid.

193. Ibid.

194. B'Tselem, "Standard Routine: Beatings and Abuse of Palestinians by Israeli Security Forces During the al-Aqsa Intifada," May 2001; B'Tselem, "In Broad Daylight: Abuse of Palestinians by IDF Soldiers on July 23, 2001," July 2001; B'Tselem, "Soldiers Abuse of Palestinians in Hebron," December 2002; B'Tselem, "Hebron, Area H-2: Settlements Cause Mass Departure of Palestinians," August 2003; B'Tselem, "Medical Personnel Harmed: The Delay, Abuse and Humiliation of Medical Personnel by Israeli Security Forces: A Joint Report with Physicians for Human Rights—Israel," December 2003; B'Tselem, "Abuse of Palestinians at the Sarra Checkpoint, Nablus District 27–31, December 2003," January 2004.

195. B'Tselem, "IDF Causes Death of Infant by Preventing Mother's Evacuation to Hospital," April 2002; B'Tselem, "Ramallah: IDF Soldiers Arrest and Beat Palestinian Man," June 2002; B'Tselem, "Border Police Officers Beat and Rob Ashraf a-Shawahin, a Peddler," July 2002; B'Tselem, "Hebron: Border Police Officers Beat Two Palestinians," October 2002; B'Tselem, "Jenin: IDF Soldiers Harass Naji Abu 'Ubeid, Age 18, and His Family," November 2002; B'Tselem, "Ramallah: IDF Soldiers Beat Ambulance Driver Emil a-Rimawi," November 2002; B'Tselem, "Hebron: Border Police Officers Attack and Delay Red Cross Ambulance Crew," November 2002; B'Tselem, "A-Ram Checkpoint: Border Police Officers Beat Two Brothers," November 2002; B'Tselem, "IDF Soldiers in Ramallah Beat and Humiliate Mohay 'Aarida," November 2002; B'Tselem, "Hebron: IDF Soldiers Beat and Abuse Palestinians in Barbershop," December 2002; B'Tselem, "Hebron:

Border Police Officers Beat Three Palestinians," December 2002; B'Tselem, "Hebron: Border Police Officers Beat 'Imran Abu Hamdia, Age 17, to Death," December 2002; B'Tselem, "Hebron: Border Police Officers Beat Hamza a-Rajabi," December 2002; B'Tselem, "Hebron: Border Police Officers Beat 'Alaa Sanukrut," December 2002; B'Tselem, "Hebron: Border Police Officers Beat Bassem Ahamra," January 2003; B'Tselem, "Hebron: IDF Soldiers Beat Ziyad a-Shaloudi, Age 15," January 2003; B'Tselem, "Hamra Checkpoint, Jenin District: Israeli Soldiers Beat and Harass Red Crescent Paramedic," January 2003; B'Tselem, "Nablus: Border Police Officers Beat Medical Personnel, Preventing Medical Treatment," January 2003; B'Tselem, "Hebron: IDF Soldiers Beat Muhammad Da'ana, Age 13," January 2003; B'Tselem, "Hebron: IDF Soldiers Beat Snack Bar Owner, Isma'il al-'Izza," January 2003; B'Tselem, "Border Police Officers Assault Palestinian Taxi Drivers with Stones at the 'Container' Checkpoint," May 2003; B'Tselem, "Huwwara Checkpoint: IDF Soldiers Beat Ahmad 'Uda," May 2003; B'Tselem, "Bethlehem: IDF Soldiers Beat Two Journalists," May 2003; B'Tselem, "Tarqumiya, Hebron District: Border Police Officers Assault Hassan Ja'afra," May 2003; B'Tselem, "Huwwara Checkpoint: IDF Soldiers Beat, Imprison, and Humiliate Four Palestinians," May 2003; B'Tselem, "Tel Checkpoint, Nablus District: IDF Soldiers Beat and Delay Civilians for Hours in Sun," May 2003; B'Tselem, "IDF Soldiers Abuse Residents of a-Tuwani in Order to Prevent Visits by Members of Ta'ayush," May 2003; B'Tselem, "Tulkarm District, Zeita: Border Police Officer Forces Man From 'Attil to Commit Sexual Act with a Donkey," June 2003; B'Tselem, "Jerusalem: Border Police Officers Beat Two Palestinians," June 2003; B'Tselem, "Wadi Batir, Bethlehem District: Border Police Officers Beat Three Palestinians," June 2003; B'Tselem, "Zeita, Tulkarm District: Border Police Officers Sexually Harass and Abuse Farmers," Summer 2003; B'Tselem, "Huwwara Checkpoint, Nablus District: IDF Soldiers Force Woman in Labor Out of Ambulance and Beat Driver," August 2003; B'Tselem, "Beit Furik Village, Nablus District: IDF Soldiers Beat Muhammad Hanani and Bury Him Under Dirt and Stones," September 2003; B'Tselem, "Surda Checkpoint, Ramallah District: IDF Soldiers Beat Muhammad 'Omar, Age 16," September 2003; B'Tselem, "Qalandiya Checkpoint, Ramallah District: Soldiers Beat Za'id Zidat," September 2003; B'Tselem, "Ramallah: Border Police Officers Beat Bassem al-Hashalmun Near the Samiramis Military Base," September 2003; B'Tselem, " 'Container' Checkpoint, Jerusalem District: Border Police Officers Beat Palestinian Student on His Way to University," October 2003; B'Tselem, "Surda Checkpoint: IDF Soldiers Beat and Detain Ambulance Driver," October 2003; B'Tselem, "Jerusalem: Border Police Officer Beats Hisham Hariza," November 2003; B'Tselem, "Sarra Checkpoint, Nablus Region: IDF Soldiers Beat Ahmad 'Abdallah and Confiscate His Car," December 2003; B'Tselem, "Sarra Checkpoint, Nablus District: IDF Soldiers Beat Nazmi a-Sheikh," December 2003; B'Tselem, "Sarra Checkpoint, Nablus District: IDF Soldiers Beat Six Palestinians," December 2003; B'Tselem, "Sarra Checkpoint, Nablus District: IDF Soldiers Beat Two Palestinians," December 2003; B'Tselem, "IDF Soldiers Beat Palestinian Ambulance Driver and Medic at Checkpoint Near Ofra Settlement," January 2004; B'Tselem, "East Jerusalem: Border Police Officers Beat Five Palestinian Workers," February 2004; B'Tselem, "Border Police Beat and Abuse A.L. in the Area of Umm al-Fahm," April 2004; B'Tselem, "al Funduq, Qalqiliya District: Border Police Officers Beat Palestinian Woman," June 2004; B'Tselem, "Soldiers Beat Shadi a-Dik and Wissam Abd al-Hakim Near Village of a-Dik," September 2004; B'Tselem, "Police Beat Zakariya Barak'a in an Attempt to Force Him to Sign a Document Forbidding Him from Entering Israel," February 2005; B'Tselem, "Soldiers Beat Muhammad Qashu'a, Age 88, in His Olive Orchard

Near 'Illar Village," March 2005; B'Tselem, "Border Police Officers Beat Residents of Beit Surik Who Block Bulldozers from Reaching Their Land on Which the Separation Barrier Is Slated to Run, Beit Surik," June 2005; B'Tselem, "Ramla Police Beat and Abuse Ilyad Shamasneh When He Refuses to Collaborate," November 2005; B'Tselem, "Border Police Prevent Red Crescent from Taking Child to East Jerusalem for Cancer Treatment, Assault Ambulance Crew, 'Anata Checkpoint," December 2005.

196. B'Tselem, "Beatings and Abuse," 2006, www.btselem.org.
197. Ibid.
198. B'Tselem, "Hebron: IDF Soldiers Beat Snack Bar Owner Isma'il al-'Izza," January 2003, www.btselem.org.
199. B'Tselem, "Hebron: IDF Soldiers Beat Muhammad Da'ana, Age 13," January 2003, www.btselem.org.
200. B'Tselem, "Policy of Destruction: House Demolitions and Destruction of Agricultural Land in the Gaza Strip," February 2002; B'Tselem, "Land Grab: Israel's Settlement Policy in the West Bank," May 2002; B'Tselem, "The Separation Barrier," September 2002; B'Tselem, "Behind the Barrier: Human Rights Violations as a Result of Israel's Separation Barrier," April 2003; B'Tselem, "Facing the Abyss: The Isolation of Sheikh Sa'ad Village—Before and After the Separation Barrier," February 2004; B'Tselem, "Through No Fault of Their Own: Israel's Punitive House Demolitions in the al-Aqsa Intifada," November 2004.
201. B'Tselem, "IDF Demolishes the Home of the a-Rimawi Family," October 2001; B'Tselem, "Separation Barrier Isolates the Zeid Family's Home from Their Village," January 2002; B'Tselem, "Al-'Aza Refugee Camp, Bethlehem District: IDF Demolishes Home of Abu Sha'ira Family," February 2004; B'Tselem, "al-Wallaja, Bethlehem District: IDF Demolishes Home of the al-'Aaraj Family," March 2004; B'Tselem, "Tulkarm Refugee Camp: IDF Demolishes Home of the 'Arada Family," April 2004; B'Tselem, "IDF Abolishes Apartment Building and All of Its Contents in Nablus Claiming Wanted Activists Inside, Nablus" January 2005; B'Tselem, "Civil Administration Demolishes Hut of al-Moher Family on Grounds That It Was Built Without a Permit, Near Zububa Village, Jenin District," June 2005.
202. "Israeli Policy of Razing Homes Draws Protests by Palestinians," *New York Times*, April 7, 2001; "Israelis Destroy Homes in Gaza Refugee Camps," *New York Times*, May 3, 2001; "West Bank Deaths Heighten Anxiety," *New York Times*, May 15, 2001; "Israelis Destroy 14 Homes of Palestinian Refugees," *New York Times*, July 10, 2001; "Israel, in Reprisal for Killings, Razes Gaza Refugee Homes," *New York Times*, January 11, 2002; "Gaza Picks Up Pieces Left by Israeli Bulldozers," *New York Times*, January 12, 2002; "Israeli Army Faces Storm for Attack on Arab Houses," *New York Times*, January 14, 2002; "Israel Demolishes 9 Arab Homes in Jerusalem," *New York Times*, January 15, 2002; "Syrian at U.N. Compares Israeli Actions to the September 11 Attack," *New York Times*, January 19, 2002; "Israeli Group Declares Limits in Making War on Palestinians," *New York Times*, January 29, 2002; "Israeli Court Stops Demolition of Homes," *New York Times*, February 20, 2002; "After the Raid, a Slum's Assessment," *New York Times*, March 14, 2002; "Hamas Members Held in Recent Bombings," *New York Times*, August 22, 2002; "10 Palestinians Are Killed in Israeli Hunt for a Militant," *New York Times*, December 7, 2002; "Israel Frees Arrested Principal of Peace School," *New York Times*, December 21, 2002; "Demolishing Gaza Home, Israelis Kill Militant's Stepmother," *New York Times*, February 6, 2003; "Israel Kills 12 Arabs in Clashes in West Bank and Gaza," *New York Times*, February 20, 2003; "Israeli Raid Snares a Foe, But Leaves Family Motherless," *New York Times*, March 4, 2003; "Israel Says

Demolition of Homes Will Proceed," *New York Times*, May 17, 2004; "Israeli Army Moves on Rafah Refugee Camp in Gaza," *New York Times*, May 18, 2004; "At a Palestinian Protest, Israeli Gunfire Leaves at Least 10 Dead, Including Children," *New York Times*, May 20, 2004; "Israeli Army Pushes Sweep in Gaza, Killing 7," *New York Times*, May 21, 2004; "Militants Force Palestinian Family into an Agonizing Choice," *New York Times*, July 24, 2004; "Israel Halts Decades-Old Practice of Demolishing Militants' Homes," *New York Times*, February 18, 2005.

203. "Policy of Destruction: House Demolitions and Destruction of Agricultural Land in the Gaza Strip."

204. "Through No Fault of Their Own: Israel's Punitive House Demolitions in the al-Aqsa Intifada."

205. Amnesty International, "Israel and the Occupied Territories: Evictions and Demolitions Must Stop" (press release), May 18, 2004.

206. Human Rights Watch, "Razing Rafah: Mass Home Demolitions in the Gaza Strip," October 2004, www.hrw.org.

207. "Israel Passes Retroactive Law: No Compensation for Palestinians," *Palestine Monitor*, July 28, 2005.

208. "We Will Not Be Idiots," *Yediot Ahronot*, June 16, 2005.

209. "Court: Palestinian Man Can Sue State Over Killing of Family by IDF," *Ha'aretz*, June 8, 2006.

210. "Trial of Palestinian Leader Focuses Attention on Israeli Courts," *New York Times*, May 5, 2003.

211. "Israel Halts Decades-Old Practice of Demolishing Militants' Homes," *New York Times*, February 18, 2005; "Israel Says Demolition of Homes Will Proceed," *New York Times*, May 17, 2003; "Trial of Palestinian Leader Focuses Attention on Israeli Courts."

212. "Israel Halts Decades-Old Practice of Demolishing Militants' Homes."

213. The exceptions were the following: "West Bank Deaths Heighten Anxiety," *New York Times*, May 15, 2001; "Israeli Raid Snares a Foe, But Leaves Family Motherless," *New York Times*, March 4, 2003; "Israel Halts Decades-Old Practice of Demolishing Militants' Homes."

214. "Israel Says Demolition of Homes Will Proceed."

215. "Israeli Army Moves on Rafah Refugee Camp in Gaza," *New York Times*, May 18, 2004.

216. "At a Palestinian Protest, Israeli Gunfire Leaves at Least 10 Dead, Including Children," *New York Times*, May 20, 2004.

217. "Israeli Army Pushes Sweep in Gaza, Killing 7," *New York Times*, May 21, 2004.

218. B'Tselem, "Policy of Destruction: House Demolitions and Destruction of Agricultural Land in the Gaza Strip," February 2002, www.btselem.org.

219. Ibid.

220. Ibid.

221. B'Tselem, "IDF Mortar Fire Kills Fares a-Sa'adi, Age 12, Burying Him Under the Ruins of His House," June 2002, www.btselem.org.

222. B'Tselem, "Demolition for Alleged Military Purposes," December 2006, www.btselem.org.

223. B'Tselem, "House Demolitions as Punishment," December 2006, www.btselem.org.

224. Amnesty International, "Committee Against Torture Says Israel's Policy of Closures and Demolitions of Palestinian Homes May Amount to Cruel, Inhuman or Degrading Treatment," November 23, 2001, www.amnesty.org.

225. United Nations Committee Against Torture, "Convention Against Torture and Other Cruel, Inhuman or Degrading Treatment or Punishment: Consideration of Reports Submitted by States Parties Under Article 19 of the Convention: Third

Periodic Reports Due in 2000: Addendum: Israel," July 4, 2001, http://www.oh-chr.org/english/bodies/cat.

226. United Nations Office of the High Commissioner for Human Rights, "Conclusions and Recommendations of the Committee Against Torture: Israel" (CAT/C/XXVII/Concl.5. Concluding Observations/Comments), November 23, 2001, http://www.unhchr.ch/tbs/doc.nsf.

227. B'Tselem, "Torture: Background on the High Court of Justice's Decision," August 2006, www.btselem.org.

228. "Israel Court Bans Most Use of Force in Interrogations," *New York Times*, September 7, 1999.

229. Alan Dershowitz, *The Case for Israel* (Hoboken, N.J.: John Wiley and Sons, Inc., 2003), pp. 134–35.

230. "Conclusions and Recommendations of the Committee Against Torture: Israel."

231. Ibid.

232. Article 1 states:
    1. For the purposes of this Convention, the term "torture" means any act by which severe pain or suffering, whether physical or mental, is intentionally inflicted on a person for such purposes as obtaining from him or a third person information or a confession, punishing him for an act he or a third person has committed or is suspected of having committed, or intimidating or coercing him or a third person, or for any reason based on discrimination of any kind, when such pain or suffering is inflicted by or at the instigation of or with the consent or acquiescence of a public official or other person acting in an official capacity. It does not include pain or suffering arising only from, inherent in or incidental to lawful sanctions.
    2. This article is without prejudice to any international instrument or national legislation which does or may contain provisions of wider application.

233. Article 16 states:
    1. Each State Party shall undertake to prevent in any territory under its jurisdiction other acts of cruel, inhuman or degrading treatment or punishment which do not amount to torture as defined in article I, when such acts are committed by or at the instigation of or with the consent or acquiescence of a public official or other person acting in an official capacity. In particular, the obligations contained in articles 10, 11, 12 and 13 shall apply with the substitution for references to torture of references to other forms of cruel, inhuman or degrading treatment or punishment.
    2. The provisions of this Convention are without prejudice to the provisions of any other international instrument or national law which prohibits cruel, inhuman or degrading treatment or punishment or which relates to extradition or expulsion.

234. "Conclusions and Recommendations of the Committee Against Torture: Israel."

235. Amnesty International, "Committee Against Torture Says Israel's Policy of Closures and Demolitions of Palestinian Homes May Amount to Cruel, Inhuman or Degrading Treatment," November 23, 2001, www.amnesty.org.

236. "UN Warns Israel Over Torture Reports," BBC, November 23, 2001.

237. "Israel Denies Groups' Charge That It Is Torturing Detainees," *New York Times*, November 21, 2001.

238. Ibid.

239. Amnesty International, "Israel: Briefing for the Committee Against Torture," May 2002, www.amnesty.org.

240. Ibid.

241. LAW—the Palestinian Society for the Protection of Human Rights and the Environment, the Public Committee Against Torture in Israel, and the World

Organisation Against Torture, "Submission Concerning Israel's Policies in the Occupied Palestinian Territories Relevant to the UN Convention Against Torture and Other Cruel, Inhuman or Degrading Treatment or Punishment," May 2002, www.stoptorture.org.

242. Ibid.
243. Public Committee Against Torture in Israel, "Back to a Routine of Torture: Torture and Ill-Treatment of Palestinian Detainees During Arrest Detention and Interrogation," May 2003, www.stoptorture.org.
244. Ibid.
245. Ibid.
246. Ibid.
247. *Amnesty International Report, 2006*, www.amnesty.org.
248. *Amnesty International Report, 2004*, www.amnesty.org.
249. *Amnesty International Report, 2003*, www.amnesty.org.
250. *Human Rights Watch Report 2003*, www.amnesty.org.
251. *Human Rights Watch Report 2002*, www.amnesty.org.
252. "Palestinian Leader Orders Force to Find Israeli," *New York Times*, June 27, 2006.
253. Women's Organization for Political Prisoners, "Newsletter June 2006," http://www.wofpp.org/english/home.html.
254. "Israelis Batter Gaza and Seize Hamas Officials," *New York Times*, June 29, 2006; "On Arab Streets and Airwaves, Shock Over Seizures by Israel," *New York Times*, June 30, 2006; "Olmert Rejects Ultimatum On Soldier by Palestinians," *New York Times*, July 4, 2006; "A Day of Funerals Across the Northern Gaza Strip," *New York Times*, July 8, 2006; "Israel Vows to Fight Until Soldier's Release, and Palestinians Mourn Their Dead," *New York Times*, July 10, 2006; "Israel Rejects Hamas Terms for Exchange of Prisoners," *New York Times*, July 11, 2006; "Israel's Two-Front Battle," *New York Times*, July 13, 2006; "The Kidnapping of Democracy," *New York Times*, July 14, 2006; "The Fever Is Winning," *New York Times*, July 20, 2006; "More Than a Cease-Fire Needed," *New York Times*, July 21, 2006.
255. Public Committee Against Torture in Israel and the World Organisation Against Torture, "Violence Against Palestinian Women," July 2005, www.stoptorture.org.
256. Ibid.
257. Ibid.
258. Ibid.
259. Ibid.
260. Ibid.
261. B'Tselem, "Torture of Palestinian Minors in the Gush Etzion Police Station: Summary," July 2001, www.btselem.org.
262. Ibid.
263. Ibid.
264. Ibid.
265. Ibid.
266. Ibid.
267. Ibid.
268. Ibid.
269. Defence for Children International—Palestine Section, "Children Behind Bars: Issue 30," February 21, 2006, www.dci-pal.org.
270. Defence for Children International—Palestine Section, "Children Behind Bars: Issue 29," December 10, 2005, www.dci-pal.org.
271. Defence for Children International—Palestine Section, "Children Behind Bars: Issue 28," October 12, 2005, www.dci-pal.org.

272. Defence for Children International—Palestine Section, "Children Behind Bars: Issue 27," September 15, 2005, www.dci-pal.org.

273. Defence for Children International—Palestine Section, "Children Behind Bars: Issue 23," June 15, 2004, www.dci-pal.org.

274. Defence for Children International—Palestine Section, "Children Behind Bars: Issue 21," December 15, 2003, www.dci-pal.org.

275. Defence for Children International—Palestine Section, "Children Behind Bars: Issue 24," July 10, 2004, www.dci-pal.org.

276. "Hamas Provokes a Fight," *New York Times*, June 29, 2006.

277. "IAF Chief: Qassam Crews Now Operating in Gaza Residential Areas," *Ha'aretz*, June 22, 2006.

278. Human Rights Watch, "Israel: Gaza Beach Investigation Ignores Evidence: IDF's Partisan Probe No Substitute for Independent Inquiry," June 20, 2006, www.hrw.org.

279. "Olmert: Israeli Lives Worth More Than Palestinian Ones," *Independent*, June 23, 2006.

280. "Probe: Hamas Bomb, Not IDF Shell, Caused Gaza Deaths," *Ha'aretz*, June 13, 2006; "Report: IDF Didn't Shell Gaza Beach," *Jerusalem Post*, June 13, 2006.

281. "Halutz Orders Probe into IAF Strikes," *Jerusalem Post*, June 21, 2006.

282. "9 Palestinians Die in IAF Strike on Islamic Jihad Rocket Crew," *Ha'aretz*, June 13, 2006.

283. "9 Killed, Including 2 Kids, in IAF Strike on Gaza Katyusha Cell," *Jerusalem Post*, June 13, 2006.

284. "Two Palestinian Siblings, 1 Teen Killed in IAF Strike in Gaza City," *Ha'aretz*, June 20, 2006.

285. Ibid.

286. "Olmert Pledges to Continue Policy of Targeted Killings," *Ha'aretz*, June 23, 2006.

287. "World in Brief," *Observer*, June 25, 2006.

288. "A Black Flag," *Ha'aretz*, July 2, 2006.

289. "Analysis: Nothing 'Surgical' About Air Force Attacks in Urban Areas," *Ha'aretz*, June 22, 2006.

290. "Don't Shoot, Talk," *Ha'aretz*, June 22, 2006.

291. "Shkedi, Go Home," *Ha'aretz*, June 26, 2006.

292. "Hamas Provokes a Fight."

293. For earlier references to "liberal hawks" and "hawks," see Friel and Falk, *The Record of the Paper,* pp. 46–87.

294. Dennis Ross, *The Missing Peace: The Inside Story of the Fight for Middle East Peace* (New York: Farrar, Strauss and Giroux, 2004), p. 726. According to Ross, Israel's final position at the Camp David summit in July 2000 was a demand to annex 9 percent of the West Bank, with a net 8 percent annexation after territorial compensation from Israel. Negotiations continued after the summit ended with no agreement, about which Ross wrote: "Aaron [Miller, Ross's aide], was always arguing for a just and fair proposal. I was not against a fair proposal. But I felt the very concept of 'fairness' was, by definition, subjective. Similarly, both Rob [Malley] and Gamal [Helal] [on Ross's staff] believed that the Palestinians were entitled to 100 percent of the territory [West Bank]. Swaps should thus be equal. They believed this was a Palestinian right. Aaron tended to agree with them not on the basis of a right, but on the basis that every other Arab negotiating partner had gotten 100 percent. Why should the Palestinians be different? I disagreed. I was focused not on reconciling rights but on addressing needs. In negotiations, one side's principle or 'right' is usually the other side's impossibility. Of course, there are irreducible rights. I wanted to address what each side needed, not what they wanted and not what they felt they

were entitled to. Our main disagreements were on the borders. I felt that the Israelis needed 6 to 7 percent of the territory for both security and political purposes. Having looked at maps with 8 percent given to Israeli settlement blocs, I believed it was possible for the Palestinians to have territorial contiguity and viability with 7 percent Israeli annexation. Gamal and Rob wanted no more than 3 to 4 percent annexation and wanted it compensated with an equivalent swap of territory" (p. 726). Throughout the Camp David summit, as described in his book, Ross frequently cited Israel's political and security "needs" while supporting Israel's proposed annexations of West Bank territory, and he rejected Palestinian rights to either 100 percent or net 100 percent of the West Bank with territorial compensation. Furthermore, Ross implies above that there would be no Palestinian West Bank contiguity and viability with a net 8 percent Israeli annexation, which, according to Ross, was the final offer to the Palestinians at the Camp David summit in July 2006.

295. See Bill Clinton, *My Life* (New York: Alfred A. Knopf, 2004); Madeleine Albright, *Madam Secretary* (New York: Hyperion, 2003); Ross, *The Missing Peace*.

296. See, for example, these Anti-Defamation League press releases at www.adl.org: Anti-Defamation League, "ADL Dismayed by UN Resolution Applying the Fourth Geneva Convention to the 'Occupied Territories,'" July 15, 1999; Anti-Defamation League, "ADL Outraged at One-Sided Use of the 4th Geneva Convention to Censure Israel," December 5, 2001; Anti-Defamation League, "Anatomy of Anti-Israel Incitement: Jenin, World Opinion and the Massacre That Wasn't," 2002; Anti-Defamation League, "Anti-Israel Bias at the U.N.," September 2004; Anti-Defamation League, "U.N. Human Rights Council Takes Two Steps Back," June 30, 2006; Anti-Defamation League, "U.N. Human Rights Council Predictably Blames Israel While Giving Hamas a Pass," July 6, 2006; Anti-Defamation League, "Human Rights Watch: Irrelevant, Immoral, on Mideast Conflict," August 2, 2006; Anti-Defamation League, "ADL Labels Kofi Annan Statements on Israel 'Blatantly One-Sided,' " August 9, 2006; Anti-Defamation League, "ADL Denounces UN Human Rights Council Anti-Israel Resolution as False and One-Sided," August 11, 2006. See also the following analyses by Alan Dershowitz at www.huffingtonpost.com: Alan Dershowitz, "The Anti-Israel Double Standard Watch," *Huffington Post*, July 11, 2006; Alan Dershowitz, "Lebanon Is Not a Victim," *Huffington Post*, August 7, 2006; Alan Dershowitz, "Terrorism Causes Occupation, Not Vice Versa," *Huffington Post*, August 11, 2006; Alan Dershowitz, "The 'Human Rights Watch' Watch, Installment 1," *Huffington Post*, August 21, 2006; Alan Dershowitz, "Amnesty International's Biased Definition of War Crimes: Whatever Israel Does to Defend Its Citizens," *Huffington Post*, August 29, 2006.

297. "Israel Urged to Adopt Geneva Convention," *Los Angeles Times*, August 25, 2004.

298. American Jewish Congress, "AJCongress Says Proposed Geneva Convention Update Affords an Opportunity to Unshackle Anti-Terrorist Forces"(press release), November 6, 2002, www.ajcongress.org.

299. "Rabbis: Israel Too Worried Over Civilian Deaths," *Forward*, August 25, 2006.

300. "U.S. Congress Okays $500M for Defense Projects With Israel," *Ha'aretz*, September 30, 2006.

301. Ibid.; "Congress Okays Joint Project Funding," *Jerusalem Post*, September 30, 2006.

302. " 'Gaza Is a Jail. Nobody Is Allowed to Leave. We Are All Starving Now,' " *Independent*, September 8, 2006.

303. For news articles that mentioned the Fourth Geneva Convention, see: "Israelis Criticized for Using Deadly Force Too Readily," *New York Times*, October 4, 2000; "U.N. Security Council Approves Resolution for Palestinian State," *New York*

Times, March 13, 2002; "Court Says Israel Can Expel 2 of Militant's Kin to Gaza," *New York Times*, September 4, 2002; "U.S. Vetoes Condemnation for Israel for U.N. Deaths," *New York Times*, December 21, 2002; "As Israelis Pull Out, the Question Lingers: Who'll Control Gaza?" *New York Times*, September 11, 2005. For Op-ed pieces that mentioned the Fourth Geneva Convention, see: "Annan's Careless Language," *New York Times*, March 21, 2002; "Life Under Siege," *New York Times*, April 10, 2002; "Israel's Tragedy Foretold," *New York Times*, March 10, 2006. See this book review article: "The Lights of Jaffa," *New York Times*, December 30, 2001. See this *New York Times Magazine* article: "Who Owns the Rules of War?" *New York Times*, April 13, 2003.

304. Anti-Defamation League, "Israel and the United Nations 1998-1999: The Fourth Geneva Convention and Resolution 181" (press release), September 14, 1999, www.adl.org.

305. David Kretzmer, *The Occupation of Justice: The Supreme Court of Israel and the Occupied Territories* (Albany, N.Y.: State University of New York Press, 2002), p. 35.

306. Kretzmer wrote: "The [Israeli] government's argument was rejected by the ICRC, leading Israeli academics, and foreign experts in international law" (Ibid., p. 34).

307. See International Committee of the Red Cross, "Implementation of the Fourth Geneva Convention in the Occupied Palestinian Territories: History of a Multilateral Process (1997–2001): International Review of the Red Cross," December 5, 2001, www.icrc.org.

308. Ibid.

309. United Nations General Assembly, "Applicability of the Geneva Convention Relative to the Protection of Civilian Persons in Time of War, of 12 August 1949, to the Occupied Palestinian Territory, including East Jerusalem, and the other Occupied Arab Territories," A/RES/60/105, January 18, 2006. For similar or identical affirmations of the applicability of the Fourth Geneva Convention to Israel's occupation, see also, for example: A/RES/59/122, January 25, 2005; A/RES/58/97, December 17, 2003; A/RES/57/125, February 24, 2003; A/RES/55/131, December 8, 2000; A/RES/54/77, December 6, 1999; A/RES/53/54, December 3, 1998; A/RES/52/65, December 10, 1997; A/RES/51/132, December 13, 1996.

310. United Nations General Assembly, "Illegal Israeli Actions in Occupied East Jerusalem and the Rest of the Occupied Palestinian Territory," A/RES/ES-10/9, December 20, 2001.

311. United Nations Security Council, Resolution 271 (1969), September 15, 1969, S/RES/271 (1969).

312. United Nations Security Council, Resolution 452 (1979), July 20, 1979, S/RES/452 (1979).

313. United Nations Security Council, Resolution 465 (1980), March 1, 1980, S/RES/465 (1980).

314. United Nations Security Council, Resolution 605 (1987), December 22, 1987, S/RES/605 (1987).

315. United Nations Security Council, Resolution 1322 (2000), October 7, 2000, S/RES/1322 (2000).

316. Security Council resolutions passed during the administration of George H. W. Bush that affirmed the applicability of the Fourth Geneva Convention to Israel's occupation of the Palestinian territories included S/RES/681 (1990) and S/RES/694 (1991).

317. Amnesty International, "Israel: Respect of Fourth Geneva Convention Must Be Ensured by High Contracting parties Meeting in Geneva," (press release), December 4, 2001, www.amnesty.org.

318. Amnesty International, "Israel/Occupied Territories: One Year After the Intifada—

The International Community Must Fulfil Its Obligations" (press release), September 28, 2001, www.amnesty.org.

319. Amnesty International, "Fourth Geneva Convention Meeting: An Abdication of Responsibility," July 15, 1999, www.amnesty.org.

320. Human Rights Watch, "Center of the Storm: A Case Study of Human Rights Abuses in Hebron District," April 2001, www.hrw.org.

321. Human Rights Watch, "Israel, The Occupied West Bank and Gaza Strip, and the Palestinian Authority Territories: In a Dark Hour: The Use of Civilians During IDF Arrest Operations," April 2002, www.hrw.org.

322. Human Rights Watch, "Letter to President Clinton," July 7, 1999, www.hrw.org.

323. B'Tselem, "International Law: International Humanitarian Law (Laws of War)," December 2006, www.btselem.org.

324. International Court of Justice, "Legal Consequences of the Construction of a Wall in the Occupied Palestinian Territory," July 9, 2004, paras. 86–101.

325. International Court of Justice, "Separate Opinion of Judge Al-Khasawneh," in *Legal Consequences of the Construction of a Wall in the Occupied Palestinian Territory*, July 9, 2004.

326. Anti-Defamation League, "ADL Dismayed by UN Resolution Applying the Fourth Geneva Convention to the 'Occupied Territories' " (press release), July 15, 1999, www.adl.org.

327. Anti-Defamation League, "ADL Urges Swiss Government to 'Make Clear Harmful Effects' Reconvening Fourth Geneva Convention Would Have in Middle East," (press release), November 17, 1997, www.adl.org.

328. Anti-Defamation League, "Israel and the United Nations 1998-1999: The Fourth Geneva Convention and Resolution 181," (press release), September 14, 1999, ww.adl.org.

329. Anti-Defamation League, "ADL Factsheet: Fourth Geneva Convention," 1999, www.adl.org.

330. Avi Shlaim, *The Iron Wall: Israel and the Arab World* (New York: W. W. Norton, & Company Ltd., 2001), p. 581.

331. United Nations General Assembly, "Illegal Israeli Actions in Occupied East Jerusalem and the Rest of the Occupied Palestinian Territory," July 15, 1997, A/RES/ES-10/3; "Illegal Israeli Actions in Occupied East Jerusalem and the Rest of the Occupied Palestinian Territory," November 13, 1997, A/RES/ES-10/4.

332. Anti-Defamation League, "Advocating for Israel: An Activist's Guide." This document was not dated but was posted on the ADL's web site as of October 31, 2006, www.adl.org.

333. Anti-Defamation League, "ADL Outraged at One-Sided Use of 4th Geneva Convention to Censure Israel" (press release), December 5, 2001, www.adl.org.

334. Anti-Defamation League, "Political Cartoonists and U.S. Newspapers Support Israel and See Hezbollah as a Terrorist Group" (press release), August 29, 2006, www.adl.org.

335. Human Rights Watch, "Fatal Strikes: Israel's Indiscriminate Attacks Against Civilians in Lebanon," August 3, 2006, www.hrw.org.

336. Human Rights Watch, "Israel/Lebanon: Israel Responsible for Qana Attack," July 30, 2006, www.hrw.org.

337. "Human Rights Watch: Irrelevant, Immoral on Mideast Conflict," *New York Sun*, August 2, 2006.

338. "Civilians Lose as Fighters Slip into Fog of War," *New York Times*, August 3, 2006.

339. "Fatal Strikes: Israel's Indiscriminate Attacks Against Civilians in Lebanon."

340. Ibid.

341. "Roth's False God," *New York Sun*, August 23, 2006.

342. Alan Dershowitz, "The 'Human Rights Watch' Watch, Installment 1," *Huffington Post*, August 21, 2006, www.huffingtonpost.ocm.

343. "Fatal Strikes: Israel's Indiscriminate Attacks Against Civilians in Lebanon."

344. Ibid.

345. "The 'Human Rights Watch' Watch, Installment 1."

346. "Fatal Strikes: Israel's Indiscriminate Attacks Against Civilians in Lebanon."

347. "The 'Human Rights Watch' Watch, Installment 1."

348. On Dershowitz's criticism of Human Rights Watch, see also Aryeh Neier, "The Attack on Human Rights Watch," *New York Review of Books*, November 2, 2006.

349. We could not locate the article, "Revealed: How Hezbollah Puts the Innocent at Risk; They Don't Care," *Sunday Mail* (Australia), July 30, 2006, on the Internet. We did find an excerpt of an article reportedly published by that title in the *Sunday Mail* at www.hirhome.com/israel/hezbollah6_2.htm. This web site included three photographs of an anti-aircraft gun reportedly deployed on a residential street in "the east of Beirut."

350. "United Nations Interim Force in Lebanon (UNIFIL)," press release, July 28, 2006.

351. "UN Contradicts Itself Over Israeli Attack," CanWest News Service, July 27, 2006.

352. "The 'Human Rights Watch' Watch, Installment 1."

353. Ibid.

354. "Canadian's Wife Wants Answers," *Toronto Star*, July 28, 2006.

355. "UN Contradicts Itself Over Israeli Attack."

356. "UN: Israel Used Precision Bomb to Hit the UN Officers," Reuters, September 29, 2006.

357. "The 'Human Rights Watch' Watch, Installment 1."

358. Ibid.

359. "Fatal Strikes: Israel's Indiscriminate Attacks Against Civilians in Lebanon."

360. "Fatal Strikes: Israel's Indiscriminate Attacks Against Civilians in Lebanon."

361. Ibid.

362. Ibid.

363. Ibid.

364. Alan Dershowitz, "Lebanon Is Not a Victim," *Huffington Post*, August 7, 2006, www.huffingtonpost.com.

365. Ibid.

366. Alan Dershowitz, "Amnesty International's Biased Definition of War Crimes: Whatever Israel Does to Defend Its Citizens," *Huffington Post*, August 29, 2006, www.huffingtonpost.com.

367. Ibid.

368. Amnesty International, "Israel/Lebanon: Deliberate Destruction or 'Collateral Damage'? Israeli Attacks on Civilian Infrastructure," August 23, 2006, www.amnesty.org.

369. "Civilians Lose as Fighters Slip into Fog of War."

370. "Hezbollah Kidnaps 2 IDF Soldiers During Clashes on Israel-Lebanon Border," *Ha'aretz*, July 12, 2006.

371. "PM Olmert Calls Hezbollah Border Attack an 'Act of War,' " *Ha'aretz*, July 12, 2006.

372. Human Rights Watch, "Israel/Lebanon: Israel Responsible for Qana Attack," July 30, 2006, www.hrw.org.

373. Human Rights Watch, "Convention on Conventional Weapons (CCW): First Look at Israel's Use of Cluster Munitions in Lebanon in July–August 2006," August 30, 2006, www.hrw.org.

374. "Israel Cluster Bomb Use in Lebanon 'Outrageous': UN," Reuters, September 19, 2006.

375. "Amnesty International's Definition of War Crimes: Whatever Israel Does to Defend Its Citizens."

376. Amnesty International, www.amnesty.org.

377. Human Rights Watch, www.hrw.org.

378. "The 'Human Rights Watch' Watch, Installment 1."

379. "Political Cartoonists and U.S. Newspapers Support Israel and See Hezbollah as Terrorists."

380. See The Consultative Council of the Lawyers Committee on American Policy Towards Vietnam, Richard Falk, chair, John H. E. Fried, rapporteur, *Vietnam and International Law: An Analysis of International Law and the Use of Force, and the Precedent of Vietnam for Subsequent Interventions* (Northampton, Mass.: Aletheia Press, 1990), p. 22. The Consultative Council of the Lawyers Committee on Vietnam, which, in addition to Falk and Fried, included Richard J. Barnet, John H. Herz, Stanley Hoffman, Wallace McClure, Saul H. Mendlovitz, Richard S. Miller, Hans J. Morgenthau, William G. Rice, Burn H. Weston, and Quincy Wright, explained further (p. 22): "In [UN Charter] Article 51, legal authorities usually invoke the classical definition of self-defense given by [U.S.] Secretary of State Daniel Webster in *The Caroline*. Mr. Webster's description of the permissible basis for self-defense was relied upon in the Nuremberg Judgment in the case against major German war criminals. This judgment was, of course, based upon pre–United Nations law and, in turn, was affirmed unanimously by the United Nations General Assembly at its first session (Res. 95(I))." The Lawyers Committee then noted "Mr. Webster's generally accepted words, [that] the right of self-defense is restricted to instances 'when the necessity for action' is 'instant, overwhelming, and leaving no choice of means, and no moment for deliberation.' "

381. "Hezbollah Kidnaps 2 IDF Soldiers During Clashes on Israel–Lebanon Border," *Ha'aretz*, July 12, 2006.

382. "Israelis Attack Just 10 Miles From Beirut," Associated Press, July 12, 2006.

383. "Nahariya: Woman Killed in Katyusha Attack," *Yediot Ahronot*, July 13, 2006.

384. "Israel Claims Hundreds of Hits in Lebanon," Associated Press, July 13, 2006.

385. "One Killed, Dozens Hurt as Katyushas Rain Down on Northern Israel," *Ha'aretz*, July 13, 2006.

386. "Israel's Two-Front Battle," *New York Times*, July 13, 2006.

387. "Israel Claims Hundreds of Hits in Lebanon."

388. Amnesty International, "Israel/Lebanon: End Immediately Attacks Against Civilians" (press release), July 13, 2006, www.amnesty.org.

389. "Aiming to Kill Hamas Military Leaders, Israeli Air Force Kills 9 Members of a Family Instead," *New York Times*, July 13, 2006.

390. B'Tselem, "Take No Prisoners: The Fatal Shooting of Palestinians by Israeli Security Forces During 'Arrest Operations,' " May 2005, www.btselem.org; Amnesty International, "Israel and the Occupied Territories: Israel Must End Its Policy of Assassinations," July 4, 2003, www.amnesty.org.

391. "Playing Hamas's Game," *New York Times*, July 15, 2006.

392. "Diplomacy's Turn in Lebanon," *New York Times*, July 18, 2006.

393. "Alternative Reality at the Summit," *New York Times*, July 19, 2006.

394. "More Than a Cease-Fire Needed," *New York Times*, July 21, 2006.

395. "No More Foot Dragging," *New York Times*, July 25, 2006.

396. "A Right Way to Help Israel," *New York Times*, July 29, 2006.

397. "Cease-Fire Diplomacy in Lebanon," *New York Times*, August 1, 2006.

398. Ibid.

399. "One Month Later in Lebanon," *New York Times*, August 12, 2006.

400. Human Rights Watch, "Israel: Investigate Attack on Civilians in Lebanon: IDF

Must Take Precautions to Protect Civilians Fleeing Areas at Risk" (press release), July 17, 2006, www.hrw.org.

401. "Israel Widening Scope of Attacks Across Lebanon," *New York Times*, July 16, 2006.
402. "More Airstrikes As Hezbollah Rockets Hit Deeper," *New York Times*, July 15, 2006.
403. "Civilians Lose as Fighters Slip into Fog of War."
404. "Israel: Investigate Attack on Civilians in Lebanon: IDF Must Take Precautions to Protect Civilians Fleeing at Risk"; "Fatal Strikes: Israel's Indiscriminate Attacks Against Civilians in Lebanon."
405. "The Child Lies Like a Rag Doll—A Symbol of the Latest Lebanon War," *Independent*, July 20, 2006; "Marwahin, 15 July 2006: The Anatomy of a Massacre," *Independent*, September 30, 2006.
406. "War Lingers in the South of Lebanon," *New York Times*, August 22, 2006.
407. "Israel: Investigate Attack on Civilians in Lebanon: IDF Must Take Precautions to Protect Civilians Fleeing at Risk."
408. Ibid.
409. "Fatal Strikes: Israel's Indiscriminate Attacks Against Civilians in Lebanon."
410. "Israel: Investigate Attack on Civilians in Lebanon: IDF Must Take Precautions to Protect Civilians Fleeing at Risk."
411. "The Child Lies Like a Rag Doll—A Symbol of the Latest Lebanon War."
412. "Marwahin: July 15, 2006: The Anatomy of a Massacre."
413. "Fatal Strikes: Israel's Indiscriminate Attacks Against Civilians in Lebanon."
414. "Israel Suspending Lebanon Air Raids After Dozens Die: Halt of 48 Hours," *New York Times*, July 31, 2006.
415. Human Rights Watch, "Israel/Lebanon: Israel Responsible for Qana Attack: Indiscriminate Bombing in Lebanon a War Crime." July 30, 2006, www.hrw.org.
416. "Night of Death and Terror for Lebanese Villagers," *New York Times*, July 31, 2006.
417. "Israel Suspending Lebanon Air Raids After Dozens Die: Halt of 48 Hours."
418. Human Rights Watch, "Israel/Lebanon: Qana Death Toll at 28: International Inquiry Needed Into Israeli Air Strike," August 2, 2006, www.hrw.org.
419. "Israel Suspending Lebanon Air Raids After Dozens Die: Halt of 48 Hours."
420. "Israel/Lebanon: Qana Death Toll at 28: International Inquiry Needed Into Israeli Air Strike."
421. Ibid.
422. "Night of Death and Terror for Lebanese Villagers."
423. "Israel Suspending Lebanon Air Raids After Dozens Die: Halt of 48 Hours."
424. Fisk, *Pity The Nation*, p. 671.
425. Ibid., p. 674.
426. Ibid., pp. 669–70.
427. Ibid., p. 681.
428. Ibid.
429. Ibid. See also "Israeli Army Says Mapping Errors Led to Shelling of a U.N. Base in Lebanon," *New York Times*, May 6, 1996; "Israel Releases Video on Lebanon Shelling," *New York Times*, May 9, 1996.
430. Fisk, *Pity the Nation*, pp. 681–82.
431. Ibid., pp. 682–83.
432. "Israel Suspending Lebanon Air Raids After Dozens Die: Halt of 48 Hours."
433. "Israel Pushes on Despite Agreeing to Airstrike Lull," *New York Times*, August 1, 2006.
434. "Peretz: Okay to Harm Lebanese Civilians If Necessary," IsraelNN.com, July 16, 2006.
435. "Inquiry Commission That Wasn't: Politicians, Army Officers and Journalists Who

Spend Their Time Covering Their Hide Should Be the First to Testify," *Yediot Ahronot*, July 31, 2006.

436. "Israeli Military Policy Under Fire After Qana Attack," *Forward*, August 4, 2006.

437. Dershowitz, *The Case for Israel*.

438. Bronner has reviewed at least eight books for the *New York Times* on Israel or the Israel-Palestine conflict from 2000 to 2006. See "Voice in the Wilderness," *New York Times*, April 16, 2000, review of Edward Said, *The End of the Peace Process: Oslo and After* (New York: Pantheon Books, 2000); "Promised Land," *New York Times*, September 17, 2000, review of Amnon Rubinstein, *From Herzl to Rabin: The Changing Image of Zionism* (New York: Holmes and Meier, 2000); "The New New Historians," *New York Times*, November 9, 2003, review of Yaacov Lozowick, *Right To Exist: A Moral Defense of Israel's Wars* (New York: Doubleday, 2003), and Dershowitz, *The Case for Israel*; "After Oslo," *New York Times*, May 4, 2003, review of Charles Enderlin (Susan Fairfield), *Shattered Dreams: The Failure of the Peace Process in the Middle East, 1995–2002* (New York: Other Press, 2003); "Exhausted Are the Peacemakers," *New York Times*, August 8, 2004, review of Dennis Ross, *The Missing Peace: The Inside Story of the Fight for Middle East Peace* (New York: Farrar, Straus and Giroux, 2004); "A Foreign Correspondent Who Does More Than Report," *New York Times*, November 19, 2005, review of Robert Fisk, *The Great War for Civilisation: The Conquest of the Middle East* (New York: Knopf, 2005); "Israel and Palestine Explored in an Unlikely Friendship," *New York Times*, October 28, 2006, review of Jeffrey Goldberg, *Prisoners: A Muslim and a Jew Across the Middle East Divide* (New York: Knopf, 2006).

439. "The New New Historians," *New York Times*, November 9, 2003.

440. "A Foreign Correspondent Who Does More Than Report," *New York Times*, November 19, 2005.

441. For a thorough analysis of the factual errors in Dershowitz's scholarship, including in the *The Case For Israel*, see Norman Finkelstein, *Beyond Chutzpah: On the Misuse of Anti-Semitism and the Abuse of History* (Berkeley: University of California Press, 2005).

442. "A Foreign Correspondent Who Does More Than Report."

443. Ibid.

444. Robert Fisk, "My Beating by Refugees Is a Symbol of the Hatred and Fury of This Filthy War," *Independent*, December 10, 2001.

445. Mark Steyn, "Hate-Me Crimes," *Wall Street Journal*, December 15, 2001.

446. Andrew Sullivan, "The Pathology of Robert Fisk," December 9, 2001, www.andrewsullivan.com.

447. Ibid.

448. "Hate-Me Crimes."

449. "My Beating by Refugees Is a Symbol of the Hatred and Fury of This Filthy War."

450. "An American Is Said to Be Killed During a Failed Prison Uprising," *New York Times*, November 26, 2001.

451. "Anti-Terror Coalition Under Fire for Refusing Massacre Probe," Agence France Presse, December 1, 2001.

452. "Fatal Errors That Led to Massacre," *Guardian*, December 1, 2001.

453. "My Beating by Refugees Is a Symbol of the Hatred and Fury of This Filthy War."

454. Ibid.

455. "A Foreign Correspondent Who Does More Than Report."

456. Fisk, *The Great War for Civilisation: The Conquest of the Middle East*, p. 472.

457. Ibid., p. 473.

458. Ibid., p. 453.

459. Ibid.

460. Ross, *The Missing Peace*, p. 668.
461. Ibid., p. 674.
462. Ibid., p. 684.
463. Ibid., p. 688.
464. Ibid., pp. 667–68.
465. Ibid., p. 668.
466. "Next Steps in the Mideast," *New York Times*, July 30, 2000.
467. Ross, *The Missing Peace*, p. 668.
468. "Yasir Arafat's Moment," *New York Times*, July 28, 2000.
469. Ibid.
470. Ross, *The Missing Peace*, pp. 688–89.
471. Ron Pundak and Shaul Arieli, "The Territorial Aspect of the Israeli-Palestinian Final Status Negotiation" (Hebrew portions translated by Noam Chomsky), The Peres Center for Peace, September 2004, p. 29, www.peres-center.org.
472. Noam Chomsky, *Failed States: The Abuse of Power and the Assault on Democracy* (New York: Metropolitan Books, 2006), p. 179.
473. Ross, *The Missing Peace*, "Map Reflecting Actual Proposal at Camp David," p. xxiv.
474. Ron Pundak, "Camp David II: Israel's Misconceived Approach," Lecture at the Camp David Seminar at Tel Aviv University, June 2003, the Peres Center for Peace, www.peres-center.org.
475. Ibid.
476. Dershowitz, *The Case for Israel*, p. 105.
477. Ibid., p. 110.
478. Ibid., p. 111.
479. *The Israel-Arab Reader*, eds. Walter Laqueur and Barry Rubin, 6th ed. (New York: Penguin Books, 2001), p. 565. Though there were five previous editions of *The Israel-Arab Reader*, we used the sixth edition to check this quote. Since the fifth edition was published in 1995 and the *Ha'aretz* piece referred to here was published in 2000, Dershowitz also must have used the sixth edition.
480. Dershowitz, *The Case for Israel*, p. 111.
481. Ibid., p. 8.
482. Ibid., p. 118.
483. "The New New Historians."
484. Dershowitz, *The Case for Israel*, p. 189.
485. Ibid., pp. 189-90.
486. Amnesty International (press release), "Israel / Occupied Territories / Palestine Authority: Killing of Children Under Scrutiny at UN," September 30, 2002, www.amnesty.org.
487. Ibid.
488. "The New New Historians."
489. See Finkelstein, *Beyond Chutzpah*, 2005.
490. Alan Dershowitz, *The Case for Peace* (Hoboken, N.J.: John Wiley and Sons, 2005), p. 185.
491. Dershowitz, *The Case for Israel*, p. 191.
492. Ibid., p. 230.
493. Ibid., p. 173.
494. Ibid.
495. Note no. 2 for chapter 25, titled, "Is Targeted Assassination of Terrorist Leaders Unlawful?," reads: "Ibrahim Barzak, Associated Press, May 31, 2003." Ibid., p. 255.
496. B'Tselem, "Position Paper: Israel's Assassination Policy: Extra-judicial Executions," January 2001, www.btselem.org.
497. Ibid.

498. Dershowitz, *The Case for Israel*, p. 218.
499. Noam Chomsky, *The Fateful Triangle: The United States, Israel, and the Palestinians*, updated ed. (Cambridge, Mass.: South End Press, 1999), p. 39.
500. Dershowitz, *The Case for Israel*, p. 123.
501. Ibid., p. 124.
502. Finkelstein, *Beyond Chutzpah*, p. 97.
503. Dershowitz, *The Case for Israel*, p. 118.
504. Ibid., pp. 118–19.
505. Ibid., p. 119.
506. " 'Moratinos Document': The Peace That Nearly Was at Taba," *Ha'aretz*, February 14, 2002.
507. Ibid.
508. Yossi Beilin, *The Path to Geneva: The Quest for a Permanent Agreement, 1996–2004* (New York: RDV Books, 2004), p. 249.
509. Ibid.
510. Ibid., pp. 249–50.
511. Dershowitz, *The Case for Israel*, p. 196.
512. Chomsky, *The Fateful Triangle*, p. 39.
513. "Hamas Provokes a Fight."
514. "Israeli Troops Move into Gaza; Bridges Are Hit," *New York Times*, June 28, 2006.
515. "Israelis Batter Gaza and Seize Hamas Officials," *New York Times*, June 29, 2006.
516. "On Arab Streets and Airwaves, Shock Over Seizures by Israel," *New York Times*, June 30, 2006.
517. B'Tselem, "Sonic Booms Constitute Collective Punishment," July 3, 2006, www.btselem.org.
518. B'Tselem, "Six Human Rights Groups to Israeli High Court: Stop the Harm to the Civilian Population in Gaza," July 11, 2006, www.btselem.org.
519. "Mother and Two Children Killed in IAF Strike in Gaza," *Ha'aretz*, July 8, 2006.
520. "Who Started?," *Ha'aretz*, July 9, 2006.
521. "Three Palestinian Teens Killed in IAF Strike on Beit Hanun," *Ha'aretz*, July 10, 2006.
522. "11-Year-Old Palestinian Dies of Wounds Sustained in IAF Strike," *Ha'aretz*, July 11, 2006.
523. "Humanitarian Groups Warn of Gaza Crisis," *Jerusalem Post*, July 11, 2006.
524. "Four Palestinians Die at Rafah Border Awaiting Entry Into Gaza," *Ha'aretz*, July 11, 2006.
525. "Nine Palestinians Killed in Israeli Airstrike," *Independent*, July 12, 2006.
526. "Israeli Army Enters Lebanon," *Guardian*, July 12, 2006.
527. "Aiming to Kill Hamas Military Leaders, Israeli Air Force Kills 9 Members of a Family Instead," *New York Times*, July 13, 2006.
528. "Israel's Two-Front Battle," *New York Times*, July 13, 2006.
529. Amnesty International, "Israel/Occupied Territories: Civilian Population at Risk in Gaza," July 14, 2006, www.amnesty.org.
530. Ibid.
531. "Playing Hamas's Game," *New York Times*, July 15, 2006.
532. Ibid.
533. "PM Haniyeh Calls for 'Serious Negotiations' to End Gaza Crisis," *Ha'aretz*, July 8, 2006.
534. "Palestinian Prime Minister Calls for a Truce with Israel and New Talks," *New York Times*, July 9, 2006.
535. "Hamas Leaders: Meshal Backs Broad-Based Deal with Israel," *Ha'aretz*, July 10, 2006.

536. "Israel Rejects Palestinian Call for Truce," Associated Press, July 8, 2006.

537. "PM: This Is a War, and It Doesn't Have a Timetable," *Jerusalem Post*, July 9, 2006.

538. "Haniyeh Calls for Talks on Gaza Crisis; Israel: First Release Shalit," *Ha'aretz*, July 8, 2006.

539. "Playing Hamas's Game."

540. "Diplomacy Is the Only Way Out," *Ha'aretz*, July 10, 2006.

541. "U.S. Vetoes UN Resolution Condemning Israel's Gaza Incursion," *Ha'aretz*, July 13, 2006.

542. "Diplomacy Is the Only Way Out."

543. "Israel Targets Hamas Economy Ministry," Reuters, July 15, 2006.

544. "Non-Aligned Movement Condemns Israeli Force in Gaza," Agence France Presse, July 15, 2006.

545. "Israel Vows to Fight Palestinians Until End of Terror," Agence France Presse, July 17, 2006.

546. "Golani Commander: IDF Soldier Likely Killed in Gaza by Friendly Fire," *Ha'aretz*, July 9, 2006.

547. "Palestinians: IDF Troops Kill 13-Year-Old Boy in Central Gaza," *Ha'aretz*, July 20, 2006.

548. "Death Toll Tops 100 in Israel's Gaza Offensive," Agence France Presse, July 21, 2006.

549. Children for Defence International, "Thirty-One Gaza Children Killed in Israeli Offensive in Thirty-One Days," July 26, 2006.

550. "Israel Ends Gaza Raid, Leaving a Trail of Death and Destruction," *Los Angeles Times*, July 29, 2006.

551. "Days of Darkness," *Ha'aretz*, July 30, 2006.

552. "Palestinians: Teenager, Woman Killed by IDF Shell," *Yediot Ahronot*, August 1, 2006.

553. "8 Palestinians Killed in Gaza Raid," *Jerusalem Post*, August 3, 2006.

554. "Prominent Hamas Politician Is Seized," *Independent*, August 7, 2006.

555. B'Tselem, "Use of Firearms: Almost Half the Fatalities in the Gaza Strip in July Were Civilians Not Taking Part in the Hostilities," August 8, 2006, www.btselem.org.

556. "Israeli Air Strikes Wound 8 Palestinians in Gaza," Reuters, August 25, 2006.

557. "Israeli Airstrike Hits Reuters Vehicle," Associated Press, August 26, 2006.

558. "Wounded Cameraman Tells of Gaza Blast," *Reuters*, August 27, 2006.

559. "Two Palestinian Militants Killed by Israeli Gunfire," Agence France Presse, August 27, 2006.

560. "Israel Detains Palestinian Hamas MP in West Bank," Agence France Presse, August 27, 2006.

561. "Fighting in Gaza Kills 4 Palestinians," Associated Press, August 27, 2006.

562. "4 Palestinian Militants Killed in Gaza," Associated Press, August 28, 2006.

563. "Israeli Fire Kills Five Palestinians in Gaza," Agence France Presse, August 28, 2006.

564. "Israel Forges Ahead with Deadly Two-Month Gaza Offensive," Agence France Presse, August 28, 2006.

565. "Nine Palestinians Wounded in Israel Raid on Gaza," Agence France Presse, August 29, 2006.

566. "Nine Palestinians Killed in Gaza," Agence France Presse, August 30, 2006.

567. "Can You Really Not See?," *Ha'aretz*, August 31, 2006.

568. "IDF Troops Kill 3 Palestinians in Separate Incidents in Gaza," *Ha'aretz*, September 2, 2006.

569. "Gaza Doctors Encounter 'Unexplained Injuries,' " *Independent*, September 4, 2006.

570. "Italian Probe: Israel Used New Weapon Prototype in Gaza Strip," *Ha'aretz,* October 11, 2006.
571. "Gaza Doctors Say Patients Suffering Mystery Injuries After Israeli Attacks," *Guardian,* October 18, 2006.
572. B'Tselem, "76 Palestinians Killed in August—Over Half Did Not Participate in the Hostilities," September 5, 2006, www.btselem.org.
573. "6 Palestinians Killed by IDF in Less Than 24 Hours," *Ha'aretz,* September 6, 2006.
574. " 'Gaza Is a Jail. Nobody Is Allowed To Leave. We Are All Starving Now,' " *Independent,* September 8, 2006.
575. "The Twilight Zone/The Boy Who Was Buried Twice," *Ha'aretz,* September 9, 2006.
576. "IDF Tank Shell Kills Palestinian Teenager, Hurts Another in Rafah," *Ha'aretz,* September 11, 2006.
577. "A Real Test for the Palestinians," *New York Times,* September 18, 2006.
578. "3 Hamas Men Killed in IAF Strike in Northern Gaza," *Ha'aretz,* October 13, 2006.
579. "Eight Palestinians Killed in Two Separate IAF Strikes in Gaza," *Ha'aretz,* October 13, 2006.
580. "IDF Intensifies Gaza Attacks: 8 Palestinians Dead," *Ha'aretz,* October 13, 2006.
581. "Collateral Damage," *Ha'aretz,* October 14, 2006.
582. "Israeli Troops Push into Gaza, 4 Palestinians Killed," Reuters, October 18, 2006.
583. "9 Palestinians Killed as IDF Raid in Gaza Goes Into Third Day," *Ha'aretz,* November 3, 2006.
584. "27 Palestinians Killed in IDF Gaza Raids Over Weekend," *Ha'aretz,* November 5, 2006.
585. "Red Cross: IDF Hit Clearly Marked Ambulance Workers," *Ha'aretz,* November 6, 2006.
586. "IAF Missile Kills 16-Year-Old, Wounds Several Others in Gaza," *Ha'aretz,* November 6, 2006.
587. "IDF Kills Seven Palestinians in Gaza; Rockets Hit Ashkelon School," *Ha'aretz,* November 8, 2006.
588. "19 Palestinians Die in IDF Shelling in Northern Gaza," *Ha'aretz,* November 8, 2006.
589. "19 Palestinians Killed in IDF shelling in Northern Gaza," *Ha'aretz,* November 8, 2006.
590. "Israeli Shelling Kills 18 Gazans; Anger Boils Up," *New York Times,* November 9, 2006.
591. B'Tselem, "The Killing of Civilians in Beit Hanun Is a War Crime," November 8, 2006, www.btselem.org.
592. Amnesty International, "Israel/Occupied Territories: Amnesty International Delegate Visits Scene of Gaza Strip Killings," November 8, 2006, www.amnesty.org.
593. Human Rights Watch, "Israel: IDF Probe No Substitute for Real Investigation," November 10, 2006, www.hrw.org.
594. Ibid.
595. "Israeli Shelling Kills 18 Gazans; Anger Boils Up."
596. "Israel Expresses Regret for Gaza Deaths; IDF Chief Orders Probe," *Ha'aretz,* November 8, 2006.
597. "A Cease-Fire in Gaza (2)," *Ha'aretz,* November 9, 2006.
598. "So Vicious, This Cycle," *Ha'aretz,* November 10, 2006.
599. "No One Is Guilty in Israel," *Ha'aretz,* November 12, 2006.
600. "How a Beit Hanun Family Was Destroyed," *Ha'aretz,* November 13, 2006.
601. "The Perils of Inaction," *New York Times,* November 10. 2006.

602. "U.S. Rejects Qatari Call for Int'l Inquiry Into Beit Hanun Killings," *Ha'aretz*, November 10, 2006; "UN Security Council to Vote on Resolution Condemning Israel for Gaza Shelling," *Ha'aretz*, November 11, 2006; "U.S. Vetoes 'Biased' UN Resolution Attacking Israel's Gaza Bloodbath," *Independent*, November 11, 2006.
603. Friel and Falk, *The Record of the Paper*.
604. "A Friendship in Disguise," *Ha'aretz*, November 11, 2006.
605. Ibid.

Index